D0312930

THE XX FACTOR

Wolf, Alison.
The XX factor : how the
rise of working women ha
[2013]

sa   10/03/13

THE XX FACTOR

How the Rise of Working Women Has
Created a Far Less Equal World

ALISON WOLF

CROWN PUBLISHERS

NEW YORK

Copyright © 2013 by Alison Wolf

All rights reserved.
Published in the United States by Crown Publishers,
an imprint of the Crown Publishing Group,
a division of Random House, Inc., New York.
www.crownpublishing.com

CROWN and the Crown colophon
are registered trademarks of Random House, Inc.

Originally published in Great Britain by Profile Books Ltd., London.

Grateful acknowledgment is made to the University of California Press for permission to
reprint excerpts from *Promises I Can Keep: Why Poor Women Put Motherhood Before
Marriage*, by Kathryn Edin and Maria Kefalas. Copyright © 2011 by the Regents of the
University of California. Reprinted by permission of the University of California Press.

Library of Congress Cataloging-in-Publication Data
Wolf, Alison.
The XX factor/Alison Wolf.—First edition.
pages   cm
Includes bibliographical references and index.
1. Woman—Employment—History. 2. Women employees. 3. Women executives.
4. Women in the professions. 5. Work-life balance. 6. Work and family. I. Title.
HD6053.W598 2013
331.4—dc23   2013011785

ISBN 978-0-307-59040-4
eISBN 978-0-307-59042-8

PRINTED IN THE UNITED STATES OF AMERICA

Book design by Jaclyn Reyes
Jacket design by Christopher Brand

1   3   5   7   9   10   8   6   4   2

First American Edition

To Martin with love

CONTENTS

INTRODUCTION

One morning in 1802, Jane Austen did something extraordinarily, breathtakingly brave. She broke off her engagement.

The previous evening she had accepted an offer of marriage from a wealthy young man, Harris Bigg-Wither. She was twenty-seven and so unlikely to receive another offer; she had no independent income. That December day, she was quite consciously depriving herself of everything that offered women status and security, namely marriage and children.

Being single and female meant a life spent in other people's homes, dependent on their charity.[1] If Austen reached old age, she would have no children to look after her. She would be single in a society with no state pensions or health insurance, without social security payments. She was choosing what was then the most dreaded of fates: to be a childless old maid.

Moreover, there was nothing unusual in her situation. She knew perfectly well what awaited her. For countless centuries before her, from the dawn of humankind, women's fates and fortunes had been defined in this way.

Today, just eight generations on, elite working women can barely imagine such terrors and such choices. *The XX Factor* is about these modern women, 70 million strong worldwide, and with the number rising daily. It is about their lives and about the choices that face them throughout adulthood; different from those of Austen's time, far more extensive, but hard choices nonetheless. And it is about the growing impact of millions of highly educated, professional females on every aspect of human society.

This is also a book about women who stand in a direct line from Jane Austen and from her novels' heroines. The women of *The XX Factor* are, like Austen's characters, intelligent and educated. They are affluent and successful but they are not the super-rich. Like the family of Elizabeth Bennet, heroine of *Pride and Prejudice*, they move in circles that include bankers, merchants and clergymen; and like Jane Austen's own family, theirs is a world of busy professionals, such as lawyers and navy officers, as well as owners of businesses and land.

The most obvious difference between Austen's world and ours is also a momentous one. Women now hold the jobs that were the preserve of husbands, brothers, sons and fathers. Women are lawyers and members of the clergy, women are bankers and business owners. In the developed world, they enter professional and business occupations just as often as men; and, among younger cohorts, they do so on equal terms.

A slow transformation of the labor market accelerated suddenly in the 1960s and 1970s. Women's expectations and behavior were transformed as elite education opened up, job opportunities changed, family structures shifted and the Pill arrived. Only now, looking back, can we see the profound differences between the lives of college-educated women today and those of college-educated women as recent as their grandmothers' generation.

We are also only gradually realizing how much the impact of occupational change ripples way beyond the workplace itself. Incrementally but irreversibly, women's penetration of the world's elites is changing both men's and women's daily activities and their personal lives. In some cases, we recognize what has changed, but in many others, as this book will show, what people believe is happening is at odds with the documented facts. And one thing that we have failed to understand is that whereas through most of human history it made sense to talk about "women" en masse, today it very rarely does.

Until now, all women's lives, whether rich or poor, have been dominated by the same experiences and pressures. Today, elite and highly educated women have become a class apart. However, these professionals, businesswomen and holders of advanced degrees, the top 15 or 20 percent of a developed country's female workforce, have not moved further apart from men. On the contrary, they are now more like the men of the family than ever before in history. It is from other women that they have drawn away.

FORTUNATE GENERATIONS

This "new class" of women has only bedded down and become numerous in the last thirty to forty years. Before that, across the millennia, hardly any women had the chance of a full, lifetime career. In my own family, mine was the very first generation to do so. Yet it was only while writing this book that I realized just how distinct a historic group we are, and how much I have lived a common story.

I grew up in prosperous, peaceful southern England. I went to a highly academic girls' high school, where it was simply taken for granted that we would all go on to college. A tiny number of my classmates went into nursing. An equally small number went straight into teacher training. The rest of us did what we called "proper," that is academic, degrees.

At one level I understood that this was new. My grandparents all left school for work in their very early teens; my parents completed secondary school but had no opportunity to go to university; my sister and I are graduates. So like millions of other postwar twentieth-century women, we were our family's first graduate generation. But because it was normal for my school and for my friends, only years later did I realize how few women, even in our baby-boomer generations, did academic, let alone postgraduate degrees, or how few had done so previously.

My sister and I were first-generation graduates, but as parents we simply took it for granted that our children would—must—get degrees. Today, unlike in my childhood, it is axiomatic that a child from a fairly affluent family, male or female, goes to college. The explosion in student numbers has been great for women in many ways; but what is equally important is their access to the best institutions. In fact, as this book discusses, it is the single most important factor in creating the genuinely co-ed elites that have emerged, especially among younger cohorts.

I went to Oxford University and to one of its then all-women colleges, Somerville. I knew, obviously enough, that Oxford in my time offered far fewer places to women than it did to men. I was totally unaware, even if I had thought about it, that this was just as true for the great American Ivy League universities—Harvard, Yale, Princeton. (Those three were the only ones I knew.) But I wouldn't have been surprised. That was just how things were.

However, the tectonic plates were shifting. Already, no important occupations were barred to me or to my college contemporaries, as they had been to graduate women quite a short time before. And in key ways Oxford was a microcosm of change. One by one the men's colleges started admitting women, and admission numbers gradually equalized. As they did, the women's colleges were forced to follow suit.

Somerville, my own college, admitted its first men in 1994. It did so for two reasons: the all-female colleges were losing the best women students to the co-ed ones; and they were unable to host university posts, all of which now demanded gender neutrality. Change, in other words, was a response to new social values enshrined in law, as well as to the rational behavior of ambitious young women. Both were important, and both, as we will see in this book, are critical in explaining our contemporary world.

Although my twenty-year-old self was unaware that higher education would soon be transformed, workplace change was a different matter. I grew up in a world where mothers stayed at home. In my early teens, I remember being pretty certain that I would stop working when my children, if I had any, were small. It was what people—women—did. Indeed, it was the right thing to do. A decade on, I did the opposite.

In going straight back to work after a baby, I was doing something that was new but would soon, for graduates, become totally conventional. In another way I was, personally, a throwback. In common with just one of my college contemporaries, I got married at the end of my senior year, straight after graduation, something that was becoming highly unusual (and which has turned out extremely well). And I had children quickly too, so that our children are significantly older than most of our contemporaries' families. I wasn't a young mother by biological or historical standards, but I had children at the same age as my mother, atypically for my graduate urban milieu and typically for her small-town professional one. It's one of the very few respects in which, quite unwittingly, I bucked the evolving trends.

One reason that today's graduates marry so much later, if they marry at all, and bear children late if ever, is the great revolution of the 1960s. Not the student revolts but the Pill. Those of us who came to adulthood post-Pill stand on another shore, an ocean apart from all generations before us. Sex can be safe. You can relax about it. Women can avoid an undesired pregnancy, completely, securely and on their own. Not surprisingly, sexual behavior has been transformed; and one result is that marriage is increasingly postponed.

Here, my generation did know that things were different. Some people were taking off for communes or endorsing "free love" and multiple partners. Lots of people were sleeping with successive fairly serious boyfriends in a way our mothers would and could never have done. I knew a few of the former group, many of the latter; wrote about sex and abortion in our student newspaper; and was well aware that the world was fascinated. (Sex, students plus Oxford is a certain hit.)

We were much less perceptive about the changing state of marriage and the family. We mostly expected to marry. In fact, we saw far less conflict between having a career and having a family than had been the case for the older and often single women who had taught us in high school, and the older and often single female academics who taught us at university.

However, we were graduating into a world where, quite unexpectedly, child-bearing and marriage patterns would be transformed for everyone—albeit in quite different ways at the top from the bottom of the income tree. Time and again contemporary women, and men, don't marry, don't have children, or do neither where once they would have done both.

It is not as simple, as we will see, as men having it all when women don't.[2] But for highly educated women, the benefits of employment have increased while the risks of giving it up have grown alongside. Both men and women today make perfectly understandable choices that are different from their parents' or grandparents' because their options—educational, occupational and social—have also changed. And as a result, many of them, by their early forties, have lives that are quite different from their teenage expectation of marriage-and-two-children.

My generation didn't see this coming. But then, as students or young professionals, we didn't and couldn't survey what society as a whole was doing. What was normal was what we, as a privileged sub-group, did. This might or might not be the same as everyone else. As it turns out, it wasn't.

THE END OF SISTERHOOD

In the half-century since 1970, human societies have studied and measured themselves as never before in history. Statistical data, high-speed computing and academic publishing together ensure a flood of empirical studies, with women a favorite subject. In writing this book I could draw on a very wide range of already published material and on widely used data sets in the public domain. (The one exception is the chapter on sex, where much of the analysis appears for the first time.)

I have used this material to examine whether contemporary women all behave similarly or whether there are systematic differences among them. And the data show, again and again, that they are very different from each other, not just in their careers, family patterns and daily tasks, but even in the bedroom. Moreover, those differences are clearly related to whether or not they are members of today's educated, professional female elites.

I was surprised that these comparisons had not been made more often. But referring to women as a single homogeneous group is the common discourse. To an extraordinary degree, people today, including feminists and professionally "female" media commentators, talk about women as though they all have common interests. We get discussions of women's pay rates ("unequal"), women's voting intentions ("liberal") and women's opinions of this or that. Far more rarely are particular groups of women compared with others.

For much of history this was reasonable enough. It was almost a century after Jane Austen that Rudyard Kipling wrote, in *Barrack-room Ballads*, that

The Colonel's Lady an' Judy O'Grady
Are sisters under their skins!

And it was true, when he wrote it, in a way that was not true for their men. Elite or poor, Irish or Indian, marriage and child-bearing were women's necessary aspirations. You married well, or badly. You bore living children to support you, or did not. On those realities, as a female, your whole life hinged.

Modern industrial societies have changed everybody's lives, but especially those of women, because the vast majority of women in a developed country can now support themselves, alone. Most women can earn salaries and live independently, whether they are single or divorced, something that was completely inconceivable in Jane Austen's day. And most developed societies now support impoverished single mothers too, replacing husbands with the state.

Nonetheless, for the vast majority of women, it is family and children, not job and career, that are the major focus of their lives, just as they have always been. Most people, including most women, work to live rather than live to work. And the outcome is two quite different groups of women. The larger group remain essentially traditional in their concerns and also in the jobs they do: namely, long-standing "female" jobs done largely by females. The other, the elite, are now very like their male counterparts. They share the latter's work habits and job choices. They share their offices, with, as we will see, some predictable and some unpredictable results. They partner and marry men like themselves.

Today's highly educated and professional women, the top 15 or 20 percent, not only have different jobs from other women; they also have quite different patterns of lifetime employment from other women. They are different in when and how much they work. They have quite different marriage and child-bearing patterns, and very different divorce rates. They bring up their children differently and they differ in how they run their homes.

I will argue in this book that all these changes are interconnected. From the opening up of the labor market, and the egalitarian values that underpin its transformation, there is a direct road to a world in which ever more graduates are childless; and where nannies are a high-growth occupation. There is a direct road to a world where the "leisure society" seems like a joke, but only for those at the top; and where old-style female altruism is a fading memory. And a direct route, also, to a new century in which change is coming much faster in developing countries than it ever did in my own, and where half of the world's self-made female billionaires live in China.

I realize, now, that mine was a hinge generation. I have always had a job; my hugely capable mother quit paid employment when she married, returning only when her children had left school. My sister and I both employed a nanny; my parents never conceived of the idea. I always worked in institutions—universities, the civil service, think tanks—where it was normal to have women as bosses, men as subordinates. I simply take for granted the presence of women as well as men in the meetings I attend.

And there are a lot of people like me; and like my agent, my mostly female editors and publishers, and like the successful women I interviewed for this book. At the start of this twenty-first century, I estimate that there were 62 million of us worldwide: women who were holding top-quintile jobs as professionals, senior managers or directors of substantial companies, and whose earnings placed them in their countries' elites. By the time of this book's publication, the number was up to 70 million and rising.[3] This is critical mass.

And yet it is all so recent.

We started with Jane Austen, who lived just a few generations ago. "She's named after Emma," said a friend of mine the other day, about her charming, talkative ten-year-old. "My favorite Austen character." And Austen's women are recognizably like modern Emma's mother. They belong to the prosperous classes; they are confident, educated, outspoken; they face difficult choices, they make decisions they sometimes regret. We identify. Yet their lives were in fact completely and unimaginably different. Their choices were those of women throughout history; the choices of today's elite women are not. And to see just how different things have become, and with what speed, where better to start than with Hillary Clinton, Margaret Thatcher and Britain's first, fabulously rich and US-born female Member of Parliament?[4]

Part One

WOMEN IN THE WORKFORCE—
A HOUSE DIVIDED

1

GOODBYE TO ALL THAT:
THE FRACTURING OF SISTERHOOD

ancy Astor became a political superstar at the twentieth century's beginning. Margaret Thatcher, the Iron Lady, was the UK's
first female prime minister and an icon of the century's later decades. And
as a new century got under way, Barack Obama beat Hillary Clinton to
win the Democratic primaries and his party's presidential nomination.

Three women. Three careers. They frame this book, and frame a
century in which educated women's lives were transformed. Astor,
Thatcher and Clinton take us from an old world to a world that is still
very new; and Clinton's defeat is as central to the story as Astor's or
Thatcher's victory.

Nancy Astor was an American, born in Virginia in 1879 and married to one of the world's richest men, Waldorf Astor. She was famous
as the first woman to enter Britain's Parliament, a society hostess and an
agitator for social reform. She became an MP in 1919, just twelve years
after Finland elected the world's first-ever female legislators, and held
a tough urban seat for twenty-five years through the Great Depression
and eight general elections. She died with the Vietnam War raging and
Swinging London already a cliché. And yet none of this would have happened if her older sister had not been stunningly beautiful.

Nancy's father, Chillie Langhorne, was a Southerner. He made his
money after the Civil War, as a contractor providing labor for the rail-
roads, and his beautiful second daughter, Irene, became a "Belle of the
Ball." For that reason, and that reason alone, his family were launched
into first New York and then European society.

White Sulphur Springs is a hot-water spa in the Blue Ridge Moun-
tains of Virginia, and was a center of the Southern marriage market

before and after the Civil War. "To get to the Springs, to lead a masked ball . . . to be a reigning Belle, was the only ideal in life worth pursuing for a southern debutante . . . Your life could be transformed by one appearance at a ball," explains Irene's great-nephew.[1] Irene Langhorne's beauty made her not only the Belle of Virginia balls, but one of America's "top four Belles"; she was selected to lead the Grand March at New York's Patriarchs' Ball, the "great annual event of the Gilded Age."[2] That meant, in 1893, instant stardom. And it was that stardom, based entirely on Irene's looks, that ushered her younger sisters, including Nancy, into New York and European top society, with a far larger and richer range of potential husbands.[3]

Yet by 1964, the year that Nancy died, a very different Member of Parliament was just eleven years short of capturing the leadership of Britain's Conservative Party. Margaret Thatcher was a graduate research chemist turned lawyer. She had already been in Parliament for five years; she would become both the UK's first female prime minister and the longest-serving British prime minister of the twentieth century. *Her* father owned a small shop in a nondescript provincial town. Her only sibling became a shy farmer's wife. And her life changed not because of a ball but through an academic scholarship to the University of Oxford.

And why is Hillary Clinton a third key figure? Why were the 2008 Democratic primaries so important? Because of why a woman lost.

Hillary Clinton entered the primaries as the front-runner. She had strong support among the female working class and she and Obama were level-pegging among the non-college young. But what mattered was the college vote, where women are the clear majority. That vote turned out in force, unlike young non-college voters. As Elizabeth Cline, in *The New Republic*, noted, "girl-power momentum" told.[4] But it wasn't behind Clinton. It was behind Obama.

Hillary Clinton's defeat by Barack Obama was a defining moment in the story of today's successful women. Not because a woman could well have taken the US presidential nomination but, on the contrary, because what ultimately decided those primaries were the votes of a certain sort of woman. And those women didn't think that the candidate's gender mattered.

For many of today's young women, being female is not the most important thing about their lives. It does not define their fate in the way it did for all females in previous human history, including women born as recently as Nancy Astor and her sisters. In those 2008 primaries, college-based voters, both women and men, signed up to Obama's promise of change. Which is just another way of saying that contemporary college women do not think there is any strong reason to vote for a woman candidate just because she is a woman.

For today's graduate women, education opens up the world, as it did for Mrs. Thatcher. These women are successful. They increasingly hold postgraduate as well as full bachelor's degrees, they do professional and managerial jobs in a world where women can hold almost any position and they earn at levels that were inconceivable a short while ago.

These women are also a minority. At most, around a fifth of the adult female population falls clearly into this group, which combines higher education, good incomes and prestigious occupations. But then, highly educated, high-earning professional men also number only about 15 to 20 percent of males in the developed world, and far fewer in developing countries.[5]

Feminists once talked of "the sisterhood," but educated successful women today have fewer interests in common with other women than ever before. As we will see, they are increasingly distinctive in their patterns of dating, marriage, child-bearing and child-rearing. But above all, women have parted company from each other in their working lives. The highly educated professional minority now have careers that are increasingly like those of the successful men they work alongside. In this shared work environment, it is entirely normal that professional women should be ambitious, and that men can and do work for women, and not just the other way round. And this drives wholesale social change.

SURPLUS SISTERS

The workplace is newly central to women's lives, but of course women have always worked. They worked in fields, gardens and homes; they looked after children, nursed the sick at home, prepared food from scratch, sewed and mended clothes. "They worked their fingers to the bone," as the saying went. It was not only the poor who worked hard. Through most of history, middle-class and affluent women also worked long hours on domestic tasks and caring for their families.

Until recently, though, only poorer women worked for wages,[6] and they, even after the Industrial Revolution, worked overwhelmingly in other people's houses. They were paid, in other words, to do the domestic jobs they would also carry out in their own homes as daughters and, hopefully, as wives.

For all classes, marriage was women's desired near-universal goal. There's a moment in the first episode of the hit TV series *Mad Men* that encapsulates not just the 1950s but all of previous history. Joan Holloway, the office manager of a Madison Avenue advertising agency, features. She is "mid-twenties, incredibly put together," says the script,[7] and she has advice for a new secretary—female, of course—who is commuting into the city.

> In a couple of years, with the right moves, you'll be in the city with the rest of us.
>
> Of course, if you really make the right moves, you'll be out in the country and you won't be going to work at all.[8]

It is the 1950s version of long-standing advice. In 1800 or 1850, 1900 or 1950, working-class girls went to work in their early teens. They worked to earn, contributing to the family finances. If they stayed single, they kept working. But if they made a decent marriage, to a man with a stable, reasonably paid job, they stayed at home.

This pattern was later-arriving for middle-class girls, and hardly applied to the rich, but only because, through most of history, these girls never took paid employment at all. Right through to the mid-twentieth century, even in the industrialized West, the most common single pattern for a woman—any woman—was to work for pay until she married and then stop.

The history of the marriage bar tells us how unquestioned all this was. From the late nineteenth century, educated middle-class girls started to enter paid employment in large numbers, as teachers, nurses or civil servants. They too stopped work on marriage. Indeed, few could have continued even if they wished. In most countries the public sector, their main employer, had a statutory marriage bar for women teachers and civil servants that lasted until startlingly recently. You stayed single or you yielded your job in favor of a male breadwinner.

In the US, economic historian Claudia Goldin estimates that the marriage bar, at its height, affected three-quarters of local school boards and more than 50 percent of all office workers. It was largely abandoned in the 1940s, but persisted into the 1950s in some places.[9] A marriage bar for teachers and the civil service lasted until 1945 in the UK; until 1957 for civil servants in the Netherlands, the 1960s in Australia,[10] 1973 in Ireland. I remember, in my intolerant teens, disapproving rather of an aunt who had quit teaching when she got married; I had no idea that, a few years earlier, she would have had no choice. She herself saw her behavior as totally normal. Staying home was what married women did.

And she definitely wanted to be married. Women did. We can barely imagine the terror that spinsterhood inspired in a world built around marriage. Being an "old maid" and being left "on the shelf" condemned you to a life with little or no respect and few opportunities. And this was true for every type of woman, middle and working class, educated and uneducated alike.

Wars were catastrophic, not just for the young men killed and maimed, but also for the women who would have married and now never could. In America, the Civil War resulted in by far the largest number of American casualties ever, in absolute let alone relative terms: well over half a million men perished, and in the Confederate States this encompassed almost one in five of all white males aged thirteen to forty-three.[11]

In 1920s England, France and Germany, it was the slaughter of the First World War that hit societies on a massive scale. Suddenly there were far more young women in the population than young men.[12] Millions of women, across much of Europe, had lost boyfriends, fiancés and husbands. Those in their twenties at the end of the war were hardest-hit: 35 percent of these women failed to marry.[13]

What had happened was devastating; but the newspapers of the time also make clear how much people's responses were shaped by a common assumption. Women existed in order to be wives. If there were no husbands, they were now surplus to requirements.

In her moving book about this generation, *Singled Out*, Virginia Nicholson quotes some comments from the British press:

"Problem of the Surplus Woman—Two Million Who Can Never Become Wives" (*Daily Express* headline, 1921)

"Britain's problem of two million superfluous women" (Lord Northcliffe, proprietor of the *Daily Mail*)

"Two millions of surplus woman-folk" (*The Times*, 1921)[14]

One of that First World War generation, her fiancé dead, remembered sitting in the train at the end of the day, "looking at the white, indifferent, tired faces opposite me [as] the wheels sang 'surplus two million, surplus two million,' and I was one of them."[15]

This was not just a problem for the educated. Nor was it just a problem for the poor. The "surplus" women came from all classes; because for all women in all classes, life as a married woman, raising children in a home of one's own, was seen as the best and natural existence. Women were indeed "sisters under their skin."

Only in the final third of the twentieth century did this global pattern vanish. And with it the commonality of human females' lives.

At first sight, this isn't obvious. Women still want to get married; and large numbers do, albeit fewer and fewer, as we will see below. A world of married women at home has been replaced by a world in which most married women work. Everywhere, they get out of the house, away from the sink, finding sociability as well as financial independence in adult employment.

But adult female employment today isn't a common shared experience in the way that tending home and family used to be. On the contrary, it sorts and separates. Women differ profoundly in how they work, when they work and why. And a good place to start exploring the change is Scandinavia.

DEGREES OF SEPARATION

Is there a female Paradise on earth? You might think so—a Nordic one, perched up above the fifty-fifth parallel, on the shores of the Baltic Sea.

Scandinavians are seen by the world, and see themselves, as flag-bearers for sexual equality. They are peaceful, egalitarian *and* economically successful; and they pioneered social programs designed to guarantee opportunities for women. As well as free nurseries and preschool provision, they offer extremely generous paid maternity and parental leave. They have declared war on the "glass ceilings" that may be blocking women's progress: most recently when Norway required all large public companies to make sure their boards were at least 30 percent female.

The Scandinavians set out to do well by women. Yet today they provide the clearest illustration of how yawning gaps open between different groups of contemporary working women. And the two things are linked.

We tend to think about discrimination and equal opportunities in numerical terms: the number of women on company boards or in the cabinet, whether there are female airline pilots, or carpenters, or marines.

Given its strong commitment to opening up opportunities for women, you might reasonably expect that in Scandinavia if anywhere men and women would be working alongside each other, equally represented at every level of every occupation.

People certainly do expect exactly that. At a 2012 book launch in New York, for example, I sat listening to East Coast Americans assuring each other that sexual stereotyping had vanished from Scandinavia; men took just as much time off when children were born as women did; and Swedish men were just as likely to be home, or on nursery duty, as Swedish women. So yes, you'd probably expect it. And you'd be wrong.

In fact, the highest levels of gender segregation anywhere in the developed world are found in the labor markets of egalitarian welfare-state Scandinavia.[16] The International Labour Organization, a diligent observer of labor market inequalities,[17] has calculated that if you wanted to make all occupations "gender neutral" about a third of all Scandinavian workers would have to move to a completely different occupation.

So is this rank hypocrisy at work? Not in the least. Scandinavian labor markets are like those of the whole developed West. They have professional occupations where women are succeeding alongside men. And then they have lower-paid occupations that are overwhelmingly female or overwhelmingly male. That is exactly what happens everywhere in the developed world; but in Scandinavia the divide between the two is even larger and sharper than for the rest of us. To understand why is also to explain how the modern workplace detaches our female elites from both history and the rest of female-kind.

INTEGRATED ABOVE, SEPARATED BELOW

Professional and managerial workplaces are increasingly integrated in gender terms. Already, by 2000, women were holding half the professional jobs across the OECD (Organisation for Economic Co-operation and Development) "club" of rich countries, even if they still occupied well under half the boardroom chairs.[18]

Imagine the job market as a pyramid. At its tip are the top fifth of the workforce in terms of pay or education—the millions of professionals, executives, business managers. Here you find elite women working, overwhelmingly, alongside the educated male elites they so greatly resemble: men and women, women and men. At this level, occupational recruitment in Sweden or Denmark looks pretty much the same as in

America: they are no worse in gender terms, and not obviously any better.[19] And America, in turn, looks pretty much like Italy or Canada, Australia, the UK or France.

Now take the other four-fifths, the fat middle and base of the pyramid. Here, by contrast, women everywhere still live and work, to a surprising degree, in a distinctively female world.

Here, in the bulk of the labor market, women are concentrated in occupations dominated by females, and often in very female workplaces.[20] It isn't what you would infer from our preoccupation with women in boardrooms and legislatures; but today "there is less sex segregation in . . . higher-grade . . . than in lower-grade occupations."[21]

Take the US. If you pick the twenty top female occupations—meaning the ones that employ the largest absolute numbers of women—you find that, in seven of them, the workforce is over 90 percent female. Make 80 percent female your cut-off and it is over half the group. Figure 1.1 illustrates just how unbalanced some of the largest occupations are, but there are plenty of other examples.[22] Of all the twenty big battalions of the female job market in the US, only three—cooks, managers and retail sales—also recruit lots of men.

And the "top twenty" are all really big, each recruiting close to or over a million women; together they account for one female employee in four—a quarter of the US female workforce. These are the sorts of

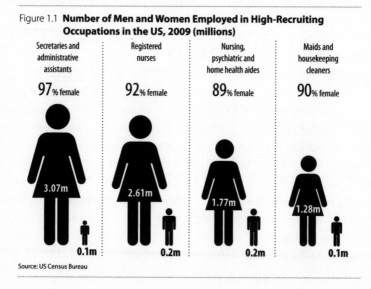

Figure 1.1 **Number of Men and Women Employed in High-Recruiting Occupations in the US, 2009 (millions)**

Secretaries and administrative assistants	Registered nurses	Nursing, psychiatric and home health aides	Maids and housekeeping cleaners
97% female	**92**% female	**89**% female	**90**% female
3.07m	2.61m	1.77m	1.28m
0.1m	0.2m	0.2m	0.1m

Source: US Census Bureau

jobs that most people do, not the jobs of the "high-skill future" over which governments obsess.[23] In 2010, fewer than 2,000 people worldwide worked for Facebook. Walmart's workforce that year numbered over 2 million, a million more than at the century's turn and up from 21,000 in 1975.[24]

There is nothing to suggest the future will be different. The US government predicts that biomedical engineers will be the fastest-growing occupation of the current decade. This sounds great; moreover, we can expect a high proportion of the new ones to be women. But there are hardly any of them to start with. The 72 percent growth that is promised amounts to just 11,500 new jobs.[25] Contrast that with home health aides: "only" 50 percent growth in the same period, as predicted by the government, will yield almost half a million new jobs.[26] Almost all of them female.

In the middle and lower reaches of the job market, across the rich developed world, *either* men *or* women dominate most occupations. Women here are as concentrated in female jobs as they have always been.[27] Meanwhile, among the hundreds of thousands of welders, vehicle mechanics, roofers, carpenters and truck operators in the US labor force, well over 90 percent are male. You can today, unlike in the past,[28] find a few female carpenters, female car mechanics and female truck drivers. But not many: not in the US and not anywhere else either.

Which brings us back to Scandinavia. In the 1990s, just under half of female workers in Norway, Sweden and Finland were working in occupations that were more than 80 percent female.[29] That is way above the global average. But it is also just an extreme version of the common pattern.

Most of the "big" female occupations in that bottom four-fifths of the world's job pyramid involve very traditional female activities, whether it is caring for children, caring for the sick and the old, or offering a warm greeting to visitors as they enter an office, restaurant or hotel. These are things that women once all did in their own homes and are now paid to do outside them. And Scandinavian countries hold the record for gender segregation *because* they have gone the furthest in outsourcing traditional female activities and turning unpaid home-based "caring" into formal employment.

These countries pioneered state-funded nurseries for the under-fives; their high taxes fund an unrivaled network of clinics, retirement homes and day centers. This is the result of Scandinavians' determination to help women out of the house and into the workplace. In occupational terms, it has had one very clear result: it has created an unusually large, new and all-female group of employees being paid to do traditional all-female tasks.[30] Scandinavian policies have huge strengths. These societies provide security and shared experiences across society that bring people together, and of course they free up the professionals. But Scandinavian truckers are still men. And parental leave is taken mostly by women.[31]

ONE OF THE CROWD

At the top of the job pyramid, it's the speed of recent change that startles—all of it in a gender-mixed direction. As late as 1870 there were precisely three active female lawyers in the whole of the US[32] and Harvard Law School finally admitted women only in 1950. But what I think would astonish most of today's working professionals is that, as late as 1970, women still made up less than 5 percent of America's practicing lawyers.[33]

And then, with the 1970s, female numbers took off. The last forty years have transformed employment's top echelons, even in such stereotypically male areas as science and computer programming; in the UK, about 40% of professional jobs in these areas are now held by women.[34] And by 2002 there were 300,000 women practicing law in America, 40 percent of those in practice.

The picture is much the same across the developed world, whether it is doctors or management consultants, purchasing managers, loan office or insurance underwriters.[35] The one exception is engineering: as late as 2009, only one in twenty of the UK's mechanical engineers was female, and the profession remains heavily male everywhere.[36]

On the other hand, look at marketing. Until I wrote this book I hadn't realized how completely women had taken over the marketing departments of our companies and nations. Lee Ann Daly talked to me at Thomson Reuters, where she was Chief Marketing Officer for the company's Markets Division after a career covering small ad agencies, radio start-ups and large corporations; and when she said about marketing that "it's getting more balanced," she didn't mean women were finally arriving. She meant it was getting to be "male and female versus all female. In my group I'm very happy to have the opportunity to hire a senior male marketer and I have, my head of brand is a male." While the other senior managers were not. It is a long way from *Mad Men*.

Working in government and universities, I've always had plenty of female colleagues. I am currently a member of the finance committee for my own university, King's College London, and as we left a meeting the other day, one of our senior administrators turned to me. "Did you notice? You were the only woman there," he remarked in surprise. I had, and for the same reason. It is such an unusual experience.

But for plenty of today's successful working women it was commonplace, and not long ago either. Lawton Fitt graduated from Brown and the University of Virginia in the 1970s, joined Goldman Sachs in 1979 and was one of the first women to make partner.[37] This was in the early 1990s, when Goldman still was a genuine partnership. She remembers: "When I joined you could put the professional women in the firm around a dinner table, and we used to do it. There were sixteen of us women; and I mean sixteen including the librarian."

I interviewed Fitt at the home she keeps in central London. She was fresh off the overnight flight from the US, and soon to take off again to Paris and Berlin. We talked on her roof terrace, overlooking the trees of Holland Park. These days, post-Goldman, hers is a transatlantic life of boards, whether investment, commercial or cultural. And as we talked, the messages were coming into her BlackBerry at a fast and regular rate.

She told me: "When I started, I was always at meetings where it was seventeen men and me. And in the first few years it was remarkable, because they all seemed to think that when they first met me, they needed to point out to me that I was the only woman in the room.

"Visibility is obviously a great place to be but it's also a minus. If you trip you trip very publicly. On the other hand, you do get noticed all the way up the chain. So when I was in there about eighteen months I got summoned to the CEO's office to have a chat about how things were and how they could make things better for me.

"There certainly were moments when I was patently discriminated against and I didn't really see it. But in a way I think that's good, because if you become paranoid and you see alligators under the bed you're going to spend a lot of time not putting your feet on the floor."

None of the younger women I interviewed described anything like Fitt's environment. At Goldman itself, perched at the top of an industry notorious for a killing work culture and male upper echelons, one partner in seven is now female, and at vice-president level it's up to about

30 percent. Fitt agrees with people who think things "tip" at this level, because "when you start to get a third of the population, a third of a board, women, it's hard anymore to actually see people immediately as a 'gender exception.' So that people don't first see you as a woman, they see you first in whatever your job or your leadership function is. And then they parenthetically see you as a woman."

Today, fewer and fewer ambitious female graduates enter jobs where they are "gender exceptions." Fewer and fewer can expect to be "female firsts." Instead, they are entering a labor market where, in 2011, the proportion of female miners in Western economies was lower than the percentage of London-listed mining companies with female CEOs.

Which explains a lot about those 2008 Democratic primaries. The US is the homeland of Betty Friedan and Gloria Steinem and of high-decibel feminism. In those primaries, where college students delivered victory to Obama, the high priestesses of the women's movement were there for Clinton. They argued that young women should support her as a fellow woman. Steinem was horrified that the women of 2008 might pass up on the chance to vote for the sisterhood. Some of them, she thought, "perhaps especially younger ones," were deluded enough to "hope to deny or escape the sexual caste system."[38] But she had no impact, and no wonder.

The young female students of 2008 have never—unlike their ances-tors—experienced anything that remotely resembles a caste system. On the contrary, at the top, men and women work together, and have work lives and habits that are increasingly similar. Elite women's lives are, as a result, increasingly different from other women's. It is a new and com-prehensive fracture.

A LIFETIME'S EMPLOYMENT?

Sometime in the 1940s, unremarked, there was a critical moment. A married woman took a job outside the home; and the world changed.

Before then, the wives who went out to work were on average less ed-ucated than married women as a whole. Employment after marriage was mostly a matter of pressing necessity, of widowhood or family poverty. From that 1940s moment on, the opposite was true. Year by year, in the US and elsewhere, the average educational level of the married women who went out to work rose compared to the average of those who did not. As economist Claudia Goldin has pointed out, that unnoticed moment, that shift in the balance, heralded the modern labor market.[39]

One reason that the change went unnoticed was that less-educated women didn't stop working. They went on working just as they always had, and for the same reasons. "When I hear people saying that 'women' . . . now work," remarks sociologist Geoff Dench, "it reminds me of the editor of a society magazine [who] on hearing that a plane has just crashed, asks, 'Anyone on board?' "[40] What happened was that ever more married women worked as well. And the biggest, fastest change was among the married and well educated.

More and more married women reentered the workplace. More and more never left it.[41] The result is that married American women today are ten times more likely to be in paid employment than they were a hundred years ago.

These changes are not just American. Terence Rattigan's recently revived play *Flare Path* is set among the English airfields of the Second World War's Allied bombing campaign—a world he knew well from his own wartime service. One vignette encapsulates pre-1940s life and attitudes, and the scale of postwar change. It finds Maudie Miller, the wife of a working-class bomber sergeant, horrified and deeply offended. A condescending civilian thinks she normally works in a laundry. On the contrary, she points out.

> "I'm new to it, of course."
> "You haven't always done that kind of work?"
> "Oh no. Not peace time, I didn't. I didn't have to work peace time. Dave had a good job, you see, and we had our own home."[42]

A few decades ago, in a world of breadwinner marriages with stay-at-home wives, far fewer women than men were in paid employment at any given time.[43] Today we assume that, in marriages and partnerships, two incomes will be the rule. Women have moved from being a minority of the workforce to almost half in most of the world's rich nations.[44] Even in Japan, where many non-Japanese assume that most women are full-time housewives, almost two-thirds of women between fifteen and sixty-four are now in employment and 43 percent of the workforce is female.

And so, today, Maudie would have a job in peacetime. But not throughout her married life and not, in overwhelming likelihood, full-time either. Because Maudie is not a graduate and is not a professional.

And in that big lower four-fifths of the job pyramid not only do women have jobs that are very different from men's, often in heavily feminized occupations. They also have very different employment patterns.

DROPPING IN AND OUT

Millions and millions of part-time jobs that did not exist in 1940 or indeed 1960 are now a major part of the developed world's economy. They are, everywhere, taken largely by women; but not by any or all of them. The less educated the women, the more likely they are to work part-time, especially if they are married. Less-educated women are also the ones most likely to drop out of the labor market for long periods of time even though, today, they almost all do return. Conversely, the more educated the women, the less likely they are ever to leave employment, and the more likely to work full-time.

Look at Figure 1.2 and you will how see how, right across the developed world, part-time work is an overwhelmingly female affair.[45] In the rich countries of the OECD, women are, on average, more than three times as likely to work part-time as men are. And this basic pattern holds whether a country falls below average for part-time working (like France or Spain) or above (like Australia or the UK).[46] The Netherlands, as Figure 1.2 shows, are record-breakers for reasons we'll return to below. But even though Dutch men and women are both more likely to work

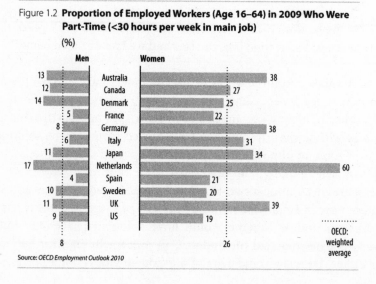

Figure 1.2 **Proportion of Employed Workers (Age 16–64) in 2009 Who Were Part-Time (<30 hours per week in main job)**

(%)

	Men		Women
Australia	13		38
Canada	12		27
Denmark	14		25
France	5		22
Germany	8		38
Italy	6		31
Japan	11		34
Netherlands	17		60
Spain	4		21
Sweden	10		20
UK	11		39
US	9		19
OECD: weighted average	8		26

Source: OECD Employment Outlook 2010

part-time than their rich-world contemporaries, Dutch women are still more than three times as likely to as the men.

Moreover, in most countries, the trend is upwards. As more women work, more of them work part-time. Except during serious recessions, surveys consistently find far more people who would like to work fewer hours than they find employees keen to add more paid hours to their working week.[47]

Part-time work is, however, much less common among graduate women than among the less educated. Of course, there are part-time professional women, and not all full-time professionals are happy with their hours.[48] But take the Netherlands, that world champion in the part-time league. Graduate women there are twice as likely as unqualified women to work full-time.[49] The US, meanwhile, has much higher rates of full-time female employment than most other developed countries. But there too employed women with a higher degree are significantly more likely to be full-time than are their least-qualified contemporaries.[50]

Men and women don't only differ in how many work part-time. They also differ, on average, in their work patterns over a lifetime. Men generally stay employed throughout their adult lives—or try to, recessions and lay-offs permitting. Many women, in contrast, spend sizeable periods not in paid employment. Not *un*employed and looking for work but *non*-employed: at home and not looking for a paid job. Many women. But not all.[51]

The educated elite are different. Highly educated women are not only more likely to work full-time.[52] They are also much less likely to drop out of employment for any significant length of time. As you might expect, having children often has a major impact on women's employment. But as we will see in detail in Chapter 3, the highly educated largely and increasingly stay employed even when they are mothers with young children. Less-educated mothers far more often stop.

Once again, the Dutch and the Americans, with their very different labor markets, show how prevalent this pattern has become. It is almost unheard-of for a graduate Dutch woman not to be employed at all, even when there's a small child around; women with less than an upper-secondary level diploma very often drop out of work completely. In the US, differences among women are huge. Among adult (twenty-five and over) female high-school dropouts just a third are employed at any given time. For female college graduates, it is about three-quarters.

A similar pattern holds for men; they are most likely to be working if they are college graduates, least likely if they are high-school dropouts. But the gap for women is much bigger, everywhere. In the US, it is twice the size of the gap for men, and in Italy it is even larger.[53]

If, as I've suggested, you think of the job market as a pyramid, with its top fifth made up of professional jobs, you can also usefully think of the female pyramid as dense and dark at the top and a lot more pock-marked and honeycombed below. The women in the top fifth not only work in sexually integrated occupations; they mostly work full-time hours, like the men, and they rarely drop out of employment. Lower down, there is far more movement in and out of employment; and, in a typical working week, far more hours spent outside the workplace too.

Why is there such a huge difference between more- and less-educated women? Kate Middleton offers the explanation.

DOING THE SUMS

In April 2011 Kate Middleton walked down the aisle of Westminster Abbey to marry Prince William, second in line to the British throne. She was certainly, in the process, ruling out any independent career. A good (and expensive) private school, good grades, a good university and a good degree had produced someone with an evident willingness, indeed enthusiasm, for life as a supportive wife.

As we saw earlier, many of today's educated young women simply do not see the world in the same way as the feminists of the 1960s and 1970s. Might Kate be the start of a counter-trend? Perhaps the employment rates and patterns that I have just described will be a high-water mark, as women reembrace the idea of getting married and then staying home.

Some people think so. The fear that American women were falling back into the trap of married dependency, living off their husbands' earnings, so horrified Leslie Bennetts that in 2007—not 1907—she fired off a whole high-octane book on avoiding the "Feminine Mistake."[54] In 2010 London the newspapers were working themselves up over another nightmare scenario, as educated mothers and teachers bewailed girls' apparent ambition to be a soccer player's wife or girlfriend, or clean up massively on a divorce settlement.[55]

Yet neither the soccer player nor the huge divorce settlement is, in practice, at all likely. There is no counter-trend emerging. Today's female teenagers will, for the most part, head for and stay in paid employment, not retreat into domesticity. The better educated they are, the more hours they will work. Just like their mothers.

Kate Middleton's mother, we should note, is half of a self-made millionaire partnership. The Middletons created a family business and fortune together: Carol Middleton was hardly brainwashing her children into the view that a mother's place is in the home. In understanding her daughter's decision, we need to take into account both tastes and opportunities, because that is how to explain Kate's choice, and that of other women. Taste, in Kate Middleton's case, not just for her husband as an individual but for the particular lifestyle of a consort and a princess. Opportunity, because the man she married is a multi-millionaire; she can, unusually, live very well indeed without worrying about the family finances.[56]

Taste and opportunity also explain the diverging work patterns of more- and less-educated women. Our work lives are the outcome of millions, and indeed billions, of individual decisions, taken on the basis of what each individual values and what different opportunities are on offer. Put together, these generate some remarkably similar outcomes throughout the developed world, because, in some key respects, our societies are very similar. They are enormously rich and productive by historical standards; they provide safety nets for the old, the sick and the very poor; and they have major values in common, including a belief in individual opportunity. Their professional job markets are integrated in gender terms, though much of the workforce is not; and women work part-time more often than men. But there are also marked differences among countries, which help explain how the general patterns arise. Compare, for example, the Netherlands and Sweden.

As we saw earlier, the Dutch have unusually high rates of part-time work. It is, predictably, more common among Dutch women with children, but it is very common indeed for women in general, encompassing over half of those without children too.[57] The large majority of Dutch women would turn down a job demanding more than forty hours a week, even at twice their current salary.[58] Only 4 percent of part-time women want to work full-time; instead, they tell surveys, they want time for friends and hobbies, as well as housekeeping and family.[59] And younger Dutch women seem even less inclined to work full-time than older ones.[60]

Clearly, a lot of Dutch women like to keep work in a second, instrumental position, and put family and personal life first. That is what I mean by "taste." Dutch psychologist and journalist Ellen de Bruin has written a book called *Dutch Women Don't Get Depressed*. It is because they work part-time that they are so happy, she argues: and this is about home life in general, not just about coping with childcare.[61] Dutch women interviewed by journalist Helen Rumbelow agreed. Educational psychologist Liesbeth Coen is single, childless and "the most I've ever worked is twenty-four hours a week . . . Sometimes I get jealous of those with flashy jobs and flashy holidays but I can fight it very easily when I remember how nice my life is." Part-timer Iris Bloem agrees: "It's financially viable if you change your way of life. I'm happy because I'm pursuing my passions."[62]

And "financially viable" is key: these choices are about opportunity as much as taste. The Netherlands' record-breaking performance in the part-time tables is a recent phenomenon. Recent tax reforms and higher childcare subsidies[63] have, as intended, got more women working—but with a huge increase in part-time rather than full-time jobs. Dutch researchers argue that this is because "relatively high-skilled work can be done part-time" in the highly productive Dutch economy and because, in a rich welfare state, "full-time work is not a financial necessity."[64] And that is true—at least for the moment, and creates an opportunity for women with particular preferences to indulge them.[65]

In the badlands of academia, there is a vicious little war going on between writers who suggest that many women have a positive liking for homemaking, and don't want to work in exactly the same way as men, and others for whom any differences in men's and women's job patterns clearly reflect continuing discrimination.[66] In the Netherlands, at least, no one seems to think high levels of employment discrimination explain why almost two-thirds of employed women are part-time and only a sixth of men. Sweden, at the other extreme in terms of the numbers of part-time women, lends support to this view.

Swedish society is organized in order to encourage full-time, not part-time, work. "Swedish women are more integrated in the labor market" is how one set of researchers puts it: meaning that they work longer hours than the European female average, and do so because full-time, not part-time, work is the norm, and encouraged by government policies.[67] But this creates its own stresses.

The European Union recently found, to its researchers' own astonishment, that Swedish families reported conflicts between work and family significantly more often than their contemporaries in apparently less "family-friendly" European countries. The differences were much more marked for women—all women, with and without children—though particularly large for Swedish mothers.[68] The reason, it seems, is that many women feel they cannot do all they need or want to do at home, or with their family, as well as hold down a full-time job. But finding a part-time job is hard in Sweden. The balance between pay, taxes and benefits pushes people down the full-time route and reduces the opportunities for a part-time choice.

It's important to remember that the large majority of these Dutch female part-timers and Swedish full-timers are not in professional or executive jobs, any more than most British, Japanese or Australian women are. They are doing jobs at the middle and bottom, not the top of the pyramid, jobs that bring in money.

I don't want to imply that money is the only reason why non-professional women go out to work. There are companionship, variety, structure and point to the day.[69] And while many of the high-growth jobs in modern economies are neither high-skill nor high-pay, there are plenty of jobs that people enjoy. Indeed, in high-skill craft jobs, such as hairdressing or carpentry, people report quite as much job satisfaction as any professional does.[70]

But a lot of the jobs done by married and single women are pretty unpleasant, as many jobs always have been. Florence Aubenas, one of France's top investigative journalists, spent a full year as an unskilled worker in the Normandy city of Caen, where factory jobs have been mechanized out of existence or disappeared abroad. Everyone she met

> warned me. If you come across a small ad for a job on the ferry
> at Ouistreham, be careful. Don't go. Don't reply to it. Don't even
> think of it. Forget it. Among the people I met . . . they all said the
> same thing: that place is worse than all the rest . . . worse than the
> oyster farmers, who make you wait for hours between tides before
> going to shake out the nets at sea, whatever the weather; worse
> than market gardening, which does your back in for chicory or
> carrots; worse than the . . . mushroom beds that leave you feeling
> completely bushed at the end of an afternoon's work . . . Those jobs
> are like being in a penal colony . . . But they're all better than the
> Ouistreham ferry.[71]

But night-cleaning on the long-distance ferry boats—the bathrooms, the vomit, the trampled cigarette stubs—was, in the end, the one job that lasted more than a week or two. Aubenas joined a workforce that was, she found, both female and part-time, making a classic trade-off between work, expenses and what they actually wanted to do, and at daybreak heading for home.

For many of the world's jobs, the question is surely not why anyone works part-time, but rather why so many women doing non-professional, non-elite jobs are full-timers. And here the differences between Sweden and the Netherlands explain a lot. The relative costs of working and not working—and so the opportunity to work part-time—differ. American experience confirms this. Like Scandinavia, the US has an unusually high level of female full-timers. It also has a very clear driver, absent from other developed economies. In America, as Vanessa Mobley, my New York editor, points out, "There's the small matter of insurance."

In America, if you have a good full-time job with benefits, then you don't need to worry about the doctor's bills, or the nightmare of a possibly disabling accident. Jobs with full health insurance tend to be full-time, not part-time. It's a pretty strong incentive.

Long-term, can our societies continue to generate the wealth that lets millions of women opt for part-time work and feel they can afford to do so? I honestly don't know. It will certainly become harder as today's developing world gets richer, its wages higher and its exports to us more expensive.

What happens will, however, involve individual women doing their sums and sizing up the opportunities. Just as they do today. And can this same arithmetic explain why highly educated women everywhere are employed for longer hours and more years than their compatriots? I think it can.

THE SAME BUT DIFFERENT

At some level, consciously or unconsciously, we are all asking ourselves the same questions. Are there jobs around that are profitable? How much do I need the money? What will I lose if I trade in paid hours for unpaid? And what do I most like doing? The workplace and the home mean more or less to different people, because people have different priorities. But across the world the equation comes out differently, on average, for particular groups. And it is consistently different for highly qualified professional women as compared to health aides, cleaners or office workers.

First of all, as a professional you're paid more. That might suggest that you can easily work less than other women, not more, because you will work fewer hours to earn a given amount. But it also means that, for every hour you put in, you clear more cash to spend on other things— eating out, taking holidays, dry-cleaning, home help: all the things that make it easier to combine going to work with a nice home and enjoyable leisure time.

Second, as a professional, staying employed affects your future pay. In their first jobs, and through their twenties, there are no real differences in average pay for men and women professionals: they are pretty much all working full-time, with male and female bankers paid the same (enormous) amounts, and male and female academics, scientists and doctors paid the same (rather lower) average salaries.[72] But as we'll see in more detail in Chapters 2 and 3, taking a long break from the labor market can have a serious negative impact on a professional's long-term pay. Most professional women can see this for themselves, even if they haven't been reading the research papers.

Third, educated women often do jobs that are pretty enjoyable. Susan Chira, the foreign editor of the *New York Times,* told me over a snatched Manhattan lunchtime that she is a classic example of women for whom work is "fulfilling, it's so woven with identity." From early on, "a big part of me was I really loved my work." But it is not just at the very top that graduate jobs are attractive. In London, university administrator Lindsey McBrayne values "the autonomy and the culture of being trusted. And I'm using the bits of my brain that I like to be activated."

And finally, a lot of professional and managerial jobs are simply not designed for part-time employees. You do them full-time or not at all; and "not at all" is a big decision to make.

Just as I started this book, I had a (rare) coffee with my stressed friend and neighbor Diana, a senior executive in a big TV company. She was longing to go part-time and spend more time with her children, and unable to find anything remotely near her current level. We were both puzzled. There is a sizeable group of professional women, mostly with children, who say they would like to work fewer hours but, like Diana, can't find a way of managing this.[73] Shouldn't employers leap at the chance this offers? Surely they could attract high-quality women at a much lower price per hour part-time than they pay them when working full-time. It's a real exploitation-of-women scenario waiting to be rolled out.

So why doesn't it happen? Is it stupidity? Prejudice?

"A puzzle for you to solve," said Diana.

Since that coffee, I've concluded that employers probably aren't irrational. If professional jobs can be subdivided easily, it is already happening on a large scale: parts of medicine and a good bit of schoolteaching have gone that way, everywhere in the world. There are growing numbers of part-time ministers, pastors and rabbis. Universities all take advantage of part-time teachers, who are cheap.[74] If other jobs aren't being subdivided in that way, if job-sharing isn't sweeping the world,[75] if work at the top stays overwhelmingly full-time, it's probably not because of institutional sexism.

In some jobs, it is obvious why part-time won't work. Lawton Fitt remembers that, in investment banking, "You give up your life. You're under tremendous stress, unbelievable stress. Standard for the things I want to do now in my life is I want to avoid doing things that make me wake up in the night in a cold sweat. Because I did that for nearly a quarter of a century."

This no doubt explains why investment banking and finance have unusually few women combining children with a continuing professional career.[76] But even coming down a notch or three, in pay and stress, basic constraints still hold. You can't run a university department properly without a calendar that encompasses a full week; ditto for a building site, a hotel, a magazine. Sue Clarke, now a government analyst, can look back at twenty years in college management: doing so, she emphasizes the need for senior college staff to commit time—and live nearby: "There's so much evening work. And recruitment. And I remember times when people said they would move closer and didn't and then they basically couldn't deliver on the job."

Full-time elite women have a lot to lose if they drop out for a while, and limited chances to go part-time. So compared to their less-well-paid, less-educated peers they take fewer breaks from employment, and many fewer part-time jobs.

Which nonetheless leaves one puzzle. Why aren't more women, and especially non-professional women, still opting out of employment altogether in favor of homemaking in a "breadwinner" marriage? Many, as we've seen, much prefer part-time to full-time work, so why are so many in employment at all? Maudie Miller, the character in Terence Rattigan's play quoted earlier, had been dragged into employment by wartime. Her generation, whether British, American, Dutch or French, weren't gasping to work in a laundry. What pulls so many of their granddaughters out of the house for a job at Walmart, Lidl or ASDA?

The answer is money again—but with a few twists to the tale.

Most women gave up paid employment on marriage well into the twentieth century even though men's earnings were generally lower in absolute terms than today; and not just because they were thrown out of occupations with a marriage bar. But women in the past also, as we will see in Chapter 4, worked longer hours at home than people do today; and they married in what was largely a no-divorce world.

Then things changed. "Homemaking," as we will see, started to take less time. The average number of children in a family fell fast. Divorce rocketed. And the job market altered. The number of good male "bread-winning" jobs began to shrink. And jobs that suited the great mass of women began to grow—including many part-time ones.[77]

For families making trade-offs between work and leisure, between paying bills and spending money on the one hand or doing without on the other, this was quite enough to create change. And for women, more financial independence, especially in a world of declining marriage and rising divorce, had to be attractive. Once started, the shift is self-reinforcing.

As soon as a lot of couples have two—or one and a half—incomes, it becomes harder and harder for others to live on one. If richer couples bid up the price of houses, if other people's children take it for granted that a "normal" childhood involves beach vacations and this year's electronic goods, if everyone else is out at work anyway and there's no one at home to talk to, why not do the same?

Today we have largely made the transition from the old world to one that is genuinely new.[78] Billions of individual decisions have produced societies in which women's lives are centered on the workplace as much as on the home. Within that world, however, highly educated women lead lives that are markedly different from those of other women.

It is true that babies, children and childcare are still central to most women's lives: more so than for most men, with all the tensions as well as the pleasures that involves. And yet even here there are stark differences between the top 20 percent and everyone else. Because it is among the new female elite, the best-educated, the most successful women, that child-bearing has changed the most dramatically. It is a change that distances them even further both from the past and from their female contemporaries.

2

THE RICH GET RICH AND THE POOR GET CHILDREN

*T*here were Seven Brothers seeking Seven Brides; and seven children in *The Waltons*, that nostalgic TV tribute to American rural life. Families of that size are almost unheard-of today and once were commonplace. Women spent their adult lives in child-bearing and child-rearing. "In pain thou shalt bring forth children," says God to Eve in the Bible, laying down her future as he banishes her from Paradise. And that is what women did.

As the world gets richer and as child mortality falls, human birth rates have plummeted pretty well everywhere. If a country's women are still having large numbers of babies across the board, you can bet, with total confidence, that it is a country at the bottom of the economic heap. And, within countries, the women with larger families are also usually poorer and less educated. Or, as the hit song of 1921 observed:

> There's nothing surer
> The rich get rich and the poor get children
> In the meantime
> In between time
> Ain't we got fun![1]

To us that is a cliché. Yet it is actually a very new state of affairs.

In the past it was not poor countries, or poor women, that boasted the largest families: quite the opposite. But today, as birth rates fall globally, it is the best educated and the most successful whose behavior has changed most dramatically. As we saw in Chapter 1, our new female elites are quite different from any that came before. And one key difference is the role of child-bearing in their lives.

Elite women are increasingly different from their contemporaries in their child-bearing patterns, as well as increasingly different from their own recent forebears. They differ in whether they have children at all. They differ in how many they have and, most of all, in when. And this parting of the ways can be traced back very clearly to the different choices that societies now offer to different sorts of women.

THE RETREAT FROM CHILD-BEARING

During the overwhelming bulk of human history, a very few individuals have been rich, a very great many have been poor and there has been a lot of breeding. Because *Homo sapiens*, as a species, shows rather little genetic diversity, many biologists believe that, at one time, our numbers must have been quite tiny (most plausibly because a natural disaster wiped most people out).[2] But once through this bottleneck, we have spread across the whole planet.

In the last few hundred years, we have multiplied at an unprecedented rate, at the same time as becoming extraordinarily rich by historical standards. Today, we number 7 billion, up from 3 billion as recently as 1960 and predicted to reach between 9 and 10 billion by mid-century. At which point, women are set to make the world's population plummet.

To see what is going on, open up the extraordinary *Gapminder* site (http://www.gapminder.org/) run by statistician Hans Rosling. On it, and with amazing ease, you can watch the world changing. Plug in "children born per mother," and "income per head," hit "play" and then watch in Technicolor as the last 200 years unfold. In country after country you can see how average family size shrinks rapidly—first in today's developed world, but then in East Asia, South America, India, and now in most of Africa as well.[3]

At the start of the nineteenth century, the US had one of the highest birth rates in the world. The UK was like China and India, and averaging between five and six births per woman; Canada and Italy were in the center of a bunched world pack. By 1900 Europe and North America were breaking free, their birth rates falling as their incomes pulled ahead; but as recently as the 1950s the average number of births per woman in the US was close to four. Today it is under two, less than replacement level (the level needed to keep a population stable over time).

In developed countries, almost no one, rich or poor, now has seven children. Fewer and fewer do so anywhere.

In many countries, including populous China, the birth rate has now dropped below replacement level; in some, including Germany and Japan, a drop in population looks imminent.[4] So in present form, having hit that 10 billion mark, population levels look set to start falling away quite rapidly. This isn't because the world's women have fallen out of love with children. But it is, to a large degree, because of decisions women make; and make in response to a world that offers new choices.

Many of the world's most highly educated women are not having babies at all. Generations are entering middle age at levels of childlessness that are historically extraordinary. When educated women do have children, they have very few. They have them later and later. Their work patterns, after childbirth as well as before it, are different from those of any previous female generation and increasingly like men's. Meanwhile, alongside them, other women—less-educated women—*are* having babies. They are having fewer than in the past, but in comparison with elite females they have more and have them younger. These women are changing their lives after and because of childbirth in ways that are quite different from their highly educated peers. The result is a widening gap between highly educated mothers and all their female contemporaries. Why? And is this permanent or just a transitional blip?

ROADS TAKEN AND NOT TAKEN

Let us start with a few numbers. In America, for example, since the mid-1970s, the proportion of American women who stay childless has doubled.[5] Figure 2.1 sums up just how common childlessness has become among educated women, and how closely the odds of having children have become linked to one's educational level.

Among American women with college degrees (bachelor's or above), between a fifth and a quarter of those born in the 1960s have never borne a child. Among graduates a few years older, it was over 25 percent. Other developed countries typically report levels of graduate childlessness just as high or higher.[6] And what Figure 2.1 also shows is that American women with graduate and professional degrees are, in the early twenty-first century, almost twice as likely to be childless as high-school dropouts of the same generation. This is a major parting of the ways.

The figures are for women aged forty to forty-four, when the overwhelming majority of women are beyond child-bearing. In this genera-

Figure 2.1 **Percentage of US Women Age 40–44 (Born 1962–66) Who Are Childless, by Educational Attainment, 2006**
Percentage childless

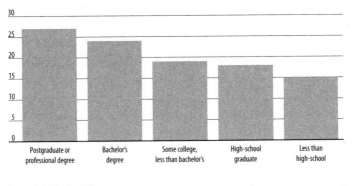

Source: adapted from Dye, 2008

tion, around a quarter of women acquired a full bachelor's degree or higher. That means there are almost 3 million US women graduates in this age range,[7] and about the same number in their late forties and early fifties. Several million of these highly educated middle-aged working women, often at the peak of their earnings and their career, have not and will not bear a child.[8]

There is nothing uniquely American about this. The picture in the UK is almost identical. There has been a growing polarization in childbearing between the most-educated women and other women;[9] childlessness is now roughly twice as high among highly educated Brits as among those with the least education.[10] In the rest of Europe the pattern is the same.

In the rich developed countries of Asia, births out of wedlock are very rare; so if you do not marry, you almost certainly will not have a child. But what you find instead is that marriage rates have diverged: in countries where marriage was once near-universal, many educated women never marry and therefore never bear a child. In Thailand, one-fifth of female graduates are single in their forties, compared to one-eighth of those who left school at eighteen. In Singapore, one-third of graduates in their early thirties are single;[11] in Japan, the fertility rate of female graduates is 20 percent lower than among those with just a junior school diploma.[12]

As college-going becomes ever more common among women, there is no sign of this pattern changing—just more of the same, more so. We can't be sure, until they reach their forties, whether today's thirty-something and twenty-something graduates will have as many, more or fewer children than the generation ahead. But age for age, so far, they are having even fewer. And in relative terms the gap between the least- and best-educated women is also not just large but growing.[13]

Figure 2.2 shows this very clearly. Fertility rates for American women have been dropping across the board. Back in 1970, you can see that every educational group was more than reproducing itself. Now, only the least educated are having babies at replacement level. But it is among the educated that fertility has dropped furthest and fastest.[14]

So much for the raw numbers. Why is this happening?

In the past it was taken for granted that women's function was to bear children. Women were "meant" to be mothers, not just biologically but because they were assumed to be intrinsically suited to childcare in a way that men were not.[15] This did not mean that our female ancestors all duly became matriachs presiding over tribes of children, sons- and daughters-in-law, grandchildren and great-grandchildren. On the contrary. According to primatologist Sarah Hrdy, for most of human history, a good half of all women in all likelihood died leaving no direct living descendants at all.[16]

But in the past, this was because so many of the children women bore died young: at birth, of starvation or disease, or killed in accidents, fights or wars during adolescence or young adulthood.[17] As for being

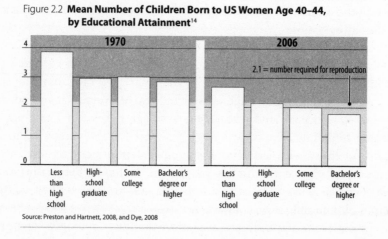

Figure 2.2 **Mean Number of Children Born to US Women Age 40–44, by Educational Attainment**[14]

Source: Preston and Hartnett, 2008, and Dye, 2008

"barren," this was viewed as a catastrophe and, in many societies, as automatic grounds for divorce.

Few people today think that women's sole function is to reproduce. Not all women want, or enjoy having, children. But was there such a huge mismatch in the past between what women wanted and what society imposed on them? Have vast swathes of women given a huge sigh of relief because they are no longer forced to be mothers against their will?

No, they haven't. Whether or not women remain childless is not, for the most part, the result of firm long-standing decisions, let alone innate preferences. A very few do realize early on that they don't want children, and never change their minds. And in the past some women were mothers simply because that was the occupation on offer. Investment banker Lawton Fitt says of her mother, "I think she's very proud of us, I think it was OK finally. But I really do believe that if my mother had been born when I was born she never would have had children. I don't think her child-raising was actually of any interest to her at all."

But this is a small minority. There is hardly a teenager to be found who has decided, definitely, to remain childless, no matter whether their grades are high, middling or low; nor is there any fall-off in aspirations through people's twenties. Young women want and expect to have children.[18]

What is more, women want larger families than they mostly have. Across the developed world, preferences for children have been remarkably stable for many years, and very similar across countries. The average preference comes out as a bit more than two—normally between 2.2 and 2.4.[19] Yet that aspiration, which reflects most people's wish for at least two children, is higher than any developed country achieves overall, let alone among its college-educated classes. For example, in 2004 a Gallup poll of Americans found that only 3 percent think a single-child family is ideal; but 20 percent of all families in modern America are "completed" by an only child.

When young, women who are now in their late forties and fifties almost all expected both marriage and motherhood. And very few elite women have a sudden deciding moment when they conclude that, after all, children are not for them. My friend Louise, a broadcasting executive who is also very active in politics, thinks she is pretty typical: "I didn't set out not to have children. But things happen or don't, and then there's that moment, in your forties, when you think to yourself: well, that's it then. And you go on to other things."

Whether specific women will, or won't, have children is not only unpredictable but in some ways fairly random. But for current generations as a whole, and for highly educated women around the world, what is happening overall is not in the least random. It has everything to do with opportunities, costs and economics. In fact, the puzzle is less that professional women have so few children, and more that they have as many as they do.

THE ROAD NOT TAKEN

If you try a couple of "thought experiments," it becomes quite easy to understand how this happens. And these experiments work just as well for men as for women—because, as I argued in Chapter 1, the lives of and opportunities for educated women and men are increasingly similar.

Imagine, for example, that you are offered an excellent new job. To take it, you have to relocate; but to an area or country you really like—New York, maybe, or Los Angeles, Sydney, Seattle, Paris, Cape Town. Take this experiment seriously. Think about it and pick somewhere you like a lot.

Right away, the move is really tempting. Now add to that being in a rut, bored with your current job. Imagine you are driven mad by your immediate boss. More points in its favor. The job itself involves a lot of travel: fine, you like travel, and challenge, and new places.

But you are in a relationship. It's going OK, but you are both busy; to be honest, you are lukewarm about it. It isn't the center of your life. Why not see how you both feel after being apart for a while? Maybe the other person will relocate for your sake. Then again, maybe not.

Try another one. You are working in a very competitive, well-paid field. You are offered the chance to join a small team working on a new, high-profile project. If it goes well, you have a real chance of promotion: you might make director, vice president, partner on the back of it; and do so sooner than most people your age, or than workmates whom you don't really rate, but who seem to be doing very well. It also means working not just late, but every weekend in the foreseeable future. It really is your choice: not everyone who is asked is saying yes. Think—imagine—hard.

Do you—did you—do it? Say yes to either of those choices and right there, if you are a woman, motherhood became significantly less likely.

These are hard decisions, and for individuals they are surprisingly difficult to predict. I know this firsthand. I got married and moved countries: the two went together. I then had children much earlier than my friends, mostly because of that move. Much of what I've done since, including opting for a relatively family-friendly academic career, has followed from those early choices—but none of it was in my plans at age eighteen. My daughter and her friends, in their twenties, are going for career, interest, risk. They know perfectly well what the statistics say, but the choices are between today's enticing options. You can't live in the uncontrollable future.[20]

The choices individual women make are unpredictable. But the choices they *can* make are not. Unlike any previous generation, millions of women born from the mid-twentieth century on can support themselves comfortably, make serious careers, start their own businesses and, indeed, raise children alone. The more highly educated, the greater the choices. Today's professional women are offered the chance to move west (or east), to open the new office abroad, to head the project team—but only *if* they make the commitment, *if* they put in the hours.

Of course, there are many childless women who regret the fact. Many find themselves caught out by their biological clocks, ready for children just as their fertility declines. But forty-something journalist Hilary Rose summed things up, commenting on a headline report about childless graduate women: "If I'd been born a generation earlier, I'd have married the man I was going out with at 25, and that would have been that, but I had options, and an education, and a fantastic job . . . I'm sure I'd have loved motherhood and I'm slightly bewildered to realize it really never is going to happen, but *c'est la vie*."[21]

And Pat McGuire, charismatic president of Trinity Washington University, a national figure in American higher education, member of multiple boards, corporate and not-for-profit, and a strong believer in a distinctive women's perspective, told me how irritated she was by the comments made about the childless and single: "I'm unmarried and have no children and I have a great life. So stop feeling sorry for me."

And so, in the US, in Europe and in ever larger parts of Asia, we find women who are more often single, far more often childless and far more often occupationally successful than their mothers were. And we also find, alongside them, more and more successful and childless men.

CUTTING BOTH WAYS

I used to believe that, while most women can't have it all, successful men mostly did. For professional women, there would be constant hard choices between family and career; for men, I assumed, career success just made it even more likely that they would get themselves an alpha wife and mother for their kids. It was obviously true historically that success bought quality *and* quantity. Genghis Khan, after all, has 16 million male descendants—one in 200 living males—and presumably just as many female ones.[22] And it still looks true at the very top today. Alpha males with serial marriages populate the gossip magazines: whether it's Donald Trump and Roman Abramovich, with classic ex-model trophy wives and girlfriends, or Rupert Murdoch and Paul McCartney, marrying wives who are decades younger, good-looking and stylish, and also financially successful in their own right.

But go outside the gossip pages, with their love of princes and showgirls, congressmen and pole dancers. Drop below the top quarter or half a percent. From there on, it isn't true at all. It is not just elite women who are failing to reproduce. Graduate and professional men, men in that top slice of the pyramid, are just the same.

Men's fertility is generally and curiously under-observed. If you look up "fertility" on the US Census website, you get a message "See under Women." But we do know what is happening to Harvard graduates.

Claudia Goldin and Lawrence Katz have analyzed marriage and child-bearing patterns for successive and recent generations of Harvard and Radcliffe graduates (Radcliffe being Harvard's sister college for women, which from the 1960s on moved toward a complete merger). And what they find are remarkably high, stable and similar rates of childlessness for men and women. A third or more of these graduates, in successive decades, have had no children. Moreover total fertility for each cohort has been well below replacement level.[23]

So Harvard graduates' children may be born with silver spoons, but there are surprisingly few receiving them. And the same is true for other elite groups, the men as well as the women. Take Germany. Professor Hermann Adrian, from the University of Mainz, looked at the family size of contemporary members of the German Parliament (the Deutscher Bundestag), omitting anyone under thirty-five.[24] This is as successful a large group as you will get, and two-thirds male. Yet half of these deputies have either only one child or no children at all. Only a little over a fifth have three or more children and, overall, deputies are well short of reproducing themselves. Broken down by political party, only one—the conservative CDU/CSU—has a majority of members with two children or more (and even there the figure is only 60 percent).

The UK has unusually good data on people's lives, and especially on those born in particular weeks of 1958, 1970 and 2000, who have been tracked carefully ever since by "Birth Cohort Study" researchers.[25] As a result we know that among people with higher degrees, men and women born in 1958 hit their mid-forties with identical rates of childlessness: 30 percent for women and 30 percent for men.[26] Moreover, among their exact contemporaries, men and women who had any form of college and tertiary education are also nearly identical in the proportions who have, or don't have, children.[27]

More generally, surveys of the British population in 1990 and 2000 showed that the proportion of men who are childless in their late thirties and early forties is significantly higher for graduates than it is for non-graduates.[28] It is true that men's biological clocks tick more slowly than women's. At ages thirty-four, thirty-nine and forty-four, more American men are currently childless than women; but men also tend to be older than women when their first child is born.[29] So, in theory, today's elite childless men in their forties could still have lots of children. But if they do, it would mean a major change in male behavior compared to previous generations.[30]

People find it very hard to believe that men and women are so similar. "Clever devils get the bird" read a headline in a recent Sunday newspaper; successful men get the girls, high-flying women have trouble finding a mate.[31] It was a story to confirm our preconceptions—only the people concerned were in fact all born before the Second World War. At work, I used to notice what I expected to see, namely the childless unmarried women and the men who remarried. But when I looked properly at fellow academics over forty in my own sizeable department, there were indeed almost no differences between women and men. Just one of us has children from more than one marriage, and yes, he's male: but childlessness, marriage and remarriage rates are almost perfectly balanced across men and women. It is indeed another way in which elite men and women have converged.

NOT OFTEN AND EARLY, BUT RARELY AND LATE

I recently took part in an all-female panel discussion about women's changing lives, along with some of London's leading female newspaper columnists and major feminist campaigners. Everyone but me strongly recommended having children later rather than sooner. That way, they argued, one's career was well established in advance of any break. I thought it was better to do the opposite, if possible: have children young and then have a clear sweep through middle age, guilt-free and relatively unexhausted. But I was not only outvoted on that particular panel; I am out of step with the temper of the times.

Having babies later and later is what occupationally successful women do. As we have already seen, large and growing numbers—unlike unqualified high-school dropouts—have no children at all. But highly educated women who do have children are also diverging from other women in when they have a child. They are having their children later and later, not only in absolute terms but compared to everyone else.

As recently as the late 1970s, not even forty years ago, having a first child after the age of thirty, let alone thirty-five, was highly unusual for women of any class. It had been equally unlikely throughout the previous centuries.[32] The idea that it would be "normal" to have one's first child after the age of thirty would have seemed completely extraordinary to any past generation.

That has changed totally. Turn up at the hospital as a pregnant thirty-five-year-old in labor and you'll be met with something of a yawn: this is routine stuff. Turn up as a thirty-five-year-old first-time mother and the yawn is only slightly smaller. Not only late childbirth but late first childbirth is now standard. Among American female graduates, the years between age thirty and thirty-five had become, by 2006, the peak child-bearing period. It is the same in the UK, where the proportion of graduates having a baby before they are thirty halved in the last few decades;[33] the same in France. The pattern is international.[34]

Live among today's graduate and upper middle classes and you might get the impression that no one even contemplates pregnancy until thirty looms. In fact you couldn't be more wrong. Most female high-school dropouts complete their families well before they reach their mid-thirties.[35] In the US four in five female dropouts are mothers by the age of twenty-five, while in Britain about half of all native-born women without qualifications become mothers by the time they are twenty-two.[36] And other, more educated but non-graduate women also have their children at what used to be a "normal" age; for those with some college or a two-year degree, the peak is between twenty-five and twenty-nine.[37]

Only for mothers with full bachelor's degrees, or more, does thirty signal the start of peak child-bearing years.[38] And only for them has there been a major change in the likelihood of having a first child after the age of thirty.[39]

NO DELAYS AND NO REGRETS

In 2005 Kathryn Edin and Maria Kefalas published a classic study, *Promises I Can Keep.* Based on an in-depth study of 162 young mothers—white, black and Hispanic—in the Philadelphia area, its main purpose was to understand why so many young women become single mothers, especially given how hard they have to struggle to support their children. The answers are equally relevant to the dramatic contrast between the *ages* at which poorly educated and well-educated women now become mothers.

The mothers in Edin and Kefalas's study were all single, either legally or—for the few who had been married—in practice. Nearly three-quarters had their first child while still in their teens. Nearly half had been or were on welfare; fewer than half were currently employed. They were also overwhelmingly positive about motherhood: "It is wonderful," "I'm *excited* when I get up in the morning," "It's like a *burst* of energy."[40]

Edin and Kefalas asked each of the mothers, "What would your life be like without children?" and the responses took them by surprise. As they explain:

> We assumed this question would prompt stories of regret over
> opportunities lost and ambitions foiled . . . But there were
> startlingly few . . . Instead, mothers repeatedly offered refrains
> like these: "I'd be dead or in jail"; . . . "I wouldn't care about
> anything"; . . . "It's only because of my children that I'm where I am
> today" . . .
> When we've told these mothers' stories to audiences around the
> country, many of our listeners are surprised . . . One woman, a
> new mother herself . . . found our claim that children bring order
> to the lives of poor mothers difficult to swallow . . . On another
> occasion, a listener told us she simply couldn't accept our contention
> that poor women express so little regret over having had children
> when and how they did. She demanded to know more about the
> "ambivalence" women must feel . . . "There has to be some tension
> or sense of regret" she exclaimed.[41]

But there doesn't, and isn't, because rewarding careers are not on offer to these women. On the contrary, they often feel rootless, lonely, without value. Children offer love, meaning and a reason to take control of their lives. As the mothers put it:

> "I got somebody that I can say that's mine . . . I know that he got love for me and I got love for him."

> "I'm proud of myself . . . I made my son what he is."

> "God's given me something . . . It's for a reason."

> "To know that I brought this person into the world and they didn't know anything and now I'm teaching and they're learning—that was a great feeling."[42]

Mothers—and indeed fathers—everywhere adore their children. But these young women have babies young, and husbandless, and without regrets, because their alternatives are so limited. It is to do with what economists call "opportunity costs": what else you might be doing with your time and what rewards different alternatives offer.

Simple arithmetic suggests that among women it is the professional and business elite who give up the most if they have children, and so will be least inclined to do so. If you work at a checkout or in a restaurant, earning $15 or £10 a hour, and quit to stay at home with your kids, that is the amount of money, and the sort of job, that you are giving up. If you are, instead, a high-salaried manager or professional, earning the equivalent of $150 or £100 an hour, then you lose ten times as much income for every hour you no longer work.[43]

And it is not just about current earnings. Young, poorly educated women do not believe that delaying child-bearing will have any major effect on their future economic prospects; and the statistics say they are right. Checkouts and waitressing jobs will still be there, paying the same, five or ten years from now.[44] For professionals, however, time out means time lost in making a career, a lower chance of promotion, losing your networks and contacts, as well as giving up something that you really enjoy.

It matters how much you lose; what also matters is how much you have left to live on, *compared to what you would have without a baby*. And this is where governments contribute to the widening divides among women, and especially between the most and least educated in our societies.

PARENTED BY THE STATE

Until very recently, no adults anywhere had tax-financed welfare states to depend on. There were no unemployment benefits and no social security. People's families were their social insurance policies: for the vast majority without private incomes, life without family meant penury. So it paid everyone to have children, as security for sickness and old age.[45]

In these societies, being a single mother was a recipe for destitution. State support for single mothers was essentially nonexistent: babies were abandoned, left with "foundling hospitals," where the death rate was astronomical, or given up for adoption. Today, by contrast, in almost all developed societies single mothers, whether unmarried, separated, widowed or divorced, have a right to benefits. These may not offer an affluent life but they certainly offer a supportable one. And the fewer your prospects, the lower your earnings before you become a mother, the better life on benefits, with a baby, will look.

For the rest of us, the arithmetic looks different. Children are a serious, if adored, expense; and we find it pretty obvious that when, exactly, people start a family will have a lot to do with money. We're used to the idea of saving for a mortgage and paying off some of our college debts first. We are, however, offended by the idea that money affects whether we have babies at all, or how many; and that this is true not just among the poor and those on welfare benefits, but right across society.

Yet while I was writing this chapter, I talked to Ludmilla. She does my ironing and is typical of London's ambitious new Polish immigrants, balancing ironing, dressmaking, part-time college and raising two kids, while her husband works long hours as a chef. "My sister and brother-in-law look at how we're struggling," she says. "They've both got good jobs here, they like having a good life. So they've decided not to have children at all."

She was shocked; but there is overwhelming evidence that money affects the birth rate. It is not just earned incomes that matter, but also government tax and spending policies. To take just a few examples:

- In the UK, single mothers (of any age) have for many years gone straight to the top of the list for "social housing"—that is, accommodation found and paid for by the state. In Italy and Spain, there are no such housing benefits. Britain has one of the highest rates of teenage pregnancy in Europe; Spain and Italy, among the lowest.

- American birth rates since 1913 seem to have been affected, in both directions, by the tax exemptions for dependents: in other words, if children earn you a big tax deduction, you are more likely to have them and vice versa.[46]

- In Israel, ultra-Orthodox Jews tend to have very large families; and almost two-thirds of the fathers are not employed, but rather spend their whole time in religious study, while the state, and child benefit, support the family. When child benefit cuts were proposed, the ultra-Orthodox campaigned against them vigorously. This was condemning children to poverty, they argued, since having babies was nothing to do with economics, but rather a religious commandment. The government cut benefits anyway; and birth rates duly declined.[47]

- In 1999 the British government introduced novel "tax credits" and more income support for low-income families with children. Overall, the reforms involved substantial sums of money.[48] Researchers estimated that, among less-educated parents, there were 45,000 additional births in a year as a result, or about 7 percent of the total number of births:[49] equivalent to filling a large baseball stadium with "new" babies every year—or, if scaled up for the US population, to filling five.

All these examples involve people having more babies—but it also works the other way around. In terms of pensions and healthcare, parents today are no better off in old age than non-parents: a complete change from the past. People today, of all classes, expect the state, not their family, to take care of their basic needs when retired, regardless of whether they have six children contributing to the tax pool or none at all; and in almost every developed country, the same is true of our health in old age as well. So there is no longer a compelling reason to be a parent as a form of insurance policy. In old age, the state is parent to us all.

The American economist Shirley Burggraf has argued strongly that "no society until recent times has expected love alone to support the family enterprise."[50] Actually, we don't quite expect that either: we do help the families of children who are very poor. The tax credit and income benefits that the British governments introduced, which quite unintentionally raised birth rates too, were quite large. For the poorest fifth of households with children, the increase in benefits for a first child amounted, on average, to 10 percent of their net household income.[51] I say the amounts were "quite large"—but only if your income was low to begin with. Ten percent of a poor family's income won't pay a nanny's taxes, let alone their wages, in Paris, Tokyo or Los Angeles.

As we have seen, the educated elite are more likely to be childless. Graduate women are also likely to have their first children at a historically unprecedented and late age. And there is a third difference between them and other women, which has a good deal to do with cost pure and simple. They are having fewer children.

This is true even when you compare mothers with mothers, rather than averaging across a whole age cohort in which many graduates remain childless. It is true whether you are looking at the US or Canada, France or Italy, Sweden or the UK.[52] It has a great deal to do with the "opportunity cost" of children, the difficulty of combining family and career. But it also reflects those nannies' taxes and wages.

While families are shrinking in size everywhere, those of graduates and professionals stay smallest. Less-educated women have their children far earlier, on average, than do graduates; but most do not, today, have more than two. However, in most countries graduate women are more likely than others to have just one child and rather less likely to have two.[53] And everywhere they are not only more likely to be childless but also much less likely to be in the small minority who still have more than three.[54]

This pattern is not particularly new, although the scale of it is unprecedented. In the mid-twentieth century, far fewer women than today had prominent careers. But among the few who did, child-bearing and fertility patterns were surprisingly similar to those of today's successful women. In the US, for example, the late 1940s was a period when married women over forty, with completed families, had an average of 3.2 children. However, for married women of this age and time who were listed in their own right in Who's Who, the average was 1.3; over half had either no child or one; and at a time when a quarter of their peer group had borne five or more children, only 3 percent reported this many.[55]

If you track today's really successful women—the CEOs of FTSE 100 or Fortune 500 companies, the college presidents, the cabinet ministers, the self-made entrepreneurs—you will also find a lot without children, and a lot with a single child. A tiny number of superwomen also keep a large family airborne. But Nicola Horlick, setting up her own asset management fund (twice) while bringing up six children, and Helena Morrissey, chief executive of multi-billion Newton Investment Management and mother of nine, are only marginally more typical of modern educated women than Prince William's bride, Kate Middleton, or Masako Owada, former Japanese diplomat and Crown Princess of Japan.

We saw above how money affects child-bearing; but those examples mostly concerned middle- and lower-income families. Money also matters for most educated parents, however; because the costs of children can be breathtaking, as we'll discuss in more detail below. As you might expect, the very rich consequently have more children than the educated upper-middle classes. Almost half of American women in the top 1 percent of households have three children or more, way ahead of the population as a whole, let alone of college-educated women overall.[56] These families can afford it.

Modern governments in developed countries are often very concerned about low birth rates, and intent on raising them. In Europe, fertility rates currently vary quite a bit and do seem to be linked to labor market policies. Fertility is higher in Scandinavia, with its large number of stable public-sector jobs for women, backed by very generous parental leave, and lower in southern Europe, with far fewer benefits for single and working mothers.[57] But policies that are designed explicitly to raise birth rates often have very modest effects.[58] France has poured vast amounts of money and effort into raising its birth rate: it is now "top" of the Western European league and yet its birth rate is only minutely larger than that of laissez-faire Britain.[59] So governments would probably have to spend a very great deal of money to increase birth rates substantially among the professional classes.

As for Asia, Singapore has for decades now been exhorting and encouraging its highly educated citizens to have more children, offering benefits and even government-supported matchmaking bodies, but to no avail. As we saw earlier, over a third of graduates in their thirties are childless and Singapore's fertility rate is currently well below even that of Japan, which has far less in the way of family-friendly policies on offer. Taiwan and South Korea, both well below replacement levels, have new policies that will certainly be costly if they work. They include very generous parental leave and flexible working rights, and a big expansion in subsidized kindergartens. Singapore's experience makes it hard to believe that anything of this sort will reverse the deep-seated changes that feed through into women's—and men's—decisions.[60]

TOO FEW, TOO LATE?

It is clear how and why so many graduate women (and men) end up with few children or none. It is from a whole succession of more or less conscious choices about career and relationships, and the relative attraction and cost of one path over another. But there's one other factor too. Sometimes, it is the unintended consequence of delay.

Few of us, as we have seen, always intend to be childless. And few of us say that we want an only child, or think that is a good idea in principle.[61] But the older you are the dicier conception becomes. Past thirty-five, women's fertility drops fast. Modern medicine seems to offer miracles, the chance to ignore and bypass biology. But at forty, fertility is way down, far more than most people realize.

Professor Peter Braude of King's College London is one of the world's foremost academic experts on fertility and assisted reproduction. I asked him about fertility as one gets older, and in particular about the chances of getting pregnant via IVF (in vitro fertilization).

"If you say what would be the likelihood that I would get pregnant at the age of thirty-five, probably about one in three will go home with a live birth. If you say what is it likely to be when I'm age forty, probably about one in ten will go home with a live birth. And if I'm forty-two, probably now we're going down to about one in twenty . . .

"We do a presentation in our own clinic for all our patients who come along every month and we show them the real figures saying that the likelihood of going home [pregnant] is so much. When patients come and they've not got pregnant, and they come back to see us, the first question I ask one of them is, 'What did you think the likelihood of going home with a baby was?' They'll say, 'Not very good.' So I'll say, 'Well, what do you mean?' 'Oh, about 80 percent.' And then I ask the other one, 'What do you think?' 'Oh, 50–50.' And I say, 'Where did you get that number from? We never told you that.' That is the wish; that is the presumption of what they're really hoping to happen. There's plenty out there in the literature, but people don't want to hear that, they really don't.'"

Part of this, Braude explains, is because of the "lucky fertile," who have babies at thirty-nine or forty, can't see what the fuss is about and say so to everyone they know. But it is also the media coverage.

"You suddenly see some film star—forty-seven—has twins and you probably think, ooh isn't that marvelous. [But] that woman had the twins because she had ovum donation using eggs from a younger woman, because she couldn't get pregnant herself.

"People come to us having had significant careers, having made a lot of money, having achieved what they really want to do, and say, OK, now's the time I'm going to have my family. And they can't pay for it, they can't buy it, they can't work hard for it and it just doesn't come.

"It's very hard when you're younger to think about the future. I mean, how many of us really are thinking about our pensions and our life insurance when we're twenty-one years old? We don't. And it's exactly the same sort of thing. When you have a good job and you're running a bank or you're looking toward running a bank, or whatever it is, you'll say, well, I'll get there when I'm thirty-five. Then I can have my family.

"It's really very difficult for women. They're at their fittest, they're at their brightest, they're making things happen and they feel they've got to keep along that track. And there is nothing that easily allows them to take a break."

Predicting the future is a game for deluded optimists; but are elite women, en masse, going to downsize their careers anytime soon? It seems implausible. In which case this century's story will be one of male and female elites who are alike in this respect too: they will have fewer children than their contemporaries, and many will have no children at all.

3

THE RETURN OF THE SERVANT CLASSES

"The hand that rocks the cradle is the hand that rules the world," claims William Ross Wallace's famous (or infamous) poem.[1] Today's women don't believe a word of it. They know where success and influence are actually to be found, and the mothers among them are getting back there at an ever-faster rate. The cradle-rocking they delegate to others.

Yet until the 1970s, educated women who gave birth behaved in exactly the same way as their less-educated sisters. They stopped work, they stayed home, their daytime lives revolved around their children's. Today, the widening gap between highly educated women and others is evident not just in whether and when they have children, but also in how they bring their children up. They—we—have reinvented the servant classes.

GOODBYE TO THE MOMMY TRACK?

As we saw in Chapter 1, unmarried middle-class women gradually entered paid employment in the nineteenth and twentieth centuries, as their working-class sisters had before them. But marriage usually meant an end to employment for both groups, and having children pretty well automatically did—often permanently. The earlier unmechanized agriculture of pre-industrial societies had dragged most women back out into the fields; but urban women of all classes, after child-bearing, quit paid employment. Obviously, they went on working, often extremely hard. But only when family circumstances were dire did they work outside the home for pay.

The women born in the first quarter of the twentieth century (many of whom became mothers in the suburban, baby boom 1940s and 1950s) were true to the image we have of them. They stayed home, kept house, raised kids. Many never returned to paid employment at all—including many of the most highly educated.[2]

Motherhood, in other words, brought with it experiences that were common across classes, whether you had left school at sixteen or were a graduate of an elite women's college. One such college, Barnard College in New York, surveyed its alumnae in depth in the 1950s and found that one of the most frequent criticisms was Barnard's failure to recognize the reality of women's roles.[3] Pre-war alumnae from the 1920s and 1930s were especially likely to wish they had received "a little better training for the womanly roles of wife and mother"[4] or "more practical training for homemaking and marriage."[5] The complaint was far from universal, but it reflected the dominant reality of this generation's lives.[6] As one member of the class of '37 explained, "Barnard did not prepare me for the life of a wife and mother—which is, after all, the main postgraduate occupation of Barnard graduates."[7]

The next generation, born mid-century, are the mothers of many of today's successful thirty-something careerists. For them, returning to work became standard.[8] As we saw in Chapter 1, the employment rate for married women took off in the 1940s and 1950s and went on climbing for decades, in large part because mothers returned to the workforce. But "returned" is the operative word: they took time out first.

Population expert Heather Joshi has calculated how long, on average, British women of the last century have stayed out of the labor market after bearing their first child. Among those having children in the 1950s, the median gap in employment after having a baby was twelve or thirteen years for all groups of mothers—meaning that it took that long for *half* of new mothers to return to any form of paid employment at all. By the time the postwar baby boomers gave birth, the median had dropped to just under six years but was still much the same for all and any groups of women.[9]

Today this pattern is transformed. There are now major differences between less- and more-educated mothers. They are different in how quickly they return. They are different in the hours they put in. They are different in how they cope with family plus work, and different in who looks after the kids.

Almost every developed country in the world now offers paid maternity leave.[10] There is pressure for it from women's groups and it is perceived as popular with women voters. Governments that are increasingly worried about falling fertility rates also hope that generous maternity leave will persuade more working women to have babies.[11] But at the end of maternity leave, paths diverge.

Many new mothers still end up staying home and non-employed for a good while; most look for jobs that fit around the family.[12] Mothers of young children have a particularly strong preference for part-time work, although, as we saw in Chapter 1, countries vary in how easy it is for them to find it, and the degree to which government policy promotes part-time working.[13]

But at the top, it is different. Here motherhood no longer transforms work patterns in the traditional way. Among the most highly educated, the most common pattern is to minimize time out and rush back to work. Harvard's Claudia Goldin has tracked and compared successive cohorts of college graduate women and concludes that those graduating between 1980 and 1990 were the first group among whom substantial numbers managed to have family and career, at the same time (something that isn't quite the same as "having it all").[14] And they did it by getting straight back into employment.

The differences are stark. It is not just that far more of the highly educated mothers are working.[15] In the "prime" age group of twenty-five to forty-four, mothers with graduate education are almost exactly as likely to be working if they have children as if they don't. Journalist Jan Murray, mother of a young daughter, points out that this can make staying at home "incredibly lonely. I struggled a lot with my decision to work when my daughter was a baby. But most of my friends were professionals like me, and keen not to drop the career they'd worked so hard for. So they were all working."

In writing this book, I talked to a whole range of successful young women—in business and finance, academia and government, publishing, museum work and journalism. I didn't set out to find ones with particular "mainstream" characteristics: these were people I knew, friends of family, friends of friends. None of them was having a child before the age of thirty; and only one was contemplating taking a full career break.

I spoke to Deirdre Eng in a coffee shop near the company where she recently became chief financial officer. She is very pretty, with feminine floaty clothes, a mile away from the old blue suit and white shirt look. She's also someone with a graduate degree in finance from one of the world's top business schools, a background in investment banking, consulting and private equity and an equally high-flying partner.

On the day we meet, she is thirty-three and newly pregnant. She explains, "From a very young age, people want to succeed at different things and I wanted to excel at academics and have a better life. At Wharton, in terms of jobs and internships, I chose investment banking because I thought the skill set would be much more leverageable, and once my eyes were set on the banking stuff I kind of settled with that."

And is it a problem, being a woman in that world?

"Not with men of my age. I don't think it was ever an issue with them. They grew up with mums at work, they grew up with women they worked with and with women bosses. It's only as you get to more senior roles—you know, becoming a woman in her mid-thirties starts to become a question mark to these men that run departments. And I was in an interview where they point-blank asked me, am I ready to do this job at this stage in my career, which was borderline illegal."

And now that she is, indeed, expecting a child?

"Will I stay home? No, that's not going to be the case. My mum stayed home with us. But it's not a reality for me."

I've quoted Deirdre, but I could have picked almost any of the thirty-somethings I talked to. Among less-educated women, there is still a significant difference in the work patterns of those with and without children at home.[16] But among the most highly educated, the difference between women with children and women without is vanishing. In the US it is now "so small as to be statistically insignificant in most years," according to economist Heather Boushey.[17]

In other words, the more educated they are, the more mothers in Western societies behave, in work and career terms, exactly like men, and exactly like women without children. This is very recent. As we saw above, Heather Joshi has calculated that, for British mothers born in the 1940s and 1950s, the median time out of the workforce was almost six years.[18] But skip forward just a couple of decades and she finds that "[w]ell over half the 1970-born graduates who had become mothers by age 33 had resumed employment within a year of their first birth": in other words, the "median labor force interruption" was down to zero. But only for graduates.[19]

Susan Chira, the foreign editor of the *New York Times*, joined the paper in the 1980s and saw the change happen.

"When I first worked there, I can't think of a foreign correspondent with a working wife. There was a traditional marriage structure. The wife went over and took care of the kids and the household management and the servants or whatever it entailed. And did not have a career. Now in many cases, they found very satisfying work, but opportunistically, it was not a career that went from A to B to C. Then it changed. And many men had to say no, I can't take this assignment because my wife's job is important. Or vice versa."

Poorly qualified mothers tend to move in and out of employment, with frequent periods outside the paid labor force.[20] Among the mothers of UK babies born in 2000, for example, over half of the least-qualified mothers were not employed at all during the first three years of their children's lives. By contrast, over two-thirds of those with any higher-level qualifications (tertiary-level qualification or above) were back at work within nine months.[21]

Right across Europe it's the same. Among mothers with children under six the highly educated are far more likely to be working than their poorly educated contemporaries. They get back to work, fast;[22] and then they stay there.

Isn't this rather odd? You would think that it is for the poor and poorly educated that the extra money would be really important. Certainly in the past, as we saw in Chapter 1, it was only when family circumstances were dire, or the country was at war, that married women, let alone mothers, went out to work routinely. Otherwise, the ideal was a "breadwinner" family, where the father earned enough for everyone and mothers could stay at home. So why, today, is it the poorest mothers who stay home and the highest earners who rush back?

It comes back, of course, to costs and opportunities, just as it did with the choice between full- and part-time work that we discussed in Chapter 1. Small children require a lot of care; someone has to look after them. If your babysitters need to be paid, then you need to earn enough to cover that post-tax. The lower-paying the jobs, the less financial sense it makes; and it is especially unlikely to make sense if you are eligible for state benefits. Do the sums and you might well conclude that you're worse off at work than not. While if you're a highly skilled professional, you may wonder if you can afford to stay home.

HEADING OUT OF THE DOOR

Vanessa Mobley, my US editor, had just had her first child when I started writing this book, and was correspondingly aware "that there is a feeling that women are severely punished for leaving the workforce, even for short periods of time. Plus who really would choose to not have a job when there are so many who have no jobs? And also you have the fact that American companies now underwrite retirement. You know, leaving a workforce would mean you were turning your back on the way companies match your contributions. That is a large part of a benefit package.

"But I also think it's so many points—it's an issue of status, and status is felt most acutely psychologically. There's the sheer fact that one doesn't want one's life to be shipwrecked by the introduction of children. I mean, why go from working in an office to wearing sweatpants every day and seeking out a living doing this and that? Why not continue to have one's identity?"

Multiple studies in the 1980s and 1990s all highlighted the way motherhood affected women's careers. Mothers earned less: theirs was a story of interrupted employment, with lower earnings and less success later.[23] Campaigners continue to insist that, for this reason, our societies need to change radically. Anne-Marie Slaughter wants women to "insist on changing social policies and bending career tracks to accommodate *our* choices";[24] Sylvia Ann Hewlett argues that "our increasingly extreme work model" clashes with the need women have to take care of children and the elderly, and that unless we can offer ways back into work after breaks and slowdowns, we will go on "leaving women behind in new ways."[25]

Today, *like for like*, women and men are paid and treated more or less equally in the workplaces of the developed world.[26] And the earnings gap for men and women has narrowed visibly and markedly compared to previous decades.[27] The point, of course, is that *like for like includes having a similar track record*. If you treat women as a single group, and add part-time and full-time workers together, you still find lower average hourly wages for women than for men, whether you're looking at North America, Europe (including Scandinavia) or Asia. This is in large part the direct result of spending substantial periods out of the labor market, which lowers your later earnings, and a preference for part-time jobs, which tend to be less well paid per hour.[28] And the most important reasons for both of these are motherhood and family.

Today's graduate mothers, going straight back to work, certainly recognize the costs and stress. Lee Ann Daly, looking back on a varied career from the vantage point of a top marketing job at Thomson Reuters, didn't feel she had ever experienced any serious issues as a female among men. On the other hand, the time came when "I did think I was having problems because I was a woman, because I had the wonderful blessing and curse of being a mother. But that is different."

In some high-stress, high-commitment jobs, things still definitely give when you have a baby. At one of the big investment banks, a vice president told me that half of the women who come back from maternity leave are gone again within a year. Columbia University professor Merit Janow, once a Wall Street lawyer herself, comments that in Wall Street firms it is "seven days a week, two all-nighters. You make a choice." Facebook's Sheryl Sandberg left entry-level jobs that were "a balanced mix of male and female" for Silicon Valley promotions where "fewer and fewer of my colleagues were women."[29] Nationally and internationally, however, the statistics are consistent and stable. Fewer women now take long breaks when their children are born, and very few graduates do so.[30] MBAs may find it hard to work continuously, but M.D.s find it easy. And while the impact of career interruptions is still strongly evident in the pay of women now in their fifties,[31] including graduates, it is shrinking. Not only is the overall male–female wage gap down but some studies suggest that for highly educated younger Americans and Europeans, including those with children, the gap has vanished altogether.[32]

Heather Joshi, who has charted the earnings penalty for successive generations of mothers, concludes that a graduate mother today who postpones child-bearing until thirty and then returns to work will probably suffer no earnings loss at all for a first child.[33] Even that extraordinarily rare beast, a graduate mother of four, will end up with wages only marginally below the childless provided she follows the new norm and goes back straight after maternity leave.[34] Motherhood now typically "costs" lower earners much more, in terms of their lifetime earnings and in comparison with men, than it does the average graduate, because it is the lower earners who most often change their work lives.[35]

Given how many academics are women, it's not surprising that data sets charting the wage histories of US graduate mothers have been squeezed pretty thoroughly dry.[36] Some studies find little or no "motherhood penalty" at all; some find significant ones, though lower than in the past; and one, rather astonishingly, found that college-educated mothers in their late thirties and early forties[37] were actually earning *more*, at the turn of the century, than their childless graduate contemporaries. But only if they had delayed child-bearing. Far from suffering a motherhood wage gap, these women were, in terms of take-home pay, doing better than non-graduate mothers, better than graduate mothers who had children in their twenties and better, even, than childless female graduates.[38]

This sounds really implausible at first hearing. Even the most Pollyanna-ish of us hardly expects our employers to promote us when and because we announce a pregnancy. And it is—so far—a one-time result, for a particular group and cohort. But it fits with another recent finding.

Among young English graduates, the women who are most keen on taking a motherhood break also tend to have lower wages at the start of their careers and to search for jobs with less intensity.[39] This makes intuitive sense: we may all face the same modern labor market, but we have very different personal tastes. Among the lawyers I know, two of the cleverest—one male, one female—switched to university teaching early on. They are both doing fine, gained control of their time, which they really wanted, and are also earning a fraction of the salaries they could have enjoyed.

The earnings results I've quoted must surely also reflect conscious choices. For women who are focused on career success, delaying childbirth means there is time to get established, and find relatively family-friendly workplaces and employers who want them for the long term.[40] Many will seek out jobs that pay very well, because that makes it a lot easier to work *and* have children. But my basic point, that taste for career and taste for motherhood affect which jobs graduates choose, also explains why chunks of Britain's civil service are becoming so remarkably female.

Just before I finished this book, I was asked to write a big report for one of our main central government departments. (Getting "outside experts" to carry out reviews is a common UK practice.) I spent a good deal of time talking to policy-making staff just below the top grades: permanent civil servants who are making what our system refers to as "fast-track" careers. These are mostly clever people in their mid- to late thirties; and time and again, I'd find myself in groups that were 100 percent female. And in groups where a good number were just back from maternity leave, or in a carefully constructed job-share, or working four or even three days rather than full-time. This degree of flexibility is almost unheard-of in the private sector; and all my civil servant friends agree that it attracts able women who want children—and then ties them in.

And it is, still, the women who think and plan ahead for children plus careers. The young women I interviewed for this book took it for granted that they would continue working if and when they had children. But I was struck that without exception and also without complaint—if anything the opposite—they saw themselves as the "primary" parent.

Take Laura Mercadier, earning a lot of money in prime brokerage, someone who had loved being a trader: "I think most women, especially my age—I'm thirty-two—would rather have a baby than promotion. And now, I think Anglo-Saxon companies especially, they're very into having women. They will create policies around being a mum."

In Oxford, student historian Kiera, ambitious and organized, re-marked that "[m]ost of my female friends, when you talk about careers they'll talk about how maybe they want to take a couple of years off to bring up children; and none of my male friends do. It doesn't seem to be on my male friends' agendas. Even when you ask them straight out, 'Do you want children?' and they go, 'Yes, yes, of course,' it doesn't seem to be figuring in their career plans in the same way."

Lindsey McBrayne is a London-based university administrator in her early thirties, whose boyfriend "changed jobs recently, and he did not think about things like whether or not there were family-friendly poli-cies. Now, if we already had a child he might have thought about it a bit more. But I don't think any of that came into his mind. Whereas for me, I keep thinking about what the maternity leave is like. And I am very aware working in a university that typically if you want to start work-ing part-time it doesn't seem to be very difficult, and if you want to take work home one day a week, again most people I know can do that.'

And in Manhattan, Amanda Kramer, a Wharton alumna, then se-nior brand manager for a global drinks company and now working for an education charity, remembered that "[t]here's a women's Wharton conference every year, and there was this panel, I'm sure they have one every year, about work–life balance. You know, five or six women on the panel who were much more established in their career. And one of them spoke of her two kids, and she's tossing them off to the nannies, and it's 'I couldn't live without my three nannies.' *Three people?* I hear some-thing like that, and I don't want to do it."

So perhaps the numbers I've cited are the crest of a wave, the end of ever-more female employment, ever-fewer breaks. Might a post-feminist generation of graduates be about to rediscover life at home and never mind the penalty?

THE OPT-OUT THAT NEVER HAPPENED

A few years ago, American newspapers were suddenly full of exactly such a supposed and dramatic change in elite female behavior. The *New York Times* carried a front-page article; so did *Time*.[41] Full-time motherhood was, apparently, back.

Lisa Belkin, in the *New York Times*, heralded the "opt-out revolution." "It's not just that the workplace has failed women," she argued. "It is also that women are rejecting the workplace." Starting with an Atlanta-based book club, made up of Princeton graduates who had abandoned work for full-time motherhood, she argued that there was "an exodus of professional women from the workplace" and a trend toward more flexibility, a new revolution in how men as well as women behave. "Everywhere you look, workers are doing their work in untraditional ways," Belkin asserted; it is about "sanity, balance and a new definition of success."[42]

"If so, it's sure not registering in the statistics" is the response of people studying the labor market: not in terms of mothers working, and not in terms of mold-breaking non-traditional workplaces either. What the statistics continue to show, just as they did a few years back, is that, in economist Heather Boushey's words, "the presence of small children at home plays a smaller role in women's labor force participation" than ever. Especially for the educated.[43]

Yes, there was a dip in female participation in the early 2000s. There was also a recession then and less work for everyone.[44] When the recession ended, employment went back up. The Atlanta book club was neither the tip of an iceberg nor the start of a trend. It was just an anecdote.

There is, however, one small exception to the rule that graduate women stay employed—small enough not to register in national statistics. It is the super-rich. They are indeed "different from us." But then, they face very different choices.

DIFFERENT FROM US

It was in Venice, as a bit player in a pre-recession bankers' "retreat," that I realized that the rich were different. These were men who had *wives*; full-time and very busy wives. Here, alive and well, were the equivalents of the eighteenth- and nineteenth-century "gentlewomen" who ran large households, with a whole "downstairs" full of staff. Of course, houses are easier to run now, and the rich employ far fewer people—but these women also organized the financial and bureaucratic tasks that once fell to propertied and leisured husbands, or their (male) agents. They were intelligent, highly educated women, often ex-bankers themselves; and they were obliged to be "non-working mothers" because their families needed a full-time house manager who wasn't always away.

Most people who are very high earners are also very time poor. This is partly because they work hard and travel constantly. But it is also because possessions (and investments) do not look after themselves. A country manor, a house in the Hamptons, a ski chalet in Davos may not require the constant attention demanded by a child, or indeed a dog. But the taxes have to be paid, the boilers serviced, the gardens maintained, the family moved there, and back, and there again. Of course many of the working poor are time-starved too. If you are ever in Venice, spare a thought for the hotel staff. They don't live in picturesque expensive Venetian courtyards but spend hours each day on a succession of boats and buses between the city and the mainland. Nonetheless, what that Venice trip taught me is that, while money may or may not buy happiness, it really doesn't buy time.[45]

As we've seen, today's highly educated women don't, as a rule, stay home after marriage or children. In that top fifth or sixth of the job pyramid, you've got dense, full-time working patterns for women and men. But have a husband who's rich enough—someone at the very tip, the 1 percent or indeed the 0.1 percent—and this begins to change. If half of a couple is very high-earning, then the other's income isn't necessary for an affluent lifestyle.[46] Media executive Karin Gilford lived in high-income Southern California with a husband in the film business and remembers that at "the private pre-school my daughter went to, of the thirteen kids in her class, only two mothers worked." At the top of the household income distribution, mothers of young children are ten or twenty percentage points more likely to quit employment, compared to those who are a little less well-off.[47] And the seriously affluent also have more children, as we saw in Chapter 2. In 2004, 41 percent—almost half—of American women in $400,000-plus households, which was about the top 1 percent, had three children or more by their mid-forties.[48] That was way ahead of the national average, let alone the college graduates'.

The rich, though, are a tiny group, leading surprisingly traditional rich people's lives. The big social change is the arrival, in their millions, of a new sort of "new mother." They are the highly educated women for whom career-making dominates the years between twenty and thirty, or, indeed, twenty and thirty-five;[49] the women at the top but not the tip of the pyramid, for whom one or two children is the ceiling. They are heading straight back into the labor market as part of a dual-income family.

I personally still think that, if you can manage it, having children in your twenties is great. Your biological clock is less advanced; you might even have grandchildren before extreme old age. And if we are all going to work till we're seventy-plus, a few years of marking time should be just a blip in your career. But "if you can manage it" is the operative phrase.

Elite children today involve enormous expenditures. Fathers-to-be do also start saving;[50] and in the equal-opportunity 2000s, the financial burden gets shared. But the burden is a big one.

Those financial pressures are a major reason why most educated mothers with ambitions for their babies not only want but need to avoid falling off the career ladder. They need to be earning enough, and be successful enough, to go back to work, afford childcare, afford home help and still come out in profit. High salaries, in other words, are what give our female elites access to something that once seemed on the way to extinction and is now necessary to their way of life. The servant classes.

"IN SERVICE"

A friend of mine, a middle-aged businessman, was born into a traditional Catholic family of first-generation immigrants. Traditional, that is, except that his mother married late. She had the first of her seven children at thirty-six and Damian was the youngest. "I used to ask her not to come to school to pick me up—I was really embarrassed that she was so much older than everyone else's mother," he remembers.

And today? Well, actually, she'd still stand out at most school gates. Not one of the young mothers, the ones without college degrees. But not one of the new late-mothering crowd either; because these older graduate mothers aren't, for the most part, there to greet their children. That's the job of the nannies and the au pairs.

Just a few decades ago, people believed that "domestic service" would vanish into history as the world grew richer. "Domestics" (both live-ins and live-outs) made up 5 percent—one in twenty—of the economically active British population in 1951; by 1981 it was fewer than one in 200.[51] In Sweden the number of domestic servants in private homes plummeted from 68,800 in 1960 to 1,364 in 1980. By 1990, with about 2.2 million women employed, Statistics Sweden listed just two.

That's just two women in the whole country of Sweden who were working as domestic servants.[52] The planet's longest-running source of female employment seemed to be dead.

THE END OF HISTORY?

Ever since human beings developed "wage labor"—doing a job, for someone else, for pay—domestic service has been one of the largest occupations on the planet. Servants were ubiquitous. "Thou shalt not covet thy neighbor's wife, nor his manservant, nor his maidservant . . ." says the last of the Ten Commandments, in a formulation suited to a world in which established families commonly had servants (as well as oxes and asses) available to covet.[53]

Outside the fields, work as a servant was, traditionally, pretty much all that women were offered. As late as 1870, almost half the employed women in the US were domestic servants; it was still a third on the eve of the First World War. These women were, for the most part, poorly paid for long, hard hours, and almost always resident in their employers' homes. Sociologist George Homans, born in 1910, was the son of a Boston lawyer and followed him to Harvard College. In their tall, narrow Boston house

> the kitchen lay below the ground level. If one went down there at night and turned the light on, swarms of cockroaches scuttled for safety. Here our long series of cooks sweated over the black coalrange . . . At the very top floor of the house, crammed into their tiny cells, with no hot water, lived—if that is the right word for their existence—our uniformly Irish maids . . . Including our cook, I think there were three of them.
>
> [At Harvard] our meals in a house dining hall were served by waitresses, and our rooms cleaned and our beds made not by ourselves but by cleaning women.[54]

The novelist and writer Virginia Woolf, a generation older than Homans, was a passionate champion of women's capacity to write, and think, at the same level as men. But born into upper-middle-class literary London, she had no idea how to cook. She is a feminist icon; and simply took for granted the need to employ maids, cooks and housekeepers whose lives moved in unseen parallel with hers and those of her set.[55]

Until a hundred years ago, being "in service" was the default job for women. Even after the Second World War, having a maid was seen as totally normal for affluent families, and not just the rich. I've got on my shelves a copy of *The Book of Good Housekeeping*, published in 1946 by the Good Housekeeping Institute for a mass readership. It is full of still-useful advice on stain removal and jam making; but "Planning the Housework" comes from a different planet. In a "Seven-roomed House Containing Four Bedrooms," there's a daily plan for the Mistress—and that is exactly what the book calls her—and another for the Maid. There are "special weekly duties" listed for a Cook-General and a House Parlourmaid, and pages of advice on Training a Housemaid.

The world for which my 1946 book was written was vanishing at speed even as it hit the presses. My grandmother was a cook: she ran the directors' dining room for a bank's head office, but she also spent years working in private homes, with no terrible and some very good experiences. Younger women, she thought, shouldn't be so negative about "going into service."

But negative they were, as was much of society. The whole vocabulary of servanthood reeks of hierarchy and disdain: "masters and mistresses," "servile" behavior. Social reformers talked of "social alienation" and "exploitation."[56] And I can remember feeling quite strongly, in my twenties, that having someone else to do your housework was a pretty disgusting idea.

By the early 1970s some sociologists were writing obituaries for the whole "primordial" and "stigmatized" occupation of servant.[57] But these turned out to be wildly premature. Millions of educated, ambitious, hardworking women might want to have it all, but they couldn't, in practice, do it all themselves. So they don't.

In Western European countries with half-decent statistics, official figures suggest that at least 4 percent of employed females now work in private homes, many for several different families.[58] This is still low by historical standards but a great deal higher than forty years ago. And around 15 to 20 percent of rich-country households are probably buying domestic labor of some sort, though far fewer admit to it.[59] Moreover, these new servants are especially important in the lives of professional working mothers. Someone has to hold the baby.

HOLDING THE BABY

Nannies now populate upper-middle-class neighborhoods across the world in the way that maids once did. I live in Victorian south London, created by the explosive growth of the nineteenth century, when the city flowed out across the fields in a century-long building boom. These were houses for the middle classes, so they all have attic rooms for the maid—and it usually was just one: a "maid-of-all-work," a term that says it all.

The maid was a taken-for-granted part of middle-class households in those days of coal fires, home cooking and mending, employed alongside (rather than instead of) the household's "mistress." When a local historian did a detailed study of a street just round the corner from me, she found that, in 1881, every house but one had a live-in servant (or two); and all the servants were female.[60] When we moved into our house, the maids were long gone, but the attic still had the narrow, dangerous ladder-like staircase and tiny leaky skylights installed by the original builders.

Modernized, expanded and weatherproofed, it became the study where I wrote this book, but also and first—as for many of my neighbors— a bedroom for the nanny. Yet when I was a child in small-town England, only one household in my parents' circle of professional families had a nanny, and they were by far the richest people we knew. Writer Caitlin Flanagan, looking back at 1970s California, remembers, "I didn't know a single child who had a nanny when I was growing up . . . We grew up in an America in which nannies were as unfamiliar to middle-class neighborhoods as Jaguars and Martians."[61] And in which the mothers of small children were not out at work.

Servants underpin elite women's lifestyles, not just because millions of us have serious careers, but because we don't have resident family. Back in 1880, a quarter of American mothers with children aged five and under had another female aged ten or older living in the same house. By 2000, that was down to 5 percent. Moreover, in 1880 most of this much-more-numerous group were family—perhaps an older child, perhaps a mother or mother-in-law. By 2000, most co-residents were not; they were unrelated, hired help.[62]

Childcare is inevitably high stress in a world where there is no one else at home to hold the baby. "I have a nanny, obviously," says Karin Gilford, forging a career as an executive in digital media via Paramount, Yahoo! and Comcast. "I never didn't have a live-in nanny," says academic lawyer and policy writer Amy Wax of the University of Pennsylvania. "I don't understand how professional women think they can have a career without."

Among the women I interviewed for this book, just one, IBM vice president Lauren States, mentioned having family in the house, as part of the "ecosystem"—her word—that enabled her to combine career and motherhood. She remembered how "[w]e were somewhat lucky in that my husband comes from a big family and one of his sisters lived with us on and off for several years. We always had an adult around the house, somehow. And I remember meeting with women in Latin America, talking about work–life balance, and after a while they said we don't have this problem, because we have people who take care of our homes and we live in a family complex. Their issues were upward mobility, not work–life balance. I don't have any servants. And I don't want to pay for them because they cost so much."

Economist Nancy Folbre points out that, in the US, even a middle-of-the-pyramid, middle-income family faces, on average, costs and payments of over $10,000 a year per child (2011 prices). That amount of money, invested rather than spent, would typically provide a nest-egg of over $1.5 million at retirement.[63] The $10,000 is without school fees, without servants. Start down the servant road and, as Lauren States points out, the money gets serious.

In the US, a live-in nanny—significantly cheaper than someone who arrives daily—costs families between $22,000 and $36,000 a year (that is £14,000 to £23,0000: post-tax, 2012 prices).[64] Not surprisingly, among families with young children, very few employ their own nanny: even among those with top quartile incomes, less than one in ten does so.[65] In London, formal childcare in 2012 was running at about £400 a week—over £20,000 a year. That is definitely more in real terms than I paid fifteen years ago, which presumably reflects rising demand; and the cost seemed eye-watering enough then.

Clara, who was our nanny for years and is now a mother of two herself, was typical for London. In the days when I used to come home to a kitchen full of socializing nannies and assorted small children, all the nannies were English, just as the maids who lived in our neighborhood a century earlier had been.[66] Typically, they were girls from stable families in outer suburbs and small towns who didn't much like academic work, and wanted to see London and the world, and for whom a childcare qualification was their ticket.

My niece, now deep in the world of young professional mothers, says that these English career nannies do still exist, "though they can pick and choose their perks"; but they no longer dominate the London nannying scene, and internationally they're a clear exception. Instead, the world has acquired a huge and overwhelmingly female "global care chain,"[67] in which "women from Mexico and Central America [are] moving into the households of . . . the United States, Indonesian women to richer nations in Asia and the Gulf region, Sri Lankan women to Greece, Polish women to western Europe . . ."[68]

Without the new servant classes, elite women's employment would splutter and stall. In Germany, as in the US, there are continuing demands for comprehensive state-funded day care of the sort for which Scandinavia is famous. But in its absence, neither German nor American professional women have been forced "into part-time work or . . . the housewife role . . . [They] are not waiting for the state or their partners to help them . . . Instead they . . . pay another person to clean their houses, take care of their children."[69]

The "global care chain" isn't just about home-based nannies and housekeepers, either. Immigrants—female immigrants—are also central to a completely new development: formal nurseries, at which affluent families pay to leave their babies and small children on a daily basis. Nannies are an old phenomenon updated. They have spread down in the world, from the day and night nurseries of stately homes to the crowded city homes of the educated middle classes. Fee-charging day nurseries, in contrast, are new; a twentieth-century phenomenon that exists entirely because, and to the extent that, mothers are intensively employed.

Susan Stein, a professional woman and mother herself, quit a litigation law firm for teaching. She runs a preschool and nursery in Manhattan, taking babies through to age five, and spoke to me against the background of a highly fragile economy. "People here pay by the month, and there are people who pay by credit card. It's New York City, they're traveling a lot, and to get the frequent-flier miles they pay by card. But I'm aware that there are people who switch credit cards from month to month, and it makes me very anxious. For us, for children under the age of two, full-time, it's $1,850 a month. And that's a lot of money. You really need to have a salary plus a second salary that can absorb that."

Susan directs the Children's Garden, a hugely sought-after establishment inside the enchanted grounds of New York City's General Theological Seminary. It's an amazing semi-secret place: a full city-block long and a city-block wide, with low-rise brick buildings, lawns, trees and flowerbeds. The nursery was originally established for the seminarians, who still get priority and a discount. The other places, Susan explains, go to a lucky few among New York City's professional families.

"I've been a teacher for twenty years. When I first started, the great majority of families had one parent working, and it was the father. There have always been these high-powered women executives, but as the years have gone on, there's no question there have been many more working families, two young professionals. I get calls all the time from these young women who are looking for infant care and cannot find it. If we were able to expand, I could fill the space immediately, and I'm sure that anybody who started an infant room, a nursery, could do that."

The parents of Susan's charges are often struggling; and yet by the world's, and even by America's, standards they are enormously well paid. They have to be, because formal childcare in a modern state is very expensive. It is bound to be, because small children are labor-intensive; and because any licensed nursery has enormous compulsory costs. As Susan explains: "We're always broke. So much of it is dependent on the particular municipal regulations. So, there are staff ratios, people need the appropriate credentials, you need a safe, clean, well-lit space, and there's insurance liability. Part of the licensing is that you must have a budget set aside for substitute teachers, and then there are the benefits and just the wear and tear on the equipment, all those things."

A full-time nanny at home means you are paying for someone's entire salary and praying they won't get ill or leave; a nursery means that you share the salary with two or three other people, and that there's backup—but also that you pay for all those overheads. Only the very prosperous, or the state, can afford either.

TAG-TEAM PARENTING

When I was in my twenties, workplace nurseries were being hailed as key to female liberation, and at one time I actually worked at a university with a good one. But it was absolutely useless to me: not just because it was a forty-five-minute journey on public transport to get there but because, at least half the time, I wasn't in the office. I was working on a research project that made me a lot more likely, come 9 a.m. or 5 p.m., to be in some industrial estate in a far-flung suburb. And, of course, the nursery kept regular and very strict daytime hours.

For the millions of couples where one or both work shifts, across days, nights and weekends, nurseries like this are little help and little used. We've seen that professional women, and professional mothers, are more likely to work full-time—but non-professionals are the ones who work across our 24/7 societies, with their late-opening supermarkets, fast food, hotels and care homes, Sunday shopping, movies and bars.[70] Nearly half of the US workforce work non-standard hours, and they tend to be less educated and in low-wage service occupations.[71] Institutional childcare often works better for more-educated, higher-income parents, and not just because of price. It is yet another way in which gulfs open up between professionals' lifestyles and the rest.

In Britain, formal childcare is subsidized, though not at Scandinavian levels;[72] and is overwhelmingly a daytime, weekday affair. Most people use informal arrangements: among employed and student mothers with ten-month-olds, only a quarter used a nanny, babysitter or nursery.[73] Children in the UK with professional/top-managerial and highly educated parents are far more likely to be in formal childcare settings than those of any other group.[74] American data confirm the pattern. Better-off families are more likely to use formal care, lower-income ones to rely heavily on informal care and relatives.[75] Low-earning couples, in the UK and around the world, often end up arranging shifts so they can share the babysitting, at the expense of time spent together.[76]

Economist Heather Boushey argues that this "tag-team parenting" is driven largely by necessity, not by choice. "Lower income families simply cannot afford to buy formal childcare," she suggests, noting that, in general, among American working wives, only 7 percent of those with graduate degrees work mostly evenings and nights, compared to 21 percent of those who failed to graduate from high school.[77] Susan Chira of the *New York Times* was struck, back in the 1990s, by how "actually, in a number of working-class households, there was more sharing of domestic responsibility. Those women who don't have a choice about working often have very unforgiving jobs where there's little flexibility or individual ability to negotiate. They don't have enough money to pay for decent childcare. But people had shifts and they alternated shifts—there was more of this than you think."

So, for the poor, it's tag-team parenting; and for the elite, it's the new servant classes.

EASTERN VALUES?

Simple arithmetic tells you that not everyone can have servants. To pay someone to work for you out of post-tax income, in a world of high income taxes, you need to be a good deal better off than them. But as the twenty-first century rolls out, there are millions of well-off households who employ the new servant classes, and keep the global supply chain going.

For successful women, it can be a straight choice between hiring help and being forced back onto the sidelines. This is true for many women at the peak of their careers, when age and illness hit their parents, and the assumption is still—on both sides—that daughters are the first point of call. But the international nexus of female careers and female servants is most in evidence when it comes to motherhood. In countries where access to childcare and domestic help is blocked, you can see how women are pushed in two directions.

Modern Japan is a clear example. Today it has high levels of female employment, high rates of female education, and birth rates that are extremely low, even by modern developed-country standards. It also has very few women in top positions, unusually little difference in the employment patterns of poorly and highly educated women, and tightly limited immigration. And all of these are linked.

I first met elegant, tiny, high-flying Kathy Matsui at a conference in Bangladesh, multi-tasking on her BlackBerry, and midway between meetings in Milan and her home in Tokyo. Kathy is an analyst, chief Japan equity strategist and co-head of Asia Investment Research for a large investment bank. But she was also, critically, born outside Japan: she has a non-Japanese passport and, therefore, as she explained, the ability to hire Filipino live-in staff. "I can manage with a Filipino nanny because I can bring one in. But when my Japanese-born colleagues ask me how to organize this, the answer is that they can't."

Only foreign nationals may; and there's no porous southern or eastern border tempting illegal immigrants, no political willingness to change immigration rules and no Japanese to do the job. Moreover, Japanese tax policies have acted as a strong deterrent to employment for women married to high-earning husbands. These are important reasons why Japan bucks the international trend. Here, unlike the developed countries of the West, highly educated married women and mothers are no more likely to work than less-educated ones.[78]

If women are really able to penetrate a country's elite, obtain high-paying, high-prestige jobs and make a serious career, then you can expect large differences in the work patterns of more- and less-educated women, and especially more- and less-educated mothers. Educated women will be much more likely to work full-time and much less likely to drop out of the labor market for periods. But when educated women face serious barriers these particular differences don't emerge, though others do.

Japanese tax and immigration policies reflect and help maintain a society in which women still find it difficult to reach senior positions, and there has been little governmental or business commitment to helping mothers get back to work. If you're a young, female, educated Japanese professional, life involves the same weighing up of costs and benefits, tastes and opportunities, as it does for women everywhere. But the choice you face is much starker than in the West. Get married, have children and stay home; or do none of these things.

Since these are also the choices that face your less-educated compatriots, sisterhood of a kind endures. Indeed, the obstacles to combining marriage, children and working are surely one of the major reasons why Japan has not only low overall fertility in all classes, but low overall marriage rates as well. But, as you might expect, the probability that a woman will choose one option rather than the other, career or home, children or none, is also affected strongly by whether or not she is highly educated.

Japan may have changed slowly. It may still have a much more heavily male elite than Western developed countries, or, indeed, many Asian ones. But compared to the past, educated Japanese women have workplace opportunities that were unheard-of even a generation ago. And if they cannot get the help they need in juggling household, family and career, a good number will opt for just the career. Japanese female graduates are, duly, less likely to marry than junior-high-school graduates. And they have a fertility rate that is 20 percent lower as well.[79]

4

PIZZA AND PARTNERS

*I*t's a November Tuesday in 1965 and in the suburbs of a New England city "Mary" is filling in her diary. She's from the generation that raised the baby boomers in the postwar 1950s, a white college-educated forty-four-year-old with an upper-quartile family income and no paid employment of her own. Today, she has spent an hour writing letters and another hour on "crafts," which sounds like primary school raffia work but was more probably knitting. She has also spent 135 minutes—a full two and a quarter hours—preparing and cooking food for sit-down family meals; and another two hours setting tables and doing dishes.

Nor is she unusual. Over in the Midwest, in that self-same month of 1965, another prosperous non-employed graduate mother, exactly the same age, recorded *her* Wednesday. "Joan" was out of the house much of the day, volunteering, and there was only one family meal for which to cook, set and clear. But she made sure of leaving herself 107 minutes—nearly two hours—to prepare it; and still had time for an hour walking the dog, and two and a half hours reading books and the newspaper.

How do we know all this? Because these 1965 homemakers kept a minute-by-minute diary of their day, as part of a "time-use" survey, just as their successors are doing today, in the US and in more and more countries around the world.[1] These diaries are not just fascinating; they are also a really accurate way of finding out what people actually did. If you ask people to estimate how they spend their time, they tend to produce days of glowing virtue that add up to a total of well over twenty-four hours. Time-use data, in contrast, allow us to see how the world actually lives, and lived.

When was the last time you saw a college-educated forty-something female spend two hours preparing a weeknight dinner? No surprise if you draw a blank, because you'd be hard put to find one. We know this, for the same reason we know about those 1965 homemakers. In 2004 Texas, we can zoom in on "Ellen" and "Frank," a graduate couple in their forties with upper-quintile income, children and two full-time jobs. On a December Friday, Ellen's diary shows no food preparation whatsoever going on in this household. Instead, they all eat out. Higher-earning graduate couples of the 2000s do of course eat in—like François and Marie-Christine, having dinner in a French city apartment on a Wednesday in November. But in this two-car, two-full-time-jobs, one-child family, forty minutes goes on food preparation, not 140.

As women's employment has changed, so has home life. In the process, the world of mid-twentieth-century educated female suburbanites has become as much of a historical curiosity as the small Midwestern family farm, or the gnarled peasants of southern European travelogues and olive oil advertisements. And there have been two major changes in how we spend our time, changes without which women, and above all female professionals, wouldn't be coping at all.

First, we have gained time by hollowing out the home. We have done this by outsourcing activities that even in the 1960s were still a central part of "homemaking." Most people think that a million female careers were unleashed by a set of machines: the washer, the dryer, the dishwasher. Wrong. It had, as we'll see, far more to do with pizza.

Second, couples have changed the way they parcel out tasks and activities. There has been a major worldwide shift toward greater equality in men's and women's workloads. Like the pizza, this shift affects everyone—top, middle and lower income. But the consequences are very different for two-career professionals than they are for most other couples. Most people are chilling out a bit more; professionals are instead running faster and further. And in the case of professional parents, both the men and the women are ratcheting up their on-task weeks in ways that no one in affluent mid-1960s suburbia could have visualized.

But let's start with the pizza.

PIZZAS AND PASTRIES

Compared to a generation ago, women in all parts of society now spend much less time on unpaid work around the house. Time-use diaries show a big drop in "unpaid work hours" for all women since the 1960s. What are they no longer doing?

We saw in Chapter 1 that many of the new jobs in our economies over the last fifty to sixty years have involved turning women's "unwaged" activities in the home into part of the formal labor market. The high-growth occupations of "caring" for the young, sick and old are among the most visible signs of change. These jobs are largely low-waged, paid by the hour, often part-time; and are held largely by the less-educated, less-affluent female majority.[2]

The growth of such paid employment takes key activities out of the home. But other changes are just as important. Home sewing and knitting are largely dead, replaced by cheap factory-made clothing, much of it imported. Most important of all, cooking has gone commercial. This is a new phase in the division of labor: one of the very last cottage industries has moved out into the marketplace.

Apart from the Israeli kibbutz, there have been no political movements or government crusades designed to socialize the kitchen and free women from the chopping board.[3] The kitchen revolution was genuinely a market creation. That may be why few people have registered just how much cooking has been transformed. Underpinning modern life there is a vast ecosystem of family-run takeout restaurants, chilled meals and fast-food empires. Other people now cook for most of us much of the time: not, unless we are super-rich, in our own kitchens but in factories turning out prepared food, in takeout kitchens and in cafés, restaurants and bars.

Our ancestors spent vast proportions of their time finding and producing food, whether as hunter-gatherers or toiling peasants. Food gathering is how all other animals still spend most of their time.[4] In the developed world, however, we buy food in. Or eat it out.

In 1978, 16 percent of American meals were eaten away from home; by the early 2000s, it was more than 30 percent. As Figures 4.1a and b show, the proportion of money spent on eating away from home has risen still faster. Moreover, much of what people eat at home consists of ready-prepared food: pizza deliveries, chilled and frozen ready meals, yogurts, soups, baked goods.

In the UK things have shifted even faster than in America. Spending on eating outside the home doubled between 1992 and 2004, at which point it overtook total spending on food eaten at home (fresh, processed and takeout combined).[5] Some of this new spending was on cappuccinos,

Figure 4.1a **Distribution of Food Expenditure, USA 1960[6] (Percentages)**

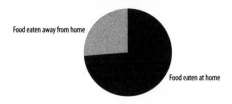

Food eaten away from home

Food eaten at home

Source: US Department of Agriculture Economic Research Service

pastries and snacks, but spending on meals out also soared.[7] France is much the same. Around a quarter of all French meals are now eaten outside the home, and not usually in temples of gastronomy either: the French are the largest consumers of McDonald's hamburgers in Europe.[8]

The first mass-produced ready-to-eat food is very old: bread, bought from bakers instead of home-baked. But until recently almost all meals were made from scratch at home. In the nineteenth century, industrial-scale canning brought cooked meats, fish and sauces to millions of homes. Takeout food started to emerge slowly; even the British fish-and-chip shop is only about 150 years old. Home freezers belong to the post–Second World War world.

Today, we fantasize about being Martha Stewart or Nigella Lawson, about putting fresh-baked cakes on the table, growing our own herbs. We buy record numbers of cookbooks, especially those of celebrity chefs. But in fact we cook less and less. Almost everyone is eating takeout pizza. And in London's railway stations, Marks & Spencer stores with a huge range of ready meals are a staple. I'm a regular in their long lines of suited commuters, male and female, calculating time to the checkout against time to the next train.

Figure 4.1b **Distribution of Food Expenditure, USA 2009[6] (Percentages)**

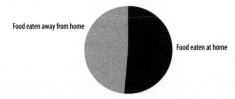

Food eaten away from home

Food eaten at home

Source: US Department of Agriculture Economic Research Service

Modern women can live and work the way they do because food preparation has moved out of the kitchen, out of the home and into the industrial economy. And we know that it's pizzas and pastries that matter, not washers and dryers, because of another of those fascinating time-use analyses, this one going way back to the early 1900s.

Valerie Ramey was able to put together data from a wealth of American diaries dating from the 1920s through to the 1960s.[9] They included the diaries of farm wives, but also two unusual 1920s samples of housewives in urban areas all of whom had graduated from elite colleges. It is remarkable how little difference there is in the time these various groups of women spent on homemaking. Even more surprising is the complete lack of change between the 1920s and the 1960s.

Farm women worked more hours in total, because they worked on the farm as well; and more hours were spent on housework in total in wealthier and larger urban homes—but the women in those homes mostly had hired help, so more people were involved in doing it. Overall, though, whether in the farm or the city, whether college graduates or early school leavers, women recorded very much the same number of hours spent on household activity, as though they had some clear internalized idea of a "normal" housewife's working day.

Of course, washers and dryers and modern cookers and refrigerators changed the home. By the 1960s it was, for example, no longer true that "if one is poor it follows as a matter of course that one is dirty."[10] Sixty years earlier, Eliza Doolittle, the London street-seller turned lady of *Pygmalion* and *My Fair Lady*, "cleans up" wonderfully when forced to take a bath in advance of elocution lessons with Professor Higgins. But then, as she points out:

> It's easy to clean up here. Hot and cold water on tap . . . woolly towels, there is; . . . soft brushes . . . and a wooden bowl of soap smelling like primroses. Now I know why ladies is so clean. Washing's a treat for them. Wish they could see what it is for the likes of me.[11]

Large numbers of non-employed American homemakers in the 1920s and 1930s had no electricity, and sometimes no plumbing either. And yet these women spent the same amount of time on their homes as the non-employed homemakers of the comfortable 1960s, with their washers, dryers, vacuum cleaners and modern stoves. These appliances were certainly labor-saving, but the labor they saved was diverted to other household tasks. It is deeply anti-intuitive and completely clear in the data: in the postwar years, through into the mid-1960s, modern appliances made no difference to the total time devoted to work in the home.[12]

This was the mid-1960s suburban world of "Mary" and "Joan," with whom we started this chapter. They spent hours of each day cooking family meals, just as their mothers and grandmothers had done. Yet they were, though they couldn't know it, on the cusp of a revolution. Just a few years after they kept their diaries, time spent cooking, and with it time spent on housework, suddenly plummeted. And not just in America. All across the developed world, there was a fall in the time women spent on unpaid household work. And total time spent on housework fell *because* of the big change in food preparation and cooking.[13] Today, even women with children at home average less than an hour a day on preparing food and clearing up; for employed women it's just over a half-hour.[14]

From primitive and early "TV dinners," families moved on to take-out pizzas, and into McDonald's; and from the late 1960s household microwaves were in the stores.[15] Less cooking and more paid employment for women fed into each other. People weren't forced to buy fast food. Women could have gone on baking and bottling the way they used to; but in practice, they opted for less time in the house and more money to spend on takeout meals. And today single professionals eat well on food bought en route for home; families can cope with two adult members on shift work, and eating out is a normal mid-week option for many millions.

SHARING THE STRESS

The other major change in how we run our households also affects every class of society. It is central to the way working couples cope. Of all the things that I am writing about in this book, it is the one I least expect readers to believe. But it is amply documented across the developed world and goes back decades. *Men and women now put in the same average number of working hours.*

Most people (and definitely most women) think the opposite. "A woman's work is never done" is an English catchphrase; most cultures have the equivalent. And as "everybody" knows, this hasn't really changed, because women still do the housework even though they are now mostly in employment too.

THE XX FACTOR

Screenwriter and author Nora Ephron once described an archetypal scene from 1970s American married life. Husband and wife sit down, draw up a list of household tasks and discuss how to deal with them in a more enlightened future.

> This happened in thousands of households, with identical results: thousands of husbands agreed to clear the table. They cleared the table and then looked around as if they deserved a medal. They cleared the table and then hoped that they would never again be asked to do another thing. They cleared the table and hoped the whole thing would go away. And it mostly did.[16]

The result, in common belief, is that twenty-first-century women come home from work to start the "second shift," toiling away into the evening while men sit slumped in front of the TV screen. For example, economist Sylvia Ann Hewlett, a prominent commentator on gender and workplace issues, claims that

> after the dust from the women's revolution had settled it turned out men's behavior had changed rather little . . . Wives and mothers continue to contribute the lion's share [of routine housework] . . . fully 40% of married, high-achieving women feel that their husbands create more work for them around the house than they contribute.[17]

One leading researcher described the "second shift" argument to me as "the most influential argument" of the last thirty years in studies of domestic life.[18] And it's not just women who take it as both a given and profoundly unfair. An international survey of labor and public finance economists—largely male, and with a professional interest in the field—found that a clear majority of each group thought that women work more in total than men.[19]

But do they? Not in the UK they don't. Nor in the US, or Canada, or the Netherlands, Japan or Israel. Or, indeed, the large majority of other developed countries. Once, probably; but not now. These days, in all these places, the average number of working hours put in by men and women in a week, a month or a year is just the same.

This does not mean that men are doing half the world's ironing, or even the grocery shopping. But if we think that housework is indeed "work," as we almost all do, then comparing workloads means comparing *total* workloads. It means adding the bits done outside the family for pay to the bits done inside it, unpaid. It is perfectly true that women on average do more of the housework. Anything else would be pretty surprising, since far more women than men work part-time, and a good many are still not formally employed. But do women generally *work* more, in total, than men? No.

Oriel Sullivan is deputy director of Oxford University's Centre for Time Use Research. She has a particular interest in the facts and myths surrounding housework, including the idea that, as women worked longer hours outside the house, "men were not picking up the slack" at home.[20] This argument has made been especially strongly in the US: apparently American men are asserting their masculinity, while American women are "performing housework" in order to endorse traditional ideas about gender and keep their husbands happy.[21]

This conjures up, when you think about it, a pretty odd scenario. Oriel Sullivan remarks that, given the attitudes of many late-twentieth-century professional women, she finds it "quite hard to imagine them hoovering under the furniture nightly in an effort to soothe the feelings of their male partners."[22] And in fact, when she and other researchers look at the vast amount of detailed information from time-use diaries, no such pattern emerges. Quite the contrary.[23]

On average, women do more work inside the home, unpaid, than men, just as we think they do.[24] But men do more paid hours outside the home, on average, than women. Moreover, compared to the past, not only are women doing more work outside the home; men are doing more within it.[25] In the vast majority of developed countries, when you take total working hours, paid plus unpaid, men and women are grinding away for the same number of hours as each other, day in, week out.[26] That is on average: it doesn't mean every single individual is doing the same amount or that all couples are totally egalitarian. But across individuals and across couples, the *average* for men and women is the same.

Figure 4.2 shows work patterns, in this sense of total working hours, for six of the world's richest countries. It is an analysis by Jonathan Gershuny, who directs the Oxford University Centre and has pioneered work on the changing division of work in families and households.[27] He uses evidence covering several decades and combines "market work," done for pay, with unpaid "household production." This is defined as things we could pay someone else to do, if we had the money, but do not

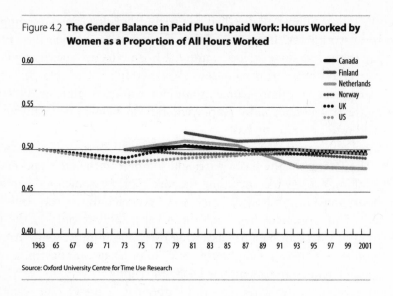

Figure 4.2 **The Gender Balance in Paid Plus Unpaid Work: Hours Worked by Women as a Proportion of All Hours Worked**

Source: Oxford University Centre for Time Use Research

get paid for when we do them for ourselves. Housework is the most obvious thing here, but there are also gardening, childcare and household bureaucracy (like tax returns).

In Figure 4.2, any entry below the 0.5 line means that women are, on average, doing less than half the total hours of work—paid plus unpaid—recorded in that country. Above the line and women are doing more than half. The Netherlands are world leaders in part-time employment, as we saw in Chapter 1; and Dutch women do seem to have been doing relatively well for themselves. In Finland, they are working that bit harder. But really, in all of these countries, and in pretty well every other developed country too, the balance is as close to perfectly equal as makes no difference, and has been for many years.

DRIVERS OF CHANGE

This equality is a phenomenon of the developed world. In poorer, less-developed countries women on average work more hours than men. So why, in developed countries, have things changed? It must surely have a good deal to do with power.

Human beings tend to exploit those less powerful than themselves and historically that has been bad news for women. However, the richer and more developed the society, the more potentially independent all women become. Modern women can live off what they earn themselves, divorce is easier and in most rich countries there are welfare benefits if things go wrong. Compared to the past, women are therefore more powerful within a relationship.

What goes on in any particular home is definitely related to women's (and men's) earnings, both actual and potential. In developed countries, men are more likely to share housework the longer their female partners spend in employment per week.[28] You can see this happening in modern families, as compared to the 1950s, let alone earlier. Kathleen Gerson, looking at the changing expectations and attitudes of the 1980s- and 1990s-born generations, found that many of them grew up in homes where both housework and childcare were shared: Jasmine, for example, remembering just such a 1980s childhood, explained, "My mom worked at a good-paying job and was doing great. My dad worked at night, so he was around when I'd get home from school."[29]

Men also put in more unpaid household hours the more money their female partners earn and also the more educated the women. This doesn't necessarily mean that educated women are more openly demanding or more feminist. But the more educated they are, the higher their potential future earnings, and this affects how couples arrange their lives.[30]

Oriel Sullivan and Jonathan Gershuny also note that, in absolute terms, those men who are the worst qualified relative to their wives do a much larger share of the housework than other men. They are also the ones who are very likely to be out of work. Sullivan and Gershuny reckon that "unemployed men are spending significant amounts of their time in the performance of housework"—though possibly not boasting about it in the pub or bar.[31]

Shifts in power, reflecting shifts in earnings and the labor market, must be one reason why men are doing more at home, and why total hours worked have equalized. But is that all it is? Values surely matter as well.

In Figure 4.2 we saw how time-use diaries report a pretty equal burden of work for both sexes in a wide range of countries; and the same is true of every rich developed country studied, with just three exceptions. In France and Spain women, on average, worked somewhat more in total than men. In Italy they worked considerably more, and it is hard to explain this just on the basis of power and pay.[32]

Italian women's total workload, paid plus unpaid, averages out at well over an hour more per day than for Italian men. It is true that Italian men are notorious—not least in Italy—for living at home into their thirties, with adoring mothers who wait on them.[33] But Japanese men are notorious in this respect too and average total working hours for Japanese women and men are equal. Italian inequality, it turns out, exists almost entirely because of the amount of time Italian women spend on unpaid work. More specifically, they spend world-record amounts of time cleaning the house.[34] Americans are generally seen as the worker bees of the developed world,[35] but Italian women are right up there with them.

The hours they work must surely reflect how Italian women feel about their homes. They like them to gleam, and gleam they mostly do. In other words, Italy's data show that culture and values make a difference. It is not simply about power, or earnings, current or future.

More generally, it seems to me—as it does to many time-use researchers—that this move to male–female equality must rest on some commonly accepted values. Ideas about what is fair and right seem genuinely to have changed, so that the vast majority of men in developed countries feel that they ought to do their "fair share" of household work and childcare. This is linked to the changes in women's employment, obviously; but men and women think about it in terms of obligations, not a naked power struggle.

While writing this book, I spoke to a number of professional women with husbands whose jobs took them away for long stretches of time, and it was clear that "making up" for this was something that both sides felt was needed. And not with purchases from the duty-free gift shop either. Media executive Karin Gilford, for example, is married to "a production designer for large feature films—you know, last year he was in Vancouver shooting a massive movie for Disney, from January to July. He works freelance; when he isn't working, which sometimes could be a week, it could be two months, or three months, he dives in. I mean he is very present at school. He volunteers, he's chaperoning field trips, he coaches Little League, every single solitary teacher, parent, principal knows him."

But this still begs the question: how do the total number of work hours average out so evenly? If—like one couple I know—you're both doing exactly the same job, in their case as heads of competing community colleges, you can figure it out pretty exactly. But for the rest of us?

Back in the 1960s, and especially in America, long serious conversations (and a lot of rage) accompanied the housework in many homes.[36] There is still a fair amount of negotiation and renegotiation about who does what in many homes (and it's worth knowing that the less clear people's responsibilities are, the more stressed everyone becomes).[37] But we are not, for the most part, standing around with calculators, working out what our actual and future incomes imply for who should do the laundry.

I think the answer has to be that we look at each other's leisure time. That, after all, is the bit of life when people—couples, friends—are together. We can't see each other at work; we can't, if we are out of the house working, see exactly how much housework other family members are doing. But we can get a good idea of how much leisure someone enjoys.[38] So one fairly simple way for couples to arrive at rough equality in their workload is by adjusting their behavior when relative leisure time gets visibly out of kilter.

And why are so many of us convinced that women do far more than their "fair" share? Partly because of the widespread publicity for those studies that apparently showed American professional women slaving away for leisured males.[39] But also because we tend to exaggerate, in tranquility, the size of our own contributions;[40] but don't notice or remember the jobs that other people did when we weren't watching. Moreover, housework and childcare are things other people often do notice, because they're around to witness them. And as we have seen, while total work hours may be equalizing, women on average still do more hours of visible at-home labor than do men.

Lindsey McBrayne, who works in university administration, resembles most of her colleagues in holding a bachelor's and a graduate degree. Like most graduates in their early thirties, she has increasing numbers of friends with young children. She is also, as we saw above, one of the people who pointed out to me, in interview, that women still typically think about babies more, and sooner, than men.

If she has a baby, she told me, "I'd expect there to be a conversation between me and my other half about how we divided up the paid work and the childcare. I would expect at least a conversation about whether or not he also went part-time. Partly I'd want to have it because I think it's fair on me that we have that conversation. But I also think it's fair that I offer him the opportunity to have that role in our children's lives.

"But that probably makes me fairly unusual, and this is something I've thought about a lot. There might be long-term serious culture change if more men did work part-time. But I don't think they're going to, not for a long time yet anyway. Maybe actually a lot of women want to work part-time because they want to have that contact with their children, because it's a slightly easier life, and they're happy to leave the men to be the ones who just carry on, and are the ones who work full-time."

As we saw earlier, highly educated mothers are overwhelmingly likely to return to work more or less right away, rather than taking the long career breaks that were common even a few decades ago. But in the two-career families that typify modern elite parenthood, it is rare for mothers to be equal, let alone higher, earners when the children are very small.

Among married and cohabiting couples in contemporary Britain, only around 10 percent of mothers with preschool children are the only, the main or even an equal earner for a two-parent household. Among graduate mothers of three-year-olds, almost three-quarters are employed—but only 20 percent, one in five, works full-time at this point. Among graduate fathers with three-year-olds, in contrast, 4 percent were part-time when interviewed, just 3 percent weren't employed, and all the rest were working full-time.[41]

Look closely at modern professional work life and you start to share Lindsey's—and my—suspicion that a good number of women may prefer it that way.

SQUEEZED AT THE TOP

A few years back, the London-based personal assistant of two bankers was convicted of theft. The pair were also a married couple and she had been stealing millions of pounds from their bank accounts.[42] It took the bankers years to notice—and the newspaper reports were greatly amused, not just because they were apparently so rich as not to miss the money, but by how much the couple communicated by email. This wasn't just when they were in different airport lounges. It was also when they were on different floors of their own home.

Full disclosure: I do the same with my family, and suspect a lot of other people do too. How else does one get the bureaucracy sorted, the calendars more or less aligned and any response at all from your spouse, your parents or your kids? There aren't enough hours in the day.

Given the changes we've seen—fewer hours on housework, a more helpful spouse—women ought surely to be less stressed and more leisured than in the past. But only "other things being equal" and other things aren't always equal at all. For many women, especially the highly educated, these changes haven't actually led to more leisure time at all.

Instead, once again, professional women's lives have become increasingly like those of professional men.

For most people in developed countries, recent decades have been a period when total work time—paid plus unpaid—has fallen. The average number of hours a week, or year, that men spend in paid employment has fallen significantly since 1965[43] and even more since 1900.[44] But none of that fall is at the top. Men in the top decile of income work just as many hours a day, on average, as they did in 1890. Meanwhile those in the bottom decile have moved from working an average of two hours a day more than the wealthiest group to averaging an hour a day less. Among unmarried employed women, the trends have been similar. The top earners are now averaging two hours a day more than the lowest.[45]

It is not that well-off women were all, once, idle. They weren't. In *The Gentleman's Daughter*, her wonderful study of eighteenth-century women's lives, Amanda Vickery quotes one of her feminine subjects writing "my time is always imployed and if I do take a pen I always meet with some interruption . . ."[46]

Bessy Ramsden, the correspondent in question, was wont to find her letters being finished by her husband: "Mrs R was called up to her Nursery or she would not have left off so abruptly," he wrote on one occasion.[47] And her description of life would have been literal and general, certainly once child-bearing began. These women were responsible for running quite substantial houses and households, and also had the main responsibility for bringing up, and for much of the education of, their children, including teaching them to read and write.

But well-off women didn't work more hours than their poorer, less-educated contemporaries. Nor did their husbands. That is totally new. Today, not only are the affluent genuinely "time-poor'; the better off the household, the more stressed for time people report that they feel—women and men alike.[48]

During the twentieth century, the length of the paid working week fell for most men. As we have just seen, men also started to put more time into unpaid domestic work, such as cooking, cleaning, gardening and shopping. These greater contributions on the home front have used up some of the time "saved" from employment, but nothing like all. Comparing leisure time today and in the past, most men still come out ahead of their past selves, or their fathers, let alone the men of the 1900s. Though not all.

The same is true for women. More of them are employed, notably among married women;[49] but, as we saw above, the time women spend on household tasks has decreased dramatically since the 1960s. And for most of the female population, the time saved on housework is greater than the extra time they are devoting to paid employment.[50] So in a given week, women in the early twenty-first century are working fewer hours in total than women were a generation ago. Most of them.

And these are not small amounts of time. For men and women alike, the *average* total working week has fallen by a solid eight hours since 1965.[51] Back then, there used to be a lot of talk about the "leisure society" and what we would all do with ourselves when we didn't have to work so much. On these figures, we seem to be getting there.

However, these averages are just that: averages. They bring together people who are working a lot less than their immediate forebears with other people who are working just as much as ever. And the latter group includes most successful professionals, male and female alike.[52]

Since the 1960s, the workloads of less- and more-educated Americans have diverged.[53] Back in 1965, there were no education-related differences in the leisure time that men or women reported: dropouts and graduates were on a par. Since then, as Figure 4.3 shows, almost every group has increased the number of leisure hours in an average week. But not at the top. Here highly educated men are working just as much as

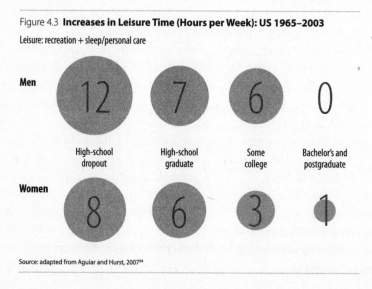

Figure 4.3 **Increases in Leisure Time (Hours per Week): US 1965–2003**

Leisure: recreation + sleep/personal care

Men

12	7	6	0
High-school dropout	High-school graduate	Some college	Bachelor's and postgraduate

Women

| 8 | 6 | 3 | 1 |

Source: adapted from Aguiar and Hurst, 2007[54]

they did. Women may be spending less time on unpaid housework—a good ten hours a week less on average—but for professionals, this is swallowed up by extra time in employment.

Lauren States, who is IBM's vice president of cloud computing, and has a host of black as well as female "firsts" behind her, confirms that "email creates a twenty-four-hour environment. And a lot of people, myself included, have global jobs. If you're going to speak to Asia you have to figure out, do you do better at night or in the morning? In that sense our jobs are continuing twenty-four-hour jobs. You have to be available and you have to be present."

We are not just talking about the very top of the pyramid either. This is about educated professionals in their worldwide millions. Two-career couples, with both employed and at least one putting in forty-eight hours a week or more, are a minority of couples, but they are not that tiny a minority—about 14 percent of all couples aged between twenty and sixty in the contemporary UK.[55] And single professionals typically work as hard or harder. Merit Janow, juggling a Columbia University full professorship with international boards and governmental appointments, remarks on her "young women graduate students, who I thought were wildly unrealistic. They thought the work–life balance had been sorted out and they were going to have it all."

My own family is certainly a case in point. For years, most days of the week, I got up early or stayed up late to work. At weekends, when the children were small, we traded Saturday afternoon for Sunday morning. I remember a moment of revelation for my daughter, then aged twelve. She had spent the whole of Sunday with a school friend and came in to find both parents glued, working, to the computer screen. "Do you realize," she inquired, wonder and fury mixed, "that there are parents who *don't work at all* at the weekend?"

Individual time-use diaries show the trends. Take America in 2003. "Tessa" is single, a thirty-five-year-old female scientist with a graduate degree. She is a home owner in Delaware and her diary shows that she was putting in fifty hours a week at the office. "Marcia," her exact contemporary, was working almost precisely the same hours. An unmarried architect, she was renting an apartment near her New York City office. The time she saved on travel went into hours at the gym. Meanwhile, "Maureen" in Texas was married with children and also working fulltime. An educator aged thirty-nine, with a postgraduate degree, she put in "only" forty-five hours at work, five fewer than the other two.

At the same time, employed American women with a high-school diploma or less were averaging twenty-three hours' paid work a week. This is an average, but not many had job commitments taking them over forty hours a week. "Marina," a married home-owning high-school graduate in California, is far more typical. In 2003, forty-three years old and with teenage children, she had a part-time job for twenty-five hours a week. And she was getting eight and a half hours' sleep on her "diary" night, significantly more than most professional women were logging. Highly educated women are far more likely to have developing careers, jobs they find fulfilling, jobs that are part of their core identity. But if you're working the hours that these jobs mostly demand, something has to give, and does.

CHANGING LIVES

Small vignettes speak to shifting lifestyles. Back in 1965, graduate women were by far the most likely to be out walking their dogs on a weekday. Very few women with just high school, or even some college, reported this as a "main activity" in their diaries. Fast-forward to the early 2000s and that difference has vanished: dog-walkers today are just as likely to be high-school as college graduates.[56] On a larger scale, changing work patterns translate into major differences in two things we all do: sleep and watch TV.[57]

In both the US and the UK, for example, women who are employed full-time average almost an hour's less sleep than those who aren't in paid jobs. Who has the least sleep of all? Highly educated full-timers, of course.[58] If you compare unemployed high-school dropouts with full-timers who have postgraduate qualifications, then, in the US today, the first group of women is sleeping an hour and a half more, on an average night, than the second.[59]

When it comes to TV, in 2003 non-employed high-school graduate mothers were averaging three hours a day watching TV or a video as a "main" activity. Graduate mothers with full-time jobs averaged just over one.[60] France in 1998 showed the same pattern.[61] And the gap is even greater in contemporary Britain: even among the employed, graduate women are watching less than half as much television as those with only low-level qualifications.[62]

We've already met Marina, that typical married high-school graduate with children and a part-time job. She managed not just eight and a half hours' sleep but five hours of TV watching on the January day in 2003 that she recorded for posterity. Down in Florida, on a September Friday in 2004, "Carol," a white forty-year-old high-school dropout and non-employed mother, was logging five hours of "direct" childcare with her three small children, and another four of housework and cooking. Even so, she not only got a good eight hours' sleep but four hours in front of the television. In contrast, when we took a random sample of ten American women with graduate degrees and full-time jobs we found that, on a typical Tuesday in 2003, half watched no TV at all. None of them spent a day remotely like Carol's or even Marina's. It would have meant choosing a totally different life.

In recent decades, the most highly educated women have cut back their hours of cooking and housework slightly, but only slightly, more than everyone else: about thirty or forty minutes a day's difference, no higher.[63] Half an hour a day does not buy a graduate careerist very much downtime. Professional women in developing countries have a far easier time in this regard. In Delhi, say my Indian friends, an affluent working couple with no children will typically have a part-time cook, a part-time cleaner and a part-time washerman or washerwoman. A business family in a smaller city would normally have at least two full-time servants, and for the better-off it will be a full-time cook, a full-time maid, a full-time cleaner, a full-time washerman, a full-time guard and a full-time driver.

Given how much money educated women are now earning, it's slightly odd that the total time people spend on non-market work seems to be so little affected by their salaries. As we saw in Chapter 3, professional women with children now hire servants as a matter of course. They have their houses cleaned. Why are they still logging so much "non-market work"?

Daniel Hamermesh, who has looked in depth at time use and "yuppie kvetch," points out that earning a lot inevitably creates a new set of demands on people's time. The more you own and the more you earn, the more time it takes to manage it, do your tax returns and, indeed, spend it. It's therefore not surprising that the working rich (and quite rich) complain of being endlessly rushed. However, when Hamermesh made this point to the staff of a large US foundation, they thought it "was typical economists' nonsense, responding, 'Can't the rich simply have lots of time by paying people to do all the work for them that they would otherwise have to do?' "[64]

This is exactly the suggestion I get in my own family when I moan about the unkempt state of our small urban garden: "So get someone in." And it's profoundly unhelpful.

In the case of my garden, it would take as long to find someone reliable whom I like as it takes to sort it out myself and I don't have time for either. That goes for a lot of other things too. Indeed, the main reason professional households end up doing almost as much household work themselves as lower-income ones may be that "buying people in" sounds easy and is no such thing—unlike phoning for a takeout dinner.

Overall, our societies are good to their affluent, educated citizens. We live longer than our ancestors, eat and drink well, travel, are entertained. If we are women, our opportunities are transformed. But modern life unquestionably demands long hours from its working elite, men and women alike, and more than it does from non-professionals. The actual differences may vary—higher in the US, lower in Germany—but the pattern is consistent, for men and women alike.[65]

Generally, if you want examples of work–life balance, you will find them among non-graduates, or among those very rare beasts, the graduate part-timer; people like the Dutch women described in Chapter 1. On a weekday Tuesday in 2000, you could indeed find, in the Netherlands, "Tina," a graduate married mother in her forties, at home reading a book, or thirty-six-year-old "Clara," spending several hours visiting friends.

But that is not the new norm. The new graduate norm is a full-time job, whether you are single or part of a couple. With no old-style wife to come home to.[66]

WILLING SLAVES

And then there are the children.

Young children dominate the lives of their parents not just emotionally but by completely upturning their lives. Take any Western country you like, and the group putting in the longest total number of working hours, paid plus unpaid, will be those with children under seven. It's true of men and women alike, graduates and dropouts, well paid or struggling.[67]

This will not surprise anyone, but another recent discovery probably will. Today, it is the graduate professionals, the ones with the longest average hours of employment, who record spending the most time with their children. It is true for men and for women. And the gap between them and other families is widening.

As we've seen, most of us today have tiny families; many people have no children at all. The years spent with highly dependent children are becoming an ever-smaller proportion of parents' working lives. But having a baby nonetheless has a dramatic impact, especially for non-graduate women, most of whom stop work for a period and then go part-time for many years. Graduate women, in contrast, mostly pay for childcare and rush back into employment.

Modern parents of all classes generally take child-rearing very seriously and expensively indeed. Our children are precious and priceless and we work hard to protect them from the rigors of the adult world. They must be kept out of the workplace, stopped from drinking, or buying cigarettes, or traveling alone. They are obliged to attend school, and be dependent on their families, for ever-longer periods.

In her fascinating book on the "pricing" of children,[68] Viviana Zelizer describes how the law, and court decisions, have reflected changing social attitudes. From the 1850s onwards, the children of America's crowded cities played in the streets; and, as automobile traffic increased, so too did child fatalities. The traditional way to assess damages and pay compensation to bereaved families and the one still in use for adults is to add up lost earnings and, in the case of the injured, costs of care. And to start with the courts did just that. The result: for a child killed by a careless driver, no compensation at all was due to its family.

The uproar this provoked quickly led to change. Juries were instructed to start putting a price, and a high price, on the grief suffered by parents who lost a child.[69] Public opinion, judges' instructions and media comment were united. Children, by the early twentieth century, had become both priceless and economically useless. The traditional practice of fostering children in homes, especially farms, which welcomed them for their working contribution, became abhorrent. Children had become, instead, "sacred."[70]

And today? As we have seen, from 1965 onwards, the time that women spent on housework fell. Meanwhile, for men and women, the average time spent on "active childcare" increased. And it is "active childcare," as recorded in people's time-use diaries, that we are talking about here. Not just being around the house while a child plays computer games or (heaven forbid) wanders up the street in search of a friend. Time where being with, and doing something for, the child is the main activity.

This has increased for all parents, but it has increased most of all for the most educated. In the US, professional parents, male and female, were already giving more time to their children than other groups in the early 1970s and they then increased their commitment further and faster. In Britain, fathers' commitment was roughly equal across social classes up to 1975; but from then on, it grew much faster at the top.

In percentage terms, professional graduate fathers have increased their commitment the most dramatically of all in recent years.[71] The result is well captured by the *Financial Times* columnist Simon Kuper:

> I have a secret life. I get up too early, serve Weetabix and then
> scrape it off the floor, hyperventilate while my daughter gets
> dressed too slowly, act as a sort of boxing referee for my two boys,
> brush various people's teeth including sometimes my own, and
> finally help my wife push all the children out the door . . . In the
> evening I rush in and perform the same ritual in reverse. I reckon
> I spend about 30 hours a week on childcare . . . Nothing in my
> childhood prepared me for this life. Admittedly my father, unlike
> many dads in the 1970s, actually changed diapers . . . Yet when I
> asked him whether raising three children hadn't driven him insane,
> he said "I never really noticed. We had a garden." No father was
> then expected to put in 30 hours a week.[72]

As for women, compared with mothers in the recent past—women who were much less likely to be employed outside the house than today—everyone, across the social spectrum, is giving their children more direct attention. Those who are not working full-time give their children a bit more time than those who are full-time employees. But among mothers, childcare time has increased the fastest for employed women with the highest levels of education.

As Figure 4.4 shows, we are talking here about substantial amounts of time. College-educated working women in the US have been doubling the time they spend on "primary" caregiving—that is, time that is focused on the child to the exclusion of other things. The pattern in the UK is the same.[73] In Australia, graduate mothers spend an average of two hours a day more on "direct" childcare than mothers with no

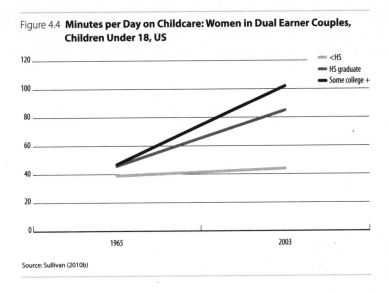

Figure 4.4 **Minutes per Day on Childcare: Women in Dual Earner Couples, Children Under 18, US**

Source: Sullivan (2010b)

upper-secondary qualifications, and an hour more than those with inter-mediate ones.[74]

Since the same thing is happening among fathers,[75] there is a sub-stantial gap between upper-middle-class, top-20-percent families and everyone else.[76] It is no wonder that, as we saw earlier, professional women aren't watching much TV and that a good number are reporting well below average hours of sleep.

Highly educated mothers are, remember, almost all employed. For most of the twentieth century, at the center of childhood memories is something different: a mother who was there, in the house, at the end of the school day: maybe busy but always there. Ten-year-old Tom, whose mother is a stressed academic colleague of mine, got great marks for a classic school assignment, writing about his life at home. He produced a lyrical description of his aproned, flour-dusted mother, baking in the kitchen on a weekday afternoon. This was not, however, something he had experienced firsthand in his whole life, though I—and Tom's own mother—certainly had.

Yet time-use diaries tell us that full-time housewives like Tom's grandmother devoted less one-to-one, full-frontal attention to their chil-dren than today's mothers do. The writer Caitlin Flanagan catches the change perfectly. For her, and she thinks she is typical, motherhood is an "exquisitely overwrought enterprise, full of the . . . never-ending sense that I'm doing too little or too much or the wrong thing."[77]

Her mother, on the other hand, she remembers as a superbly competent housewife. "That children came along with the deal was simply assumed" by her, as it was by anyone else of that generation marrying and setting up home.[78] "Housewives didn't trot after their children the way I trot after mine: Junior All-Stars! Karate! Art for Tots! Their children trotted after them. I whiled away a childhood leaning on the counters of dry cleaners and shoe repairers, and I was happy to do it. I liked being with my mother."[79]

There are two caricatures of graduate-motherhood out there in the media: the driven professional who rarely gets back before the kids are in bed and offers them small amounts of "quality time" in recompense, and the super-schedulers, rushing from one activity to another, polishing their kids' future CVs at every opportunity. The fact that graduate mothers spend so much time concentrating on their children suggests super-schedulers have won the day; but why?

Judith Warner, in her bestselling book *Perfect Madness: Motherhood in the Age of Anxiety*, refers to a new cult of "sacrificial motherhood": a dedication to 100-percent mothering that is not a "lifestyle choice [but] . . . a spiritual calling."[80] There is plenty of anxiety on display in the "Mommy wars," with upper-middle-class mothers, in print and in chat rooms, worrying away endlessly at the pros and cons of being a "stay-at-home mother" (though not a housewife). But is this really all about cultural angst and guilt, born of more widespread paid employment? I doubt it.

First, it's not just elite women but also elite men who are increasing their childcare commitment massively. Second, this is not a phenomenon specific to one or two countries;[81] in fact, quite the contrary. This suggests that there are some more deep-rooted social forces at work.

Two leading female experts on time use suggest (rather bleakly) that elite parents' activities have a lot to do with "investment." "Parents of young children invest time and money in high-quality care," they write, so that "higher-quality children" will "on average . . . do better in school and in the labor market."[82] Families in the 1960s, or indeed the 1950s, the 1940s and for centuries before, were hardly indifferent to their children's futures. But in today's world, this is an area in which highly educated parents have been seized with severe anxiety.

In rich countries, the huge twentieth-century expansion in middle-

and upper-middle-class jobs has leveled off, and competition to sell goods and services is global. Neil Kinnock—now Lord Kinnock—who came from a mining background to lead the Labour Party for many years, acknowledged the issue very clearly a few years back. Whether you're on the left or on the right, he observes, if you've made it to the top yourself, you'll do (almost) anything you can to stop your children sliding.[83] Today's top parents, surveying the globe, are not sure if anything will be enough.

And they are right to worry. Formal education is becoming more and more important as a gateway to the sunny uplands of high-earning careers, and finely tuned CVs are passports to the right schools, the right colleges, the right shortlist. Highly educated parents don't love their children any more than other families do; but they do know about this obstacle race. If activities, chauffeuring, tutoring come at the expense of leisure time, then that is the price that today's parents are determined to pay. It will be well worth it if their sons and daughters win not just an education but the right educational prizes.

5

MAKING IT

At the top the future looks bright. Listen, for example, to Sadaf. She is in her third year of studies at Oxford University, with some clearly worked-out plans. "Hopefully in ten years I will have done a master's in either international development or conflict resolution. I hope to perhaps be working for the Foreign Office as a diplomat and be setting the foundations for my move into the UN or any other world organization."

Her friend Liz, meanwhile, expects that ten years from now she will "be working in law somewhere. I haven't decided exactly where yet, but I hope that I will be working in a City [of London] firm and then perhaps move across to the bar."

The ambitions are realistic enough. These women are presidents of prestigious student societies, attend one of the world's top universities and personify the next generation of successful professionals.

"There's nothing I've wanted to do that I haven't been able to because I've been a girl," says Sadaf; and Linda, another successful third-year, joining us for coffee on a damp gray Oxford afternoon, agrees. "I look around at my friends, and I think these are incredibly smart women, and I'm really excited. I think our generation will do even greater things."

Half a world away, the ambitions and confidence are just the same. Drishya is in the second year of her university degree and considers that "ten years from now I might be working in the UN. I want to do an international law master's, international law and human rights."

Among Drishya's classmates, Sumpa plans to be a professor and Shivalaxmi a lawyer. Mingzhu Ha, planning for a master's and doctorate and her own NGO, believes, "Once we get educated, we can do whatever men can do."

Two sets of women, both on track for elite positions courtesy of their studies. But while the Oxford group attend one of the world's oldest elite universities, Drishya and her friends study at one of the newest. And while Linda, Sadaf and Liz came to Oxford from comfortable middle-class homes in England, the others have come to Bangladesh from all over Asia, from small communities in which education for women is a very new idea.

I spoke to the Asian students on a winter's day in Bangladesh. Winter there means warm sunny days and evenings that are almost cool. The air is as clear and the sky as blue as they ever get in this humid delta nation. Their university, AUW, the Asian University for Women, exists to educate exceptional women in a region where many girls are still denied an equal chance. It is sponsoring a conference and its hand-picked students are attending.

We talk in a modern conference center in teeming gridlocked Dhaka; over in the corner a couple of guys, shadowed by bored teenage boys, are checking out the sound system. But sitting at our white-linened table on the main floor of the hall, swiping at the mosquitoes, we're all female. We are all, except for me, very young, and we are living examples of how modern professional elites are formed: namely, in top universities.

This group have come on full scholarships from all over the region: from Bhutan and Nepal, from China's far Northwestern Province, from India and rural Bangladesh. They left homes with little or no English and are taking demanding degree courses taught in the English they all now speak to near-perfection. Mingzhu Ha is from a village where most girls drop out after primary school, while Sumpa, daughter of a carpenter and a housewife, is from a village where most of the women "aren't educated, they're illiterate, and the men don't care about them. But I think if we are educated we can change the world."

These girls are extraordinary in their independence, risk-taking and willingness to leave for a strange country, with a visit home once a year at best. But they are also uncannily like the Oxford students. They don't think everything will be easy: the Oxford women told me they thought there was still bias; the AUW women know that they live in what are still male-dominated societies, and they face pressures from their families to marry before it is "too late." They all know about recessions and political turmoil. But none of them, at AUW or Oxford, thinks that being female will place serious obstacles in her own path, and all of them think that their education offers a fast route to the top.

And they are right. Modern higher education is serving women very well indeed. This chapter explains how, and why, this happens.

THE EDUCATION EXPLOSION

All over the world, education is a growth industry. Indeed, it is replacing agriculture as the biggest industry on the planet. In the UK, for example, there was one person in education, whether preschool, school or college, for every two in employment by 2010.[1] And the education workforce accounted for 8 percent of employment, larger than any other sector apart from health.[2]

As education grows, so does women's share of it. Back in 1950, across the globe, women received on average about three-quarters as much education as men. Today the average is close to 90 percent. Even in regions such as South Asia, where girls are still much less likely to be in school than are boys, the gap is closing fast. And in the developed world, it has reversed. Women acquire more education than men; more years in school, more certificates, more degrees.[3]

At the end of the nineteenth century, in the rich developed countries of Europe, less than 1 percent of young men and far less than 1 percent of women attended university. In England, higher education for women dates back only to 1871; a decade later, Oxford's Somerville College, the women's college that would produce the only British female scientist to win a Nobel Prize (the chemist Dorothy Hodgkin), as well as the first female prime ministers of both India and the UK, had a total of eighteen students.

By 1900, in English universities there was still only one full-time female student for every six men. On the eve of the First World War, Vienna was the crucible of modern art, architecture and philosophy; and at the University of Vienna only 120 of the over 9,000 students were women.[4] Overall, higher education was something for the few. As late as the 1950s, in France, Britain, Australia and Italy, less than 5 percent of young people went to university. And well under half of these were women.[5]

Today, everywhere, people are flocking to university. And women flock faster than men. They number the majority of university students in every developed country and in a growing proportion of developing ones. And they have overtaken men in just a few decades.

To understand the size and speed of change, look at Figure 5.1 and Figure 5.2. They demonstrate, using four different countries, both how enrollment has exploded generally and how the number of female students in higher education has overtaken the number of men. The US was one of the first countries where this happened;[6] France is typical of Europe. But one could pick pretty much any developed country—Canada, the UK or Australia[7]—and find the same pattern. As one could in Jordan. Or Peru.[8]

Some of this is smoke and mirrors: traditional and high-recruiting female jobs have moved their training into universities while traditional male ones haven't. Back in 1900 the US was unique in having almost as many women as men in higher education, though by mid-century the gap widened considerably and in men's favor. However, America was different largely because its elementary-school teachers were being trained in university departments, unlike the rest of the world's. Now more or less everyone has university training for all teachers.[9] And in more and more countries nurses (mostly female) now have to be graduates, whereas electricians (mostly male) so far don't.[10]

Nonetheless women are also increasingly evident, and indeed dominant, in high-prestige courses. In the US, for example, females make up way over half of enrollments not just in four-year institutions, but also at the postgraduate level, and are now the majority of PhD candidates

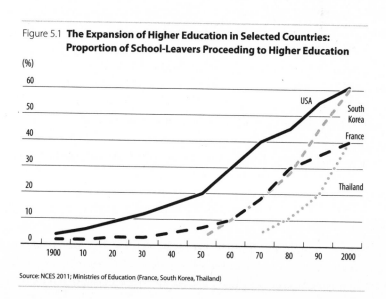

Figure 5.1 **The Expansion of Higher Education in Selected Countries: Proportion of School-Leavers Proceeding to Higher Education**

Source: NCES 2011; Ministries of Education (France, South Korea, Thailand)

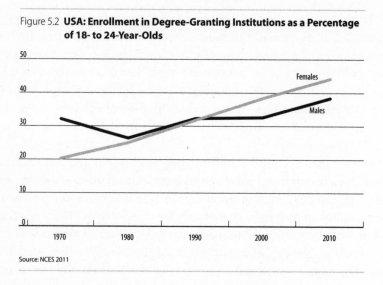

Figure 5.2 **USA: Enrollment in Degree-Granting Institutions as a Percentage of 18- to 24-Year-Olds**

Source: NCES 2011

as well.[11] Universities have become overtly meritocratic in the criteria they use for admission, and so it has become harder and harder to justify limiting the number of places made available to women. Take, for example, the formal admissions process that controls access to a top US law school today.

As a candidate, you apply only after gaining a score on a national test,[12] delivered in high-security conditions and taken by tens of thousands. Each application you make will be dealt with by a dedicated admissions office; each one will be reviewed and read—maybe by a committee giving a holistic judgment, maybe by several faculty members who give a numerical score. Each one will be scrutinized for what an admissions director at one top school calls the "quantitative" and the "qualitative" factors. Everything will be recorded along the way.

This change from a far more informal past isn't just about scale. It's also about what is legitimate and legal. And it is very good for women. If they score well in this formal process, they will be admitted to a top school. And many of them score very well indeed.

COLONIZING THE CAMPUS

The young professional women I interviewed for this book had all gone to good universities and almost all had graduate degrees. None of them had felt outnumbered in class, let alone overwhelmed. Deirdre Eng, a

Wharton alumna and company CFO, never even noticed the gender balance in her business school class, and had to think quite hard before telling me that "it was probably . . . maybe 40 percent women. Yeah."

Amanda Kramer, brand-managing for Diageo, the huge drinks company, went on to business school from Washington University in St. Louis and was similarly vague about gender balance in the classroom. "Back in my undergraduate business class, I felt like it was fifty-fifty. Maybe it wasn't, but it didn't feel like I was anything unusual at all."

Almost 60 percent of medical school students in the UK are now female; in US medical schools, women have made up just under half of entering students for the last ten years.[13] And in the developed world it is now the norm for law faculties to have a majority of female students. In a recent letter to *The Times*, a British female lawyer remembered that when she studied law in the 1960s there were forty-three students in her class, just three of them women. One of her two female classmates also wrote in the next day: "How about the only ten males in my [daughter's] class of 2010 at veterinary school?"[14]

The change isn't uniform or universal. Women are colonizing the law faculties and medical schools en masse, and at elite US business schools a good third of the entering students are now women, but engineering stays firmly majority-male. In France, universities are not the institutions that matter most. That accolade belongs to the *Grandes Écoles:* small teaching institutions from which the overwhelming majority of the French elite graduate. Many focus on engineering and these are still heavily male. But among those *Grandes Écoles* that are business- and commerce-focused, the student body is now more or less 50/50.[15] Move across to the *Grands Établissements*, the top research and postgraduate institutes in science as well as social science and the humanities, and once again women are the majority.[16] And in French universities, it is 60 percent.

One reason women are doing so well at university is simply that they do better, on average, in high school. The Programme for International Student Assessment (PISA) studies run by the OECD are high-profile comparisons of teenagers' performance in a wide range of relatively developed countries. In the 2000 reading survey, females scored higher than males on reading in every single country that took part, and the differences were often substantial.[17]

Countries' own tests and examinations consistently find the same thing for both reading and writing, just as they also find girls to be more likely to read for pleasure.[18] The picture for mathematics is more complex. Until a couple of decades ago, girls consistently did worse at math than boys: there used to be all sorts of research projects and educational initiatives aimed at closing the math gender gap. Today, even in math, girls and boys are performing about equally in most of the developed world's elementary and high schools.[19]

And why do women do better? In substantial part, simply because they work harder. Much of the grind, and many of the key decisions in modern education systems, take place at a time when young women are often markedly different from men, in ways that education systems reward. Girls in their teens are, on average, more conformist, diligent and forward-thinking than boys.[20] It's not just stereotype. They really are the ones most likely to color in their worksheets beautifully, the ones with organized, clean folders of work.

"The girls don't argue, they just sit there and take notes," as my older son used to complain after revision sessions for the public examinations controlling university entry in the UK. Sure enough, classroom studies show that boys ask, and respond to, teachers' questions more often than girls. But they also show that teachers interact more with boys than girls, in large part not because teachers are favoring boys but because of the time they spend telling boys off.[21]

Not all women are more conscientious than all men, obviously; there are plenty of fiercely competitive, hardworking alpha males out there, as well as plenty of unmotivated females doing the minimum.[22] But the average differences exist and they add up. In the annual American National Survey of Student Engagement,[23] female students, whether in their first or final year, are consistently more likely than males to be highly conscientious in preparing papers and assignments, more likely to work "harder than you thought you could" to meet an instructor's expectations and less likely to admit to turning up without having completed readings or assignments.

Women are set up to perform well at exactly the time that our societies' meritocratic guillotines crash down. And that matters a great deal for their futures, because not only are universities bigger and more open to women than before, but education is also ever more important in determining our future lives.

A NEW RELIGION?

"Be good, sweet maid, and let who will be clever," wrote the influential Victorian clergyman and novelist Charles Kingsley. It is impossible to imagine this being said by any respected national figure in the developed world today. Poverty and misfortune bar the way for many millions, but deliberately and unnecessarily to deny someone an education? That is as close as you get today to a universally acknowledged cardinal sin.

And this isn't just true of the developed West. The same attitudes prevail, increasingly, across eastern and southern Asia, Africa and Latin America. They are evident even in countries that explicitly reject female equality: those of the "religious" Middle East.

Isobel Coleman knows these societies well. She directs the Women and Foreign Policy program at the Council on Foreign Relations and writes of how, in even the most fundamentalist Islamic circles, women's actual lives increasingly conflict with narrowly defined traditions. One of her most telling examples concerns Sheikh Yusuf al-Qaradawi, the controversial Egyptian whom she has described as a "paunchy octogenarian religious scholar–cum–Islamic televangelist who, by virtue of his prominence on al-Jazeera, is one of the most recognizable Muslim clerics in the world today."[24]

He gives fiery sermons, insists that women must veil themselves and thinks female circumcision acceptable and often desirable. And yet, Coleman told me, his four daughters are highly qualified scientists, one with a master's from the University of Texas, the other three with full science doctorates from British universities.

I spoke to Coleman in her elegant New York office, a place of polished wood and book-lined walls, high in the Council's Upper East Side mansion. It seems a long way from the world of women (or men) in Iran, Iraq and the countries of the Gulf, where she has worked and traveled widely. And she is not pretending that life in these countries is in any sense equal for men and women, or that they will, tomorrow, become like liberal New York. But she argues emphatically that education, and the emergence of a large educated female middle and upper class, reflect and drive change.

"Even though you have a traditional religious leader, Sheikh Qaradawi, he lives in a modern world. He is not a liberal, he's not a progressive by any means. But on this topic of women the lived reality of his existence is that he has PhD daughters, and they're not PhDs in home economics. It used to be, in a place like India or Persia or wherever, that women were 'inferior, they need to be under the control of men because they're weak, and they don't know any better.' And there was nothing to disprove this theory. But today everywhere you look, these restrictions and notions are disproved on a daily, on an hourly, on a minute-by-minute basis, so that it's become almost ludicrous."

Iran is a theocracy, in which the ultimate authority rests with highly conservative male clerics. But it is also a country where more than 60 percent of university graduates are female and where educated women, as well as men, are at the forefront of resistance to the regime.[25] As Coleman remarks: "Women's education was started under the Shah. But nevertheless it became an important bragging right for the Islamic regime to say, look, we can educate women *and* be conservative and traditional. You know they haven't been able to do what they thought they could do, which was to tightly control curriculum and educate women as good Muslim women and leave it at that. It doesn't work that way and that tension is so evident on the streets of Iran today. This very educated class of women is questioning restrictions on their lived reality. I mean, the regime dropped the age of marriage to nine, and then after much pressure raised it to thirteen. But in Iran people are not marrying their daughters off at thirteen. The average age of marriage in Iran is high, late twenties." And the birth rate has more than halved since 1980.

The fact that Iran's regime has consistently boasted about its education of women shows how deeply people have internalized the idea that education is good: even people who are quite deliberately "reactionary." Contrast this with England, only a little over a century ago, where a world-famous center of learning publicly rejected the idea of access to learning as a universal right. In 1897 the University of Cambridge faculty voted down the proposition that women should be awarded full degrees. The undergraduates cheered them on and a roaring mob of young men celebrated the vote by trashing the town center.[26]

Today, controlling access to university education on any grounds other than "merit"—brains—is increasingly illegitimate. Governments and universities may sometimes champion "affirmative action" as a way of righting past wrongs, or tackling serious political tensions.[27] But they see it as something that is intrinsically questionable, has to be justified carefully, and that they hope will be temporary. In principle, modern societies believe that you shouldn't get favorable treatment because your family has quartering on its shields or is one of the state's "first families." You should not be admitted to a degree course only if you have the right religion, caste, color. Or the right gender.

This is part of a change in values that goes well beyond higher education. Imagine yourself catapulted a few generations back. You left school and you looked for a job, mostly locally. To find it, you tapped your—and your family's—networks and contacts. Some people might have gotten apprenticeships through their fathers and uncles. Some went into the family firm. For others, family connections took them to a City of London or Wall Street brokerage, or the newsroom of a national paper.

Or rather, took young men there. The occupations I've mentioned were all closed to women: no father would ever have raised the issue on a daughter's behalf.

Today, it is not just universities but employers who are under pressure to hire on the basis of meritocratic criteria and to demonstrate that they have done so. Hiring someone because you knew their father or mother happens, but as something to gloss over, not broadcast. And it is illegal for employers in most of the developed world to discriminate by sex when they advertise or hire for a job.[28]

In this world, what could be safer and more praiseworthy than hiring on the basis of educational qualifications? Good grades are transparent. They are earned in institutions that proclaim their dedication to merit and equal access. And so formal qualifications are increasingly the entry gate to a successful career. They may not guarantee a great job, but without them you don't even get to the starting block. No wonder 98 percent of newborn babies' mothers want their child to go to college.[29]

GET EDUCATED, GET RICH?

A college degree has become the most reliable way to get ahead in life. It doesn't guarantee success, and some people manage without, but it is a very good bet. The "returns" on a degree, meaning the extra amount that college graduates earn compared to those with lower qualifications, have held up or even increased throughout the world, even though there are more and more graduates.

This is partly the result of genuine changes in the economy. There are more jobs today not just for engineers, scientists and mathematicians, but for people who can write the sort of analytical, extended prose that gets you high marks on a coursework essay. There are more lawyers in our complex, regulated economies, and more accountants too, almost all of them now university-educated.[30]

A lot of it, however, has rather little to do with economic "need."[31] Many governments pour money into higher education because they believe that it automatically generates innovation and boosts growth. But, as I and others have argued at length, there is in fact precious little evidence that producing more and more graduates does anything for a country's growth rate.[32] It does, however, change the job market.

The more graduates there are, the more employers hire them in preference to non-graduates. After all, graduates are likely to be relatively intelligent, relatively hardworking and a much safer bet than a dropout. Many of the jobs now taken by graduates have not changed their skill requirements since the days when they were done perfectly well by high-school graduates who had never gone to college. But now you need a degree to get hired.

All of this generates a self-propelling inflation of degree requirements, with more jobs demanding graduates and more people heading into higher education. Once upon a time, Trinity Washington University in Washington, DC, was an exclusive liberal arts institution, whose students included Nancy Pelosi, first woman Speaker of the US House of Representatives, and Kathleen Sebelius, two-term governor of Kansas and Obama's Secretary of Health and Human Services. And it was called Trinity College. But as its president Pat McGuire explained, "Increasingly, American higher education is moving in favor of the 'university' word, and the consumers of American higher education think that a university is a much more important experience. So we wanted to recognize the reality of who we are. The growth in degrees is enormous. Given the current economic climate, we see a lot of students who feel they cannot have enough credentials. And we've seen the ratcheting up in credentials, which means there are over-credentialed people who are under-employed. There are not enough places to employ all those MBAs right now."

This isn't just about entry to high-paying business careers. Caroline Marcus works in a sector that combines terrible pay with enormous competition for jobs: museums and galleries. For years she had a portfolio life, freelancing at big London institutions such as the National Gallery and the Imperial War Museum; today she combines this with a permanent position as Head of Learning at London's Jewish Museum. And along the way she did a master's degree, "which was a massive stepping-stone for me career-wise. My CV was very strong in terms of my experience but I was looking at roles in places where they have a screening test before you're even put forward for a possible long-listing or shortlisting. I didn't have an MA, which automatically ruled me out."

Just recently, she told me, "We advertised for an administrator job at the museum, on a relatively low salary. It was fascinating interviewing people for this position. They were interested in being administrators but they were actually looking at it as a way into the sector."

A basic administrative low-salary job, but it attracted over seventy applicants. And the large majority, Caroline said, had master's degrees. Credentials may not always open doors, but in their absence more and more doors stay firmly shut. It is hard to see how this could change in the face of today's burgeoning universities, and our laws, values and attitudes. And it does play to women's strengths.

WINNER-TAKES-ALL

In 2010, Elena Kagan became a Justice of the Supreme Court of the United States. Her confirmation meant that the nine-member Court had three female justices for the first time ever. It is a Court with Catholics and Jews, a black justice and a Hispanic one. It is also, in the second decade of the twenty-first century, made up entirely of justices who were educated at either Yale or Harvard law schools.

In the UK, graduates of Oxford and Cambridge universities— "Oxbridge"—dominate politics across the spectrum. In 2010, British voters handed the premiership to the Conservative David Cameron, Oxford-educated like his famous predecessor Margaret Thatcher.[33] He faces, across the chamber, the winner of the 2010 contest for leadership of the Labour Party. This was a contest involving five candidates: four men, one woman, three from highly educated professional families, two from very ordinary ones, four white, one black. And every one of them a graduate of Oxford or Cambridge.[34]

In France, as we noted earlier, the institutions that really matter are not the universities but the small and super-selective *Grandes Écoles*.[35] Politics is dominated by graduates of one in particular, the École Normale d'Administration, or ENA, a small postgraduate institution that recruits largely among students whose undergraduate studies were also at a *Grande École*. Since 1970, nearly half of France's prime ministers and three of its six presidents have graduated from ENA. And it could have been four presidents out of five if Ségolène Royal, the Socialist Party candidate and runner-up, had won in 2007. François Hollande, Royal's ex-partner and the father of her children, was the victor in 2012; he's another ENA product and so is the woman he beat in the primaries, Martine Aubry.[36]

As higher education has exploded in size and scale, elite institutions stand at the top of ever-larger pyramids. This expansion has not damaged them. On the contrary, the more people there are waving degree certificates, the more employers want to know which ones are "best." "No one ever got sacked for buying IBM," they used to say. No one gets sacked because they hired a woman or man from Tokyo, Oxford, Peking or MIT either.[37]

Going to a "top" institution definitely has a positive effect on your future earnings, compared to other graduates. However, the difference between a mid- and lower-ranking one isn't nearly as clear.[38] That is entirely consistent with a university world that has a few instantly recognized names, and hundreds or thousands of other institutions whose individual worth it is impossible to know. Robert Frank and Philip Cook have charted the rise of such "winner-take-all" markets in a number of areas: sport, finance, the media and American higher education.

> Consider the CEO of a floundering Fortune 500 company faced with the task of hiring a management consulting firm. He interviews the consulting teams from two firms and finds that they are indistinguishable in terms of their ability to respond to his concerns and formulate initial strategic plans. One team, however, consists of graduates of Stanford, Harvard and Chicago, while the other is made up of graduates of less distinguished institutions.
>
> With nothing more to go on, the CEO will have a compelling interest in choosing the former team. He wants, after all, to tell his board that he got the best advice available . . .[39]

Frank and Cook were studying 1990s America, and noted that high-achieving college students were becoming ever more concentrated in the "top" institutions; and a decade on, Stanford economics professor Caroline Hoxby confirmed the pattern. She notes that anyone who spends time at the events of "certain colleges" is likely to hear alumni exclaim that their college is so selective today that they would not be admitted were they to reapply.[40] But it is only "certain colleges" that have changed. The top 10 percent are ever more selective. The majority are not.

This parting of the ways between the elite and the rest is now global. Elite employers hire from around the world; and students travel to study, in pursuit of the most valuable degree course to which they can both win admission and afford. The result is that national and international league tables, which rank "top" universities, are increasingly important. In every internationally competitive university that I've worked in or know secondhand, the latest rankings are pored over in senior management meetings, trustee meetings and meetings of council. People debate ways to rise and how not to fall. But for most universities, the international league is an irrelevance. They are not players.

Pat McGuire of Trinity Washington University sees academic hierarchies as not only long-standing but inevitable. "We see an interesting example of this right now with the whole controversy around whether Yale and Harvard should have a lock on the Supreme Court of the United States. But when I went to law school, all of us who went to Georgetown Law School felt we were in a pretty good place, but we also knew sort of instinctively that we weren't going to go to the same place as the Harvard and Yale gang got to, because in the law it really is stratified by where you go to school. So I think the future of elitist behaviors will continue to be very strong. At the top levels of government and the top levels of certain industries, like law and so forth. You know, that's part of life."

America is far from the most extreme example of university hierarchies, in spite of those Supreme Court justices. In Japan, Tokyo University is out there in front for what sociologists call "elite formation." It has educated almost half of all postwar prime ministers and, in a "normal" cabinet, well over a quarter of ministers will be its graduates. Behind it come a couple of other long-established public universities and a couple of top private ones; everywhere else is an also-ran.[41] And in France, it is not just whether you went to a *Grande École*, but exactly which one that matters for the whole of your adult life. Laura Mercadier, trader and banker, is herself a graduate of one of the *Grandes Écoles Supérieures de Commerce* and told me how, in her final year, "I interviewed for internships and people told me, OK, so you went to this school and so you will have this salary to start. And I was, like . . . so *why* don't I have the same salary as others? More than some and less than others. 'Because of your school.' So your salary depends on the ranking of your school."

All this means that, when the student body changes in the top institutions, so do the world's elites. Women do well in formal education. Women do well in admissions to elite universities. And since the space at the top is limited, elites are changing in their turn.

THE CHANGING OF THE GUARD

Over the last few decades, women have become an ever-higher proportion of students in the most selective institutions. This means that employers now recruit from classes that were once male, and are now mixed or, in some cases, majority female.

America's Ivy League undergraduate colleges are among the most famous and selective in the world, and their recent history, illustrated in Figures 5.3a and 5.3b, encapsulates the change.[42] Figure 5.3a shows the overall proportions of undergraduate men and women in the Ivy League and in the prestigious Seven Sisters colleges of the early 1950s, a time when none of the Seven Sisters admitted men and most of the Ivy League men's colleges had yet to admit a woman to their undergraduate courses.[43] It's a familiar picture: far fewer places, and so far fewer opportunities, for women's brightest and best.

Now look at Figure 5.3b, which covers the same elite private colleges, Ivy League and Seven Sisters, sixty years on. There are now far more places available in total, at these top undergraduate institutions, for women than there are for men. The Ivy League colleges have opened their doors; the Seven Sisters, meanwhile, have created only a few places for men. And in case you think that the "real" prestige belongs only to the Ivy League schools, a look at their enrollments, taken separately, confirms the change. The Ivy League colleges, so recently all-male, now have a small majority of female over male undergraduates.

Remember, too, that these institutions have expanded in size only a little since the 1950s. Education here is a glittering prize that has held

Figure 5.3a **1950–1951: Undergraduate Enrollments, Top Private Colleges, Northeast US**

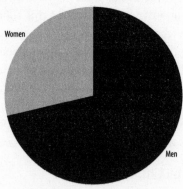

Source: College admissions officers

Figure 5.3b **2009–2010: Undergraduate Enrollments, Top Private Colleges, Northeast US**

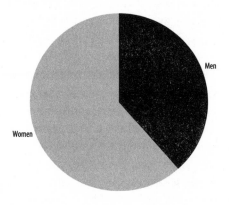

Source: College admissions officers

its scarcity value. And because of these changes, the absolute number of young men in the Ivy League colleges was smaller in 2010 than it was in 1950. Thousands of young men who would have had an Ivy League undergraduate education in the old all-male days now don't and won't. Many thousands of young women have taken their place.

A contemporary employer who is fishing in that special, limited pool is now choosing from a very different group of people from his or her predecessor in the 1950s, let alone before. And the same is true in other countries' elite institutions. As recently as 1970, only a little over 10 percent of Oxford's and Cambridge's students were women; today it is close to half and half.[44] Even in Japan, that bastion of male elites, the University of Tokyo aims and expects 30 percent of its students to be female in the very near future.

MAKING CONNECTIONS

For many pioneers of women's schooling, education was about the opening up of eager minds. My own academic all-girls high school was founded in the nineteenth century by just such women. They lauded scholarship and rather despised sport, let alone needlework and cookery ("domestic science"), and the school motto was "Knowledge is now no more a fountain sealed." However, the reason why the graduates of top universities do so well in life has only partly to do with the quality of the education they get. And it is only partly because employers' eyes light up at the sight of the institution's name on a CV. It is also about contacts and networks, stretching into the years ahead.

Jane Austen, realistic as ever, and herself barred, as a woman, from ever attending university, was well aware that higher education is not just about learning. In *Pride and Prejudice*, she introduces Mr. Collins, the nightmare suitor for the hand of the novel's heroine, Elizabeth, by observing that "Mr Collins was not a sensible man, and the deficiency of nature had been but little assisted by education or society . . . Though he belonged to one of the universities, he had merely kept the necessary terms, without forming at it any useful acquaintance."[45]

To go through university[46] without making any useful contacts at all was a glaring omission. It was the mark of either an unworldly saint or an incompetent. You don't do a physics PhD because of the contacts you will make. But why else would anyone do an MBA? Wharton alumna Amanda Kramer was quite clear that it "gives you the credentials. I knew it would set me up better if and when I wanted to take breaks or make kind of big career switches. Why Wharton? Because I wanted to stay on the east coast of the US, that's my life. It has one of the best reputations. And a big class—so again the network."

I talked about contacts and networks to Christie Whitman, one of the most successful Republican politicians in recent New Jersey history, as well as its most prominent female officeholder. She was the state's first female governor; the first Republican woman in the US to defeat an incumbent governor; and the first Republican woman to be reelected to a second gubernatorial term. Although she came from a prominent political family, she won the primary for the governor's race with no support from the state party apparatus. "And it was great because I didn't owe anybody anything. But as I've said to a lot of women, it's not necessarily because the men are sexist, it's just that people tend to go and support people they know. And guys know other guys; they don't go drinking beer with the women, they'll go with another guy, or play golf."

It's the washroom syndrome as well as the golf club. It's the fraternity and the college reunions. Only now, increasingly, it is women as well as men drinking beer as freshmen; women and men working together in the academic pressure cooker of a final year; and women as well as men calling men and other women on behalf of alumni networks.

Christie Whitman went to Wheaton, a tiny private liberal arts college, all-female in her day: the not-so-distant 1960s, when Harvard, Yale and Princeton were still all-male and none of the men's colleges at Oxford or Cambridge admitted female undergraduates. Her daughter, however, went to highly selective and formerly all-male Wesleyan,[47] a college that along with Williams (women admitted 1970) and Amherst (women admitted 1976) is one of the very top liberal arts colleges in the US.

These colleges are less well known outside America than the big research universities, but they are super-prestigious, and a route to the top, as Vanessa Mobley pointed out to me. She is my New York editor, an alumna of Williams, with a string of Pulitzers on her CV. Growing up, she went to excellent parochial and selective college prep schools. She also lived in Florida, a long way from the centers of power. "You know, America is a large country and an overwhelming number of people never leave where they're from. I always wanted to do better, wanted brighter horizons. That means that you're going to compete on the national stage. And competing on the national stage means competing in college admissions. I personally never had a sense that I was going to be among the most talented; but I certainly wanted to be as talented as I could be, right? And without parents in these power centers, if I wanted to be part of this, I was going to do so under my own steam. That required me to attend a college where my classmates were part of these worlds, and where the leap to them wasn't quite as great as it would be if you attended a second-tier college."

THE RISE OF THE CRAMMER

I said earlier that the ever-growing importance of college was great news for well-educated women, if rather less so for men. But it isn't quite an unsullied picture. Our formalized, meritocratic system also puts extraordinary pressures on children of both sexes and on their parents.[48]

This isn't a completely new phenomenon. Candidates for the imperial Chinese civil service, would-be mandarins with their family's hopes on their shoulders, studied intensely for years, then endured days of competitive exams. They took these immured in tiny individual tents in the Forbidden City's examination courtyard, so that no one could confer or cheat. But the scale and worldwide reach of "exam hell" *is* new.

The pressures are even more evident in the booming economies of Asia than in the West. The Chinese invented modern examinations. During the Cultural Revolution, an unfettered Mao abolished serious university study, and threw students and faculty out into the countryside. Today, examinations are back with a vengeance. In modern China, men and women graduate at a roughly equal rate, within a system where institutions are clearly and publicly ranked. How they perform in the national university entrance examination, and how prestigious a university they consequently attend, decide a Chinese teenager's life. And consequently they work toward it, days, evenings, weekends and holidays, within a grinding regime that parents hate and that seems irreversibly self-perpetuating.[49]

As for India, the Indian Institutes of Technology (IIT) are recognized as world-class engineering and technology colleges, and face almost half a million applicants a year for 8,000 places. One result is modern Kota. It is a small city in western India whose main industry is now running crammers: institutions that exist entirely to prepare teenagers for university entrance. In some cases, parents send their children, male and female, away for a whole two years' preparation, and think it well worth the price if they get into an elite college at the end of it. Pramod Maheshwari, Kota's single biggest operator, currently enrolls 18,000 students, almost as many as in my own large research university; his company, Career Point, is listed on the Mumbai Stock Exchange after a 2010 IPO (initial public offering) that was forty-eight times oversubscribed.

It is hard to see how any of this can go into reverse, short of total economic meltdown. It is also hard to see how it can fail to entrench women's access to the elite. Which leaves us with something of a puzzle.

The economy as a whole benefits if organizations can employ the best-educated and most-competent workers of both sexes. But the number of "top" universities, "top" firms and glittering political, academic and business prizes is by definition limited. If women couldn't be CEOs, then some additional men would have had the chance to head Pearson, IBM, Pepsi, Hewlett-Packard. If women couldn't be politicians, then men who have never made it into contemporary politics would be senators, MPs and ministers.

Why did the top institutions, staffed by men, run by men, for men, ever let women in? The answer is partly values: the growing belief in meritocracy that drives current practices. But it was partly, and paradoxically, self-interest.

WHAT WERE MEN UP TO?

At the end of the Second World War, egalitarian and democratic values were acclaimed by politicians. As colonies became independent nations, they automatically adopted universal suffrage for women as well as men, something that the colonizing powers had not done until they were much richer and more developed. And the idea that women "obviously" should not do certain jobs was in retreat.

Scandinavian governments of the era were attacking gender inequalities head-on. In France, although the proportion of women in universities was still below half, no elite institution discriminated overtly on the basis of sex. On the other hand, at Oxford, which now had Margaret Thatcher as a student, overt discrimination against women was still the accepted order of the day.

Oxford and Cambridge were, it is true, unusual. No other UK university had their policy of reserving a given number of places for women, and a given and much larger number of places for men. On the other hand, postwar Harvard, Yale and Princeton were all-male. These universities were, and are, the super-elite. They could have held out much longer than they did. But by the 1960s they no longer wanted to.

Was this because of feminism? Not in any obvious, direct way. American feminism was far more militant than elsewhere, but also deeply schizophrenic on the subject of mixed-sex study. Many early American feminists believed passionately in the importance of women's colleges, separate from the oppression, or distraction, of men.

However, by the 1960s, the same changing values that fueled feminism, spread universal suffrage and demanded meritocracy in the labor market had been adopted by university leaders. They found it increasingly difficult to justify or believe in anything other than gender-blind admissions policies. And there was something else, which helped American Ivy League presidents open their doors to women, and resist the complaints of horrified alumni, including those of Yale, who staged a full-scale revolt against admitting women. Being single-sex was bad for business.

In his history of how co-education came to the Ivy League, Jerome Karabel argues that a determination to stay ahead drove change at Harvard, Yale and Princeton.[50] These three institutions sit firmly at the top of the academic hierarchy—the White House has been occupied by one of their graduates for fifty of the years from 1900 to 2010—but like all top universities they worry incessantly about whether their place is secure. And in the 1960s it was increasingly clear that they were losing some of their best applicants to co-educational rivals.

More and more "alpha males," it turned out, wanted to study in institutions that also admitted alpha females. Far from disliking the idea of having women compete with them in class, they were prepared to turn down all-male Yale or Harvard and go to Chicago or Stanford instead. In Oxford and Cambridge, co-education came piecemeal, college by college, but with the same underlying dynamic. Many of the best male candidates, and almost all of the best female ones, chose co-educational colleges over those that remained single-sex.[51]

As higher education grew, it became more and more a place where students not only acquired skills, diplomas and networks, but found their spouses as well. And most men did not, as it turned out, want to marry ditzy, adoring and uneducated homebodies. They wanted to date and marry women like themselves.

This also takes some explaining; and is a subject to which we will return in detail in Chapter 11. But the major reason is, surely, parents' desire for "quality" children. As Chapters 2 and 4 discussed, people want the very best for their offspring, and in our societies that makes education crucial. And as parents, the most useful thing you can do to further your children's education is to be educated yourself. Both of you.

This chapter has focused on the last century and on the importance of universities for today's new-style female elite. But education was central to success in industrial societies far before that. As economies industrialized and modernized, subsistence farming and low-skill laboring jobs gave way to office jobs for literate workers. If, as a potential mother, you wanted the best for your children, you would need a husband who could afford to keep his children in school, not send them off to work at the first possible moment. And as a potential father, you would want a wife who could help your children succeed in school, not just keep them washed, fed and clothed. In other words, an educated woman.

In wealthy Western families, mothers had for centuries played a major role in teaching their children to read and write.[52] But as it generated wealth and a fast-growing middle class, the Industrial Revolution spread formal, extended education to hundreds of thousands of women. For men, marrying an educated wife became an important step in securing good jobs and a good life for your future sons.[53] The demand for formal education surged: elementary education for ever-larger parts of society, plus secondary education for the sons aiming for white-collar and professional jobs and for their future wives. And as we will see in Chapter 7, this surge in demand for schooling was met, in large part, by training and employing female teachers.

So for many decades, while top jobs and elite universities remained all-male, and women's aspirations still centered on a "good" marriage, family success was served by having two educated parents. When elite institutions and professional schools opened up, they did so within a society where women were already highly educated. Women could and did flood through the doors.

6

THE WAY WE LIVE NOW

I started to write this chapter one November day in 2011. That same random day, I opened up the *Financial Times*. In the big "Companies" section, which deals with private sector business and big money, the front-page lead was banks in the euro crisis. On page 2 it was the appointment of a new head for mainland China by the world's second largest hedge fund manager. Page 3 carried the *FT*'s regular weekly "CEO profile": this time, the new CEO of EasyJet, a huge European budget airline.

Why is this relevant? Because the newly announced "China head" of Man Group was a leading businesswoman in her forties, Yifei Li. She is a former head of MTV in China, a former martial arts champion, a graduate of both an elite diplomacy school and an American university. And because the new CEO of EasyJet was Carolyn McCall. Her previous job was as CEO of the Guardian Media Group, which owns the *Guardian* newspaper along with a range of other publications.

As for the euro crisis, the single most important protagonists that day, and indeed that month, were Angela Merkel, chancellor of Germany, Europe's dominant economic power, and Christine Lagarde, head of the International Monetary Fund. Nor was there anything special about that particular issue. The previous day, one of the main stories had involved Anglo American, the vast South African mining group. Its CEO was Cynthia Carroll, a geologist with a Harvard MBA.

As previous chapters have shown, the number of successful, high-earning, professional and business women has exploded. In 2012, about 70 million women worldwide belonged, in their own right, to either the

upper-middle class of "highly educated professional and salaried" workers and affluent business owners or to the tiny group of super-rich.[1] And
the number is climbing fast.

Seventy million people is an enormous number. It is larger than the
population of the UK or France. It is larger than the estimated population
of the whole Roman Empire. It is only slightly less than the population
of the US in 1900, by which point America was already a superpower.

But 70 million is also a small minority. Many women in rich developed countries have low incomes, limited possibilities and unpleasant
jobs. These profound changes involve our elites; women are not advancing together in a vast sisterly phalanx. Worse, many millions of women
across the globe are still oppressed on account of their sex.

On the very same day as the FT wrote about Yifei Li and Carolyn McCall, other newspapers were carrying the stories of Gulnaz and
Farida. Nineteen-year-old Gulnaz was jailed for adultery in Afghanistan
after she went the police to report that she had been assaulted, raped
and left pregnant. Farida is also in an Afghan jail for "moral crimes,"
after she fled a violent husband who clubbed her with an iron bar when
she attempted suicide.[2] Forced marriages and "honor killings" remain
common in rural Pakistan; genital mutilation—female circumcision—
continues to occur in parts of Africa; girls in India are far more likely to
be illiterate than boys; women in Saudi Arabia will get the vote in local
elections from 2015 but are still forbidden to drive.

In other words, many millions of women still lead lives that are profoundly unequal simply by virtue of their sex. And yet that randomly
opened copy of the Financial Times also demonstrated something else.
Change is happening much faster and more comprehensively in today's
developing world than it did in the West.

This is partly because of the pressures and opportunities of a global
economy. It is also because changing values create their own uncontrollable dynamic. The students I met at the Asian University for Women
encapsulate this revolution, and it is why one cannot conceive of a return
to the past. Famine, disease or holocaust may one day destroy all continuity between future societies and our own. But short of that, we are not
going to recover the historically unquestioned assumption that women's
activities—all women's activities—should be defined and constrained
by the shared fact of being female. It is unimaginable in the developed
world and, as we will see, in the developing world as well.

THE XXFACTOR

FASTER–AND FURTHER? WOMEN IN THE DEVELOPING WORLD

Cut it which way you like, most of the self-made female billionaires in the world are Chinese. Most of the top ten. Most of the top twenty. And most of the top fifty too.

Take Cheung Yan. She is worth more than twice as much as Oprah Winfrey, the wealthiest self-made American woman. Worth, in fact, somewhere between $5 billion and $6 billion, all from a scrap-paper and recycling business that she launched in the mid-1980s with start-up capital of $4,000. "In any business transaction, it's not sex that makes the difference. It's actually that you should use your intelligence to win," she told CNN.[3] Dong Minzhu's style is even more direct. Boss of China's largest air-conditioning manufacturer, author of a bestselling business book, she's famous for never taking a vacation and for telling an interviewer that "I never miss. I never admit mistakes and I am always correct."[4]

Women like Dong Minzhu are genuinely self-made. In her early thirties, having lost her husband, she left her son with his grandmother, moved to the booming south of China and took a sales job with a small state enterprise. Her performance shot her to the top: she took the company public and transformed it into a global player. Rags to riches too for Chen Lihua, named the third richest self-made woman in the world by the Shanghai-based Hurun Report. She left school early because of family poverty, opened a small furniture repair shop and parlayed this into the Fuhua Group, a conglomerate that has brought her a $4 billion fortune.

And that is before you get to the property developers. Former journalist Wu Yajun was worth over $6 billion by the time she was in her mid-forties. Xiu Li Hawken is a Chinese literature graduate, married to a London teacher. She lives in a modest suburban house when at home with her English family and is a self-made billionaire from developing underground shopping malls in China. Or there is Zhang Xin, photogenic and charming: she worked on Hong Kong assembly lines before winning a scholarship to Sussex University, then joined Goldman Sachs and is now, with her husband, a billionaire developer of luxury apartment blocks.

China's explosive growth offers extraordinary opportunities; and of course, in a developing country with very low wages, successful women can afford a lot of home help. But what is truly extraordinary is the contrast between the developing world today and the West at a comparable stage of economic change and wealth: a period when women also had large low-waged servant classes to rely on.

THE WAY WE LIVED THEN

Two hundred years ago, mainland Britain was on the cusp of becoming the first industrial nation. It had abandoned subsistence agriculture and embraced a fully market-based economy a century and a half before.[5] Its economy was being transformed by entrepreneurs, business owners, investors and inventors. Yet hardly a single one of them was female.

Through most of the nineteenth century, British women were actually less empowered politically than they had been in many previous centuries. They were barred from voting by their gender even if they were property owners and property tax payers, and if they were married, their property was at their husband's disposal.[6] The 1851 Census lists a sum total of nine female law clerks and twenty-two female "scientific persons," and not a single woman lawyer, physician, surgeon, surveyor or engineer.[7] Forty years on, in the 1891 Census, there were still just 101 female physicians, and not a single female who had made herself a million or more by starting a company.[8]

China's economy is already huge, but its income per head, in the 2000s, was still at the level of America's a century before.[9] Yet in the early 1900s, with its economy booming, the US did not have a single Dong Minzhu or Wu Yajun. It did not even, in 1910, have a single female judge, justice or magistrate or a single female veterinary surgeon.

China is a front-runner in this respect. The 2009 Grant Thornton International Business Reports[10] estimate that, among large privately held businesses in China, women occupy about 31 percent of senior management positions, one of the highest in the world; and that more than 80 percent of such businesses have senior female managers. But it's not just China.

There were no women anywhere in 1910 who resembled Indra Nooyi, the Indian-born and Indian-educated global CEO of PepsiCo. Or Vinita Bali, who turned around India-based Britannia Industries, a food manufacturer that now has 35 percent of the Indian biscuit market; or Kiran Mazumdar-Shaw, creator of India's, and indeed Asia's, largest biotech company. Or anyone like Saudi Arabian Nahed Taher, the first woman to head a Middle Eastern bank, and one that she co-founded. America in 1910 had no such women. The nations of Europe had no such women. Nowhere did.

It is not that today's developing countries have always had an enlightened attitude to women. On the contrary. My friend Padma Desai is a professor at Columbia University in New York with a Harvard PhD. But she grew up in a provincial India where for a girl to be widowed very young, as many were, was a catastrophe. "There is a pronounced cultural stigma prohibiting a Hindu man from marrying a widow or divorcee," Padma explains in her memoirs.[11] As a childless widow, you had no options but servile dependency on whichever relative would take you in.

Padma's memoirs are dedicated to "Kaki who endured." In her childhood, Kaki, the widow of her father's brother, was "no more than a shadow in the household," though one who loved and pampered the children. "I do not remember Kaki wearing sandals. She did not need them because she hardly left home . . . She always covered her head. She had to because it was shaven."[12]

As for China, it was a country where girls were quite recently so little valued that they might be just numbered at birth, as First Daughter, Second Daughter and so on, rather than given names of their own.[13] Many Chinese families still value boys more than girls; and "doing"—that is, killing—an unwanted newborn girl was apparently commonplace in rural areas as late as the 1990s.[14]

Most developing countries are far from achieving across-the-board equality between women and men; in many, the birth of a boy remains a greater cause for celebration than that of a girl. Yet in all the big and successful developing countries of today—China, India, Muslim Indonesia—women play a significant role at the top of the job market, among the educated and well-off. Thailand is not highly rated for gender equality; international agencies and academics argue that inherited attitudes and "cultural norms" are at odds with female success.[15] Yet in family-owned and private companies—which are extremely important in the Thai economy—women have been doing very well indeed. Among large, privately held businesses, most of them family firms, the Grant Thornton International Business Report found that, in 2009, 38 percent of senior-level positions were held by women, making Thailand a world leader on this measure.[16]

Adam Quinton spent many years with Merrill Lynch, where he was a champion of greater diversity and more women at the top; his career

included years in Asia as head of Asia Pacific Research. In his experience, "You get quite a few successful women there, they're quite visible, and it's no big deal that they are women. That's not the issue. You do well, whether you're a man or a woman, and that's fine, you get on with it. There is much less residual gender discrimination."

And that is certainly consistent with what is happening in top Asian multinationals today. A century ago in the West, hardly a single woman had penetrated the middle, let alone the top ranks of business and commerce. Today, it is not just in the highly developed countries of East Asia that women are making it to the top. Large numbers are doing so within the continent's developing countries, at unprecedented speed. The proportion of female managers at the top of multinationals in China or India is already close to that in their developed neighbors, and orders of magnitude greater than in the US a century ago.

MODERN VALUES?

Why is today's developing world so different from our own? Clearly it is not because its elites were historically more open to women than ours: in many cases, quite the opposite. So is the explanation essentially economic, namely that later-developing countries are readier to use female talent because, in a global economy, they need to? Or is there something more profound at work?

Certainly today's developing economies use a very different skill mix from Britain in 1810 or Germany in 1870. Today even small commercial farmers and manufacturers are part of a global economy, exporting by air and interacting with suppliers and purchasers constantly, online as well as by phone. More generally, developing countries are playing "catch-up," orienting themselves to the technologies of developed countries as they are today, not the much less-educated and technically advanced societies they once were.

But that doesn't actually explain the differences. Developing countries almost all have an oversupply of skills (as, indeed, does the developed world),[17] so there are plenty of underused male skills and abilities out there. European countries were all able to grow perfectly adequately with very little female participation in middle-class and professional jobs, right up until the Second World War. So, in principle, could today's developing countries.

One has, instead, to look to ideas and values. Outside a very limited number of countries, the world has—as we saw in Chapter 5—accepted

that men and women should both have full access to education. Isobel
Coleman of the Council on Foreign Relations explained to me what a
major impact Iran's acceptance of this entitlement has had. She also
writes about emerging female Islamic theologians in Pakistan and the
emergence of top-class women's colleges in Saudi Arabia.[18] All bear witness to the way in which certain ideas and values have spread across
the contemporary globe, and with far greater consequence than designer
labels or hamburger brands.

"Education for all" is not the only idea with global heft. Most contemporary nations sign up to a large number of common values and
practices, including political democracy. Here too there is overwhelming
acceptance of equal access. Rich and poor, men and women, should all
enjoy the same rights at the ballot box. Of course, many political leaders pay lip service to universal values while undermining them as best
they can. But in explaining the rapid progress of women in the developing world, the legitimacy of these values is crucially important, because
it makes them impossible for leaders to ignore. And if women have an
equal right to vote, if women have as much formal right to enter politics
as men, then you set up a dynamic process that changes societies.

MADAM MINISTER

Comparing politics in the developing world today with those of Western countries a century ago is as instructive as it was for business and
commerce. It was only in 1916 that the first woman was elected to the
US House of Representatives. Until 1929, UK women, having finally
won the franchise, had to be older than men before they voted: Barbara
Wootton, one of the most eminent British women of her generation,[19]
became a magistrate in 1925, at the age of twenty-eight, two years before
she would be allowed to vote! In Switzerland, women finally got the vote
at federal level in 1971, but the last canton (state) held out till 1991.

Outside the Gulf, no recently independent or recently developing
country has behaved similarly. Moreover, the countries that are world
"leaders" in terms of female representation in politics are as likely to
be developing (and often African) as Western. As Table 6.1 shows, the
Scandinavians are predictably high in the "female legislators" rankings;
but it is poor, landlocked Rwanda that is top, and more than half the top
twenty-five are developing nations.

At the end of 2011, when Germany's Angela Merkel was laboring
to save the euro, eleven other countries were also being run by female

Table 6.1 **Legislatures with the highest female representation: 2009 (percentage)**

1. Rwanda	56.3	13. Norway	36.1
2. Sweden	47.0	14. Belgium	35.3
3. South Africa	43.5	15. Mozambique	34.8
4. Cuba	43.2	16. New Zealand	33.6
5. Iceland	42.9	17. Nepal	33.2
6. Finland	41.5	18. Germany	32.2
7. Netherlands	41.3	20. Belarus	31.8
8. Argentina	40.0	21. Uganda	30.7
9. Denmark	38.0	22. Burundi	30.5
10. Angola	37.3	23. Tanzania	30.4
11. Costa Rica	36.8	24. Guyana	30.0
12. Spain	36.3	25. Timor-Leste	29.2

Note: No. 19 is the tiny principality of Andorra.
Source: Inter-Parliamentary Union. Figures calculated for lower or single legislative house only.

prime ministers. As many again had female presidents.[20] And while non-democratic China stars as a place for women to do business, it is Southeast Asia that best demonstrates how fast women are rising to the top of developing country politics.

India, Sri Lanka (then Ceylon) and Pakistan became independent countries with a full adult suffrage only in 1948. In 1960, Sri Lanka became the first country in the world to elect a female prime minister. Six years later, India became the second. Pakistan acquired its first female prime minister in 1988. Bangladesh,[21] one of the world's largest Muslim countries and a parliamentary democracy, has two large political parties. In 1991, twenty years after independence, Khaleda Zia became the country's first female prime minister; in 1996, she lost to Sheikh Hasina, female head of the main opposition party. The two women have been slugging it out ever since.

These women have all come from high-profile political families; but having a charismatic father or (assassinated) husband is no longer a prerequisite for success.[22] India, for example, now has very powerful female politicians with no family base, such as Kumari Mayawati, J. Jayalalithaa and Mamata Banerjee.

Mayawati in particular attracts devotion and fierce criticism in equal measure. She is "sister" to her millions of supporters, many of whom are, like her, Dalits ("untouchables"); to her opponents, she is an autocrat who lines her own pockets. At thirty-nine, she was the youngest politician ever to become chief minister of Uttar Pradesh (population 200 million) and has to date served four terms.[23] Her huge birthday bashes are splashed across the media and she has raised massive sandstone statues of Dalit leaders all over the state. They include herself, standing tall and clutching a trademark that the British under Mrs. Thatcher would have found familiar: a large square handbag.[24]

What unites the developed and developing worlds is a self-reinforcing dynamic. It may start with tokenism; but tokenism provides women with a springboard to power and influence. The number of "visible" women rises; soon, having powerful women in politics seems perfectly normal. And in the process it becomes less and less acceptable to discriminate, and harder to do so without an outcry.

Christie Whitman was one of the most prominent US female politicians of the 1990s and 2000s, not just as a two-term Republican governor of New Jersey but also as a member of George W. Bush's administration. Tokenism, when she started out, was rife. "I first went on the county college board. I was asked to serve on that. And there was a woman on the board, and she'd resigned. It was a five-member board, four men and one woman. And so that was sort of the woman's seat; you know how it was. Then I was asked if I wanted to run for office by the county chairman, then by the Republican Party state chairperson, at that point female. And she asked me if I'd run for a Senate seat that they'd had a woman run for before.

"The men were not terribly accommodating, but it tended to be 'a woman's seat' or 'a woman's turn.' And this was against then-Senator Bill Bradley and the woman who ran against him six years prior had lost by sixteen points. I think the reason they didn't fight me when I said I'd run for it was that they reckoned whoever ran for it was going to get beaten. And then they'd be able to at least say a woman had run.

"I didn't win but I came so close. I was their worst nightmare because I didn't go away, and it gave me name recognition nationwide, not just in the state of New Jersey. He spent $12 million and I spent less than $1 million and he beat me by just three percentage points and it had been a big-deal race."

Three years later, having won a successful primary campaign running against the state's party hierarchy, Whitman was governor of New Jersey.

Christie Whitman's career illustrates perfectly how unstable and short-lived "tokenism" tends to be. But it was important that the political establishment felt a need for token women. It gave her a start, just as the similar desire of a UK prime minister for a woman in his cabinet gave Mrs. Thatcher hers. Both were a reflection of profound underlying changes in mainstream values and attitudes.

FOLLOW THE MONEY

"Follow the money" is pretty good advice when you want to know what's going on.[25] Women are now a substantial proportion of the world's high earners, as well as its high spenders. And while changing values and the contemporary day-to-day normality of female elites are the main reasons that it is hard to imagine women's opportunities going into reverse, hard cash is another. Money is power.

There are two things that most people "know" about money in modern societies. One is that women are paid less than men. The other is that a tiny percentage at the top are getting richer and richer, while middle incomes stall. Both are true (up to a point).[26] But in understanding the world of educated working women today, we also need to be aware that hundreds of thousands of those top-of-the-tree high earners are women.

In recent years, there has been a general move back to a world of rich and super-rich individuals and away from the relatively equal incomes of the mid-twentieth century, and what economists such as Tony Atkinson refer to as the "Great Compression."[27] However, the trends have been very different for women compared to men. While men's average incomes have tended to flatline or even fall, women's average incomes have grown: in the US, for example, they have grown further and much faster than men's fell.[28] And something else is completely new. This time, as high earners draw away, women are a substantial part of the pack.

Meanwhile, women on average do still earn less than men, for the big (and immovable) reasons discussed above. The majority have babies; they are the ones who take the main childcare role and most take time out for this. Women generally prioritize family, they work part-time and they are concentrated in traditionally "female" jobs, which are often fast-growing, often secure, but also, often, low-paid.

But none of this applies to the highly educated. Across the Western world, as we saw above, women now occupy half of professional jobs.[29] And in every OECD country, the proportions of men and women in the highest-earning quintile are correspondingly very similar.[30] Like for like, younger women and men are now paid the same, and accumulate wealth at the same rate.[31] And the increased income inequality of recent decades, though it has hit non-elite men particularly hard, is not just a male phenomenon.[32] Income inequality among women has also risen. Since the mid-1960s, the percentage of total female earnings going to women in the top earnings groups has doubled.[33]

Detailed analyses of American private sector employees[34] show that among the top one in 100 American earners, the proportion of women rose from about 2 percent in 1980 to almost 14 percent in 2004.[35] That is a sevenfold growth in the course of a quarter-century. In the UK women are a little more common at the very top than in the US: about one in six of the UK's top 1 percent of taxpayers are female.[36] And if you look at wealth—not just current earnings, but stocks, bonds, property—you can also see the impact of "women rising." In the top 2 percent of Americans, the one-in-fifty group, women's share has been increasing steadily since the 1940s and by 2000 they were a full half of the group.[37]

Since the total share of national income going to top earners has been rising in many countries, the result is a lot of very well-paid women ready to spend.[38] Of course, women in the past also had a sizeable amount of spending power. But it was of a very different kind. They didn't, for the most part, earn it themselves. They were deeded it, sometimes by their fathers though largely by their husbands, in life or after death.

This meant, among other things, that the greater the proportion of a society's wealth that was held by women, the worse the economic outlook. Columbia University academics Lena Edlund and Wojciech Kopczuk[39] have shown that, from 1675 until very recently, the more wealth was held by women, the more economically stagnant the economy. That was because, in a stagnant economy, inheritance was the main way to get rich; and inheritance benefited women as well as men.

In more dynamic times, men created new wealth and new fortunes. But until very recently indeed, women did not. Creating a new fortune was not an option for them, however inventive and able. So economic dynamism was associated with more wealth going to men, because the relative importance of inheritance declined, and vice versa.

If you look at today's super-rich, who number in the hundreds rather than the hundreds of thousands, the traditional pattern is still very obvious. The women in this group have generally inherited great wealth rather than made it. In the US, *Forbes* magazine publishes an annual list of the 400 wealthiest Americans;[40] women are a small minority, and a fairly stable one, hovering between 12 and 19 percent over the last three decades.[41] In Britain, the *Sunday Times* Rich List publishes a similar annual roundup of the 1,000 wealthiest Brits. In 2004, women were only 7 percent of the main list; in 2011 that was up to 11 percent. The German "rich list" of people with huge multi-million-euro incomes, typically from industry, comprises about 640 individuals; only one in six (17 percent) is female.[42]

Whichever the country, these super-rich women are still overwhelmingly the beneficiaries of inheritance, as daughters, wives and widows.[43] Typical of seriously large female fortunes are those of Lisbet and Sigrid Rausing, philanthropists whose grandfather, uncle and father revolutionized packaging with Tetra Pak; or of Liliane Bettencourt, heiress to the huge L'Oréal cosmetics company created by her father; or of Christy Walton. She is the top woman in the Forbes 400 list, and is there simply because her father-in-law founded Walmart. On either side of her sit men like Mark Zuckerberg and Warren Buffett, who made their own gigantic fortunes.

When you go beyond the Forbes 400 to the larger but still very rich group of the wealthiest 0.01 percent, you can see how women's share of such wealth has gone up and down because of economic changes. A quarter of these people were women in 1925 and this rose to 50 percent in 1969.[44] By 2000 women's share in this list of the "top one-in-ten-thousand" was back down to a third. That wasn't because opportunities for women had declined. It was because earned incomes and new wealth had become more important again, relative to inheritance, and the really huge new fortunes were male.

But even here, among the plutocrats, there are signs of accelerating change. First, more and more of the women who inherited fortunes based on family companies are also actively involved in running them. The Fortes are one of the richest families in Britain, because of the hotel business created by their father, Charles; in this generation, daughter Olga is as actively involved as her brother Rocco. Norwegian sisters Helene and Marianne Odfjell run the huge oil-drilling and shipping company made over to them by their father. Georgina Rinehart is Australia's richest individual, not just its richest woman. When she inherited the HPPL mining group founded by her father, it was on the skids; today it is a giant.

Second, a completely new sort of woman is starting to appear, women who have made their own money from scratch. There's Oprah, of course; and J. K. Rowling, author of the Harry Potter books. But they followed quite long-established routes: women have always been involved in entertainment. More significant are the women making fortunes in areas that were once all-male. The new Chinese billionaires may be the most dramatic examples, but they are not unique. There is former eBay chief Meg Whitman. Or Mary Perkins, a self-made billionaire who sells spectacles. Lynn Forester de Rothschild, who made herself a fortune in broadband Internet while also a single mother, told me that one of her great moments was when she walked into her fifteen-year-old son's bedroom "and he was on the phone, saying 'When I grow up I want to be as successful as my mother.' "

These self-made female fortunes are important not just in themselves, but as the tip of an iceberg. The societies that make them possible also support the careers of the hundreds of thousands of women making salaries that most of the world barely dreams of, and the thousands whose businesses make them multi-millionaires, albeit two figures, not three. This amount of money, made by women and not just inherited and spent by them, changes the world's balance of power.

BE GOOD TO YOURSELF

The *Financial Times* is currently the newspaper with the wealthiest, most international readership on earth. And fashion in the *FT* is for *FT* readers, not for stay-at-home wives and girlfriends; fashion for readers who are mostly high-earning and, increasingly, high-earning and female.

Vanessa Friedman is the fashion editor: a super-thin, super-elegant born and bred New Yorker with a Wall Street family. I asked her about the buying habits of affluent women. Not the super-rich, not couture, but were there lots of buyers funding their own upmarket clothes habit?

"Affluent? You mean people making over a quarter-million dollars a year?"

Actually, being an academic, I'd thought affluence started a good deal lower than that. But this level, to Vanessa, was pretty standard: there were plenty of women out there making that. As there are.

In 2008, in the US, CPS figures indicate that 187,000 women were earning Vanessa Friedman's benchmark salary of a quarter-million dollars or more. A few of these are breathtaking CEO salaries: $47 million for Carol Bartz during her Yahoo! Inc. incumbency, $26 million for Irene Rosenfeld at Kraft.[45] But what is really astonishing is the average annual income in Vanessa's group of "the affluent." It was $475,000. Roughly the same number of women were making between $200,000 and $250,000 a year.[46] We are talking here about a group of salaries that start from four or five times the average income for full-time male American workers (and it's an even higher multiple of the female average).[47]

Or look at the change another way. If the patterns of fifty years ago had held constant, then the top 2 percent of wealthy Americans—the top one in fifty—would contain 300,000 more men than it does today, and 300,000 fewer women. Those are big numbers.

And these women spend. Fashion and female luxury brands have become ever more profitable and high-profile in international markets. A friend of mine who runs a charity was recently a pro bono participant at a training day for top-flight female executives. At one point, the women were all asked to take their shoes off for a "barefoot" session. "I think I'm in the wrong job. They were all wearing Louboutins and Jimmy Choos except for me," she reported.

Vanessa Friedman covers Prada, Dior, Gucci and other top-range off-the-rack fashion houses for the *Financial Times* and told me, "When you talk to these brands, they say that increasingly women are buying stuff for themselves with their own money. They buy their own toys."

As men have always done?

Vanessa agreed. "That has been the traditional thing. Like, it's OK, I earned it, I can go and buy it. I remember the story about my father-in-law—he manages mutual funds—getting a big account and coming home with a new Porsche. There was absolutely no consulting with his wife about it. And I also remember a woman I knew at J. P. Morgan in London—she'd have been in her late thirties and she'd worked really hard on some deal. So one day she left the office at five, took a cab, went straight to Chanel on Bond Street and bought a handbag. She said, 'I wanted to remind myself of why I do this.'"

Yes, women are still a minority at the very top, and yes, a Chanel bag can take you up to $15,000 a throw, but it isn't quite a Porsche. However, Vanessa is right. And while these women are a minority of the wealthy, there are now a lot of them.

The young professionals I spoke to were well aware not just of their own privileged salaries, but of a world quite different from their parents'. Laura Mercadier is the French-born and -educated banker who explained to me just how hierarchical the French system of *Grandes Écoles* can be. Of her current life, as a thirty-something banker with a City-based fiancé, she commented, "It's very new, it's unheard-of, this kind of lifestyle. I like fashion so I like the big brands; and because I can afford it, I buy it. I just spent the weekend in the south of France; a week in Provence beforehand and then a long weekend in St. Tropez with our friends, most of them working in the finance industry. We are all young, in a five-star hotel and going out to restaurants."

The growth of women's earnings has helped to make the luxury market remarkably recession-proof. Standard and Poor's analyst Alessandra Coppola is deputy head of equity research in Europe, and was one of the first to predict that luxury spending wouldn't collapse in the wake of the 2008 financial crisis. But even she underestimated just how resilient the market would be.

I met Alessandra in London's Canary Wharf, in an upmarket restaurant full of men and women in their late twenties and thirties and with not an overweight person in sight. Canary Wharf, the financial district downriver from the City, is a self-contained island of tower blocks, underground shopping centers, damp winds off the Thames, and wealth. A graduate of Bocconi, Italy's top university, Alessandra is small, elegant and understated, with shoulder-length dark hair and no designer tags in sight. But visible labels are, she explains, enormously important, especially to women in fast-growing Asian economies.

"Women buy for themselves. And they buy all the time. They're resilient consumers. And the new Asian economies have very different markets from ours. You are showing status with what you wear.

"Women spend what they've got, rationally and more continually, through good and bad. I was one of the first to say that established customers for luxury goods wouldn't collapse in 2008, but I thought the aspirational customers would—and I was wrong. Sales held up and did well right through the crisis. And now, with the finance industry picking up again and so many well-off women there, they are definitely going up. And will do so even more in the future."

The shift in purchasing power isn't just about luxury markets, of course. It is also about big purchases: cars, pension schemes and, increasingly, houses.

Ashley Milne-Tyte is a New York journalist and broadcaster. She is well established but with earnings a good way off super-rich levels. And she drew my attention to the number of single women who—like her—were buying homes and finding themselves getting "gooey over a home improvement commercial."[48]

Between 2000 and 2003, for example, one US home buyer in five (20 percent) was an unmarried woman: there were over 3 million such buyers. Over half of these women were under forty-five—and well over half of this group had never been married.[49]

Put another way, single women spent over $550 billion on US real estate between 2000 and 2003; and while some were divorced and downsizing, much if not most of that money was directly from their own earnings. Of course, many of the purchasers were not high earners and were purchasing quite modest homes. But a sizeable minority of single women buy at the high end—much the same size as the proportion of single men purchasing in this bracket. Again, the absolute numbers are large: 141,000 single women bought a house worth more than $300,000 between 2000 and 2003. And if you're an American or European reader of home improvement and decorating magazines, you'll probably have noticed how many of their covetable featured homes are now created by single women.[50]

As societies get richer, more and more people aspire to home ownership and more and more become owners. What this means among our contemporary, unisex professional classes is that couples quite routinely own two homes. I remember my sister and brother-in-law selling the houses that they had each bought as single, employed professionals. When they married they pooled the money for a new house, which seemed, and is, entirely normal behavior. But only now, only today; because this sort of female home ownership encapsulates our modern female lives.

Which is why this chapter ends with my colleague Sue Clarke. A few years ago, she took a policy-related job in central government in London; she continues to live in Oxford with a commute that strikes me as horrendous. Why didn't she move?

"Well, I had a house by that time. In Oxford. And I had a new partner. Though we each had a separate house. It's only since then that my partner and I have moved in together. So we rent out one house and live together in another." And in the morning he heads off to a commute in one direction, she in another.

When Sue describes her life, it involves exactly that balancing of job opportunities, geographical moves and relationships that is characteristic of modern professional life. She spent twenty years in college management, moving up the hierarchy via new projects, new initiatives, new appointments. And fixing on and staying in Oxford because "I wanted to be somewhere fairly central. I had a partner who I knew was on a very upward trajectory and I knew that he was going to move around a lot, and I thought there's no good me doing that. If I ever get a job in Liverpool he will get a job in Devon. And he did indeed move around a lot and our relationship didn't sustain that. But while I stayed static, I seemed to get a different job and exposure and career opportunities every year."

And a house. And, later, a London job and a new partner. It is not how educated women used to live, but it is certainly how we live now.

7

SOMETHING TO REGRET?

*T*oday's labor market welcomes women. For the earnings gap to shrink, individual employers have had, time and again, to choose a female as the best candidate. They have duly done so; and so among young professionals men and women now are evenly treated. Banks and hospitals, law firms and manufacturers all hire women where they once hired only men; and women, correspondingly, earn, work and progress to their and their employers' benefit. After all, what is there not to like about a larger pool of talent?

And yet for some organizations, the century prior to the 1960s was the special one. From the mid-nineteenth to the mid-twentieth century the "caring" sector enjoyed its own golden age. For the first time, large numbers of well-educated women were entering the workforce, and the institutions that catered to the young, the sick and the old could take their pick. For a hundred years, the most brilliant and energetic women in society worked for them, either as paid employees or by giving enormous amounts of time for free.

Increasingly, they do neither. The best and the brightest have mostly left the caring professions behind and we think none the worse of them for it. "Female altruism" is vanishing into history.

AN INTERLUDE AND WAY STATION

By the eighteenth century, upper- and middle-class women in the West were educated, cultured and well-read. The original "Blue Stockings," or female intellectuals, were a highbrow literary discussion group founded in England in the 1750s. Its members lived in a society in which middle-class literacy was universal and where publishers sold ladies' magazines, fashion plates and novels to a large, less highbrow and specifically female market. But, as we have seen, educated women had no careers open to them other than marriage.

Then, in the nineteenth century, Western education was transformed and, with it, women's options. A network of formal schools for all classes developed across North America and Europe: schools whose workforce was rapidly feminized as the century progressed. For a full century, teaching could rely on attracting large numbers of a country's most academically able women. To be a professional woman was, in effect, to teach.

Alongside these changes came a vast expansion in organized volunteering and charitable work. The charities of the nineteenth century were staffed overwhelmingly by women, largely unpaid. They were also for the most part created and run by women. Charities offered a range of services: financial help, medicines and medical advice, recipes, clothing, links to potential employers. And many of a country's most able women gave enormous amounts of time to these organizations, especially once they married and left any form of paid employment.

When educated women first entered the labor market, they were admitted to jobs that were extensions of traditional female pursuits. Affluent mothers had educated their children at home for centuries, and women were duly seen as suitable to teach the young of the nation at large. Women traditionally offered personal charity and care to the sick, the old, the unfortunate; these became large-scale activities as societies were upended by industrialization. Medicine was relatively early in opening its doors, though it was far behind teaching in offering many opportunities to women. Social work was female and voluntary in its early days, and then female and paid. It was all very "womanly," just as work in the lower parts of the female job pyramid remains today.

But further up, teaching is now simply one option among many, while the old-style middle-class female volunteer has all but vanished. Voluntary organizations are increasingly run by professionals. And teaching no longer enlists the brightest and the best of each generation.

Of course, this reflects the changing opportunities that previous chapters document. Earlier generations of educated women worked largely in schools, or volunteered in the community, because little else was on offer. But the able women of seventy or a hundred years ago did not regard their occupations as simply second-best choices, to which they were condemned by male oppression and from which they longed to escape. On the contrary, these women mostly saw their work as a vocation. Many of them lived in a world that took for granted the value of duty and service to others. They shared an openly expressed idealism, and a belief that their jobs mattered—especially to the future of other women.

These values were inextricably entwined with religious faith. Pioneering female professionals of the nineteenth and early twentieth centuries were imbued, in an unself-conscious way, with the language and values of religion. Duty to God and duty to one's fellow women and men were one of a piece. This was true of those who were active believers, but the same basic values characterize those who had lost any specific faith.

If we do not understand this, we will not understand how profoundly different the world of modern elite women is from that of their grandmothers and great-grandmothers. Or, indeed, from the generations before that. Most educated women of two or three hundred years ago regarded the traditional "women's work" of caring for home and children not with 1960s feminist disdain, but with the values of their time and society: love and duty, fortitude, propriety and resignation. These women were not saints, but they saw the world differently.[1]

Care's golden age carried its own destruction within it. Once women were more educated and once educated women were employed, limiting their opportunities became ever harder to justify or maintain. And looking back today, we could, though with very partial truth, dismiss the beliefs of past generations as an opiate of the educated female classes, developed to reconcile them to unequal lives. But in that case we should see our own obsession with female pay and occupational success as an ideology too. Understanding how we live now, and why, also means understanding what we have lost.

FROM CLASSROOM TO CLASSROOM

Today, as have seen, school and college propel academically successful women into a unisex professional elite, where no jobs are barred to them. But for a century before that, a closed female circle took academically successful girls from high school to college and then back again.

In 1851, the British Census counted 42,000 schoolmistresses, plus 21,000 governesses (but not a single female physician or surgeon); by 1890, a quarter of a million British women worked as teachers. Clever working-class girls progressed from "pupil teachers" to schoolmistresses, while growing numbers of middle-class girls also entered the profession.

Among Americans born in 1900, over 90 percent of the college-educated women who entered the labor force were employed as teachers.[2] Until the First World War, any employed graduate of the country's elite female colleges was almost certainly a teacher. Among Wellesley graduates from pre-1915 classes a full 85 percent of those who entered any employment at all reported this as their occupation. At Vassar it was a mere 80 percent. At Mount Holyoke, it was close to 90 percent.[3]

The alumnae records of Somerville College, Oxford, one of the first and most academic of Oxford University's women's colleges, confirm how many brilliant British women made their lives in the classroom. In 1888, at the end of the college's first decade, only three ex-students were reported to be working other than as active teachers. As late as 1920, we find a (much larger) class matriculating of whom just two, an art dealer and a director of an iron foundry, made "non-caring" careers.

Teaching, at school or occasionally at university level, remained the dominant occupation for this 1920 generation, accounting for 80 percent of those who reported recent or current paid employment. By contrast, among the Somerville women who matriculated in 1980 just over 10 percent report a schoolteaching career. In this 1980 group, there were already more accountants than teachers, while both bankers and marketing managers outnumbered university lecturers and librarians.

Thirty years later still I interviewed another group of female Oxford students. They were from a range of different colleges (all now co-ed) and different disciplines, and from very varied ethnic and social backgrounds. I asked them, "Have any of you ever thought of making schoolteaching your career? Honestly?"

Their replies:

"I personally haven't considered it as a career."

"Me neither."

"Me neither."

"Not at school level."

"No, I didn't ever think about teaching. I want to go out there and push the borders and find something new."

Half a world away, the students at the elite Asian University for Women come from societies that are developing but still poor. Widespread education for women is very recent; but, as we saw, these societies are changing and opening up to women at far greater speed than did the developed world. And none of the AUW students I talked to was planning to be a schoolteacher either.

Contrast today's female opportunities with America in the 1860s. In her famous American novel *Little Women*, Louisa Alcott describes a family of four girls whose father has lost most of his money. When I read the book as a child, I was caught up by the personalities of Meg, Jo, Beth and Amy, and was barely aware of their precarious lives and limited options. But precarious and limited they were. As Alcott tells the reader at the start of the story, when financial disaster hit:

> The two oldest girls begged to be allowed to do something
> toward their own support, at least . . . Margaret found a place as
> nursery governess, and felt rich with her small salary . . . Aunt
> March . . . was lame and needed an active person to wait upon
> her . . . She proposed to take [Jo] for a companion. This did not
> suit Jo at all; but she accepted the place since nothing better
> appeared.[4]

Compared to the March sisters' opportunities, to be either a governess or a companion, working in a "proper" school was liberation. Jane Eyre, one of English fiction's great early heroines, was first a governess and then a teacher in a small rural school. Her story draws on the experiences of Charlotte Brontë, its author. The penniless daughter of a clergyman, she was the only Brontë sister to escape—for a while—from Yorkshire and tuberculosis. She did so for a Brussels classroom; but she also worked as a governess, and at one point she and her sisters attempted, with total lack of success, to set up an "Establishment for the Board and Education" of a "limited number of Young Ladies" in their own family home.[5]

And then there is the Wollstonecraft family. Mary Wollstonecraft was the celebrated feminist author of *A Vindication of the Rights of Woman*, published in 1792. The pamphlet's passion, fury and logic made her famous in her own day as well as now. But in her early twenties she and her two sisters were typical "members of the respectable middle classes . . . [who] were more or less completely without means and . . . could not look to their families to keep them out of the gutter."[6]

Mary duly seized the only opportunities available to women in this sizeable group. She worked as a lady's companion and as a governess and she ran a school with her sisters. She then, utterly atypically, went on to publishing fame, bore an illegitimate child, married a renowned philosopher and died in childbirth. Eliza and Everina Wollstonecraft enjoyed a far more common fate. They struggled through life as governesses and teachers, and ended their days in Dublin running a small more-or-less solvent school where one of them taught the girls and one the boys.[7]

As Western economies grew, formal education became an increasingly important stepping-stone to good jobs and career success. Large numbers of parents would pay for their children's education, and the consequent demand for teachers was met from the growing ranks of educated girls. In the late nineteenth century, England was the most industrialized country in the world, and the English Census was recording almost as many women in its "professional occupations" as it was men.[8] But being a female professional was pretty much synonymous with being a teacher and remained so for many decades, even as the professional workforce exploded in size.

THE BRIGHTEST AND BEST

Genuine higher education for women started in 1830s America, at Mount Holyoke in Massachusetts, but gathered pace from the 1860s. Vassar in upstate New York was founded in 1861, while in England Girton and Newnham in Cambridge were founded in 1869 and 1871. In the 1870s came Wellesley, Smith and Radcliffe, all in Massachusetts, while in Oxford Lady Margaret Hall and Somerville opened. In 1881, the women's École Normale Supérieure at Sèvres brought elite female higher education to France.

In France the whole purpose of Sèvres was to produce female teachers for new academic *lycées* (upper secondary schools) recruiting girls, in parallel with the established boys' *lycées*. To be *Monsieur* or *Madame le Professeur*, in one of these schools, was very different indeed from working as an ordinary teacher or instructor in the main state system. The graduates of Smith and Wellesley, Somerville and Girton similarly taught in academic high schools, or occasionally in the universities themselves, not in the elementary schools that were employing women in their thousands and hundreds of thousands.[9]

Whether or not women's higher education was explicitly designed to educate "top" teachers, teaching was the occupation actually on offer. And teaching was duly what the earliest graduates did. As a result, on the eve of the First World War, just under half of women secondary-school teachers in the UK were already graduates with degrees in academic "subject" disciplines.

Secondary school principals and headmistresses commanded salaries that were the best on offer to women and way above the female norm. There was enormous competition. By 1900, a typical head teacher's salary in Britain was £300 for a small secondary or high school, more for a larger one:[10] this at a period when an annual salary of £500 took you into the top 1 percent of *all* earners, and not just female ones, and a good wage for a skilled male manual worker was £125 a year. In a world where, as one small-town woman teacher commented, "[t]he only alternative to teaching seemed to be working in a shop,"[11] it was no wonder that teaching got the best.

In the US, we know in detail what happened to the alumnae of the elite women's colleges from their foundation through to 1915. A comprehensive survey was carried out in 1915, at which point a very high proportion of all these colleges' alumnae, ever, were still alive.[12] And as Figure 7.1 shows, teaching was to an overwhelming extent the most common occupation and a majority pursuit.

Even after the First World War, things changed slowly. At Barnard College in New York, one of the top "Seven Sisters," the class of 1918 were surveyed in the 1950s, toward the end of their careers. These were

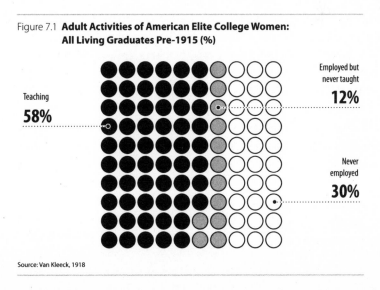

Figure 7.1 **Adult Activities of American Elite College Women: All Living Graduates Pre-1915 (%)**

Teaching
58%

Employed but never taught
12%

Never employed
30%

Source: Van Kleeck, 1918

prosperous women, with three-quarters reporting regular household help.[13] Around one in six had never been employed. Among the rest, teachers now formed a minority, but only just; they were by far the largest single occupational group.[14] As late as the graduating classes of the 1950s, a large majority of Oxford alumnae "taught at one level or another, sometimes after time spent in some other occupation."[15]

And then it stopped. Among girls born in Britain in 1970, only about one in ten of those scoring in the top academic decile chose teaching as a career.[16] Among Americans of the same generation, young people scoring at this level were less than one-fifth as likely to become teachers as their 1964 counterparts had been.[17]

France was the same. We know what proportion of *lycée* teachers completed the rigorous "*classes préparatoires*" that educate eighteen- and nineteen-year-olds for entry to the super-selective *Grandes Écoles*. Among those who qualified before 1955, two-thirds of the women teachers had done so; among those qualifying after 1966, only a quarter.[18]

A few elite graduates, men and women, do still become schoolteachers. A few more, in both the US and Europe, teach for a year or two as part of a program serving challenging inner-city schools.[19] But for most high-achieving and highly educated women, schoolteaching no longer looks that appealing.

Why did this flight from the classroom happen? Not, anywhere, because men pushed women aside. On the contrary.[20] Schoolteaching has been feminized for a century and a half: by 1870, two-thirds of American teachers were women. Recently it has become even more so. At nursery, kindergarten and elementary levels, teachers are overwhelmingly female; at high school and post-secondary, majority male workforces have given way to balanced or majority female ones.

The change, the departure of so many "top" female brains from teaching, comes from two simple factors: opportunity and pay. Today, clever girls can be lawyers, entrepreneurs or army captains; run a cable channel or a government department. Meanwhile, teachers' wages have fallen relative to other graduates, both in Western Europe and in the US.[21] To modern eyes, the result seems obvious and predictable. We assume people will follow high salaries, and that education is primarily "about" getting a better job. So a mass exodus by clever women was inevitable.

And did indeed occur. But to see this as simply a liberation of pressed labor is to misunderstand, profoundly, these early generations and how they viewed the world. Early female educators, in schools and universities, lived and breathed a moral seriousness that is far removed from anything in elite education today. They were not all chafing against the constraints of an occupation they were forced and doomed to follow. For many of them, teaching was a vocation and a calling.

MATHEMATICS AND MORALITY

Service was a key word in the early girls' schools. Many of the educational pioneers were highly religious; some were not religious at all. Nonetheless they all lived in a world where actively "doing good" was both a major part of many women's lives, and intrinsically linked with religious faith and instruction. For Dorothea Beale, the celebrated headmistress of Cheltenham Ladies' College and founder of St. Hilda's College, Oxford, "moral training is the end, education the means." Her near-contemporary Lydia Rous encouraged the teaching of advanced mathematics to her female pupils; but also a "Christian view of life as service."[22]

This emphasis on service was not specific to one country. In France, the new girls' *lycées* were in part a deliberate attempt to reduce the influence of the Catholic Church over women's education. The École Normale Supérieure at Sèvres opened the road for *"Madame le Professeur"* to staff these elite state schools, and demanded the highest academic standards of its graduates. But staff and students also saw teaching as a vocation that was as much about values, duty and morality as about the imparting of secular knowledge.

Julie Velten, Madame Jules Favre, was the extraordinary and eminent first director. Characterized by a "moralistic idealism," she sent her students out to "take charge of souls" as well as minds.[23] Madame Favre was also a passionate supporter of the Third Republic, which had been established after the disastrous 1870 war with Prussia and the deposition of Emperor Napoleon III; she believed that "individual moral growth" was "indispensable for national strength." She also insisted, "To do one's duty . . . is the goal of life," and that teaching provided the opportunity to pass a "personal sense of moral obligation on to young people."[24] And like most of her contemporaries, she believed that girls and boys should be educated in different ways, for different lives.

Of course, praising duty and service, and talking without embarrassment about virtue and charity, did not automatically make people better, kinder or more honest than today. But it would be quite wrong to think that this was hypocritical playacting by people who were otherwise just like us. As late as the 1940s and 1950s, Western governments' education policy, as articulated in policy documents, speeches and legislation, still talked the language of morality and idealism without embarrassment. Today's equivalents are concerned almost entirely with the individual economic benefits of schooling and the delivery of occupational skills.[25]

Governments' preoccupations mirror the priorities of mainstream feminism, which is equally focused on the workplace and on occupational success—and which evaluates female advance accordingly. The educational values of earlier times are, for better or worse, extinct and more or less forgotten. Meanwhile, schools have been big losers in the occupational stakes. Once, they had, as teachers, large numbers of women with top-flight degrees and a passion for their academic subject. Today, in much of the world, teachers are seen as functionaries struggling with classroom discipline. As one of the Oxford students I quoted earlier explained, "A major reason that I didn't think about teaching is salary and that's an awful thing to admit because I think that teaching's really important. But it's not as simple as salary. It's also about status."

However, while teaching has suffered, it is not just through the schools that the wind has swept. The revolution in female opportunity and the spread of full-time work among educated women have also had a huge effect on local communities, grassroots politics and above all on charities.

CHARITY BEGINS AT HOME

Back in Chapter 4, we met "Joan": a married college graduate, non-employed and recording her day's activities. On that typical American Midwestern Wednesday, as recently as 1965, she had spent half the day out volunteering. In this, she stood in the line of generations of women who provided unpaid leadership and day-to-day labor for a huge range of voluntary and charitable activities.

Once upon a time, and not so very long ago, many educated women never worked for pay. Of the rest, we have seen, many stopped when and if they married, and most of the others when and if they had children. But today there are no more Joans, in the Midwest or anywhere else. The old unpaid female workforce is now busily employed for pay.

It is not that no one volunteers. Almost half of all Americans say they do, men and women alike;[26] so do almost half of all adult Canadians, whose official statistics body reports figures under the title "Caring Canadians, Involved Canadians." In fact, there is generally a lot of self-congratulatory cheerleading on the subject, whether from governments, corporations or the organized "voluntary sector" itself.

So yes, a lot of people volunteer. And a lot don't. But more importantly the average amount of time that people give today is tiny.

Take Britain. It sounds good to be told that two British people in five volunteer every year;[27] that volunteers are "inspirational but not unusual" and that, in the words of one recent prime minister, the country "is filled with people sharing their talents so that others can realize theirs."[28] It is a lot less impressive to discover that only three in a hundred people are volunteering on any given day; and less impressive still to learn that the average amount of time donated, across the adult population, is four minutes a day, or less than half an hour a week.[29]

Everywhere, paid employment displaces volunteering. American time-use surveys show this clearly: more hours in employment are associated with a drop in volunteering.[30] Among British adults every hour a day extra in employment has a clear and substantial negative effect on the amount of voluntary work people record.[31] And vice versa. Among the full-time homemakers who remain, volunteering has actually increased.[32] In France, by far the most active female volunteers are college graduates not in paid employment. But these are a small and shrunken group.[33]

Forty years ago, on any given day, almost a third of female graduates—like "Joan"—reported time spent volunteering in their detailed time-use diaries. Fewer than one in ten female high-school graduates did so. By the early 2000s, as Figure 7.2 illustrates, the number of female high-school graduates volunteering on a given day had barely changed. The numbers of college graduates, however, had plummeted.[34]

Among the alumnae records of the elite women's colleges, you can find example after example of educated women who turned their talents to a life of voluntary activity and unpaid public service. As Figure 7.1 made clear, almost a third of the early "Seven Sisters" graduates were never employed. The numbers varied greatly from college to college, reflecting their rather different student bodies: some affluent, some very affluent indeed. Vassar lived up to its socially exclusive image, with record numbers of "non-employed" alumnae, and Mount Holyoke to its origins as a teachers' seminary.[35] But both differ dramatically from the present, when a Vassar or Mount Holyoke graduate can barely conceive of a life

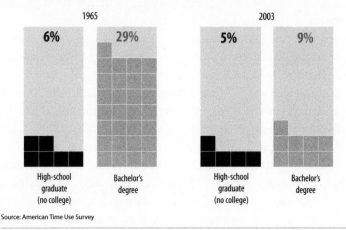

Figure 7.2 **Percentage of Women Age 25–44 Reporting That They Have Volunteered on a Given Day: US**

1965

6% 29%

2003

5% 9%

| High-school graduate (no college) | Bachelor's degree | High-school graduate (no college) | Bachelor's degree |

Source: American Time Use Survey

spent outside the labor market. And in between came generations of able graduates who turned their energies to volunteering.

At Barnard College, New York, where the class of 1918 was surveyed in detail in the early 1950s, only 20 percent, one in five, failed to record serious involvement in one or, more often, two, three or four voluntary and philanthropic activities.[36] Obituaries pulled almost at random from Oxford alumnae magazines similarly encapsulate that world: "A lifetime in adult education . . . supporter of many voluntary organisations . . . President of the Women's Liberal Federation . . . a model of concerned and constructive citizenship";[37] or a life spent largely outside paid employment as "a campaigner . . . lay reader . . . chairman of the Compton and Shawford Festival Choir. Problems relating to mental health and unemployment were to concern her . . . as [unpaid] Director of the Institute for Industrial Therapy, founder of the Southampton Industrial Therapy Association."[38]

There will be few if any such obituaries for the classes of 1990 or 2010.

KINDER, KÜCHE, KIRCHE?

Children, cooking, church—these were the traditional occupations for women in the days when society held them firmly in their domestic place.

And one common view of volunteering is that it was all of a piece, a way of maintaining separate spheres for men and women, and providing "a social role for under-occupied middle-class women"[39] who would have been much better off with proper jobs.

But it is also possible to look at recent history rather differently. Medical insurance, unemployment benefits, the welfare state all became widespread only after the Second World War. Go back just a little further and private charity is the main source of help in fast-growing, fast-changing societies. Western countries were urbanizing at speed and their cities were crammed with recent migrants, from the countryside or much further afield. Many of them were very poor.

Nineteenth- and early-twentieth-century citizens responded by creating myriad charities. Almost all of these relied heavily on female volunteers. Very many of them were also church-linked or religiously affiliated. This is hardly surprising. Religious affiliation and the importance of religion were still taken largely for granted. What could be more logical than to extend and adapt old charitable practice, itself overwhelmingly associated with the churches?[40]

District or household visiting developed in the cities as a forerunner of formal social work. It grew out of the casual, informal visiting of country parishes, and with the same underlying assumption: that impoverished people and benighted souls could be saved by another individual who took a direct interest in their physical and spiritual well-being. To an overwhelming degree the two went together. Visitors were for the most part concerned with both body and soul. They were also mostly women, and they numbered in the hundreds of thousands.

Historian Frank Prochaska estimates that, on the eve of the First World War, there were close to 200,000 volunteer "district visitors" in England, linked to one or other of the churches: more people than were employed by the entire civil service of the day. Visitors "became a feature of city missions, hospitals, homes, temperance societies and settlement houses. The largest single type was connected to churches and chapels. Whatever their affiliation, they instructed the ignorant, nursed the sick, comforted the dying and 'glorified God in all things.' "[41]

In 1893, the reformers and analysts Louisa Hubbard and Angela Burdett-Coutts estimated that, in Britain, about 500,000 women were working for charities "continuously and semi-professionally," though unpaid, and another 20,000 worked as paid officials of charitable societies.[42] To put this in context, at that time the largest employer of women, other than as domestic servants, was cotton manufacture, in which 333,000 British women worked—far fewer than in the charities.

Certainly there was plenty of misery to relieve. William Booth, founder of the Salvation Army, described visiting, in an urban slum in the north of England,

> a hole, unfit to be called a human habitation—more like the den of some wild animal—almost the only furniture of which was a filthy iron bedstead, a wooden box to serve for table and chair, while an old tin did duty as a dustbin. The inhabitant of the wretched den was a poor woman, who fled to the darkest corner of the place.[43]

In New York, Jewish organizations responded to mass immigration from Russia and the Pale of Settlement. Lillian Wald, visiting the Jewish tenements of the Lower East Side, described case after case like that of

> Annie P., 44 Allen Street, front tenement, second floor. Husband Louis P. came here three years ago and one year ago sent for wife and three children . . . two months ago he deserted her, though she stoutly maintains he returned to Odessa to get his old work back. The youngest, Meyer P., age five years, fell from the table and injured his hip . . . is in pain and cries to be carried. They had no rooms of their own but paid $5 a month to Hannah A., a decent tailoress, who allowed the family to sleep on her floor. Sunday I saw them . . . Tuesday I went to Hebrew Sheltering Guardian Society, saw superintendent and obtained promise of place for the two well children by Thursday . . . They have absolutely no one in America but their mother.[44]

Of course, the motives of these visitors were no doubt mixed, as human motives are; they could gain status, friendships, gossip, an escape from unhappiness at home. They also did much good.

Voluntary work offered middle-class women the opportunity to create and run substantial organisations. The first female-controlled charity in New York, the Widows Society, dates back to 1797, receiving a charter in 1802. Historian Kathleen McCarthy, who directs the Center for the Study of Philanthropy at the City University of New York, has described how "[f]rom their inception, female-controlled charities . . . subsisted on a mixed portfolio of donations, investment, public allocations and generated funds,"[45] all of which had to be managed. The female trustees entered into contracts with the state and municipalities for the delivery of services, as well as generating large amounts of money themselves.

Nineteenth-century charity fairs, benefits and bazaars were an enormous business and a more or less entirely female one. Million-dollar profits were raised during the Civil War for Union troops through fairs organized and run by women under the auspices of the US Sanitary Commission (and $1 in 1863 was worth close to $19 today).[46] In Britain, fairs and bazaars, run entirely by unpaid women, were a major source of income for both charities and big single-issue political campaigns.[47] Later, it was women with backgrounds in charitable work who would administer government-funded welfare services, and serve on school and hospital boards.[48] Frank Prochaska concludes, "If we are to isolate one profession that did more than any other to enlarge the horizon of women in nineteenth century England, it would have to be the profession of charity. It was more often unpaid than paid . . . but it was a profession none the less."[49]

Women also campaigned, successfully, for political and social change, and not just to get the vote. Harvard University's Theda Skocpol is a highly distinguished social scientist, and a past dean of Harvard's Graduate School of Arts and Sciences. She has analyzed how women won support for public social spending after the Civil War, in spite of deep skepticism about the ability of the government to administer social programs well. They won the argument, she writes, because they were seen to rise above narrowly partisan positions—but also because their own voluntary networks had shown that social programs could be administered both cheaply and without corruption.[50]

"TO BENEFIT MY FELLOW CREATURES"

The importance that volunteering once held in the lives of educated women was bound up with their everyday networks and social lives. But it also reflected a profound difference between past society and ours. Their lives reflected the shared assumption that educated and privileged women should and would naturally undertake "good works."

This was brought home to me by historian Gillian Sutherland's account of the Clough family, eminent Victorians on both the male and female sides. The Cloughs provided, in Annie and Thena, the first and fourth principals of Newnham College, Cambridge, one of the very first institutions in the world to offer higher education to women. Thena, the fourth principal, died only in 1960, which in the scale of human history barely registers as time past at all.

And yet their world—that of Thena, as well as Annie—seems immeasurably distant. Sutherland calls her book *Faith, Duty and the Power of Mind*, and this title encapsulates the values that drove and structured these women's lives, and those of their contemporaries.[51] Annie was a deeply believing Christian, whereas Thena was an unblinking atheist from an early age. But the idea that one's life should be based on duty and obligation to one's fellows, and the constant attempt to be "good," ran through both their lives and writings as a constant thread, as it did of those around them.

"If I could only do something to benefit my fellow creatures," Annie wrote in her journal at the age of twenty-one;[52] and the determination to be good, combined with a fierce commitment to "the best and the finest in thought and sentiment," was the core of these women's actions.[53]

Now, on a twenty-first-century day, you may still find a good few working-age female graduates out volunteering. But the full days of charitable work that characterized US Civil War fund-raisers, or volunteers at the slum "settlements" ministering to the nineteenth-century poor? Or the near-full-time commitment to volunteering that still, in the 1960s, characterized so many women's lives? Only one in 250 women graduates, less than 0.5 percent, reports that sort of commitment today.[54] And though it would be nice to think that we all start volunteering like crazy in retirement, in fact we do no such thing.[55]

Among my own friends and acquaintances, I can think of just one highly educated and professionally qualified female who dedicates her life to community activity rather than paid employment, and has done so since her mid-thirties. She has done so in community, religious and political organizations, and she is fantastic. But in my generation, she is also the exception who proves the rule. A path once followed by able women across the developed world has been abandoned.

DO-GOODERS AND LADY BOUNTIFULS?

Highly educated women have disappeared from large-scale unpaid social service in large part because alternative opportunities opened up, and, as we have seen, the 1970s were the decade of accelerating change. Banker Lawton Fitt described to me how her own mother "would have had my life had she been born in a different generation. When she graduated from university, she wanted to go into business management. She came from Ohio to Boston to go to the Radcliffe Management Institute or whatever it was then called, worked as a management consultant for a bit and then stopped when we were all born. Because in the 1950s that's what you did.

"But she always had charities. She was on boards of many charities and did all this at a very professional standard. I certainly was a latch-key kid, from very early. When I got home she was out.

"My mother also felt she should be doing the cleaning herself, but she wasn't any good at it and we didn't have a lot of money. So we all had assigned chores plus au pairs who were a series of pregnant unwed soon-to-be mothers out of a local home. I think it was my mother's compromise way of getting help and at the same time feeling she was doing something socially valuable.

"And then on her fortieth birthday she got admitted to the doctoral program at Harvard Business School and was one of the first two women to graduate with a doctorate from Harvard Business School in 1973. And was made an instructor, went on the faculty at Harvard and had a very active career. She was one of the first people to bring management discipline to the arts."

And she no longer made volunteering a central part of her life.

My own mother was also a superbly effective volunteer and unpaid fund-raiser and returned to employment in her late forties. I remember her wondering if maybe volunteering's time had come. It demeaned people, she felt, if they had to ask for charity, knowing it might be refused. Getting a clear entitlement from a public service should avoid that.

A widespread disdain for the unpaid volunteer reinforced the lure of a changing labor market and encouraged women to turn away from "good works." People weren't just affected by the money, but by the status and the attitudes that my mother described to me. Geraldine Peacock, when head of the UK Charities Commission,[56] expressed this attitude perfectly. The growing number of big charities headed by salaried female professionals was a welcome sign of change, she said, given that until recently "the sector still smacked of volunteerism" and so put off "women who wanted to make a career."[57]

Disdain for volunteering was not new: back in the nineteenth century, we find Lucy Aikin complaining that "a positive demand for misery was created by the incessant eagerness manifested to relieve it."[58] But as the twentieth century progressed, the balance of opinion shifted.

Unpaid activity was increasingly seen, across the developed world, as "amateur" in quality and morally questionable. It required people to be grateful for help to which they were actually entitled, as citizens with equal rights. And volunteers were often regarded as "idle, vain and uninformed women . . . conservative and more or less misguided."[59]

But be careful what you wish for, as they say. You may get it.

Dr. Kathleen McCarthy's Center for the Study of Philanthropy is in the heart of New York City: a city of foundations, charity lunches and vast philanthropic gifts from the super-rich. But not, anymore, of non-employed upper-middle-class wives in their thousands who devote large parts of their week to charitable endeavors. Among today's highly educated professionals, philanthropy typically takes a very different form. It is also a form that is increasingly the same for men and women, both in what they do and in the time they are willing to give.[60] As Kathleen explained, "If you're climbing the corporate ladder, whether a man or woman, it's expected that you'll be involved with nonprofit organizations for any number of reasons. It builds skills and it builds a portfolio constituency within the community, so it's an important form of corporate outreach. And that's always been part and parcel of how American corporations work."

The difference today, she argues, is that men and women are involved in the same way, not differently. "If you're a professional woman you're probably still involved with volunteer work but at a different level. You're not licking envelopes anymore, you're on the board. And so the positioning has changed."

And outside corporations? Do women scientists, for example, often volunteer?

"Probably not outside the sciences. Do they raise funds? Sure, if you're asking about raising funds for women scientists. But I wouldn't be surprised if I were the only member of my faculty who's served on boards and things like that."

Meanwhile, the "professionalization" of social services, health and welfare has not transformed society in quite the way that people once hoped. Today's public services are staffed by millions of paid staff, who depend on the existence of "clients" but also have a great deal of power over them. As Michael Lipsky pointed out in his seminal work on "street-level bureaucrats," lower-level front-line staff are human beings with their own interests to pursue. And all too often "the experience of seeking service through people-processing bureaucracies is perceived . . . as dehumanizing [and] the phrase 'human services' is often understood as ironic by all but those who work under that label."[61]

Direct help from a charity volunteer in return for a thank-you or a prayer starts to look less intrinsically demeaning and less undesirable from the vantage point of our own imperfect present.

———————————

In her book *Diminished Democracy*, Theda Skocpol showed that the mass-membership cross-class organizations that thrived from 1860 to 1960 have all but vanished from the US. They have been replaced by professionally staffed advocacy groups concerned to influence policymakers and the direction of public funding. And speaking to me in her Harvard office she emphasized how much the lives of the highly educated and affluent have changed.[62] Today, she told me, "most of the civic activism of the privileged . . . is channeled through check-writing to support professionally run advocacy or social-service groups. To be sure, Americans still volunteer a lot by international standards . . . But much of today's voluntarism is managed by professionally run agencies and involves short-term or one-shot commitments from rank-and-file contributors."

As we have seen, highly educated women are the group whose involvement has also changed the most rapidly across the developed world.[63] This is partly because they are the ones being offered great new job opportunities. But Skocpol pointed out to me that in America, particularly, such women are also among the social groups that have moved furthest away from a life focused on church and religion.[64] "Churches do still provide community and the infrastructure for voluntary activity. But it's not people like us who are the churchgoers. For people like me, if we go to anything we go to professional associations.

"It's hard to see it reversing. The sorts of professional women who in the past would have been speaking for mothers and children—even if with a viewpoint we now find silly, like temperance—aren't there. Professional women with PhDs are all working their tails off."

And if you doubt that the old housewives' army of female volunteers has gone, ask the Girl Scouts and Girl Guides. Scouting and Guiding are themselves redolent of a vanished past. Yet their founder, Baden-Powell, understood exactly what excites and interests children, and the movement has twenty-first-century children lining up at the door. What it lacks are adult leaders.[65]

A SHRUNKEN AGENDA

In a 2006 interview for BBC radio, the feminist author and cultural theorist Angela McRobbie observed:

> there has been a marked shift away from what feminists used to
> call the ethic of care. It was a defining feature of women's lives—
> caring for others, caring for children, caring for the husband,
> caring for elderly people. And that of course often extended into the
> community.
>
> It stands to reason that as women enter the labor market their
> time is going to be limited for caring. The easy answer is to say
> that caring rightly has become a profession in its own right, and
> there's a lot of sense to that. On the other hand, we all know the
> debate about the wider values that accrue to giving care in society.
> If that's replaced by ruthless individualism, by straightforward
> competitiveness, then I think that does raise all sorts of problems.
> It's kind of a toxic brew.[66]

McRobbie's concern over "caring" has hardly been the conventional feminist position. That measures progress by whether men and women are equally represented at all levels of every occupation, all paid and at equal rates.[67] Nor was McRobbie proposing or expecting that women retreat from most of the labor market. But her comments also highlight the gulf between the iconic female advertising slogan of today—"Because I'm worth it"—and the world of our educated female forebears.

If you look at women's pages and chat rooms today, the issues that dominate are the "glass ceiling" and the "Mommy wars." Arguments over whether or not mothers should stay at home with small children and whether employers should be making life easier for mothers usually attract a large and emotional mailbag. Ditto rape, abortion and a topic we will be turning to below: sex and the sexualization of society.

When I interviewed Theda Skocpol about current trends, she argued that we had seen "a radical *narrowing* of women's voice. American women in the past were always testifying and petitioning like crazy, way before the modern period. In fact, what has happened is that female advocacy has shifted from being about everything to being very narrowly about women.

"It is particularly significant that this has happened because, in the absence of a strong labor movement, [American] women were the ones who stood up for welfare, and made the case for the public good, for everyone. Now it's all so narrow."

It may also be inevitable. The daily lives of elite women today are, as we have seen, dominated by employment. Whether single or married, they work long hours, as do their partners. They give their children hours of dedicated attention. There isn't much energy left.

Back in 2006, I wrote an article that was the precursor of this book. It was about the divergence of professional and non-professional lives.[68] But it was also, quite specifically, about the disappearance of the hardworking, non-employed women of my own childhood and of centuries before, and about what a genuine loss this was to society. It appeared in a British journal called *Prospect*, whose readers are an academic, center-left sort of bunch, and I expected to get a torrent of criticism: Lady Bountifuls and Goody-Two-Shoes, the lot of them, and good riddance to a world that produced them.

But I didn't. In fact a lot of people, and especially professional women, told me how much they agreed. "Those wonderful women," said one friend. "It's time we appreciated them properly."

Their world has been replaced by one that is more egalitarian, more open to female ambition and achievement. And so, inevitably, these women have gone. But they deserve to be missed and mourned.

Part Two

DOMESTIC SPHERES MADE NEW—
WOMEN, MEN AND FAMILIES

8

SEX AND THE SINGLE GRADUATE

Once, as we have seen, to be unmarried was a woman's nightmare. Marriage was the only serious career open to middle-class and educated women; but women wanted to be married not just for security, not just for children. It was also to avoid lifelong celibacy.

This book began with Jane Austen breaking off her engagement. She was brave, clearheaded, her readers are the beneficiaries, but was the decision right? Years later she was to tell her niece, "Anything is to be preferred or endured rather than marrying without Affection." But by then she was a published and successful author. In between, she must have wondered.

In *Emma*, when the novel's disappointed heroine decides to contemplate life without marriage, her protegée Harriet is horror-struck.

> "But still, you will be an old maid!—and that's so dreadful!"
> "Never mind, Harriet, I shall not be a poor old maid; and it is poverty only which makes celibacy contemptible to a generous public! A single woman, with a very narrow income, must be a ridiculous, disagreeable old maid!—the proper sport of boys and girls—but a single woman, of good fortune, is always respectable . . ."[1]

Today, the very term "old maid," with its accretions of dread and unhappiness, is vanishing from our language. It is doing so not just because single women can lead full, prosperous lives outside the home, but also because "respectable" single women today are almost never maids.

Women's roles in the workplace have been revolutionized; educated

women have lifetime careers in the same way as men do. But the transformation goes beyond the workplace itself. The chapters that follow
focus on how personal relationships between men and women have
changed. Family dynamics are different. Physical appearance and sexual
signaling operate in new ways. And most dramatic of all are the changes
to sex itself.

NEW WORLDS AND OLD

Whatever films and bodice-ripper novels like to imply, premarital sex
used to be rare and seriously risky. Because "risk-free sex" was a pipe
dream, female sex happened overwhelmingly after (as well as mostly
within) marriage. Pregnancy was more likely to be a prelude to a shotgun marriage than to an illegitimate child;[2] but if the man couldn't be
persuaded or forced to do the "right thing," then women faced social
ruin, and their babies, for the most part, a miserable fate.[3]

With the Pill, everything changed. At that moment of its launch in
1960,[4] we entered a world where pregnancy is under women's control,
and where they can avoid it, with near-total reliability, if they will. They
can plan a serious career. They can commit themselves to periods of
stress-free childlessness. And they can do this without signing up to either total abstinence or a willingness to abort.[5]

It is hard today for most of us to imagine the stress associated with
sex if you are desperate not to get pregnant and contraceptives are either unavailable or seriously unreliable. But, pre-Pill, that was everyone's
world. It was also one where, in most countries, abortion was illegal. So
even if you had no serious moral objections—or did, but were desperate
enough to abort anyway—ending an unwanted pregnancy meant breaking the law, and taking risks that often led to infection, infertility, even
death.[6]

It wasn't just career-minded women who were liberated. Everybody's
life was changed. In "Annus Mirabilis," the poet Philip Larkin (born in
1922) observed that

> Sexual intercourse began
> In nineteen sixty-three
> (which was rather late for me)—

Post-Pill, young women of all classes and backgrounds began, rapidly,
to behave in ways that were totally different from Larkin's 1920s and

1930s childhood, let alone the centuries before. Scholars estimate that in 1900, only 6 percent of American teenagers would have engaged in premarital sex.[7] Today, around three-quarters of American and British teens are sexually active.[8] Among young women in their twenties and thirties, fewer than one in ten reports going without sex for the whole of the previous year.[9] And with the typical age for first marriage—if people marry at all—heading toward thirty, much of this sexual activity is, by definition, extramarital.[10] We are looking at a sea change in behavior.

What people do, not just when and with whom, has changed. When I was eight, it was a thrill to sit with the boy next door and look up "rude" words in the dictionary. Today, the Internet offers instantly accessible pornography on a worldwide scale.[11] In developed countries, images have gone mainstream that, even two decades ago, would have been top-shelf or under-the-counter stuff. Ours are the first societies where pornography is sold routinely in places populated by "respectable" women, including just about any hotel room. Cozy female magazines like *Woman's Home Journal* or *Woman and Home* carry large color ads for "A vibrator that really works . . . perfect for play by yourself or with a partner" alongside the recipes, diets and home decor.[12]

These changes are society-wide. But they mask important, underlying divergence. More- and less-educated women all behave sexually in ways that no women in previous centuries would have believed possible. But the more and less educated are also significantly different from each other. Sexually, as in the workplace, gaps have opened up, because of the very different opportunities on offer to the elite at the top of the pyramid, compared to the 80 percent below.

OLD HABITS, NEW CLOTHES

For two quintessential websites of the sex-and-soft-porn age, try Girls Gone Wild or Nuts. Both sit firmly within the law and have the same determinedly unembarrassed "this-is-all-normal-and-fun" delivery. They have similar content, and some utterly gorgeous girls on view. On GGW, you're taken straight to "Vote for the hottest girl in America," with photos plus descriptions of the "wildest thing" they've ever done and their "biggest turn-on." On UK-based Nuts, it's "Assess my breasts" the minute you log on, with photos posted—unpaid—by girls from San Francisco to South Africa, as well as London, Edinburgh and Birmingham.

Journalist Ariel Levy was one of the first to write about the rise of female "raunch culture." She went out on the road to watch Girls Gone Wild cameramen filming "young women flashing their breasts, their buttocks, or occasionally their genitals at the camera, and usually shrieking 'Whoo!' while they do it."[13] It was, she discovered, amazingly easy to find them: America is full of gorgeous girls willing to strip for Girls Gone Wild, and to do so for nothing but a baseball cap. As a GGW tour manager told her, "It's amazing . . . People flash for the brand."[14]

Britain is the same. There are thousands of girls desperate to become "glamour" models, which means posing almost-but-not-quite naked.[15] At any given moment, perhaps a dozen such models are making good money. But "there are so many girls coming through," one model agency head told journalist Natasha Walter, "you don't even have to pay [them] . . . all these girls, milling around, all desperate to bag a footballer and be a glamour model."[16]

Run a competition in a nightclub to find a new face for Nuts and, as Walter saw, there will be girls lining up to present a "crotch in stretchy, tight red pants to the camera" and obey shouts to "show some skin" or get a thonged "arse in the air" in front of an audience of cheering young men.[17]

One of *Sex and the City*'s stars is Samantha. She is promiscuous, financially successful and "trysexual" (try anything once); and she wants her partners to leave "an hour after I climax." She's become a world-famous character—but typical of professional women now, or the wave of the future? No, and nor are the GGW flashers.

When Ariel Levy went out on the road with Girls Gone Wild, the tour manager was Mia Leist, a twenty-four-year-old woman who had graduated from expensive, private Emerson College in Boston. Nineteen-year-old Debbie, in rhinestones, white stilettos, tiny shorts and body glitter, was one of Leist's finds.

"Crazy Debbie," said Leist. "I love her. She gets so many girls for us."

When Levy then asked Leist if she would ever appear in a GGW video herself, she said, "Definitely not."[18]

Running these businesses and working in them are not, it turns out, at all the same: not for yourself, definitely not for your daughter. Phil Edgar-Jones was the creative director of *Big Brother*, the hugely popular reality TV show whose later series often recruited actual and would-be topless models and porn stars. He also had a young daughter. Walter "asked how he would feel if she wanted to . . . do glamour modelling. 'I'm a middle-class parent so I'd be . . .' Then he stopped himself . . . 'I would hope she would have different aspirations. I encourage her to read books. Other people have different backgrounds.' "[19]

As for David Read, the director of a big "glamour model" agency, when asked what he would think if his daughter wanted to be the next Jodie Marsh, famous for the size of her breasts, "he was frank: 'I would die to think that she'd try to follow in her footsteps.' "[20]

He doesn't need to worry. The girls stripping for Girls Gone Wild, the girls posing thong-clad on all fours, backs arched, in search of "publicity": these girls are traditional to the core. They are not the educated professionals discussed above. Instead, they are following the most long-established pursuit for single females: promising, flaunting, offering and selling sex to men. Sex for them remains the basis of their fortune and their career. As London-based Phil Hilton, a founding editor of *Nuts* magazine, told Walter, "Let's be realistic, and take an honest class perspective here—are you going to say to those girls, why do you want [to model]—why don't you want to be a cabinet minister?"[21]

But while sex can still be valuable and is still in high demand, as a female launchpad, sex isn't what it used to be. Many girls, well-educated girls, like Read's and Edgar-Jones's daughters, now have different high-return opportunities. Sex still matters to successful professional women; indeed, with secure contraception and far safer childbirth, they almost certainly enjoy sex more than their female ancestors did. But sex is not absolutely central to making any career, as it once was for all women, whether as a route into or outside of marriage. It has less impact on how their whole lives turn out than was the case for women in the past; and they behave accordingly.

A FEMALE MONOPOLY

Heterosexual sex is something that only women can give to men, and heterosexual sex is something that men really, badly want. At least the 96 percent of men who tell researchers they are totally straight certainly do.[22] Women have, historically, squeezed everything they can out of this. Sex has been women's route to power, possessions and position; indeed, the only route open to girls with no money to their names. For them, "my face is my fortune," as the well-known ballad says.

For some women, the payoff was staggering. Empress Cixi, who died in 1908, came to the Chinese court as a teenage concubine and became the last imperial ruler of China to possess real power. She ruled for nearly fifty years, first through her son, then, after his death, through her nephew. When the latter challenged her policies, he was placed under house arrest. And when this nephew's favorite concubine made a bid for influence and power she ended up at the bottom of a well.[23]

Cixi is unusual only in being recent. Marozia, back in the tenth century, was mistress of one pope, mother of another, and seized power over Rome in a coup d'état, before being deposed by one of her own sons. In Byzantium, a number of emperors chose their brides from the participants in a selective "bride show." Among those who became empress in this way was Theodora, a provincial beauty whose triumph in the bride show made her a future regent, saint of the Orthodox Church and one of the most influential rulers of medieval Byzantium.[24] Roxelana, sold as a slave into the Turkish royal harem, became the favorite, confidante, adviser and wife of Suleiman the Magnificent. Her son succeeded as sultan; the original heir-apparent was killed on suspicion of rebellion, almost certainly at Roxelana's instigation.

Sex, children; children, sex. In a world run by men, these were women's routes to power.

In pre-Pill, pre-sexual-liberation days, men got regular sex with respectable girls only by marrying them. Looks and sex appeal were thus the way to make a better-than-expected match. Some women played successfully for extremely high stakes: Anne Boleyn, mother of England's Elizabeth I, refused to become the king's mistress. And Henry VIII wanted Anne badly enough that she became his wife and queen, albeit one who ended on the scaffold.

All over the world, sexual desire fed directly into the marriage market. This had mixed results. Some marriages were, we know, very happy.[25] Often, though, it was "flames for a year, ashes for thirty," as Count di Lampedusa put it in his great semi-autobiographical novel, *The Leopard*. But sex proffered, sex withheld were the main assets that girls possessed, and one on which, for the overwhelming majority of men, they had the monopoly.

Of course, the value of looks hasn't vanished. The world's remaining royal families amass stunning wives: Queen Rania of Jordan; Crown Princess Letizia of Spain; Sheikha Moza bint Nasser of Qatar; or, indeed, Kate Middleton, now Duchess of Cambridge and wife to Prince William. So it's not that sex and looks no longer matter at all—that would be a nonsensical thing to claim. But sex isn't the key to women's fates in the way it was and certainly is no longer the main source of female business opportunities. As, for many millennia, it used to be.

FLOATING WORLDS, COURTESANS AND MADAMS

Cities of the past had larger, more visible "vice districts" than those of today's developed world, in part because most girls didn't. And it was in France's demimonde, Japan's "floating world," New Orleans' French Quarter, that women could make their own fortunes as owners and managers, alongside men. Sex was the one industry in which, histori-cally, women were not only the workforce but most of the managers and owners too.[26]

Becoming a madam was one of the very few ways in which women could make (as opposed to marry or inherit) serious money. Generally ex-prostitutes themselves, they ran small businesses—typically with be-tween four and twelve girls—in challenging circumstances.[27] Running the establishment, which at the top end would provide food, wine and comfort as well as women, recruiting new staff, managing relationships and keeping in with local police and politicians made for a demanding life. But it was one that could make women very rich.

Lulu White, one of the most famous New Orleans madams at the end of the nineteenth century, ran the large Mahogany Hall brothel. It cost about $40,000 to build then—a good $1 million in (2008) dollars—and by 1906 White had built up savings of at least $150,000 (equivalent to several millions today).[28] In the early 1900s, sisters Minna and Ada Everleigh were the wealthiest self-made women in Chicago. They were also madams, whose Everleigh Club was a brothel of unprecedented lux-ury. Pictures survive of its gold piano, Oriental Music Room and Japa-nese Throne Room; it was frequented by men from the top of Chicago society.[29]

The sex trade offered huge rewards to the lucky or to supremely talented risk-takers, as well as a dismal end for the losers. The French actress Sarah Bernhardt is one of the very few pre-twentieth-century women whose fame owed nothing to birth and has outlasted them. Bern-hardt's celebrity value far outstripped, in her day, anything that Mari-lyn Monroe or Princess Diana could summon up a century later: there were vast crowds at the docks when she landed for overseas tours; streets were named after her, plays written for her. A "Sarah Bernhardt" day sponsored by France's cultural elite culminated in a "Hymn to Sarah Bernhardt."[30]

Bernhardt was the daughter and niece of courtesans.[31] She belonged to the French "demimonde"; actresses, then, mostly did.[32] She took her own first lover, of many, in her teens. Her younger sisters, Jeanne and Régine, became courtesans in their turn; as one of the gossipy Goncourt brothers recorded in their for-publication Parisian journals: "Overheard in Brebant's restaurant: 'The Sarah Bernhardt family—now, *there's* a family. The mother made whores of her daughters as soon as they turned thirteen.' "[33]

Three girls, close in age. But Régine died at nineteen, "after a miserable life of neglect and prostitution."[34] Jeanne, her mother's favorite, succumbed to drug addiction. Only Sarah thrived. For every *"grande horizontale"* not just amassing, but saving, a fortune, there were plenty of others who never made it off the streets, or who slid down there as they lost their patrons and wealthy lovers.[35]

And today? Theater has turned respectable, but pornography and gambling have boomed; so there are still plenty of ways to make money out of sex-related businesses. But women are now offered more and very different business openings. Chinese female billionaires are making their fortunes in chemicals, paper, household goods. Highly talented businesswomen like Lulu White and the Everleighs could and probably would make larger fortunes with far less risk than in their own time, when brothels were the best opportunity going. In the sex-and-entertainment world, meanwhile, a new gulf has opened between the owners and the hired help.

WRESTLERS, BUNNY GIRLS AND RAMPANT RABBITS

Linda McMahon, the Republican candidate for a Senate seat in the 2010 and 2012 Connecticut races, ran a self-financed campaign with money she made as a promoter of professional wrestling. And not just any wrestling—semi-naked, bloodied, female wrestlers are the company's speciality and a big export line. Not that she was ever one of them: raised in a conservative Catholic home, she has a BA in French, got teaching certification and has been in business with her husband ever since they both graduated from college.

Playboy Enterprises, owner of *Playboy* magazine, with its pages of female nudes, and Playboy Clubs (with their recently resuscitated Bunny Girls), was created in the 1950s by Hugh Hefner. Hefner is famed for his lifestyle with a mansion full of girls and glitz. But from the late 1980s until 2009, the chairman and CEO of Playboy Enterprises was his daughter Christie, surrounded by a heavily female senior management team. And Christie Hefner was certainly never a Bunny. She didn't come up through the business like the old-style madams did; rather she looked, at all times, the professional, financially astute, expensively educated executive she was.[36]

A century ago, women who ran "vice district" businesses generally knew them from the inside. No one, however, is suggesting that naked female wrestling has become a mainstream occupation for upper-middle-class girls. Instead, there's an uncrossable line drawn between the female CEO and the girl in the ring or on the center spread.

The graduates of exclusive Boston liberal arts colleges don't strip for Girls Gone Wild; but they're perfectly happy to tour-manage. When the Everleigh sisters ran their Chicago brothel, they were beyond the social pale; Christie Hefner was a respected member of Chicago's business elite. In the UK, college-educated, middle-class Anna Arrowsmith was a parliamentary candidate in the 2010 UK general election. She is a highly successful maker of British pornographic movies.[37] And a CEO called Jacqueline Gold is a favorite of the mainstream UK media and especially its women's magazines.

Gold wins awards and praise for her business acumen: a national business organization named her "business communicator of the year"; she is a regular attendee at the country's annual "Women of the Year" gathering. Why? Because she turned around a struggling sex-toy retail chain, Ann Summers, and made it a major commercial success. She did so by copying the techniques of those Tupperware parties of the 1950s and 1960s, where housewives invited their friends to buy plastic food containers over lunch or coffee. At an Ann Summers party, the goods on sale are sex toys and sexy lingerie.

My daughter studied science at Cambridge University. Her richly endowed college gives its Women's Society a generous annual grant to help promote women's interests, one of which turned out to be hosting an Ann Summers party. On a cold fenland evening, budding female members of the global elite happily spent a good chunk of their society grant on refreshments—alcohol, not coffee—for a lingerie-and-sex-toy event. Top seller, the Rampant Rabbit vibrator.

None of them, however, was dreaming of glamour-modeling or a job as a hostess on the Las Vegas Strip. None of them was contemplating a future in which making a good "catch" decided pretty much everything about your future—including whether you would have a regular sex life or any sex at all. And it's a safe bet that this group's sex life, up to this point, had been rather different from that of their less academic contemporaries.

CONVERGING AND DIVERGING

John is a high-school junior: sixteen years old, middling grades, regular sort of kid. Yes, he tells the researcher, it's true. Guys in his school often have underage sex. Yes, with girls in their class. The researcher is surprised. Haven't girls all gone studious? Surely they are the ones getting all the grades, leaving the boys behind?

"It's not girls with straight A's," John corrects her. "Girls with A grades are virgins." He is, he feels, stating the obvious.

The figures bear him out. Take American women aged twenty-five to forty-four, surveyed early in the new millennium. The average age of first intercourse for this group of women was seventeen years eight months.[38] But among women this age who went on to gain a higher degree, more than half reported that they were over nineteen when they first had intercourse. Among high-school dropouts, by contrast, half reported having had intercourse before their sixteenth birthday.[39] Looked at slightly differently, among high-school dropouts, first intercourse now takes place, on average, almost three years earlier than among those with law or business school in their sights.[40]

This isn't because college-stream girls have been slow to catch up with the sexual revolution. This particular gap is new. It is also widening. Among American women just a little older, currently in their late thirties and early forties, the average difference is significantly less: a bit over two years. The UK reports similar trends.[41]

Historically, we know, very few girls anywhere had intercourse before the legal age of consent and marriage. And among British women born in the decades before 1965, very few girls had intercourse before the age of sixteen (the legal age of consent in the UK). Among those born in the 1950s and 1960s, early intercourse grows significantly more common among the later-born but not by a large amount, and increases were spread fairly equally across the cohort.[42]

But among younger women a gulf then opens up between those who will later be educationally successful, and hold full bachelor's degrees, and their less highly educated contemporaries. In Britain, as in America, "underage" sex became and is far more common for girls who are not on a college track.[43] The Essex suburbs of London are legendary; New

Jersey, even more so. My friend Nigel, who still lives in Essex, swears that girls he grew up with really did keep notebooks and compare tallies of the men they bedded—numbers and performance. But only some of them. The ambitious, just as in America, were working at their grades.

These basic patterns, detailed in the Appendix, also hold for men. Reported median ages at first intercourse were and are lower for British men than for women.[44] However, high-achieving boys are very like high-achieving girls in key ways. They are much less likely than their contemporaries to report underage sex. And, in addition, far more of them, proportionately, start having sex late, after the age of twenty-one—something that is also true of high-achieving girls.[45] By age nineteen, 70 percent of contemporary American girls in the bottom decile of household income have experienced sex; in the top decile it's just 47 percent.[46]

This isn't because academic kids are so nerdy that they don't even think about sex: as we'll see later, in their twenties and beyond graduates are as sexually active as their contemporaries. But at sixteen or eighteen, academic grind can have a big influence on your chances of success in life, and apparently that, for the moment, takes priority. As sixteen-year-old John observed, in their mid-teens modern girls with straight A's stay virgin. And so, he might have added, do quite a few of their academic male competitors.

SUMMERS OF LOVE?

Can we really be confident about either these major changes in teenage sexual behavior or the way they are related to education? Sex doesn't sound like something most people will talk about openly and truthfully if you walk up to them in the street. Remarkably, we can. Today's data come from large national surveys, and are credible and good.

It was the advent of AIDS that convinced governments that they needed reliable information on sexual practices; and around 1990, a good number of countries collected it.[47] Before that we got lots of titillating stuff, but from self-selected volunteers. The 1990 surveys, by contrast, report reassuringly similar and very undramatic findings on, for example, how much sex people were having and with whom.[48]

Of course, some people may nonetheless be reporting what they think they should do, or what they wish had occurred.[49] The most valuable data are from countries where follow-up surveys asked the same questions and where reported changes are very likely to reflect genuine change. The US and Britain are, for that reason, the main source for the rest of this chapter (and since much of the analysis is new, the Appendix provides some detailed tables).[50] As we will see, on any measure that is directly comparable, the two countries' figures are usually very close. Since the surveys are entirely independent, this suggests that the results reflect quite general aspects of modern Western behavior.[51]

And one thing they show is that while college-bound girls are today's teenage virgins, sexual revolution came first to the campuses. Summer of Love, Woodstock—like the 1968 student revolts, these were upper-middle-class, college phenomena, with student baby boomers in the vanguard.

The adult world was fascinated or appalled. As the Palisades High School alumni who authored the bestseller *What Really Happened to the Class of 65* remark, "[N]o aspect of [our] life has received so much publicity as our sexuality."[52]

As privileged Los Angeles teenagers, their high-school years were in fact nothing very new: most graduated from high-school as virgins. Lisa Menzies, expelled for coming to school drunk, was the exception in her determined sexual activity and remembered that "between the ages of sixteen and eighteen, I actually counted how many men I went to bed with. I counted four hundred and twenty-five and then I stopped."

No one else reported anything remotely similar. But what followed was late 1960s campus life, and by then premarital sex was common, the Pill was the norm—and so was parental disapproval.[53]

When, in 1990, *Sex in America* thudded down, reporting on the sexual history of American eighteen- to fifty-nine-year-olds, you could see how sexual revolution had duly rolled across the country. People in their fifties at the time of that survey were pre-war babies, already adult in 1965. They were much more likely to have had only one sex partner in their whole lives, and much less likely to report more than ten sex partners since they turned eighteen than were younger cohorts.

Moreover, as Figure 8.1 shows, change had indeed hit the campuses first. It was American college graduates who in 1990 were reporting the largest numbers of sexual partners. College graduates were more likely to report between five and ten, more likely to report ten to twenty, and twice as likely to report more than twenty-one as respondents with just a high-school diploma.[54]

It is not that everyone at university took to free love. Plenty of young women went through college without engaging in full sex at all. Among the prime boomer generation, born in the decade straight after the war,

Figure 8.1 **Percentage of US Adults Aged 18–59 Who in 1990 Had Had More than Four Sexual Partners (Lifetime to Date)**

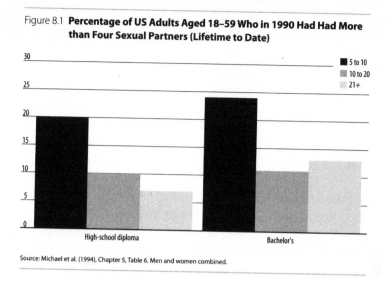

Source: Michael et al. (1994), Chapter 5, Table 6. Men and women combined.

40 percent of graduate women report that they first had sex at the age of twenty-one or over.[55]

It was, however, on the college campuses that today's mainstream behavior first evolved and from there that it spread. This was true in the US and equally true in the UK, as Figure 8.2 shows for women taken as their own. At the 75th percentile, the point dividing the most active top

Figure 8.2 **Number of Male Sexual Partners Reported by Non-Graduate and Graduate Women, Age 25–44, Britain (Lifetime to Date): 75th Percentile**

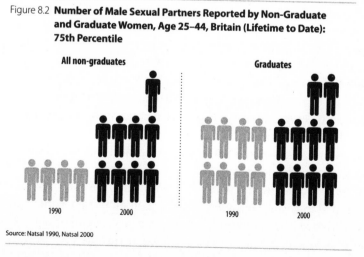

Source: Natsal 1990, Natsal 2000

quarter from the rest, graduate women in 1990 were reporting twice as many partners as were non-graduates. By 2000 non-graduates had pretty much caught up.[56]

THE END OF SPINSTERHOOD

Not so long ago, before the Pill, millions of educated women were virgin spinsters. In the late 1960s, living together before marriage was confined to a tiny minority; now the vast majority of married couples have co-habited first.[57] Men couldn't, pre-Pill, enjoy sexual relationships with a series of "respectable" girls.[58] Nice girls really didn't. Now they do.

Winifred Holtby was one of the finest English novelists of the 1920s and 1930s, and a chronicler of pre-war middle-class life. She served in France in the First World War, as an army auxiliary; she was an Oxford graduate, a feminist and socialist. Like so many of her generation, she never married; and in 1934 she wrote a much-quoted essay: "Are Spinsters Frustrated?"

It is a passionate expression of people's need for fulfilment, and insistence that this can be found in other than sexual ways. It talks about achievement and creativity. It also, accurately and realistically, takes for granted that women in her position will indeed be "spinsters." "At the moment, life seems very pleasant; but I am an uncomplete frustrated virgin woman. The psychologists, lecturers and journalists all tell me so. I live under the shadow of a curse," she wrote sardonically. But while she was determined to prove that there could be far more to life than marriage and children, her novels also depict vividly the dread, as well as the sexless lives, experienced by millions of single women.[59]

Now it has become entirely normal for women to have a sizeable number of sexual partners over their lifetimes: women between twenty-five and forty-four are reporting five partners on average, and many are up to ten or more. This is not, as we will see later, because the suburbs are full of swinging couples. It is, rather, a combination of sex among single adults, ever more delayed marriage and more couples splitting and re-forming.

Modern behavior started in the campuses; but by now, as we have seen, there tend to be few differences between graduates and non-graduates in total numbers of partners over a lifetime (for men or for women).[60] However, Figure 8.3 looks at contemporary American women slightly differently, comparing cohorts ten years apart in age. And what it shows is how different women are in their timing.

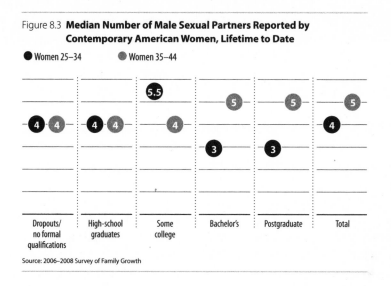

Figure 8.3 **Median Number of Male Sexual Partners Reported by Contemporary American Women, Lifetime to Date**

● Women 25–34　　　● Women 35–44

Dropouts/ no formal qualifications	High-school graduates	Some college	Bachelor's	Postgraduate	Total

Source: 2006–2008 Survey of Family Growth

Among the younger women, graduates report fewer partners than non-graduates; since they generally start having much sex later, this shouldn't be a surprise. Graduate professionals also marry later and have children much later than the less educated. And sure enough, Figure 8.3 shows that in terms of total numbers, graduate women in their late thirties catch up and indeed draw ahead of some other groups: highly educated women report a higher median number of partners than high-school graduates or dropouts.[61] All that high-school grind may have postponed sex, but it didn't spell a lifetime of abstention.

As Figure 8.2 showed, many graduates today are into double figures when it comes to adult sexual partners: a quarter of British female graduates aged twenty-five to forty-four reported at least ten male sexual partners to date. But are there many women with a backlist so long that they're hard put to remember the names? Not twenty-five-year-old women reporting hundreds of partners—they are likely to be prostitutes—but women with ten, fifteen, twenty times the median number. How much of a prototype is *Sex and the City*'s Samantha for today's career graduate?[62]

In 1990s Britain, for which we have very detailed responses, "high activity levels" were concentrated among the campus baby boomers—as they were in the US. Women with more than twenty partners were significantly more numerous among the graduates than the non-graduates.

But there weren't many of them even there. Among graduates aged twenty-five to forty-four, about six in a hundred reported more than twenty partners to date. For non-graduates, it was only just over one in a hundred.[63] And well under one in a hundred women reported more than forty partners. Then, and later, most people were bunched pretty close to the median figure.[64]

By 2000, the Samantha prototypes were somewhat more numerous: one in a hundred women aged twenty-five to forty-four reported fifty or more partners to date.[65] And around 5 percent reported more than twenty: higher than a decade before but still a tiny proportion. Meanwhile, the gap between graduates and non-graduates had shrunk (just as it did for median and 75th percentile numbers). Among the 5 percent of British women reporting over twenty-one partners to date, differences by education were no longer statistically significant.

As for these real-life Samanthas: among the graduates, women with over fifty partners were mostly in their thirties, not married (though sometimes cohabiting at the time of interview), and the majority, but not all, were childless.[66] And somewhat surprisingly, only about half lived right in the city—though London and its suburbs do figure large.

STAID OR SEX-SATURATED?

So spinsterhood has vanished into the mists; but leaving what? A world of sex toys and one-night stands? Or something rather more pedestrian?

Much of the information I'm reporting here I owe to Cath Mercer, a University College London academic and one of the world's foremost sex researchers. Sitting right above the desk in her small, tidy office there is, of course, a copy of the dun-colored 500-page tome in which the British team reported their 1990 results. "Welcome to the world's most boring-ever book about sex," Cath remarks.

It seems an odd reflection of a revolution. Sex and marriage have been divorced; so have sex and pregnancy. Cohabitation is usual; multiple sex partners the norm. Put "sex-saturated culture" into a browser and you'll come up with 21 million hits in an instant—none, as far as I can tell, questioning the "self-evident" fact that we live in one. And yet academic reports on our sex lives are not boring because they are draping swinging lifestyles with deadening prose. On the contrary, they are boring because the sex lives of most people are very staid.

Certainly, today's adult normality includes being sexually active. In a given year, almost 90 percent of American young women aged twenty to twenty-four report having sex, and so do 90 percent of Brits.[67] Among those a little older, figures are even higher, as we've seen; in both Britain and the US, fewer than one woman in ten aged twenty-five to forty-four reports having had no sex at all in the previous year.[68] As for having had sex in the five-year period previous to interview, in 1990 only three in a hundred British women aged twenty-five to forty-four reported no sex over that whole period; ten years later, figures were much the same.[69] And this holds for all types of women.[70]

So sex, yes. But lots of sex? No. If you look at Figure 8.4 you'll see how often people say they have been having sex in the last four weeks. And the answer? On average, once a week.

The number of people who are having wild sex every night is, it seems, vanishingly small.[71] In twenty-first-century America, in twenty-first-century Britain, the median response, for a four-week period, is four. That's sex four times every four weeks. Once a week. Get to twice a week, eight times a month, and you're up in the sexually active top quarter of the population.[72]

Back in 1990, only one woman in five in the twenty-five-to-forty-four age group reported having sex *more* than twice a week.[73] In 2000, the figure was essentially the same. And since other Western countries were just like the UK and US back in 1990, it seems safe to infer that they haven't changed much in the meantime either.

Figure 8.4 **Median Numbers of Times Women Had Sex with a Male in the Last Four Weeks**

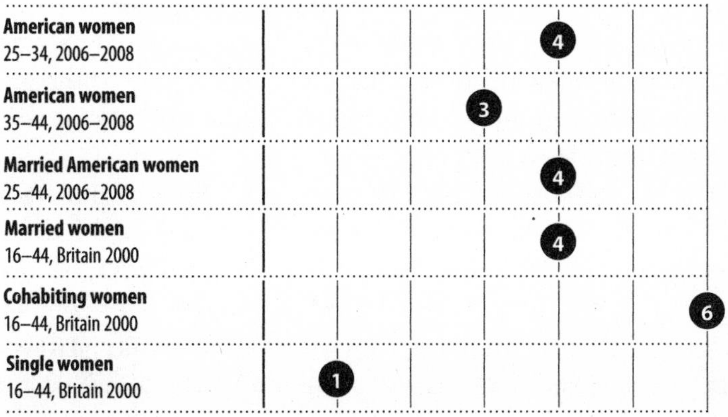

American women 25–34, 2006–2008	4
American women 35–44, 2006–2008	3
Married American women 25–44, 2006–2008	4
Married women 16–44, Britain 2000	4
Cohabiting women 16–44, Britain 2000	6
Single women 16–44, Britain 2000	1

Sources: US Survey of Family Growth 2006–2008; Natsal 2000

And those swinging singles? What Figure 8.4 also shows is that single women in the 2000s are having much less, not much more, sex than married ones. As was also the case in 1990.[74]

The famous Gilded Age actress Mrs. Patrick Campbell used to talk of "the deep, deep peace of the double-bed after the hurly-burly of the chaise-longue." And the picture most of us have is of singles playing the field—*Sex and the City* again—and exhausted dull marrieds. But the reality is closer to the opposite. It is those tame settled partnerships that are having the most sex—and with each other.

The reason is actually fairly obvious. If you live with someone there is someone there at hand, night after night. You don't have to go looking. So married couples have sex far more often than single people; and the most sexually active women (and men) are cohabiting but not married— as you might expect from a group that is younger and on average much closer to the start of a relationship than are married couples. Which isn't to say that many cohabitees have been enjoying sex every night either, or anything remotely close to it. Even the most sexually active group in the US statistics—unmarried but cohabiting high-school graduates—were only averaging a couple of times a week.[75]

So not much sex in 1990; and not much in 2000 either.

Is everyone just too tired? If so, you might expect professionals to be the hardest hit. As we saw in Chapter 4, they are the ones who are working as many hours as ever, with no increases in leisure time and a great deal of reported stress. Does this show up in the sex surveys?

Perhaps, but only at the very top. When asked about the last four weeks, very highly educated American women report substantially less sex than other groups. This is the case even among married women, where this sub-group reports less sex than most.[76] True, it is only women with postgraduate degrees—the most career-oriented group—who register levels lower than other groups.[77] Nonetheless, in the workaholic 2000s, the boomer effect is history.

Most of us today—women and men—are following quite a similar, if novel, pattern. We change partners relatively often at the start of our sexual careers and then settle down for years on end with just one other person. In both Britain and America, about a quarter of contemporary women in their early twenties report two or more sexual partners in the previous year; for the rest it is one or, more rarely, none. Post-twenty-five, it is overwhelmingly just one.[78]

The number of British twenty-five- to thirty-four-year-old women reporting more than one partner a year did almost double between 1990 and 2000.[79] But the claim sounds a lot less dramatic when you realize that the change is only from 7 to 12 percent of people.[80] As for four or more partners in the last twelve months, those proportions are tiny. For young British women it was about 3 percent in 2000;[81] while in America, the proportion of twenty-five- to forty-four-year-olds reporting four or more partners in the last year was, in the period 2006–2008, about 3 percent for high-school graduates or women with some college; and just over 1 percent for dropouts and graduates.[82]

And once and while married, adults everywhere report being over-whelmingly faithful to their spouses. Less than 2 percent of American married women, whatever their educational background, report having had more than one partner in the previous year.[83] And while, of course, they may not all be telling the truth, overall, it's not just goodbye to Woodstock and Haight-Ashbury.[84] It is welcome to the not-so-swinging suburbs.

MUTUAL INCOMPREHENSION?

I'm a pretty conventional married academic; so is Cath Mercer, the expert demographer who provided me with so much of this chapter's information. And yet there we sit in an upmarket Carluccio's coffee shop near St. Paul's Cathedral, poring over data on sexual practices. Maybe our equivalents would have done this happily, in a public space, back in 1990. Not, I think, twenty years before that.

Adults today have transformed their sexual behavior; yet physically and emotionally, we are the same creatures we were a generation or ten ago. Many authors argue that men and women have different sexual tastes and desires, just as they always have: men think about sex more, women have less interest in experimentation and place much more emphasis on romance. And some have argued that there is a very large "sex deficit" between men and women, which kicks in the minute women have children or reach middle age.[85] From that point on, they say, men want a lot more sex than women do; and nothing about the Pill or the sexual revolution has changed that.

Is that true? There's a huge literature on how men and women talk and think past each other: the "women from Venus, men from Mars" genre. But are contemporary men and women still very different in their sexual tastes and attitudes? Are women in all social groups unlike men, but like each other in this way? Or is this another area in which education makes a difference?

The British Natsal surveys, with their large national samples, tell us the most about changing attitudes and habits. Older adults (over forty-five) weren't surveyed in 2000, so all the respondents in the most recent data reached adulthood after the sexual revolution. But we can compare adults aged twenty-five and forty-four in 1990 with those of the same age in 2000. And what they show is that men and women are still quite different in a number of ways; but that the differences between more- and less-educated women are also large, and often larger.

ANYTHING GOES?

While our "sex-saturated" society may be a good deal less sexually hyperactive than the media would have you believe, we are nonetheless very different indeed from our ancestors. Changes in behavior generally affect what we think is "right" as well as what we think is normal.

This has certainly happened for sex. Our attitudes and tolerance for others' behavior have been shifting quite rapidly, because of what we talk about as well as what we actually do. And, as with actual behavior, graduates are usually the moving force. The data show that non-graduates' opinions in 2000 have shifted closer to those held by graduates a decade before. However, graduates have also changed in the meantime, and there are still significant differences between the groups.

One-night stands illustrate this. Few female graduates are actually reporting a life full of one-night stands, certainly not once they hit twenty-five: as we saw above, the number of women leading a *Sex and the City* existence is pretty tiny. But graduates are much less disapproving of them than non-graduate women.

Between 1990 and 2000 the proportion of twenty-five- to forty-four-year-old British women thinking one-night stands are "always wrong" fell from a third to less than a quarter among graduates. It also fell among non-graduates, from well over half to a third.[86] However, that still leaves a big gap between graduate and non-graduate women: the graduates are far less disapproving, at least in theory. Moreover, while men are generally less negative than women, graduate women in 2000 were actually less disapproving of one-night stands than male graduates had been in 1990, and only a little more so than graduate men in 2000.[87]

Women graduates have also been opinion leaders in their attitudes to male and female homosexuality. Women, both graduate and non-graduate, are consistently much less negative about homosexuality than men, and also make no observable distinction between male and female homosexuality. (Men, especially the non-graduates, are less tolerant of male homosexuality than they are of female.)[88] But female graduates are quite particularly tolerant.

In 1990, well over twice as many British non-graduate women thought male homosexuality to be wrong as did women graduates.[89] And the gap between graduates and non-graduates has stayed sizeable and significant even though both groups showed major shifts between 1990 and 2000. By 2000, the proportion of female non-graduates thinking male homosexuality is always wrong had shrunk to just under a quarter. That is still a lot more than the 10 percent of female graduates who continued to think so; but both figures reflect a sea change in social attitudes, and both sets of women were much more tolerant than equivalent men.[90] Indeed, looking at society as a whole, life before the Second World War seems, in this domain, like something from another planet.

LIKING IT

There is a well-known story about middle-class Victorian English-women. On the night before their daughters' weddings, they would give them time-honored advice on the sex that lay ahead. It was "Lie back and think of England, dear."

Apocryphal or not, our sexual habits are light-years removed from those of nineteenth-century women. It is not just that "spinsters" have vanished. We have now had decades of *Cosmopolitan* magazine, where typical features offer "Twelve freakiest sex tips that really work," "Let's get sexting" and "Doing it doggy style."[91] Women talk about sex a lot more. But, just as with attitudes to others' behavior, there are differences among women in how they feel about sex for themselves.[92]

As we have seen, it is widely believed that men always want a lot more sex than women do, even if they don't get it, and that the difference is especially large once children arrive. And there are grounds for seeing this as quite hardwired into our biology. In 2000, British researchers duly asked people if they had lost interest in sex for a month or more anytime during the last year.

The replies seem, at first sight, to confirm the "sex deficit" claim. There is a big gap between women and men and it doesn't wait for middle age to cut in. Twice as many women as men answered in the affirmative:

yes, they had lost interest for a month or more. And the numbers weren't small either. Of the twenty-five- to forty-four-year-old women 39 percent said yes compared to 18 percent of men.

But vary the question a little and you get a very different picture. Asked whether they enjoy sex "always," "most of the time" or less, men are more likely than women to say "always." But add together the two positive choices—"always" and "most of the time"—and the totals are very high for women as well.

Indeed, if you look by age group and education, you find that in every female group but one, at least 80 percent—four in five—register high satisfaction with sex. The exception is the youngest, non-graduate group, the under-twenty-five-year-olds, who are also the group that started having sex youngest. And when you look at the men, you find exactly the same pattern: the young non-graduate men are the dissatisfied outliers.[93]

In 2000, British adults were also asked whether they would like to have more sex or less sex than at present (or whether the amount was just right). Again, at first sight, the "sex deficit" looks alive and well: a majority of men but only a minority of women aged twenty-five to forty-four would like either much more or more than they are having. However, looking at figures for women as a whole conceals a major difference.

The majority of graduate women would like more sex, please. They don't think that what they have now is enough; and in fact the percentage of graduate women saying they would like "more" or "much more" sex is pretty much the same as for men. It's non-graduate women who are giving very different answers from men. Most of these less-educated women think they are having quite enough already—or indeed would like a break.[94] The data don't tell us why; it may be because of their earlier sexual histories, it may be because of other things in their lives. But the difference is significant and sizeable.

There is one other puzzle in women's changing views of what "good sex" demands. British women were asked, in both 1990 and 2000, the same slightly convoluted question—do you agree that without orgasm, sex can't be satisfying for a woman? And here, once again, you find differences by education; but also some real convergence. In most cases, as we have seen, non-graduates have become more like graduates in the last decades. Here, it is graduates who have come round to the non-graduates' point of view.

Between 1990 and 2000, the proportion of female graduates definitely agreeing—yes, orgasm really matters—rose from 17 to 27 percent. In 1990 that was a much lower figure than the one for non-graduates and in 2000 it wasn't. And the number of graduates who definitely disagreed—that is, the number who thought female orgasm really wasn't crucial at all—fell sharply.[95] The change is statistically very significant. But the data don't offer any explanation, and I don't have one to offer either.

INSIDE THE BEDROOM

Education-related differences also extend to tastes and practices, and are not confined to Britain. Back in 1990, for example, US researchers asked people whether they found something like using a vibrator, oral sex or sex with a stranger appealing.

Graduates were different. Female college graduates were considerably more likely than less-educated women to like the idea of something over and above "straight" sex.[96] Not that this was saying much: adult American women in the late 1980s were a pretty conservative bunch, with only 1 or 2 percent thinking that group sex, or watching sex, or having sex with a stranger, sounded very appealing. (Men, on this occasion, fancied being a lot more adventurous.)[97]

In 1990 America, graduates were also the ones most likely to report

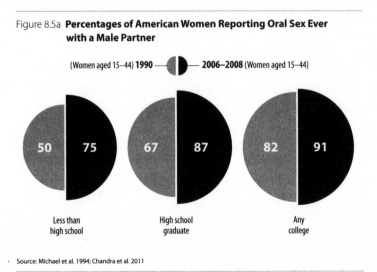

Figure 8.5a **Percentages of American Women Reporting Oral Sex Ever with a Male Partner**

(Women aged 15–44) **1990** —————— **2006–2008** (Women aged 15–44)

Less than high school	High school graduate	Any college
50 / 75	67 / 87	82 / 91

Source: Michael et al. 1994; Chandra et al. 2011

Figure 8.5b **Percentages of American Women Reporting Anal Sex Ever with a Male Partner**

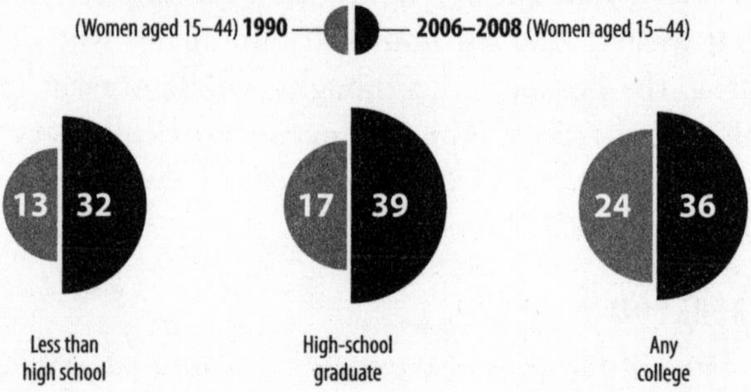

(Women aged 15–44) **1990** ———■▶—— **2006–2008** (Women aged 15–44)

13	32		17	39		24	36

Less than high school   High-school graduate   Any college

Source: Michael et al. 1994; Chandra et al. 2011

actually engaging in varied sexual practices, though this particular graduate boomer phenomenon isn't obvious in the 1990 British data.[98] It is especially clear with oral and anal sex, neither of which was approved of—or, in many cases, even legal—a few generations ago.

Compare 1990 with 2006 and two things are obvious. As Figures 8.5a and b show, there has been a sizeable increase in the reporting, and probably the practice, of oral and anal sex by all women; and, as happened with numbers of sexual partners, graduate–non-graduate behavior has converged.[99] We may not have the exhaustingly active sex lives of TV fantasy, but it seems that we do do sex differently from people in the past.

And yes, this world is liberated. Yes, it is more tolerant. It is a world where women can enjoy sex and can control their fertility; and where sex is constantly on display. But it is also a world that retains some old taboos. In particular, it still abhors the sale of sex for money. We may be easy about one-night stands, but, as the next chapter will explain, the oldest female occupation on the planet is still beyond the pale.

9

WORKING GIRLS

he tale of Eliot Spitzer is a story of the new and the old. Spitzer was a crusading New York State attorney general. He spent his career prosecuting organized crime in the garment industry, and securities and Internet fraud. And for just one year, from 2007 to 2008, he was the elected governor of New York State.

Just one year because he was effectively forced out of office. The *New York Times* exposed his use of call girls and his days were numbered. His story is new and modern in that Spitzer was a client of an international agency, with the strong Web presence that is typical of modern prostitution and porn, and left a long trail of electronic exchanges. But also old. Old because this sort of incident has been destroying public careers for over a century. Old because the girls were of an entirely traditional type, making money on the fringes of the entertainment industry. And old, finally, because in this age of easy sex, they were commanding the same high fees as their predecessors.

Spitzer is estimated to have spent as much as $80,000, over a period of a few years, on girls from Emperors Club. The club's top escorts charged $3,000 or $4,000 an hour; and for the short tryst that hit the headlines, Spitzer apparently paid $4,300. It took place in the upmarket Mayflower Hotel, a few blocks from the White House in Washington, DC, something that shouldn't have surprised people. Hotels are a call girl's regular turf. Indeed, as Belle de Jour, a London call girl and publishing phenomenon, explains, "In a world of twelve-year-olds in sexy boots and nans [grandmothers] in sparkly mini-dresses, the surest way to tell the prostitute walking into a hotel . . . is to look for the lady in the designer-suit. Fact."[1]

Today, sex outside marriage and a series of sexual partners are, as we saw in Chapter 8, the new female normality. Moreover, a third of young British graduate women now think one-night stands are "rarely or never" wrong.[2] And yet here we have girls charging hundreds or indeed thousands of dollars an hour, and a working environment of luxury hotels and rich clients. The question, surely, is, why isn't everyone doing it?

Which they are not.

Selling sex—sex for money—is the last great sexual taboo. The rest of this book deals with all the things that today's educated women can do, and do do; many of them for the first time in female history. This chapter explains why, in this new world, an old attitude and an old barrier prevail.

NICE GIRLS DON'T

Prostitution is the oldest female profession, and the most widespread. We meet "working girls" very early in the Bible.[3] Brothels and camp followers characterize every previous civilization that we know. And as we saw in the previous chapter, the sex industry was historically one of the very few where women could own and run their own businesses.

In this not-so-long-ago world, where marriage was women's main objective and main career, extramarital sex carried huge risks of pregnancy, disgrace and ruin. When it came to a career in the demimonde, a few women, typically actresses, achieved fame and fortune, often as the mistresses of kings and princes. A few whores and madams made fortunes; a few became respectable married women. But very few. For any girl hoping to make a good match, or, much later, a respectable professional career as a teacher, nurse or civil servant, the risks of selling sex hugely outweighed the benefits.

Today, acting, singing and dancing are admired occupations that have moved well away from their origins. There are so many wannabe actors that their marginal price—what you pay to hire an extra one—is zero. Thousands of struggling actors would, if allowed, act for nothing. In contrast, being a prostitute, and especially a top-class one, is still something most girls won't touch. How do we know this? *Because* their fees are so high.

Normally, if a job pays very well, a lot of people want to do it; if they succeed, this then drives pay down. A number of things can stop this, and keep pay and prices up. The job may take years of expensive training: medicine is the obvious example. It may require skills that only a few people have, like pro football. Or the people in the job may be able to erect legal barriers to keep other people out. The rationale for licensing is that it stops clients getting poor-quality service from "cowboys." But licensed occupations are also able to keep their prices high because they restrict who does the job.

But sex? What possible barriers to entry or need for training can there be? Ours is a world where millions of women, and millions of pretty women, are already doing it for free. If they are not also offering sex-for-sale on the side, and driving down the breathtaking fees charged by top escort agencies, something must be stopping them.

What might that be? There are two obvious explanations, both frequently offered and both inadequate. The first is that "sex work" is so degrading and dangerous, even in luxury hotels, that only the desperate, the enslaved and the trafficked will do it. The second is the law. In many modern countries, brothels are banned and soliciting is forbidden. It may even be a crime to pay for sex. Fear of a criminal record may be keeping people out of prostitution and off the streets; maybe escorts charge a lot to offset the risks and costs of an illegal activity. Maybe. But let us look at the evidence.

HUNTING THE TRAFFICKERS

In modern societies, prostitution triggers moral panics. In early-twentieth-century America, "white slavery" was the rallying call. Campaigners were convinced that many thousands of young girls were being kidnapped and sold into prostitution, and that "60,000 white slaves a year" were dying in the United States.[4] Only a small number of girls were ever found who appeared indeed to have been overtly bought and sold, but there was a wave of anti-prostitution activity and legislation that transformed American life, and especially its underworld.

More recently, in Europe, campaigners and media have demanded action to stop "traffickers" who are allegedly smuggling thousands of unwilling girls across borders to work in massage parlors and on the streets. In Britain, between 2007 and 2009, figures of "25,000 sex slaves" were given in parliamentary debates; "18,000" trafficked victims, coming in at the rate of "4,000 a year," were figures quoted and requoted in the press. A few genuine victims were identified, but again, their numbers were tiny. They were also deeply unrepresentative of modern British prostitution.[5]

In developed countries, prostitution is not, by and large, something forced on women by brutal pimps, nor is it based on the trafficking of tricked or kidnapped girls. As a growing mass of evidence makes clear, this is not the case today and was not the case historically either. Ruth Rosen, a leading American historian of prostitution, remarks that "I am struck again and again by most prostitutes' view of their work as 'easier' and less oppressive than other survival strategies they might have chosen."[6] This does not mean that it was the job of their dreams, or pleasant, or that there weren't many other things they would rather have been doing. What it means is that, for very many women, it was and is a rational economic choice.

This was especially obvious in the days when there was precious little else on offer for women, and when "immoral" earnings were far higher than the pay of industrial workers, let alone domestics.[7] As one Victorian (male) campaigner for women's rights observed, "It costs a man money to indulge in vice but for a woman it is money in the pocket."[8]

Ruth Rosen reports that, in the early 1900s, it cost at least $9 a week to support yourself as a single woman in America; and that before going on the game prostitutes had earned $6 a week on average in a labor market that barred them from skilled trades and occupations. As prostitutes they could make $50 to $400 a week—anything from eight to sixty times as much.[9]

The letters of Maimie Pinzer tell us precisely how it looked from the prostitute's end. Maimie worked as a prostitute in early-twentieth-century New York; a clever girl, born into a Jewish immigrant family whose fortunes plummeted when her father was killed. She left school to help her mother in the home, something she deeply resented, and from the age of thirteen she started to date young men. "Of course the inevitable thing happened. Some young chap took me to his room: and I stayed three or four days."[10] Her mother had her placed in a reform school; it was the start of eleven years of life with lovers, working as a nude model, drug addiction, an unhappy marriage, intermittent prostitution. We know Maimie's story because of her later long correspondence with the upper-class Bostonian Fanny Quincy Howe,[11] and she makes clear just how much better prostitution paid than almost anything else a working- or middle-class woman could do. "I just cannot be moral enough to see where drudgery is better than a life of lazy vice," she observed; Maimie describes how, faced with the bare and meager reality of life as the wife of a "respectable" working-class man, "I gave up in disgust and . . . began to use what charms I might possess to make it possible to have a few of the luxuries."[12]

And today?

It is always difficult to know how much prostitution is going on in a society. It is doubly difficult when, as in many Western societies, large parts of the market involve illegal activities: for example, because of bans on advertising, soliciting in the street or curb-crawling. However, only a tiny proportion of US women report today that they have ever been paid for sex, far lower than in either the past or in poorer countries today.[13]

Those who do, like Maimie a century ago, are often very clearly "in business." In the UK, an increasing number of entrepreneurial sex workers get custom entirely through the Internet, and benefit from "Punternet," on which punters (customers) post moderated field reports. Indeed, academic expert Teela Sanders, who has interviewed a wide range of sex workers, and clients, reports that "an increasing number of women with web-authoring skills manage their own websites."[14]

Among her interviewees was Natasha, who charges £250 for each service, and remarks that "[a] lot of the people who see me only do after reading a good report . . . obviously they are paying a lot of money and they want to know what they are getting is good. I quite like that." And Krystal is also a field report fan: "I know I am good at what I do, so [the reports] are always going to be pleasant."[15]

The authors of a long-term study of licensed Nevada brothels reached conclusions very much in line with Sanders's and with Ruth Rosen's work on nineteenth-century prostitutes. "Labor market dynamics," in their view, explain why women come and work in the brothels, where they operate on a self-employed basis with a cut to the brothel owner. It pays better than the low-level service jobs that are these women's alternative, and they need the money. "None of the women we interviewed in the brothels told us stories of being forced into the brothels. Around half . . . had never sold sex illegally [and] a great many come from service industry jobs . . . the majority were not career sex workers." And turnover was duly enormous.[16]

Street prostitution is something different. Compared to working out of a brothel or massage parlor, or your own home, street prostitution has enormous and obvious drawbacks. In countries where on-street soliciting is tolerated, many of the street prostitutes come from much poorer countries. Italy is an example: the girls who appear on seafront streets every summer evening are, to English or American eyes, extraordinarily lovely for the trade they ply. But hardly a single one is Italian: they come from Eastern Europe or Africa.

In Britain and the US, by contrast, many street prostitutes are native-born, and feeding a drug habit. As one john, now a user only of massage parlors, explained, "To be honest I feel it's exploitation. The people on the street are there because they're desperate . . ."[17] And another, using parlors and Internet sites, hated street prostitution: "You know it's all drug-related. It's a grim life and it's bad."[18]

The most detailed study of street prostitutes, carried out in Chicago, found that 83 percent of the full-timers were indeed drug addicts. (There were also a number of women who only turned tricks on holidays, when demand surged; and they weren't addicts.) At this end of the market, there was a fixed price—customers didn't differentiate and nobody lingered. Violence was common.[19]

Compared to a century before, relative wages for street prostitutes have fallen fast: there are a good many jobs in a modern economy that pay women better than this. However, even at this bottom end, where you are down to $25 or $30 a trick, not just hourly but annual wages still tend to be above the national female average.[20] It is unpleasant and frightening, and that keeps supply down. Imagine, instead, selling web-cam sex, talking and performing for invisible, paying spectators. This is so easy to do, and carries so few risks, that one big conglomerate boasts 900,000 signed-up performers ready to strip and talk dirty from their own bedrooms. Some webcam girls make very good money; but for many, hourly earnings are, as you might predict, right down to the national average or below.[21]

And at the top end? Between the escorts in hotels and apartments and the working girls on the street there is an earnings gulf. Researchers estimate that, on an hourly basis, escorts are making between eleven and twenty times as much as street prostitutes. Only a tiny proportion make the sort of money Eliot Spitzer was paying. But a sizeable number command fees between $250 and $400 (£150 and £250) an hour, in 2008 prices. Columbia University economists calculated that, on average, "escorts who provide sex command some $280/hour, a wage rate that on a full-time basis would place them in the top 0.5 percentile of the US earnings distribution or roughly in the top 0.05 percentile of the female earnings distribution."[22]

If these top-end women aren't enslaved, if their work isn't totally terrifying and degrading, then is it just the law that keeps lots of women away and the prices high? Economists tend to assume so—a top-earning prostitute, they argue, "would be distraught if prostitution were legalized, because her stratospherically high wage stems from the fact that the service she provides *cannot* be gotten legally."[23]

It's true that a criminal record isn't good for your career. But as a full explanation, this just doesn't hold up. Even in countries where prostitution isn't illegal, such as the Netherlands and Australia, the stigma endures and call girls stay pricy. And pay rates seem to be pretty similar in the UK and the US, even though the law is less hostile to sex work in Britain than it is in the States.

So we need another explanation. Swedish-born economist Lena Edlund has one. Marriage and the marriage market.

THE MARRYING KIND

I met Lena Edlund in her office in Columbia University, New York. It was a glorious day as I walked across campus to Lena's office. Students were sitting on the library steps and on the grass, and there were plenty of long tanned legs, low-cut tops and well-applied makeup on view.

There was also a lot of accumulated debt. There are students at Columbia paying $20,000 a year in fees, and that's before they have to find the money for New York City living. They're taking out loans, working in bars at night, hustling for summer jobs. And yet I'm certain that those Columbia girls were not flocking into the call-girl business.

Lena has a special interest in the economics of sex and marriage. In particular, she explained, "I am interested in why prostitution pays so well. I was particularly puzzled by it, because we now live in a very promiscuous society. But there's a very clear distinction between being a prostitute and being promiscuous. What exactly is it that makes being a prostitute so bad?"

Her curiosity was sparked not by recent scandals, but rather by a memory from her Swedish childhood: "I was eight maybe, and there was a television series, imported from the USA, called *Rich Man Poor Man*, with Peter Strauss and Nick Nolte; they played brothers. One becomes the center, he's a manual worker, played by Nick Nolte. And there's a scene where he picks up a woman, I guess in a bar, and they go to a motel. Then there's the next scene, where she wakes up and he has left.

And she looks around her, and she sees a dollar bill on the nightstand. And she starts crying.

"And I'm thinking, why's she crying? It's really interesting, because there's nothing factual that has changed. Everything that happened, happened. And now the bad news is that there's money on the table. Why is that bad?"

As Lena argues, there is a real puzzle here. Why is it so terrible when someone pays you, after the event, for sex? Only about 2 percent of American women say they have ever been paid for sex, and that includes informal payments, not just people who have worked in the sex trade. A few upper-end encounters would make a big dent in your student loan. Promiscuity is pretty common and having many sexual partners over a lifetime has become completely normal. And yet girls don't.

Prostitution, in the past, paid well at the cost of being "ruined": respectable men used prostitutes but did not normally marry them.[24] Lena argues that this is still in fact the case. Men don't marry prostitutes. And because of this, prostitution still carries a huge penalty.

If prostitution and marriage are indeed largely incompatible for women,[25] then you are taking a huge risk if you sell sex. Most women prefer marriage to early repayment of their student loans; more generally, most women with reasonable career prospects will think that an escort's earnings, good as they are, do not offset the costs of getting in the game. So they don't. And the prices at the top stay high.

There still is a marriage market out there, not just a market for sex, Lena insists. "I think there will still always be a market for wives. And men don't like marrying former prostitutes. So, being a prostitute has this extra cost. You can't marry, you destroy your marriage market. And that means that for women to go into prostitution it needs to be very well paid."

However, as she and her colleagues have noted, "The bottom has essentially fallen out of the under-class marriage market in the US":[26] something that we already noted in Chapter 2 and will discuss further below. The least-educated and lowest-earning women therefore have few marriage prospects that they might be putting at risk by undertaking sex work. Accordingly, there's a plentiful supply of women at this level, and prices have been driven down from historically higher figures.

As for the women who do appear on escort agencies' books and websites, they are, Lena reckons, "fantastic looking . . . but my guess is that they're still pretty average women: we're not talking about very high-end trial lawyer material. It seems unlikely that they were all top models, or neuroscientists. And it's unpleasant work, right?"

ALL IN A DAY'S WORK

There is confirmation of Lena's arguments in the firsthand account of someone who spent a good many years in the trade. "Belle de Jour" was a publishing phenomenon in the early 2000s: a London call girl who clearly knew what she was talking about. Belle also was—is—that apparently unusual creature, a graduate for whom this was good money, better paid and much more amusing than the alternatives on offer.

She makes it sound easy. Search the Internet. Find an appealing agency. Call the manager. Meet; get glamour shots for the site; manager pleased. And then the manager calls and asks, " 'Can you do something for me? Can you write something about yourself for the portfolio? Most of the other girls, I write something for them, but you should do this very well . . .' "[27] Which bears out Lena Edlund's point. Girls with degrees, alpha girls who write well, just don't.

Top-price escorts, Belle explains, have to be not just physically attractive, but smart, trustworthy, good at acting and talking dirty. They must be willing to wax, make-up, make-up, wax—and able to "pass" in a business environment. Even at the top end it's not simply an occupation that many people would find unpleasant; it can indeed be dangerous. At the end of a job, she writes, it's "text or ring the agency . . . If the manager can't get through she'll ring the client, then the hotel, her own security if they're nearby, then the police. She knows."[28]

Belle has now come out as an American-born, UK-based, unmarried research scientist. And she was a phenomenon because she was so unusual, not because she had a typical tale to tell.[29] Although it was on the campuses that the sexual revolution took off, the escort business is not a mainstream postgraduate pursuit, least of all for graduates of the top universities.

The female students of Cambridge (and Oxford) University are happy to host an Ann Summers party and giggle over Rampant Rabbit vibrators or candy-floss lubes and licks. But they're not planning to exit the safety zone. My daughter, a recent Cambridge graduate, told me about "Oxbridge Dating." It was launched to offer businessmen and tourists an evening with a pretty, cultured Oxford or Cambridge undergraduate. No sex, at least not officially; several hundred pounds a shot.

But "basically, no one signed up," said my daughter—even though lots of her friends were very hard up. I searched for it everywhere on the Web, but in vain. If Oxbridge Dating still exists, I certainly can't find any trace.

Is it really the prospect of marriage, or rather the loss of it, that holds women back? After all, men commonly have sex with a considerable number of women before they marry; and women do the same with men. What is it about sex-for-money that makes it different?

Lena Edlund suggests that we turn the question around. Why, nowadays, do any men get married at all? And her answer: children. "The key feature of marriage is that men obtain paternal rights. And then they want a wife who's going to give them their biological kids. A wife can't be a prostitute if you want this: you can't do marriage and prostitution in parallel and you can't do it sequentially because men don't like marrying former prostitutes."

Why not? Because, compared to having a number of partners in sequence, and being faithful to each while it lasts, prostitution is about having multiple partners all at the same time. And if someone did this once, why not again? The last thing you want, as a man, is to worry about the legitimacy of your offspring.

Men care about sex, and female looks, just as they always have. And they care about having children—again, as they always have. So gorgeous girls can make money selling sex if they want to. But they mostly don't, and won't.

10

PRETTY GIRLS AND PEACOCKS' TAILS

mma is a high-flyer at an elite university. She is president of its most prestigious student society and she thinks that "a lot of times people concentrate on the fact that a girl's pretty or that's the main thing that will be pointed out. Like it's, 'Oh, she's president. Oh, she's pretty,' not, 'Oh, she's president. Oh, she did a fantastic job.' There will always be that problem of girls being in a position because they were seen to be prettier than the rest of the university and girls will continue to struggle with that, I think."

"Some struggle" might be the tart response of the men Emma beat for this position, and of the men and the less-attractive women who lose out to her in the future. But she is absolutely right in one sense.

Whether you see looks and sexual attraction as useful weapons, as things that stop men taking women seriously, or both, they matter. And they matter way beyond the bedroom or the nightclub floor. "The world is a sexy place. It's primal," is how the founder of Victoria's Secret puts it, and he has a high-end lingerie chain with a $3.5 billion annual turnover to prove his point.[1]

Heterosexual men—which is over 95 percent of them[2]—are attracted to women who are young, but also to specific features that are associated clearly with youth and, therefore, by implication, fecundity.[3] That covers firm breasts, clear skin, an hourglass figure. These features are consistently attractive to men across very different cultures, which strongly suggests they have been attractive for a long time now.[4] Not surprisingly, the overwhelming majority of young women possess these qualities to some degree, and so must have inherited them from women who possessed them, bore children and have living descendants.

It is true that sex plays a smaller role in determining the fate of clever well-educated girls than ever before in history. Nothing this chapter says will contradict that. But it is a smaller role, not no role at all. And sex is still, often, very important indeed.

Sex is about mating and marriage and having children, and as such it is central to our personal lives, men's as well as women's. It also marks out the sort of life that an individual woman leads, because, as Chapter 8 demonstrated, the divide between highly and less-educated women works its way into how early a woman has sex and the numbers of partners she has had by when.

But sex also has new and important repercussions for today's mixed-gender professional workplaces. It does so partly in obvious but also in less obvious ways. Women and men send sexual signals to each other directly, if often quite unconsciously, and that affects their behavior in the workplace. In addition the characteristics associated with "being attractive" matter, for men as well as women and for reasons that go well beyond immediate sexual encounters and fantasies. Here, too, behavior and responses are often quite unconscious; and in a world where men and women work and compete professionally both within and across genders, they are changing the dynamics of the workplace.

SEX, COMPETITION AND THE PAYOFF TO BEAUTY

Sexual attraction was always an important part of the competition to mate and bear children with desirable partners. That was *the* crucial competition where women were concerned; for men, it was not the only one, but it was important nonetheless.

Sexually, women's beauty and physical appearance matter more to men, and are a more predictable way of attracting them, than male looks and appearance matter to women.[5] It is the major reason why female college students use makeup twenty times as often as men.[6] (It's just surprising the difference isn't higher.) And as we have already noted, many of the things that men find beautiful and attractive in women are linked to likely fecundity.

Women, meanwhile, are attracted by male characteristics that are likely to signal health, power and wealth. Good looks are nice, but relatively less important than they are to men. In other words, both women and men are attracted by the characteristics of potentially good mates. And to a large degree we respond to these characteristics subconsciously, and intuitively.[7] Just looking at photos of good-looking members of the opposite sex makes us feel better.[8]

Which takes us back to competition. In the past, when women's only routes to the top were domestic and sexual—they were born, married or slept their way up—it was in those worlds that they competed. They entered the marriage market. Or, as we saw in the previous chapters, they sold sex.

Today, professional women are where men have long been. Mating is not the only competition, though it still matters. But in addition, these women compete at work, and in the same environments, and for the same jobs, as men do. In that work environment, brains, determination, energy and connections all tell for men and women alike. But so, it turns out, do looks. In fact, they matter *to* both men and women and *for* both men and women as well. Though rather more for women, and in a two-edged way.

This does not mean we are simply prisoners of our genes, or driven entirely by our hormones, or anything close to it. But a lot of what happens in human societies, beyond the obvious contexts of dating, marriage, child-bearing and divorce, cannot be explained without recognizing that we respond to sexual signals. And it is not just that we respond differently to the people (and gender) we personally find attractive. We are also affected by signals that we consciously or, very often, unconsciously recognize as being powerful and positive for other people, not just ourselves.

THE EYE OF THE BEHOLDER

"Beauty may be only skin deep, but that is deep enough to confer an unsettling array of advantages," comments academic lawyer Deborah Rhode in her review of the "beauty bias."[9] This payoff is not just an offshoot of sexual desire and possible mating: people reward beauty in their own sex too. Human beings like being around people they find attractive to look at. And they also, often quite unconsciously, ascribe other positive qualities to those who are good-looking.

This is true across cultures. And there is also remarkable agreement, not just across cultures but across genders, on what makes for a beautiful face. We like symmetry (and respond to it from earliest infancy). We also like faces that are "feminine" in the sense of having plump lips and big eyes.[10] This latter point is especially true for female faces, whether the observer is male or female herself.

THE X̶FACTOR

People don't actually realize how important looks are. Only one-third of Americans think that, in their workplace, the attractive are more likely to be hired or promoted. But "a cottage industry of studies indicates that popular assumptions are wrong."[11]

Daniel Hamermesh, of the University of Texas at Austin, has been studying the effect of beauty on earnings for many years and finds that it has an astonishingly wide and significant impact.[12] "Ugly people earn less than average-looking people; and average-looking people earn less than the beautiful . . . bad looks hurt us," he concludes.[13] But how can we be so sure? The labor market isn't a speed-dating exercise. Can our looks really matter so much?

The reason we can be sure is that people agree so strongly about what and who are physically attractive. That allows researchers to get highly consistent "beauty ratings" using photographs. And when they look at the lives of the less and more highly rated, the findings are unequivocal.

Whether they are men or women, people who are better-looking receive higher pay, while plain-looking people earn less than average, other things equal.[14] And these are not tiny differences either. The average difference in pay between people rated above average and those rated below average is more than the difference associated with an extra year of college or five years' work experience.[15]

Your looks affect the votes you get in a TV reality show; and they affect whether you're chosen to join a group or team.[16] In political races, the better-looking non-incumbents are more likely to win the primary or the election itself (although once you're in, looks seem not to matter anymore, compared to bringing home the gravy).[17]

There are plenty of jobs where your looks might seem to matter in an obvious way: jobs like receptionist, fitness instructor or sales assistant on a cosmetics counter. In much of the world, employers are permitted to use explicit beauty criteria; in these cases, advertisements for such jobs will openly demand physical attractiveness, and, generally, express a preference for females.[18] What is much more extraordinary, however, is the impact of looks where most of us would not expect them to matter.

Among economists, that driest of professions, Hamermesh reports that you were significantly more likely to be elected an officer of the American Economics Association if you were in the top half of the list on looks.[19] Students (and especially freshmen) give much better evaluations to better-looking lecturers and instructors.[20] American lawyers, it seems, earn (even) more than normal when they are better-looking—and the further out from law school they get, the stronger the effect becomes. Better-looking attorneys are, by mid-career, billing at higher rates, and not just billing more hours.[21] Private sector lawyers are also, on average, better-looking than public sector ones, and the difference becomes more marked over time, as lawyers actually switch sectors.[22]

This isn't just about men responding to women. Good-looking men also do better. The wage effects for lawyers are just as clear for men as they are for women. And data for Dutch advertising agencies indicate that agencies with more attractive managers (male and female) have significantly higher sales revenues.[23]

Why is this? Some of it is "straight" sex, the effect of being more or less sexually attractive to people one encounters. But a lot of it is about a rather more complex sort of signaling; something that involves the same characteristics, but with no expectation, or hope, that anyone will end up in bed. Let's start with the sex.

BEDMATES AND BOARDROOM RIVALS

Historically, we know, the only way for men to have sex with the vast majority of girls was by marrying them. The more a girl possessed certain physical characteristics, the more attractive she was, and the more likely to make a "good" marriage. Those physical characteristics are well mapped. They are also especially important when it comes to first impressions.

Psychologists emphasize that people—men and women—respond differently when considering the possibility of a long-term relationship rather than a possible casual date or short-term sexual encounter. That makes immediate physical attraction more important in choosing potential sexual partners than is the case for lifetime mates.[24]

When it comes to the workplace, we are not, most of the time, focusing on lifetime partnerships. Our working days are, however, full of first impressions. Lynn Forester de Rothschild, who made a fortune in broadband, remembers that early in her career "I had to contend with things just because I was a woman. For example, I remember an important meeting, I was the only woman there, my first time with that group. And I said something and it got glossed over. And then fifteen minutes later, a man said exactly the same thing, and everyone said, 'Brilliant.'

"So I asked a friend later, am I mad? And he said, 'What do you expect, Lynn? Everyone was sitting round that table thinking about ****ing you.'

"But I also got breaks because I was a woman. Times when I probably wouldn't have been noticed if I'd been a man. And they wanted a woman in that room. I probably wouldn't have been there otherwise."

Sociologist Catherine Hakim argues that, because of men's greater interest in sex, women have a built-in surplus of "erotic capital."[25] The "laws of supply and demand determine the value of everything, in sexuality as in other areas," she writes. Male sexuality has little value, because there is more of it on offer than women want: the reverse is not true and this "gives women the upper hand in sexual bargaining and private relationships."[26] Hakim is absolutely right that men really are more interested in sex. As we saw in Chapter 8, women's sexual behavior has changed dramatically in recent decades; but men remain, to an overwhelming degree, the main purchasers and users of pornography.[27] Yes, there is "Mommy Porn" (think *50 Shades of Grey*) and a tiny "male stripper" industry. But you don't find hundreds of lap- and pole-dancing clubs catering to female middle-managers. There are no sex holidays in Thailand being marketed to women in Rotterdam, Vancouver or Chicago. There is no "Punternet" website for women, where they can rate male prostitutes for the benefit of future customers. All of these are big for men.

When Harry Met Sally is a film, scripted by Nora Ephron, about two friends who do, eventually, fall in love and marry. Its most famous scene involves the actress Meg Ryan (as Sally) demonstrating, in a restaurant, how easy it is to fake an orgasm. But it also contains this encapsulation of male/female differences:

Harry: You realize, of course, that we can never be friends.
Sally: Why not?
Harry: Men and women can't be friends because the sex part always
    gets in the way.
Sally: That's not true! I have a number of men friends and there is
    no sex involved.
Harry: No you don't.
Sally: Yes I do!
Harry: You only think you do.
Sally: You're saying that I'm having sex with these men without my
    knowledge?

Harry: No. What I'm saying is that they all want to have sex with
you . . . Because no man can be friends with a woman that he
finds attractive. He always wants to have sex with her.

Sally (smugly): So you're saying that a man can be friends with a
woman he finds unattractive.

Harry (thinks it over): No, you pretty much want to nail them, too.

What does this mean for the workplace? Does this male/female difference give women a built-in advantage, as Hakim suggests?

In the past, employed women were overwhelmingly junior and low-
status. They might find a husband and "progress" out of work into
marriage. They might also be harassed by the more powerful men they
worked for—as, in some places, they still can be. When power is completely unequal, Hakim's sexual "imbalance of supply and demand" is
only a small part of the picture.

However, in modern developed societies, women are no longer barred
from well-paid jobs and careers, and sexual harassment is increasingly
both illegal and socially unacceptable. Hakim is then surely right to see
"erotic capital" as a potential source of competitive advantage at work,
albeit one to be treated with care. It was something I asked all of my
younger female interviewees about, and something on which they were
all agreed. Yes, the sexual element is there. And yes, some women use it.

Kerry Miller is a vice president at Goldman Sachs. I met her at their
vast headquarters building in lower Manhattan: a weird mixture of
Lords of the Universe and hotel conference suite, with two tiny reception
desks marooned in the echoing space of the entrance hall, nowhere for
visitors to sit and some great art on the walls. Kerry is tiny, blond, perfectly dressed—cashmere, suede, beautiful shoes, low-key makeup—and
she told me that "I'm going to speak on behalf of my women friends in
finance, we talk about this, it's a reality. Women do use it, especially, I
would say, women in sales roles. Yes, 100 percent. I had this friend at
Barclays and one day we met for a drink, and I was, like, wow, you look
fantastic. And she was, yeah, I had a meeting with so-and-so today, so
I wanted to play it up. She's a brilliant girl, as smart as it gets, but that
extra she can play off of—she would."

Does it work? It's obviously hard to find out what happens in the
worlds of bond sales, private equity and trading floors. But it definitely
works for fund-raising. A research study by a group of University of
Chicago economists showed very clearly that door-to-door fund-raising

works much better—indeed twice as well—when it is done by attractive women.[28] Compared to other doorstep solicitors, attractive white females were significantly more likely to get contributions. This was mostly when and because men answered the door. And gentlemen do prefer blondes; Caucasian men do anyway. A follow-up study comparing the fund-raising success of girls who all had equally high beauty ratings found that blondes did best of all, because white men gave them more.[29]

CORPORATE CAUTION

Calling up your "erotic capital" can backfire, of course. As the American Psychological Association has established, a woman who applies for a professional-level job dressed in an overtly sexy way is much less likely to be considered for it than someone dressed conservatively.[30] More generally, if you are involved in a long-term working relationship, rather than a one-time sales encounter, being too overt will mean you're not taken seriously.

Kerry Miller, working in compensation and recruitment strategy, explains that, compared to her New York friends in sales, "actually I pull back. I'm at an operating committee meeting here, with the senior managers, every two weeks, and I tone down my personality. I normally have a suit on, my hair back. Probably if they saw me outside of work they would be shocked, because I'm so friendly, big personality, and I'm the complete opposite with a lot of them. Because I want them to see that I have my eye on the prize and I know what I want to communicate and let's get the job done."

Senior managers, and especially human resource chiefs, are terrified of sex-in-the-office. Visions of harassment suits dance in front of their eyes. At extremes, they erect sandbags in the form of strict rules about language, physical contact, meetings, relationships outside the workplace. It is a bit like trying to dam the Amazon: many people mentioned, and wouldn't name, colleagues and ex-colleagues who had furthered their careers via full-blown affairs. But the codes, and the worries, do affect office behavior. Especially in America, or so Laura Mercadier has concluded.

Laura is the Paris-born banker whom I've quoted above on the subjects of babies, wealth and the ultra-hierarchical nature of French higher education. She has worked with Credit Agricole and BNP Paribas, and, when we talked in her airy apartment in west London, had moved to the private banking side of Credit Suisse, dealing with the bank's rich individual .clients. But she got her start in finance on a New York trading floor.

"It was a very, very good experience. It was very young people, and you felt very much in a team. There were just two women. But I liked this kind of environment, because it was playful; and for me, Americans with women at work, they are a pain. Because they feel like they cannot talk to you normally. And I'm a very blunt and happy person, I've not been raised with that kind of political correctness. I didn't really enjoy the relationship with some Americans at the office. This was the only thing I didn't like. Because they 'take distance.' It's pretty much the opposite of how you should be with each other, so it's a bit weird, you feel ostracized, pulled apart. But then it's the culture and you have to understand the culture if you want to be involved in this American world. And it is not true in London at all.

"I think when a woman is very professional, very good, brings new ideas, and she also speaks like a woman, likes to joke or charm a little bit, because it's part of a woman, then it's very good. It's ten times better than a man. So I don't see why you would try to be like a man to please them, because for me it's not as effective. It's more effective being as good as them in content but in the delivery still like a woman. Not flirty, just charming. Giving a warm feeling. I would hate myself if I would become a very successful woman but lost my feminine side. For me that's a failure."

Few men will object to the presence of pretty girls determined to charm (even if some of them are a bit paranoid on office territory). And as Laura pointed out to me, banking, like a lot of other occupations, is very much about personal contacts and address books: "You're twenty-five, in the markets, you need to build up your networks, you have a lot of energy, you go out every night, you meet people, they're interested in you for whatever you bring to them. Plus I think women are very social when they're young, especially before they have kids. So I think it was kind of innate; it was easy for me to meet people, to introduce myself, tell them what I was doing. And especially in the finance industry, everybody is interested to know what you do in your bank, what you sell, what could be an advantage . . ."

Attractive women in sales, good-looking women collecting a lot of money on the doorstep for charity: they are clear examples of Catherine

Hakim's notion of "erotic capital," and of how men's sexual responses can work for women. The "distance" that Laura refers to is the flip side: a pulling back, often for good reason, that can work against them.

In the next few "mixed gender" meetings you're in, take a look at how people choose to sit. You'll find women taking a seat next to another woman, or in small female groups, far more often than you'd expect if seating choices were random. Men (fortunately?) don't notice. My husband thought I was talking nonsense till he did as I asked and started watching. And then checked with the next three really successful women he talked to—a CEO, a journalist, a politician—all of whom told him that yes, that did indeed happen.

We are hardly dealing here with women who are scared to open their mouths in meetings. So it must, I think, be about avoidance—about not, inadvertently, sending the wrong signals to men by where you choose to sit. Like so much of our social behavior, it involves decisions so instant and unconsidered that they are largely instinctual.[31] What has changed is that giving and avoiding giving sexual signals are now a far larger part of work life than in the past.

Lee Ann Daly, formerly of Thomson Reuters, with experience in a variety of business settings, told me that "one of the real challenges, in the upper half of organizations, continues to be getting men to feel comfortable knowing more junior women and having the kind of relaxed relationship that they can have around more junior men. Say you're the senior-most level and you want to cultivate a relationship with a woman who's three levels down, it looks weird. I think that so many times young men get selected for stretch roles and opportunity roles because there's just a greater comfort level there. It's 'Bob will do a great job because I know Bob and we're friends' versus 'Cindy . . . boy, she's done really top-notch work but I haven't actually spent time with her.' If you were to talk to my boss, for example, he'd say, 'Oh, it's not taboo for me to go and have lunch with somebody three levels below me who's female.' But how much does he actually do it?"

Thinking back to how she got promoted in the past, she remembered an advertising agency where "frankly part of it was because I had gone on a couple of road trips with the president of the agency, up to Toronto, and been stuck in an airport eating Canadian candy bars and talking about the difference between the Mars bar in the USA and Canada . . . stupid little things, except they're not. You have to have idle time getting to know the other person."

So, on the one side, being pretty, being sexy, can help. Women signal automatically; men automatically respond. And first impressions, as we know, can be very important (and quite often correct).[32]

But on both sides, a determination not to give the wrong signals, a desire to avoid sexual encounters, can also work against women. And does some of that quasi-automatic behavior, that "being feminine," lead to women behaving, around men, in ways that hold them back?

DO WOMEN ASK?

Just the other day, at a London event, I heard a well-known female columnist singing the praises of a recent program on the BBC. There had been three economists discussing the latest dismal news, she said, all women, and the moderator was female too. "And they were all so nice and polite and kept saying how much they admired the others' work. Not like men would be at all."

Well, maybe. Perhaps the producers just failed to find a good cross-section of economic opinion that evening. Two weeks after that conversation I was at a symposium in Amsterdam. There were three economists on the platform, all male; and the moderator was male as well. And they were all very nice and very polite and they all kept praising each other's work as well.

There is some much-publicized evidence that "women don't ask" for a high starting salary, a raise, a promotion, in situations where men would.[33] There is also well-publicized research suggesting that, in specially staged competitive environments, women are more likely than men to shy away from competition, and men to embrace it.[34] There's evidence that higher testosterone levels lead to greater risk-taking and, on real trading floors, are associated with greater success.[35] And then there is a whole wealth of evidence showing that boys tend to be much more physically aggressive and openly competitive than girls in the way they play, and in their liking for teams, games and keeping score.[36]

It is this sort of research that leads some people to argue that women will never break through glass ceilings without special help;[37] and others to speculate that, if there had been more women involved in finance ("Lehman Sisters"), the banking crashes of 2008 would never have happened.[38]

Yet overall, the evidence from psychology is—as so often—surprisingly mixed. Women don't always hold back in mixed company; and even when the men are clearly competing harder, the absolute differences are not always as large as you might imagine from the headlines. As for "not asking," being less aggressive at work, more risk-averse: yes, the evidence suggests there are male–female differences, and yes, they may be hardwired. But we also know that young men and women these days earn the same, like for like. So even if there are these differences, they don't seem to be having any very serious effects.

On balance, young women today probably benefit from the sexual signals and sexual dynamics of the mixed workplace. And certainly all the successful young women I interviewed for this book were attractive too. That wasn't my intention: my interviewees were friends of friends, colleagues of colleagues. But every single one was slim and groomed, with good hair, good skin and good clothes. I would also bet a lot of money that, if I'd been interviewing their male counterparts, I'd have found almost exactly the same thing: maybe a couple of exceptions, but no more than that.

Being good-looking, being slim and radiating good health are all sexually attractive. But the signaling involved goes well beyond the sexual, because the things to which men and women respond are not random sexually or otherwise. They have bedded down in our species because they are signs of a general "fitness."

People with certain characteristics are likely to make good mates because they are more likely to be healthy, long-lived and successful. They seem likely not just to breed but also to keep the children alive and well. But as humans, our adult lives are about a lot more than reproduction and giving the impression that you are a good bet as a parent. In these other parts of our lives first impressions also matter. In order to do well, we need to convey to other people that we are competent, trustworthy, superior, someone they want to hire and have around. One of the ways we do it is through the characteristics associated with sexual attraction; things that other people respond to automatically, but for good reason.

That is why signaling is not just directly sexual, but general. It is an important part of why beauty pays, and good-looking lawyers earn more. And it is why appearances, and the responses they evoke, don't fade into irrelevance once a professional woman hits her late thirties. As we can infer from a peacock's tail.

PEACOCKS' TAILS AND COSTLY SIGNALING
Upriver from London, the Thames boasts a succession of manicured riverside pubs. On sunny days, you can drink in the company of Thames

Path walkers, owners of small boats, waterbirds, and, at my favorite, peacocks.[39] The cocks stroll around among the drinkers and the peahens, displaying their extraordinary tails on a regular basis. They also fly up to the pub roof, to make their ugly calls. If you only ever saw the birds on the ground, you wouldn't think such flying was possible; and in a world of fast-moving predators—wild cats, foxes—these tails seem crazy. Which is why they have fascinated evolutionary biologists from Darwin on.

Darwin deduced that, way back, peahens started to prefer mating with males who had large showy tails. This meant that the larger the tail, the more offspring a peacock was likely to have, and over time tails got bigger and bigger still. But why would dowdy, sensibly camouflaged peahens prefer this to a lean, mean fast-flying bird? "Costly signaling" is the answer.

Costly signaling is behavior that is very costly in terms of resources—time, energy, risk or, in humans, money—and also conveys information that has potentially big returns for the signaler. For example, a huge tail takes energy to grow and maintain, and handicaps and endangers its owner. But a peacock with a fine tail therefore proclaims that he is physically a fine, strong and fit specimen who can easily cope with all these demands. And is a desirable mate.

Among nonhuman species, signaling is all about mating and choosing a good parent for your offspring. Among humans it goes much further. We are also interested in choosing people for a much wider range of activities. However, the basic problem is the same. There is a lot about people that we don't know and we are trying to evaluate their future potential as well as their current worth, as employees, employers, trustees, political leaders.

This is even harder in today's large and complex human societies than it was in the small groups of our hunter-gatherer past. As we saw in Chapter 5, one reason why there is such intense competition to enter a select few of the world's universities is the signal that their degree certificates send: not about "reproductive fitness"—that is, the likelihood you'll produce top-quality offspring—but about your intelligence, application and general fitness for top jobs.

Certificates, however, only take you so far. A lot of human signaling remains face-to-face, whether it's for elected office, the CEO's suite or just the good graces of someone you want on your side at work. There, first impressions take in physical attributes, but also the way you dress and behave, and what these seem to say about your backstory. To understand just how powerful these signals can be, look at the story of Alexander Korda.

PERCEIVING AND DECEIVING

Alexander Korda, the legendary pre-war film director, was a naturally brilliant signaler who understood two things. First, signals are just that: they are not the reality and so they can be faked. As the world's greatest evolutionary biologists emphasize, in relation to the whole animal kingdom, "Any animal that can perceive can be deceived."[40] And second that, if you are bidding for the top, costly signals are the way to go. Korda knew that things that are expensive and visible proclaim your possession of a really valuable characteristic, whether it's wealth, health or intelligence.[41]

Korda was born into a Jewish family in a tiny settlement on the vast, featureless Hungarian plains. His father died when he was just thirteen, leaving the family penniless; his initial efforts to succeed in Paris ended with his being sent home to Hungary as a charity case. But soon after, starting as an errand boy in the experimental world of pre–First World War cinema, he first became a director and then raised the money to buy out his studios. "He . . . discovered that you can get somebody else to put up all the money for a company, still own half of it yourself *and* manage it as you please!" as his nephew and biographer explains.[42]

In the chaos of inter-war Europe, this was a feat he had to repeat time and again, as countries disintegrated, economies failed and central Europe became increasingly unsafe for Jews. His advice to his family was "Always go the best hotel and eat at the best restaurants—and sooner or later someone will appear who will give you money."[43] He dressed well; his appearance was impeccable; he always lived like a millionaire even when he was far from being one. Don't ask for appointments with bankers, he advised, which is a signal that you want something from them. Instead invite them to dinners full of beautiful people they want to meet. "After that you can sit a banker down with a glass of brandy and a good cigar and propose to him something he wouldn't even *listen* to in his office."[44]

It helps to have Korda's level of charm. And, of course, it mattered that he could and did make fine and memorable films with the money he raised. But what he was explaining here is the quintessence of costly signaling.

Research on beauty confirms, time and again, that in the labor market, men benefit or suffer just as much as women: for example, as we saw earlier, male lawyers with good looks gain just as much as good-looking female ones. This seems puzzling at first, since women place much less weight on appearances than men do when choosing husbands: fecundity matters less to women, resources more. However, as we have just seen, signaling by humans goes well beyond specifically sexual encounters. We see physical characteristics as evidence of underlying quality; we like to be among the successful and able. And we definitely like to think that the people we hire are from the top half of the distribution.

Talking about "beauty" makes people think of facial features, but that is only part of it. Body weight and height also matter. Of course, there are individual exceptions; but tall men do significantly better in the labor market than shorter ones, after controlling for education, class, race and general health. And it is not just the very short who suffer a penalty; men in the whole bottom fifth for height are significantly affected.[45] People associate height in men with strength, energy and resources, which is why short male politicians often wear stacked heels; and the labor market data indicate that our perceptions translate into concrete advantage.

Obesity, meanwhile, is bad for your earnings as well as your health, especially if you're a woman. In laboratory studies, people claim they won't discriminate against the obese, and then go ahead and do just that.[46] Labor market data for the US and the UK confirm that obese women really suffer for their weight, even more than men do for their height.

This isn't just because obesity is more common among the poor, although it is. The finding holds true even after controlling for education, family background and health. Obese white women earn a lot less on average than their otherwise-similar peers.[47] I suspect this goes well beyond aesthetics and signals of fecundity. In modern societies, which value slimness and sport, an obese woman is "read" as someone who has little self-control or ability to stick at something difficult (like exercise or a diet). This is then generalized into their likely value as an employee.[48]

All of this helps explain why, in 2010, "of the sixteen female United States senators between ages fifty-six and seventy-four, not one has visible gray hair; nor do 90 percent of the women in the House of Representatives."[49]

Academic lawyer Deborah Rhode, who pointed this out in her attack on the "beauty bias," finds it demeaning verging on despicable. But these women are behaving in a rational and sensible way. As rising UK politician Liz Truss explained to me: "In politics, one's gender is quite an important factor in the way people look at you. If you're an analyst or an accountant, the output is the set of accounts, the report. Whereas if you're a politician the output is the person. Your physical appearance is more important, the way your voice sounds, your backstory, all of those are important in a way they're not in many other careers. And the initial impression is very strong."

Initial impressions are critical for undecided voters on the eve of an election. They are critical on the campaign trail. In the UK system, they are critical in getting your party's nomination. Local branches of the major parties decide on their candidate at selection meetings at which shortlisted contenders speak and are quizzed. Your performance at such a meeting and the image you project decide your fate.

None of this is specific to women. Elderly Chinese male politicians all have black hair because it's dyed, not because the Chinese don't go gray. But signaling and first impressions have very particular implications for women, because looking young and looking healthy, with gleaming hair and clear skin, are prime female signals.[50]

If you're a female politician, you don't try to look like a would-be topless model. But you do, for very good reason, try to look slim, healthy, attractive and reasonably young. The US senators who worry about gray hairs are not trying to attract mates; their ages are matters of public record, and they are interested in power and influence, not reproduction. They know, however, that age in women is not associated with power and fitness: it is the wrong signal and not one they want to emit. And I bet none of them is obese, either.

THE BEAUTY INDUSTRY

It is because female appearances count for so much that great fortunes were built on cosmetics and creams. Liliane Bettencourt, sole heiress to the L'Oréal fortune, is one of the world's richest women; the Lauder and Revson family fortunes are built on perfumes and creams.[51] But the beauty industry was, until recently, heavily oriented toward the young.

Today, there has been a real shift, not just in ambition and scale—cosmetic surgery, body sculpting and fillers, hair extensions and transplants—but in the industry's "demographic": the people who provide it with substantial portions of its revenue. More and more of them are successful working women, not just in their thirties and forties but in their fifties and sixties too.

My friend Peggy recently hosted a sixtieth-birthday get-together. Ever since I've known her, she has managed to combine looking utterly elegant at any time of day or night with three children, an impeccable home and a full-time, ongoing semi-political career.

"You look fabulous," I said, which was the truth.

"Well, I guess I should. The amount I'm paying my colorist, I could fund a preschool program."

Nonsurgical beauty treatments are a huge and growing industry, with the advantage of a lot of repeat trade. Botox has to be topped up; so do fillers. Skin peels need repeating. Dr. Roy Lowe is one of the world's leading "beauty" dermatologists, a Botox pioneer who practices in both London and California. He just recently began to offer Saturday clinics and appointments, and they were instantly oversubscribed. But then, Saturday best suits the growing number of full-time, overstretched professional women working to keep up their appearance.

It's not that women in the past stopped thinking about their looks entirely the moment they married or turned forty. That would be a nonsensical claim. People like to look good because of the attention and status and self-respect it brings. And since being married for life didn't necessarily mean being happily married for life, there were strong reasons to help marital relationships along by looking good for your husband. "She did him credit," said of a well-dressed, good-looking wife on someone's arm, gets to the heart of how status works in any human society.

But as plenty of people before me have pointed out, women in the past didn't work anything like as hard as we do to look twenty years younger than they were. They went gray. They put on weight. Some of the shift is because of changing divorce laws. When marriage is for life, wives aren't concerned about sexual competition from other females to the extent they are today. The speed with which the dumpy Italian housewife vanished post–legalized divorce was extraordinary.

But much of the change is because of the workplace, not divorce and marriage. Professional women in their fifties are not in the business of having babies. They are very much in the business of chasing and holding a serious job. That is a large part of why, in the UK, the cosmetic surgery industry has an estimated £2.3 billion turnover;[52] while in the US, there were nearly 14 million cosmetic plastic surgery procedures in

2011 alone, costing somewhere between $10 billion and $13 billion. And according to the American Society for Aesthetic Plastic Surgery, about nine out of ten cosmetic surgery patients are women.[53]

There is a huge amount of money being spent here. Projecting health and youth as you get older can be not just very expensive, but hard work too: just look at all those male politicians out for runs with their personal trainers. But the basic asymmetry between the sexes does mean that, among the successful middle-aged, women put proportionately far more work, and far more cash, into their appearance than men.

Which brings us back to that surprisingly recession-proof sector of luxury goods and high-end fashion. As we saw in Chapter 6, this is a rapidly growing part of the consumer market, selling increasingly to women who spend their own earned money. It is growing and also changing: not just because women are wealthier in their own right, but also because of what they spend their money on and why.

MAKING A STATEMENT

Dressing neutrally is a contradiction in terms. Uniforms can be imposed on you, as they are on soldiers, prisoners and many schoolchildren. They then proclaim your status and position to anyone you meet. Otherwise, every time you choose what to wear, you are telling the world what sort of person you are, or how you wish to be seen. High-school students dress like the rest of their clique. Male defendants turn up to court clean-shaven, hair cut short, in suit, shirt and tie. As feminist Susan Brownmiller complained, "Who said 'clothes make a statement'? What an understatement that was. Clothes never shut up."[54]

Clothes have always been an important way of signaling wealth and status. This isn't just about women's clothes. The world's art galleries, palaces and stately homes are full of "swagger portraits" that proclaim the wealth and taste of both male and female sitters through the clothes they wear. There are silk, braid and velvet; glorious armor; gorgeous jewels. The wealthy seventeenth-century burghers of Holland's golden years wore Calvinist black and then showed off their wealth with the size and fine quality of their lace ruffs and shirt cuffs.

Today is no different, though the swagger is a little more subtle. Academic lawyer Deborah Rhode complains, "During my term as chair of the American Bar Association's Commission on Women in the Profession, I was struck by how often some of the nation's most prominent and powerful women were stranded in cab lines and late for meetings because walking any distance was out of the question."

She thinks their taste for vertiginous heels is crazy and dysfunctional. I disagree: on the contrary, it involves signaling in just the same way as dressing for your day in court, or spreading your peacock's tail. The heels proclaim that their wearers are wealthy, stylish and therefore not ready to be pensioned off; that they spend their time on soft carpets, not pounding the city streets, and that they are rich enough to take taxis, often. Of course, to get the full message, you need to recognize that the shoe in question is a Manolo rather than a cheap catalog purchase. But most women will manage that without much difficulty.

Men's clothes today are much less colorful than in the past, and the world's professionals and businessmen dress similarly, in suits, blazers, overcoats. Even so, there are plenty of ways to signal both wealth and taste. The *Financial Times* has a weekly "power dressing" feature in which top business people—mostly men—talk about what they are wearing, and why. *FT* fashion editor Vanessa Friedman says, "It usually takes about fifteen minutes of wheedling. First of all, especially if it's men, they say, 'I don't think about what I wear at all.' And then you say, well, when you go to a meeting do you always wear a tie? Do you look at people's shoes? And they actually get quite involved in it. It's not about the object in a vacuum. It's about the way they relate to people, and what sort of people they want to be. Consciously or not consciously, people use fashion to say something about themselves."

However, while men also dress to impress, especially in those crucial first few minutes of a presentation, meeting or sales pitch, women's clothes attract far more attention and dedication from wearers and observers alike. People sometimes comment that "women dress for other women," as though this shows deep irrationality. It is true, and totally rational.

Women dress to attract men and they dress to impress men. They also dress to impress other women—in the past, as rivals in mating, marriage and society,[55] these days as rivals in the workplace too. Women dress, in other words, to show other women what sort of people they are.

In the past, high-status clothes were by definition clothes in which you couldn't do a hard day's labor. They proclaimed that you did not need to. This is as true of a dress kimono in Japan as it is of the buttoned dresses and corsets of the nineteenth-century West, which no one could get into or out of without a maid to help. Today, however, successful women are employed. They therefore need clothes that tell the world that they are serious working professionals: they are not the maid, not a housewife and not a trophy wife either.

For a short time, it looked as though working women would simply mimic Western men's working uniform. Businesswoman Lynn Forester de Rothschild, a couture client, remembers that when she started in business thirty years back "I dressed in a blue suit, white shirt, low pumps, hair pulled back. A friend said, 'You look like an air hostess.' We all did."

It couldn't last. Why would any millionaire businesswoman, or any top female lawyer, want to look indistinguishable from an air hostess or a middle-manager for Sears? They wouldn't, and they no longer do.

We have already met the high heels, signaling wealth, taste and "fitness." More generally, over the last twenty or thirty years, new sorts of working clothes have evolved that signal "elite woman." They are instantly recognizable as office wear, but also clearly expensive and high status—and a lot less monotonous than the male equivalent. The *FT*'s Vanessa Friedman, an acid observer of the "dark blue suit, white shirt and blue tie" syndrome (UK male politicos) and the "dark blue suit, white shirt and red tie" syndrome (American ones),[56] argues that "really expensive [women's] clothes done well deserve their price tag, they make you feel absolutely appropriate and functional. So you can run around waving your arms trying to get a cab, and you can lean over, and nothing will show and nothing will escape. I think that, if you're running a company, that is worth quite a lot of money."

Christine Lagarde, former French finance minister and current head of the International Monetary Fund, made the 2011 *Vanity Fair* best-dressed list with exactly this kind of dressing. It's the black/gray/cream/taupe palette; beautifully cut dresses, trousers that don't crease; natural fabrics. In Lagarde's case, it's mostly Chanel, though not at all the instantly recognizable gilt and multicolored tweed end of that label. This is low-key, serious, working-woman stuff. She and the clothes look great. And it is definitely very costly signaling.

The importance of good dressing is likely to increase, for the simple reason that there are more women out there, competing with each other and trying to impress both male and female clients and superiors. Moreover, the apparent exceptions tend to prove the rule. One of the few major professions in which dressing well is not important, and even frowned on, is my own, namely academia. This isn't from poverty. Academics are reasonably well paid, unless you take corporate lawyers and bankers as your benchmark; and while it is true that they want to project seriousness and intellect, there are plenty of very smart female trade unionists and left-wing politicians.

The key point is surely that academia is one of the few professions where you can make reliable objective judgments of individual people's work, over time. Academics have publications you can examine; grants gained by them, personally, and the grades their students award for teaching quality. There is less payoff to costly signaling in this context and so less pressure to engage in it. In most other occupations, the precise contribution and achievement of a single individual are much harder to assess for anyone outside their team, let alone their workplace. Costly signaling is therefore a lot more effective. And with us for the long term.

11

ONE OF YOUR OWN KIND

"One of your own kind, stick to your own kind!" sings Puerto Rican Anita in *West Side Story*. But when we watch Maria ignore Anita's advice out of love for white-boy Tony, or Juliet calling down to Romeo from her balcony, or Verdi's *La Traviata*, whose doomed courtesan loves upper-class Alfredo, our hearts are with the heroines.

And in real life? Most people take Anita's advice. They marry their own kind.

Social scientists have a word for own-kind marriages. They are an example of "assortative mating": males and females mating with partners who are like them in the ways that matter for lifetime success. Around the world, assortative mating has always been common and the marriage market a cold-blooded affair. As Jane Austen pointed out in one of literature's most famous sentences, "It is a truth universally acknowledged that a single man in possession of a good fortune must be in want of a wife."[1] But the richer the family, the more tightly they controlled marriages, and the more these were negotiated on the basis of wealth and family status.

Today, most people are free to follow their hearts. But it turns out that we follow them in a largely materialistic direction. Assortative mating is actually on the rise. As more women develop successful careers, men are free to use the same criteria as women traditionally did when weighing up potential husbands; and it seems that they do just that. Increasingly, successful men and women marry each other.

WHO MARRIES WHOM?

In fairy stories, a goose-girl may marry a prince. But in late-twentieth-century America, the odds that high-school dropouts would "marry up" in educational terms fell substantially for both men and women.[2] A high-school graduate and a college graduate were much less likely to marry each other in the late 1980s than they had been in 1940; college graduates in particular became less and less likely to marry down. By the turn of the twenty-first century, there was only about a one in ten chance that a female college graduate would be married to a high-school graduate (let alone to a high-school dropout).[3]

Women often suspect that men like to marry women much less intelligent, or educated, than themselves. If that were true, they could certainly go on doing so—but they don't.[4] On the contrary, "the like likes the like."[5]

Male doctors, in the past, couldn't expect or plan to marry female doctors, because there weren't many. Male business executives couldn't marry female ones. They married nurses and secretaries instead. Equally, many more able and academically successful girls became nurses and secretaries in the past than now. Today, the educational attainment of men and women is far more equal than it was.

But that isn't the whole story.[6] Increases in educational matching and mating go beyond what you'd expect simply from the increase in women with bachelor's and graduate degrees.

In France, for example, graduation rates have soared, as they have everywhere else. But even allowing for this, there is an "increasing aversion" to marrying someone with a different educational level. People marry within it twice as often as you would expect if education didn't matter.[7]

In the UK, researchers again find increasing rates of educational matching, with the biggest increases involving graduates marrying graduates.[8] You can see this happening among top British politicians. The male prime ministers who preceded and followed Mrs. Thatcher had "traditional" wives. But then there came a generational shift; and among today's party leaders and rising stars, it is all two-career, high-flying partnerships involving lawyers, designers, journalists, senior civil servants and company directors.[9]

In Israel, it's the same. Graduate men have become far less likely to marry "down," instead marrying fellow graduates. Meanwhile women, since they are now equally educated, marry "up" less—but are also much less likely to marry "down" than they were in the 1980s.[10] So too in Italy and the Netherlands, so too in Germany and Slovenia. There are individual exceptions, of course,[11] but increasingly people marry someone at the same educational level.[12]

The sorting isn't just by education either. Money married and still marries money. Partly, it is because education and earning power are closely related. But only partly. Researchers interviewed women who were teenagers in the 1970s, 1980s and 1990s, and subsequently married, and looked at the current and likely future earnings of their husbands, using not just husbands' education, but occupation and current earnings too. They found that the women with the highest current earnings tended to have the husbands with the highest current earnings; and that, over those decades, high-earning women became *increasingly* likely to marry men with high expected earnings.[13]

Moreover, among American married couples in the late 1980s, husbands and wives were vastly more likely to have the same level of parental wealth behind them than one would predict if wealth were irrelevant to getting wed. This is surprising, because in rich and growing societies there are more opportunities for people to make, rather than inherit, money. And it is not just because the more educated tend to be from wealthier backgrounds, even before they start earning. Parental wealth mattered even after controlling for education.[14]

In *Bobos in Paradise*, his book on the new American elite, *New York Times* columnist David Brooks observes modern assortative mating, as displayed weekly in his paper's wedding pages. In the late 1950s, he writes:

> wedding accounts . . . didn't emphasize jobs or advanced degrees.
> The profession of the groom was only sometimes mentioned, while
> the profession of the bride was almost never listed. . . . Ancestors
> were frequently mentioned . . . Even the captions would be
> unthinkable today: "Mrs. Peter J. Belton who was Nancy Stevens."
>
> [Today] I'm not sure I'd like to be one of the people featured on
> the *New York Times* weddings page, but I know I'd like to be the
> father of one. Imagine how happy Stanley J. Kogan must have been,
> for example, when his daughter Jamie was admitted to Yale. Then
> imagine his pride when Jamie made Phi Beta Kappa and graduated
> summa cum laude . . . Jamie breezed through Stanford Law School.
> And then she met a man who . . . did his undergraduate work at
> Princeton, where he, too, graduated summa cum laude. And he, too,
> went to law school, at Yale . . .
>
> These two awesome résumés collided at a wedding ceremony in

Manhattan . . . The rest of us got to read about it on the *New York Times* weddings page . . .

When America had a pedigreed elite, the page emphasized noble birth and breeding . . . [Today] it's Dartmouth marries Berkeley, MBA weds Ph.D., Fulbright hitches with Rhodes, and summa cum laude embraces summa cum laude (you rarely see a summa settling for a magna—the tension in such a marriage would be too great).[15]

So, in fairy stories, penniless girls marry princes; and in the twenty-first century, alpha men may manage to land a high-earning wife. But why should assortative mating be on the increase? And how does it actually happen?

AN EXCEPTIONAL SPECIES

We humans don't just mate. We marry. Ours is the only species that makes a formal separation between mating and a legal state of marriage (though other species practice long-term relationships, and what looks very much like adultery).

We are also alone in having separated mating from reproduction. As Chapter 8 described, reliable birth control has brought with it huge changes in human sexual behavior. "Respectable" people can and do have lots of sex outside marriage. Many successful women today don't marry. Many less successful women don't marry either: a decline in overall marriage rates characterizes every single developed society. But that doesn't mean that they have given up sex.

And, starting very recently, we have separated reproduction— childbirth—from marriage on a hitherto undreamed-of scale. In Western societies childbirth increasingly often happens outside marriage. Illegitimacy and single-motherhood exist at levels that would have been inconceivable even half a century ago.

And yet marriage still matters. Especially at the top.

The number of out-of-wedlock births has exploded. But they remain very rare among the successful. Divorce is increasingly common everywhere. But it is much less common among the affluent and educated. There, the majority, once married, stay that way.

In the developed West—though not the developed East, as we'll see later—marriage is actually becoming more common for graduate than non-graduate women. As a result, 2008 statistics showed for the first time ever that American graduate women were more likely to have married by age thirty than non-graduates.[16] They weren't more likely to be mothers—quite the opposite; but a higher proportion had married, while a far smaller proportion were unmarried mothers. Older American women, aged thirty to forty-four, are much more likely to be (still) married if they are graduates than non-graduates. Why?

The answer lies, as always, with the choices individuals make, albeit within a context of social change. Most men and women still want to marry, and see marriage as the best background for bringing up children. And in the past, child-bearing took place overwhelmingly within marriage because, as we will see, it was the only way to rear human children successfully, on a society-wide scale.

Today, many poor women, in the US and elsewhere, have almost no marriageable men on offer but can survive as single mothers, and are so from the start.[17] Our focus, however, is on the top. And here, there are strong incentives and disincentives of a very different sort.

RINGS ON THEIR FINGERS?

A lot of people remember, correctly, that successful and highly educated women used very often to be single. If you grew up in the 1960s, 1970s or 1980s, you were very probably taught by female teachers who had been born pre-war, and possibly treated by a female doctor of that same generation. For both these groups there was still a stark and evident choice between marriage and career, as there had been for the educated women before them.

At Vassar, alumnae records show that over a third of the graduating classes of 1902–1906 never married; a decade later, it was still over a quarter.[18] Among all American women born in 1890, those with college degrees were four times as likely to remain unmarried as women without degrees. The 1950 US Census showed that 93 percent of non-graduate women in their mid- to late fifties were or had been married, but only two-thirds of college graduates.[19] Even among women born in 1950, female graduates were still half as likely again as non-graduates to stay single. In contrast, for men of these earlier generations there was no difference between graduates and non-graduates in propensity to marry.[20]

Today, marrying is increasingly a graduate pursuit. Bluestocking girls, girls-who-wear-glasses, nowadays marry, in the US, as often overall as other women and a lot more often than some types of women do. People tend to find this implausible. What about all those career women?

What about the growing numbers of childless graduates described in Chapter 2, many of whom are also unmarried? And, indeed, they exist. But there are also very large and growing numbers of non-graduate women who are unmarried. This is partly because people marry later; but largely because so many never marry at all.

Marriage rates have plummeted across the whole of Europe.[21] In America, rates are still fairly high by rich-world standards, and the decline has been fairly slow for whites (though very fast for blacks).[22] Substantial declines there have nonetheless been.[23] Meanwhile, in the European Union as a whole, over a third of all live births in 2009 were to unmarried women. In France, Sweden and Norway, it was well over 50 percent; in Belgium, Denmark and the UK, in the upper 40s.[24] In the US, the overall figure is about 40 percent.

However, these averages conceal enormous differences between different groups. Graduates and non-graduates, in particular, are progressively parting company. Figure 11.1 illustrates this, using data for contemporary America. (I have used figures for whites only, because there are enormous differences among racial and ethnic groups. However, *within* these groups, the differences between graduates and non-graduates are always marked.)[25]

Figure 11.1 shows both the gulf between graduates and dropouts and how very few graduates have out-of-wedlock births today. Moreover,

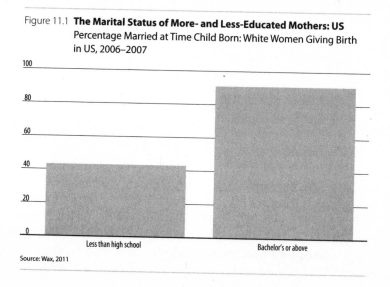

Figure 11.1 **The Marital Status of More- and Less-Educated Mothers: US**
Percentage Married at Time Child Born: White Women Giving Birth in US, 2006–2007

Source: Wax, 2011

there has also been little change among graduates in the last fifty years. *Less than 5 percent of births to white American graduate mothers were extramarital in 1965 and less than 5 percent are today.* As Amy Wax points out, "Well-off whites have largely maintained traditional patterns of family."[26] Meanwhile, among high-school dropouts the numbers of single mothers have soared.

In the UK, graduates are more likely to have out-of-wedlock births than American graduates are. But British graduate mothers—and graduate fathers—are still much more likely to be married than not. Among the cohabiting parents of UK babies born in 2000, about 85 percent of graduate fathers and mothers—more than five out of six—were married, compared to 70 percent of cohabiting couples overall.[27] New mothers who were single at the birth—neither married nor cohabiting—were overwhelmingly from lower educational groups. Only one in thirty British mothers with a full bachelor's degree or above was single at the time they gave birth,[28] and throughout the West, out-of-wedlock births are far more common among less-educated (and poorer) women than they are among the educated and the financially secure.

To understand how and why this is happening, we need to think about what it takes to rear a child: not just to have a baby, but to rear it successfully to adulthood. Humans are, obviously, very different from other creatures—not least, though not only, in their invention of both marriage and contraception. But to understand our current behavior, and why it changed so quickly, a good place to start is the primates, the order of mammals to which we, *Homo sapiens*, belong.[29] All primates share some common problems in child-rearing. And understanding what is constant also helps to explain why our particular human solutions have changed.

BIRTH IS JUST THE START OF THINGS

Male humans, like other male primates, have the physical capacity to father a very large number of offspring.[30] Women, like other female primates, have a fixed and limited number of eggs. Human babies take nine months to mature in the womb and then need very regular suckling over long periods.[31] In this we are out at the extreme, but still basically in line with other primates. Compare a baby monkey, helpless and clinging tightly to its mother's back, with a newborn foal, ready to move off behind its mother, let alone a baby turtle, hatching and heading off alone for the sea.

Males need to impregnate a female in order to reproduce, and one obvious way to increase their chances is by having sex with as many females as possible. In Chapter 10, I quoted a famous interchange from the film *When Harry Met Sally*. Harry tells Sally that "no man can be friends with a woman that he finds attractive. He always wants to have sex with her." And when Sally retorts that in that case a man can be friends with a woman he finds unattractive, Harry tells her, "No, you pretty much want to nail them, too."

All primate males, including human males, do indeed have a large and rather indiscriminate appetite for sex. It is easy to jump from that to seeing society as made up of sexual predator males, impregnating and moving on, and earth mother females, left holding and nurturing the babies. A good many discussions of human behavior duly make it sound as though male promiscuity is "natural."[32] But this is deeply simplistic—as well as completely untrue to the way human societies actually operate.

In reproductive terms, it is completely pointless for a man to impregnate lots of females if none of the children survive. Human offspring require large amounts of resource-intensive mothering; a human female's offspring thrived historically to the extent that she found, and kept, a good male mate. The men who left numerous progeny behind won't, on the whole, have been lifelong wastrels.[33]

This highlights a primate-wide problem. All primates have to provide support to nursing mothers of helpless babies. Interestingly, they do so in a wide variety of ways. You get monogamous Titi monkeys with fathers holding the babies; you get baboon harems sharing the load.[34] And in some species, such as chimps, who are our closest surviving relatives, family groups of sisters, daughters and nieces forage together without much male assistance.[35]

But human societies are built around male–female pairs. The key requirement for an ambitious female human, from the time *Homo sapiens* appeared until the very recent past, was therefore a resource-rich and reliable father for her children.

SURVIVING AND THRIVING

As eminent primatologist Sarah Hrdy explains, it is an iron rule that in societies, "daughters born to high-ranking . . . females rise in the hierarchy, and, in turn, pass on the advantages of their acquired rank . . . to daughters . . . Daughters who grow up surrounded by high-ranking kin give birth at an earlier age to *offspring more likely to survive* . . . [and] social advantages are transmitted across the generations."[36]

Hrdy is talking about primate societies in general. Take human societies in particular and, until very recently, it was the pattern for us too. Right up until the nineteenth century it was wealthier couples, *not* the "teeming masses," who raised larger families, because more of their children survived.[37] Only today can we associate large families with poverty.

Women want their offspring to survive and they want to secure "the best" for them. That means, by definition, having more resources than their peers. So women have always been in competition with other women. Chimp mothers manage and compete without much male help by operating in female family bands. But it was virtually impossible for a human female, in any pre-modern society, to raise a child successfully without male support. Fatherless children were, bluntly, very much more likely to die. Even if they did not, it would be harder for them to thrive, make a good match or, indeed, have many living progeny of their own.

This is not because men shared childcare equally; they never have, though they do more today than in the past, as we saw in Chapter 4.[38] The key point is rather that, until modern formula was invented for baby humans, we were just like other primates—breast milk was the only food an infant could digest. Infants survived if they were tied to a mother or, possibly, a wet nurse who could suckle them instead. Otherwise not. And someone had to help support the burdened mother and nurse.[39]

An illegitimate or abandoned child's prospects were therefore dire. From the fifteenth century and into the nineteenth, the growing cities of Europe set up foundling hospitals for babies whose mothers could not care for them successfully. Babies were left there, in their tens and hundreds of thousands; and the large majority died. There were too few wet nurses, infection was rife. According to Sarah Hrdy, "The scale of mortality was so appalling, and so openly acknowledged, that residents of Brescia proposed that a motto be carved over the gate of the foundling home: 'Here children are killed at public expense.' "[40]

Which brings us back to marriage, as well as mating. Human babies need direct and extensive support from their fathers and so societies have developed ways to provide it. Our ancestors worked hard, and often with cruelty, to deter women from adultery, so that men would be confident about parentage and provide that support. They also worked hard to stop men from walking away from their obligations. Bed-hopping, then vanishing was not a good all-around strategy for men who wanted to have living children, but it was and is a temptation. Males can, after all, sire another family, in another place, another day.

In spite of repeated Western fantasies about sexual idylls (mostly in the South Seas), no known human societies, including ours, have ever operated a sexual free-for-all with no socially enforced consequences.[41] On the contrary, they have all had a well-recognized institution of marriage, with husbands incurring a legal responsibility to support any children born within it. Society after society has had rules and sanctions, often draconian, designed to force men who had fathered children to wed the mothers, and to deter married women from bearing children by a man other than their husband.

All of this was obvious and natural to our ancestors. It isn't to us, because we have uncoupled sex from reproduction so thoroughly. We don't need to outlaw premarital sex because of the terrible costs of the illegitimate child-bearing that will follow, and we don't need shotgun marriages.[42] As a result, the sexual behavior of young unmarried women is completely different from that of any previous human societies.

And there are other ruptures. The arrival of easy sterilization, breast pumps and formula means that mothers can be away from their babies with no need for a wet nurse. Most important of all, it is no longer necessary for a woman to secure a man's support in order to raise his child. A man need not stick around if he wants that child to live and reach maturity. If the woman can't provide support herself, as many do, then the state will do it for him.

So why does anyone marry?

AN INDIVIDUAL LIFESTYLE CHOICE?

A surprising number of commentators see marriage today as an expression of nothing more than personal beliefs: a lifestyle choice that some embrace and others reject. Exhibit A, in this argument, is often Scandinavia, because Scandinavian countries were among the first to have very high levels of out-of-wedlock births and yet are obviously cohesive, prosperous countries.[43]

Both outside observers and some Scandinavians talk about marriage in their countries as though it had no particular importance. American researchers Betsey Stevenson and Justin Wolfers, for example, refer to the "Nordic model" of the family, and the "emerging norm in Sweden that children and formal marriage need not be linked."[44] Gøsta Esping-Andersen, the eminent Danish sociologist, states that "in Scandinavia, cohabitation is now de facto the same as marriage."[45] And *The Econo-mist*, in 2011, fell in with the consensus that "[i]n Sweden . . . marriage is disappearing as a norm."[46]

But is it? Economist Lena Edlund, Swedish-born and US-based, was prompted to question this by Americans' fascination with her country. "A sociologist in Chicago asked me, why are so many people in Sweden choosing not to get married? And I felt I had this really dull answer. I said, Oh there's no difference between marriage and cohabitation in Sweden. Which first of all, is not true and second, does beg the question, is it totally random, the people who get married and people who don't? No, that is not the case. I mean, the king got married."

Indeed, and so did the Swedish crown princess, and so did the over-whelming majority of my own Swedish friends, a highly respectable bunch of academics, civil servants and school principals. They mostly have got married and stayed married; and the ones who never married stayed childless.

We saw earlier that in the US, and many other developed countries, highly educated people are by far the most likely to marry and have chil-dren in wedlock. Sweden is no different. Among twenty-nine- to fifty-five-year-olds, the highly educated are almost twice as likely to marry as are less-educated Swedes.[47] Moreover, while every single other OECD country saw a decline in "crude" marriage rates[48] between 1970 and 2009, Sweden did not; and instead of being way below, it is now slightly above the OECD average on this measure.[49]

In other words, everywhere in the West marriage survives, and ev-erywhere the most affluent and educated mothers are the least likely to be single, whether it is Seattle or Stockholm, Oslo or Ottawa. The rea-son, I would suggest, is that marriage is still seen as best for children, and that most alpha women are only willing to bear children within it, and within marriage to an alpha man at that.

AN ULTIMATUM FROM THE ALPHA FEMALE

People (and other primates) want children. And they want the best for them. This isn't only about women. Most men are the same. Just as women want "top" fathers for their children, so men want "top" moth-ers for theirs.

If a man wants such a woman to raise his family, then he has, in most cases, to offer marriage. And the result? The overwhelming major-ity of children born to the elite 20 percent of highly educated people, anywhere in the world, are born to couples who are both married and assortatively mated.

This does not mean that people only marry in order to have children. On the contrary, people marry—just as they form partnerships—because they want love and companionship.[50] And values do have an effect: as Amy Wax points out, the different marriage rates for different American ethnic groups can't be explained in purely economic terms, but have to involve different attitudes as well.[51] But if you want to explain the enormous differences between the social classes in rates of marriage and out-of-wedlock births, then women's different choices, plus the occasional ultimatum, offer an answer.

The logic was set out for me very clearly by my friend Helen Joyce, one of those exceptions who prove the rule. She is an ex-academic turned journalist, currently *The Economist*'s bureau chief in Brazil, and the sole breadwinner for her "husband, wife and two children" family. Her husband looks after the kids.

Helen is a classic successful professional woman in every respect but this, including the fact that she is married. Her family's role reversal is very unusual. "I don't know another person in my situation, not one other. I'm not a road map for anybody," she says. I don't know anyone else like her either. While researching this book, I kept asking people whether they had friends like this. Typically, they'd know at most one such couple personally, maybe a couple more by repute. That was it.

Helen points out that successful families, successful children, depend on the quality of the men and that "a lot of men out there aren't doing anything very much. And there are lots of men who'd be perfectly happy to do no work. But most of them are just not a great option; they're not very marriageable."

To judge whether someone is a reliable, long-term option as a father for your children, you need evidence, she argues. "If you pick somebody who can prove their drive and determination by the fact that they've reached this job by thirty, they're earning this, they're holding it down, then you know that they're not slackers. There probably are plenty of nice laid-back people who aren't slackers; but you know, you bear a big risk as a woman. You carry the baby; they can walk out on you. The ones who aren't doing much, they could be wonderful. But they're not proving it. I certainly wasn't willing to end up with a slacker. And Andrew proved himself many times. He's very competent, he isn't a lazy person, he's a very clever man."

In other words, the sort of father Helen wanted for her children.

The Millennium Cohort Study, which is tracking thousands of British babies born in 2000, confirms Helen's view that she is very unusual. Couples where the mother is the sole earner at the time of a baby's birth are rare: just over 5 percent in total, less for married couples, more for cohabitees. By the time the child is three they have become rarer still, down to below 2 percent of couples. In most cases, either the father now has a job or the parents have split; and these couples also have a much higher chance than others of splitting in the first three years.[52]

At the time of the babies' births, there were also many more equal earners, or couples where the mother was the main earner, than was the case among the couples who were still together three, five or seven years in. Of couples with a newborn, 17 percent fell into one of these categories; five years on this proportion had more than halved.[53]

Each time I interviewed a successful young woman for this book, I asked her how she felt about marrying someone less successful than she was, and also about being the sole or main support for the family. One or two of the students were open to the idea. In Bangladesh, among the elite students of the Asian University for Women, Tshering, from Bhutan, thought that "as long as there's a sense of sharing, and you understand each other, that's OK," while in Oxford, Emma told me that being the main breadwinner "would be an empowering thing. It would be brilliant. I wouldn't have a problem with it, but I think men would."

But they were a small minority. As for the young women who were already well into their careers, they might be open to sharing—but basically, they wanted successful husbands, husbands like them. Banker Kerry Miller spoke for them when she said, "I don't know anyone who would be able to have a stay-at-home husband."

As for Helen and Andrew, they didn't plan their future this way. She did her PhD in mathematics at University College London (one of the UK's top universities), where her husband had done his law degree, "and realized rather early this was a really foolish mistake. What he actually liked was theater—doing lighting, front of house, whatever. When I had my first child, I took maternity leave, then went back full-time. Andrew was doing lighting, very well paid but incredibly long hours. And we decided that this was not a sustainable way to live.

"I didn't fancy not going back to work, and then not seeing my husband, not even seeing him at the weekend. He was earning more than I was then, but doing a lot more hours. So we decided that he would take a career break. We were thinking about it quite rationally. Andrew was really at the peak of his earnings, the most he could ever earn in a career where no one stays till sixty-five. Also he had a bad back. It was OK, but financially quite tough, going down to the one salary.

"He hasn't worked since. We had a second child and he's looked after the kids. Nearly all of my female colleagues here are extremely jealous. But I didn't make any more of a decision about it than they did really. Except at some point I decided that I was willing to live on too little money rather than not see my husband."

As Helen says, today's successful, educated women take major risks if they have a baby. When there are other positive things on offer in your life, unmarried motherhood on an insecure income has little appeal. Combining a serious career with parenthood is tough enough in a two-career partnership, almost impossible for a single mother without amazing energy, unusual talent and a good deal of money.

Most successful women will therefore only have a baby given the clear commitment and the financial insurance offered by marriage: marriage, that is, to someone at or close to their own educational and income level, who can help raise a "high quality" child,[54] and with whom their children will have full inheritance rights. No marriage, no baby.

SWEET CHILD OF MINE

It is clear why successful women would want a stable marriage. But you might expect successful men to prefer serial wives and more children, and to dump older wives for younger ones on a regular basis. Or, alternatively, to opt for a wife plus a mistress.

Some men do behave this way. Lucian Freud, the painter, had at least fifteen children, three of them born to three different women in the same year. James Goldsmith, billionaire tycoon, was famous for remarking, when he married his mistress, that "when a man marries his mistress, he creates a vacancy."[55]

In many, perhaps most, societies of the past, rich men routinely practiced polygyny. They had multiple female partners who were theirs alone, sometimes as wives, often as concubines. It was a reward for wealth and success.

Today, however, developed societies are strictly monogamous. Divorce laws mean that marriage also carries new financial risks. Among economists, Nobel Prize winner Robert Lucas is famous first for his divorce settlement and only second for his theories. His wife had a clause inserted into their divorce settlement, entitling her to 50 percent of the $1 million prize money should he win the Nobel Prize. Which he duly did, for work on "rational expectations": something his ex-wife had certainly shown and on which she duly collected.

Moreover, men now live in societies where, when single, they can have sex with plenty of girls like themselves. They don't feel the same "biological imperative" as women. They can and sometimes do father children well into old age. Meanwhile, in most developed countries, men are expected to be not just monogamous but totally faithful once married, whereas in the past, extramarital sex, with mistresses or top-end prostitutes, was seen as normal for successful married men. All this makes marriage today sound much less appealing to successful young men than to successful young women. So why are men marrying at all?

Many of us know unmarried couples with children where one would be happy to marry and the other won't; the latter is usually male. Most of us can also quite easily think of young women—intelligent, accomplished and nice women—who have found themselves alone after years of cohabitation because the men "wouldn't commit."[56] It is behavior that can, should and does worry young women, and might seem to follow logically from modern mores plus male biology. It is devastating for those on the receiving end. Yet it is far from the dominant pattern. Nor is serial marriage.

The majority of elite men still marry and they marry women like themselves. The overwhelming majority of graduate fathers are married when their children are born. The average fertility of graduate men—the number of children they father—is the same as that of graduate women, as we saw in Chapter 2, which means it is low, just like theirs.[57] And highly educated husbands work as many hours in total as their wives and contribute an increasing amount of time to childcare.

There is also nothing to indicate that more successful men are more often adulterous. In Britain, more highly educated men are somewhat less likely than other men to describe their ideal relationship as "married with some sex activity outside marriage."[58] (And less than 10 percent of men overall choose this option.) The highly educated and well paid are also no more likely than other men to report paying for sex with a woman.[59]

And what really surprised me was to discover that the average age gap between men and women at marriage hasn't changed. Men, it turns out, don't routinely dump thirty-three-year-olds to marry twenty-three-year-olds, any more than graduate men routinely flee spiky graduates in favor of admiring and less-educated women. The average age of men at first marriage has risen considerably, just as it has for women, but not any faster: the average is, across the developed world, for men to be two or three years older than their spouse, but no more.[60]

Perhaps it shouldn't be surprising. As I've emphasized, men, like women, want to have families, not just procreate and move on, and they too want high-quality children. The best way to get both is to marry a "top" female. These are exactly the women who are very disinclined to have children on any other terms than marriage, and monogamous marriage at that.[61] They are also not ready to settle down at age twenty-two.

In almost every country the father of a legitimate, born-in-wedlock child continues to have rights as well as duties in relation to that child that he doesn't for one born out of wedlock.[62] As a "legitimate" father your rights of access to your children are established even in the event of divorce. Economist Lena Edlund argues that human "marriage" is essentially about fathers' rights.

"Anthropologists, when they went out to look at the world, had this feature in their back pocket and they call a practice 'marriage' if it has it. The feature is that the husband is the presumed father of the children. Historically it has been very easy to assign or link the mother to the child. But the father, who is he?

"This feature of 'marriage' also means that men *obtain* paternal rights from it. For instance, in Sweden, if you are not married, as a man, and your partner has a child, first of all your partner has to sign off on your being on the form at all. And second [if] you're the designated father you still have quite limited parental rights. So you don't have custodial rights. But if you're married you have them automatically. And if you split in Sweden now, if you divorce, the default is that you maintain joint custody, whereas there is no such rule if you're just cohabiting. There's no presumption that unmarried fathers have custody at all."

Scandinavian experience certainly suggests that fathers' rights are strongly linked to marriage rates. Among the Scandinavian countries, which all have similar values and income levels, the highest extramarital birth rates are found in Iceland—64 percent compared to 54 percent in Sweden, or 47 percent in Denmark.[63] Iceland also gives unmarried fathers the fullest access rights and the same paternity leave entitlements as married ones. But even in Iceland, people do still marry.

THE X FACTOR

MARRYING MORE, DIVORCING LESS

Something else follows too. As we saw above, among American women in their thirties and forties, graduates are the women who are most likely to be (still) married.[64] This is not just because today's most-educated Westerners are most likely to marry before they have children. It is because they also stay married the longest. Graduates are much less likely to divorce than non-graduates.

The differences are more pronounced the younger the age group, and are very pronounced indeed. The US Census Bureau recently calculated how likely it was that married adults would divorce in a given year. For people in their late twenties, the rate was twice as high for non-graduates as for graduates; people in their late thirties were much the same.[65] Across the country, Democrat-voting "blue" states have lower divorce rates than "red" Republican ones. This isn't because Democrats are closet moral conservatives, or vice versa. It simply reflects states' average levels of education.

All across Europe it is the same. Having a higher level of education makes you less likely to divorce. It is far from the only thing that matters, but it does matter, and significantly.[66] Yet this was not true when divorce first became quite widely available.[67] For example, in Sweden, educational level had rather little effect on the likelihood of divorce pre-1980. It now has quite a strong one.[68] And among older US cohorts there was much less difference than among younger ones.

So, with lots of individual exceptions, the most educated get married before they have children and tend to stay married. Meanwhile, among the least educated, as we saw earlier (Figure 11.1), there has been a collapse of marriage. As Edin and Kefalas discovered in *Promises I Can Keep*, their landmark study of low-income single mothers, these young women love the idea of marriage. But not, on the whole, to "their" men.

"After everything is situated the way I want it to be situated, then I'll be ready to get married," is how one seventeen-year-old mother put it.[69] But there is no great optimism that this will happen. Instead, these women explain that, "I don't want no relationship [where] the first woman he sees turns his head . . . I'm afraid that would happen. That's the only reason why I would never get married at this point."[70]

When it comes to finding trustworthy, decent men, they argue, "You might have to go somewhere far away to find one," and in thinking about who might be worth marrying, "Not anyone from *this* neighborhood."[71]

And among the large majority of people, the broad middle classes? It comes down one way for some people, the other way for others. It is still more common for women in middling income and education groups to be married than unmarried at the time they give birth; but there is also a much larger proportion of never-married mothers here than among the most educated.[72] And this pattern is then compounded by differing rates of divorce.

Think yourself into a typical position, as a middle-income woman. You'd like to be married (and plenty of your friends and family are). You badly want a child. The guy won't commit. Having a child out of wedlock is not the catastrophe it once was and plenty of other people are doing it. Your job is OK, but just a job: you won't lose as much as a high-flying professional would by pulling back for a while; and having children and a family are top of your priorities. If things go wrong and you end up on benefits, that is tough, but not the end of the world. Not surprisingly, a good many women opt for the baby without the ring.

It is similar with breakups. It is usually women who sue for divorce, and their decision to stay married or quit can be shifted not just by husbands' behavior (arguments, adultery) but also by bread-and-butter issues. How poor will you be, how deprived will your children be, if you go?

Huge increases in divorce across the globe have followed changing work opportunities for women that make it possible for them to support themselves. But government policies are important too. As we saw in Chapter 3, shifts in tax rates and benefits that lead to more money for single mothers can trigger more marital breakups. It's not that everyone walks out—but at the margin, a few more do so. And conversely, the more you have to lose by quitting a marriage, the more inclined you are to stay.

And that is why, in today's America, women aged thirty to forty-four are much more likely to be married if they are graduates than non-graduates, while in the low-divorce world of the 1950s, the exact opposite was true.[73] But if, at the root of change, we find men's and women's hardwired desire for children running up against modern economies and modern welfare systems, why are things so different in affluent Asia?

ASIAN EXCEPTIONS?

So far in this chapter, the data I have been discussing come from the developed West. But there is a dramatic difference between it and the rich countries of Asia. In the West, it is the least educated who are the least likely to marry. In Asia, the biggest declines among marriage involve the most educated women. Does this mean that the whole argument is flawed? No.

The reason for this contrast is not that graduate women in Japan, Korea, Taiwan and Singapore have dramatically different desires, or behave quite differently from their European and American counterparts. It is the non-graduates, and the least educated, who are different. Because, in Asia, all mothers marry. In Japan, for example, less than 2 percent of births are to unmarried women. And its rich Asian neighbors are the same—whether it is Hong Kong, Taiwan, Singapore or South Korea, the proportion of births out of wedlock remains tiny. And if all mothers marry, then you can't, statistically (or in reality), have a situation where graduate mothers marry more.

Why is this? The contrast cannot be explained simply by the level of benefits for single mothers (meager though these usually are in Asian countries). It is rather that in rich Asian countries, extramarital births are still deeply disapproved of: values do matter. So you don't find large and rising numbers of less-educated women taking the traditional route of child-bearing but without a husband. What you do find is rising numbers of Asian women who don't have children, and often don't marry either; and, as we saw in Chapter 2, this is especially common among the most educated, for whom marriage and career are very hard to combine.[74]

So, in the rich West, we have declining marriage rates and rising illegitimacy rates.[75] In the rich East, we have declining marriage rates and a tiny incidence of out-of-wedlock births. In both cases, that result is the product of individual decisions, some in response to worldwide economic change and others in response to factors as local as tax credits for single mothers and whether you can get a visa for your nanny.

And around the world, whatever the country, like marries like and educated women link to educated men. It is a universal pattern; but how does it actually happen?

MATCHMAKER, MATCHMAKER, MAKE ME A MATCH . . .

"Assortative mating" is hardly new. Boston's top families (the "Boston Brahmins") intermarried to a remarkable degree in the nineteenth and into the twentieth centuries. Theirs was a society that was educated, fairly non-ostentatious, civic-minded, but

Where the Lowells talk only to Cabots
And the Cabots talk only to God.[76]

Sociologist George Homans was born into this now-vanished Boston: his mother was an Adams, the closest thing to blue blood in America.[77] His family lived

> on an ethnic island, largely Yankee, which was also a class
> island, largely Brahmin . . . [It] was also what is now called an
> urban village . . . many of the families had known each other for
> generations. The surest sign of it was that, when I met some lady
> or gentleman hitherto unknown to me, she or he would be sure to
> say: "George Homans? Oh, yes, of course. You must be Abigail's [or
> Robert's] son," and then go on to climb down the family trees until
> the branches met in some common ancestor.[78]

The men went to the same schools—elite boarding schools and colleges, all in New England. The women's career was marriage; they lived at home until that occurred, and the people they met and might marry were defined by social contacts almost as tightly as they were for a nineteenth-century Hungarian prince.

But today? In order to marry someone, you have to know them. Stanford's Paula England suggests that the increase in assortative mating could be partly because young people's lives, these days, are very socially segregated.[79] Certainly neighborhoods and schools in the US are more segregated, not just by income but also by culture, than they used to be.[80] And the high-achieving students who converge on recognized, elite universities come predominantly from well-off homes.

However, people also marry much later than they did a generation or two ago, and years after they graduate. Compared to nineteenth-century Boston, elite men and women today live in a far more traveled society. Women as well as men leave home for employment. They also still marry men who are several years older, on average—and therefore weren't even in the same class at school.

So today's assortative mating can't be fueled just by proximity in one's teens and early twenties. Instead, it works two ways. People do meet at work, and educated professionals work in mixed workplaces to a far greater degree than other men and women. But there is also a lot of active legwork by the men and women concerned, some virtual and some real.

The virtual bit is unisex. Both men and women have replaced the flesh-and-blood matchmaker with the virtual one.

Matchmakers, like servants, went out of fashion in the West. I remember one attractive college friend of mine bewailing this when we were both nineteen. At the time she specialized in serial high-stress breakups; since then, she has made a lot of money in oil trading, hasn't married, and last time I saw her, still thought arranged marriages were a pretty sensible idea. Matchmaking remained and remains important in some non-Western cultures: in India, for example, it's a regular event for top "Bollywood" film stars—Karisma Kapoor, Madhuri Dixit—to have arranged marriages.

But the whole idea is at odds with the romantic ideal of marriage. Western girls were expected to just meet a future husband and fall in love. This sometimes worked but often didn't. So matchmakers have been reinvented.

Go online and you'll easily find sites offering escort services, sites displaying "pretty Russian women," sites for men in search of a beautiful Thai wife. But you'll also find information on a whole range of Internet dating and matchmaking sites. In just a few years, these have moved from doubtful fringe to respectable mainstream, with increasingly specialized clienteles: Gray and Farrar, of London, Los Angeles, Paris, Milan and beyond, charges membership fees of over $20,000 for men and women alike.

I have only one female professional friend who's the breadwinner for a traditional-style family, but I now know a good few couples who first linked up online. And while photos may make a big difference to first impressions, Internet dating sites are also striking for their up-front approach to marriage-market criteria. Most Western users are slightly less blunt than the highly educated Chinese woman who recently specified not just "master's degree or more, no smokers, taller than 172 cm, parents who are still together; annual salary over 50,000 yuan," but also "at least two girlfriends, but no more than four."[81] But the underlying approach is the same.

And real, physical legwork? That is a female speciality, and one we know about courtesy of Carrie in *Sex and the City*: "There are 1.3 million single men in New York, 1.8 million single women, and of these more than 3 million people, about twelve think they're having enough sex."

Carrie is totally right in her numbers. New York does indeed have far more single women than men. It's true of London and Stockholm as well; I'd happily take a bet on Paris and Tokyo. East German young women have moved West at great speed following reunification, leaving many of the men behind.

But surely that suggests that ambitious, able young women are putting their careers first and don't really care about marriage? No, quite the opposite, says Lena Edlund: many are following the eligible males. Lena is the Swedish-born economist we met earlier who thinks hard about modern escort services, and who argues that paternity rights explain a lot about marriage. When we talked in her Columbia University office, she also told me that "for ages, we have actually seen more women than men in urban areas. It's a striking pattern. And what do we know about urban areas? Well, they are wealthier and they have more skilled jobs. Women these days are fairly educated. But that's recent and the pattern is also there in countries where young women are not as well educated as men.

"I propose that you think about this as a market. There's always a scarcity in the partner market. So some men are going to be on the highly in demand side, and the best outcome for young women will be for these 'high demand' men to be partnering with them. And where are these guys? They are in cities."

Lena's point is that there is always, by definition, "excess demand" for highly desirable partners. We'd rather partner up than down. Hence, more women would like "alpha males" than can have them—we can't, never mind don't, all marry the stuff of our teenage dreams.

But if the best men are in the cities, women who move there will have some chance, probably quite a good chance, of meeting one. They may not manage it; but if they stay in places where the number of "good men" is extremely low, their chances of a good match will be very low indeed. If you can't have certainty, a good chance is better than a poor one.[82]

If women are flocking to cities to compete for the alpha males who are working there, you might expect men to do the same, because there will be desirable girls left over. However, today's urban job market works against men at middle and lower levels. There are a lot of mid-level city-based occupations to which recruitment is heavily female. For men, in contrast, many of the reasonable middle-income jobs remain firmly outside the honey-pots of the metropolis.

Visiting New York as an outsider, I've been struck by the groups of chic women—just women, no men—dining in expensive restaurants. However, even though her university office is bang in the middle of Manhattan Island, it wasn't the all-female groups in its bars and restaurants that caught Lena's attention.

"In a big city it's not actually so visible. What I was aware of is like the butt of a Swedish national joke; this municipality in the north that can't retain its young women. It's called Pajala. One local politician even proposed a package deal to get women from Russia: you could get them not just as women, but as medical doctors. It would solve two problems, because they can't get doctors to stay either. Of course, this was treated as a gaff. But there have been various speculations about why this happens—climate, or lack of movie theaters or museums, things that women are supposed to be interested in. And then I saw a ranking of income. And Pajala was just one of the poorest.

"However, what has happened recently is that Asian women, especially from Thailand, move into these poor areas. The men aren't competitive on the national marriage market but they are very competitive in, say, Thailand. And then the market becomes very visible. Because, you know, you'd think the further north you travel the more indigenously Swedish, the more reindeers, but no . . . actually, you get Thai food. And when I spoke to someone up there, he said, 'You know, that's always been our solution. It just used to be, we took women from Finland instead.' "

Which no one outside noticed, since there were no obvious physical differences. And which is impossible today, when Finland has moved from a dirt-poor dependency of Russia to one of the richest and most technically advanced countries on the planet.

Lena and Jane Austen are as one. If you want to understand marriage, think of a market. But also think children. Even more than in the past, it is children—the desire for them, the raising of them—that drive elite marriages. And with the assortative marriages of graduate high earners, elite families are also being transformed.

12

FAMILIES UNLIMITED

riends was the iconic sitcom of the 1990s: six young professionals, whose friendship group is the center of their lives. *Sex and the City* spoke for the 2000s: four women who turn to each other for advice, support, secret-sharing. Social networking now eats up hours of many people's days. So are friends the new family?

No. They are not. Friends are not family, and families still matter. Successful young professionals who live thousands of miles from where they were raised all got there through their families' efforts. Their children, if they have any, will be the same. Women's increasing independence and penetration of elite jobs haven't reduced the importance of families. On the contrary, it has greatly increased successful women's ability to do well by their offspring.

THICKER THAN WATER

To understand the importance of family, visit Postman's Park. It sits just north of St. Paul's Cathedral, in the City of London: a typical little urban park, with trees, seats, a bit of green, a few flower beds—and the Memorial to Heroic Self-Sacrifice.

Beneath a loggia is a wall hung with ceramic memorial tablets. Each one commemorates someone who sacrificed their life to save that of others. Or rather, to save someone who was *not* their parent or their child. "Heroic self-sacrifice" doesn't, on the whole, embrace what we do for close relatives, and certainly not what we do willingly for our children.

It is perfectly normal for a parent to rush into a burning house or rough seas to try to save a child. Not doing so might be understandable, but it is also pathetic, a source of shame. Twenty-three-year-old

John Cranmer, saving a stranger's life while drowning himself; William Goodrum, who perished saving a fellow railwayman from death under an approaching train; stewardess Mary Rogers, giving up her life preserver on a sinking ship: these are the people honored on the Postman's Park tablets, not fathers and mothers putting the lives of their children before their own.

Not all parents do care for their children at all times. But we are shocked when they don't, because it is so rare. As for favoring your kin, it is so normal and common that it has its own name: nepotism.

The operative word here is "favoring." It means that people don't play fair. They don't treat non-kin in exactly the same way as they treat family. For that reason, modern states and laws try to prevent nepotism. It flies in the face of contemporary universalistic values; values that, as I have argued above, are an important reason why modern societies no longer find it legitimate to discriminate against women and in favor of men.

Any state or organization that wants to be efficient, never mind fair, worries about family favoritism. Imperial China could run a vast, populous and long-lived state because of its extraordinary state bureaucracy.[1] Officials were selected on the basis of formal examinations, and once appointed, were sent far from home.

How could a mandarin be objective, free from corruption and a reliable servant of the state, if his family was close by? Anyone naïve enough to doubt the power of blood ties needs only look a few yards across the Forbidden City from the courtyard where the civil service examinations took place to the Inner Court, the imperial family's quarters. There, emperors' wives and concubines were engaged in a time-honored and far more widespread pursuit: scheming to promote the interests of their sons. The women's natural allies, in China as in other empires, were the court eunuchs. Eunuchs could never seize power directly, but they could obtain enormous power through a young emperor or his mother. And because they could never have children of their own, they could, up to a point, be trusted.[2]

In this respect, humans are like every other living creature. We want to protect and help our own children most of all; not all the children in our community equally, let alone "society" as a whole. No wonder that wicked stepmothers figure so large in fairy stories, whether they feature Cinderella, Hansel and Gretel, or Snow White as the victims. And no wonder, too, that the killing of human babies and toddlers is about *seventy times* more likely in homes where the natural father is absent and another unrelated man present.[3]

Human families do not just look after their children. They also look after each other in sickness and old age. If it weren't for the support that families provide, even the most generous welfare states would buckle and fail. For every father or mother worrying about university entrance, there is a son or daughter worrying about a parent's failing health and independence. But when it comes to deciding a society's winners, and its structure of power and wealth, it is parents and children who are the key players.

This has always been true, but two major and related changes mark today's families. First, as we saw above, modern assortative mating means that, in many cases, mothers with careers can promote their children's interests in much the same ways as fathers do. And second, among elite families, daughters' interests and future success are now promoted in exactly the same way as sons'. Moreover, this happens in large part through the efforts of besotted fathers around the globe.

DADDY'S GIRLS

There is nothing new in fathers loving their daughters. Yes, there have been societies where another daughter was a cause for mourning: a useless mouth to feed, another dowry to find. But religious texts, myths, literature and history are also full of beloved daughters: Cordelia, Emma, Electra and, indeed, the goddess Athena, a full-blown daddy's girl. Genghis Khan, the great Mongol conqueror and mass murderer, consistently trusted his daughters rather than his sons, leaving power in their hands in his absence.[4]

For girls in the past, marriages could turn disastrous, with husbands who were drunk, violent wastrels. In a world where divorce was often impossible, fathers and brothers offered the only possible recourse and protection. And many did their best, within the limits of contemporary laws and values.[5]

More recently, parents of daughters, and especially those with daughters but no sons, have supported feminist policies such as equal pay and affirmative action more than parents with sons alone.[6] Voters are also more likely to vote in a "left-wing" way after giving birth to daughters than they were before.[7]

This is probably because women are more likely than men to need state support at some point, to help them care for children and family members; contemporary left-of-center parties generally attract more support from women than men and it is almost certainly for this reason.[8] Having daughters rather than sons probably makes parents, in turn, more aware that their children might need state help one day, and so more supportive of parties associated with generous welfare and benefits.

At a political level, men with daughters have pushed for legislative change that promotes women's causes.[9] In America, abortion is a highly polarizing issue that has created a close alliance between major "pro-life" church denominations and the contemporary Republican Party.[10] However, in the period 1997–2004, US congressmen with daughters generally voted in a more liberal "pro-choice" direction on reproductive rights issues than you would expect from either their party or their individual voting record.[11]

I asked many of the women whom I interviewed about their fathers. Among the younger ones, whatever the continent, virtually every one had a father who was not merely supportive but took it for granted that daughters should strive and succeed just like sons. Marketing executive Lee Ann Daly, sole girl in a family of boys, remembers how her father "wanted me to know that there was nothing I couldn't do. And he gave me a book when I was about eleven years old, a book called *Girls Are Equal Too*. And he inscribed it, 'To Lee Ann, welcome to the widest of all possible worlds.'"

Paris-born banker Laura Mercadier remembers that her father "wanted us to be independent financially and he always kind of pushed us to be top of wherever we were. Like I always had to be first; and I was!"

So is a highly supportive father something that marks out today's female high-flyers? I would guess not.

Having nonsupportive parents can clearly mess you up. But I suspect that supportive fathers were ubiquitous among my younger interviewees not because these women are different from their peers, but because they are typical of their generation. Modern educated fathers generally support and root for their daughters' success as routinely as they do for their sons'. It is those who don't who are the odd ones out.

This may seem a curious claim. After all, across the world a large number of families still have a strong preference for sons over daughters. The normal ratio for babies at birth is something between 103 and 106 boys to every 100 girls. But selective abortion is currently producing some enormously skewed birth ratios, notably in China, where in the early 2000s 124 boys were born for every 100 girls. Families' determination to have a son means that "one child" families in China end up as disproportionately "one boy" families, while in families with several children, repeated male births are accepted happily, but not repeated female ones.

China is the most extreme, but some other countries are not that far behind. South Korea was up to a 117:100 ratio in the 1990s, though it has since dropped back. For India as a whole, the ratio is only slightly above normal, but in some states—notably in the northwest—it is well over 120:100. The new states of the Balkans and the Caucasus are also way outside the norm in the numbers of male babies born.[12]

Highly uneven sex ratios are not uniquely modern. They were also achieved by some previous societies through widespread infanticide and neglect.[13] Parents—mothers as much as fathers—would consistently give more food and care to boy children because they were of more potential value to the family. Even today, we can find clear evidence of such treatment in developing countries with a strong "son preference."[14]

But while India and China are vast countries, and so creating a global "male surplus" in absolute terms, they are culturally atypical as well as still very poor. There is no "worldwide war" on baby girls,[15] because most contemporary countries do not have an overwhelming preference for sons. Countries that manipulate birth rates this way are a minority.

Modern prenatal technology means that parents can, if they feel strongly, shift birth ratios without recourse to the horrors of infanticide. China and India manage it in spite of their continued poverty; the rest of us could too, if we were determined. Balanced birth rates, like unbalanced ones, are now a choice. And in our increasingly low-fertility world, the ideal is usually a two-child, not a two-boy, family.

Meanwhile, even in developing countries with unbalanced birth rates, and even in those boy-biased countries where the daughters of the poor receive far less education than their brothers, the elite has changed. Here we see an explosion of female dynastic power. Widows, sisters and a very large number of daughters from leading political families are vaulting into elected office.

Equal-opportunity political dynasties are especially evident in Asia. To take just a few examples from 2012:

- Bangladesh's prime minister, Sheikh Hasina, is the daughter of the country's first president. She succeeded Khaleda Zia, ex–prime minister, leader of the opposition and widow of the country's seventh president.

- The president of India's ruling Congress Party, Sonia Gandhi, is the widow of the assassinated Rajiv, a former prime minister. Rajiv's mother and Sonia's mother-in-law, Indira Gandhi, was herself assassinated while serving as prime minister. Indira herself was the daughter of India's first prime minister, Jawaharlal Nehru.

- Thailand's prime minister is Yingluck Shinawatra, a businesswoman and accomplished campaigner, and the youngest sister and anointed successor of the deposed and exiled Thaksin Shinawatra. Thaksin is a former prime minister who created the Thai Rak Thai party, whose heartland was Thailand's poor, rural areas. His sister led its successor organization (the Pheu Thai Party) to a landslide victory.

- Burma's most prominent politician is Aung San Suu Kyi, who took on the mantle of political leadership from her father, leader of Burma's independence movement. She endured years of house arrest and separation from her family under Burma's military dictatorship, and in 2012 led her party to victory in elections for the lower house of parliament.

- Park Geun-hye, elected in 2012 as South Korea's first female president, is the daughter of Park Chung-Hee, who ruled South Korea for eighteen years, made himself president-for-life and was assassinated in 1979.

In Pakistan, the assassinated Benazir Bhutto was the daughter of Zulfikar Ali Bhutto, himself executed by his political enemies. In Sri Lanka, Chandrika Kumaratunga, president from 1994 to 2005, followed in the footsteps of her parents, both of whom were prime ministers.[16] Indonesia, Malaysia and the Philippines all have women from famous families in prominent positions; and in all of them, women garner votes and support from men and women across the social spectrum.

The female politicians of Asia operate in countries where democratic politics are still recent, and the charisma of early leaders and founding fathers lingers. But they also illustrate two more general trends. First, the individual who inherits a leader's mantle, the child on whom the stardust settles, is as often a daughter as a son, as often a sister as a brother.

Second, there are still family trades. Women across the world are benefiting from the spread of universalistic values, and the accompanying intolerance for discrimination by gender, race, sexual orientation or any other "marker." But alongside that, not only do families promote their children's interests in society at large; they are also keeping the family firm in play.

For the Bhuttos or the Gandhis, the family trade is democratic politics. For the Hefners of *Playboy*, as we saw in Chapter 8, it is soft porn. But family enterprises run the gamut, and so do the women who head them. In a world of professional women, not just families but family firms are thriving, and thriving because of the women among them.

ALL IN THE FAMILY

Some family enterprises are very long-lived indeed. I know one, currently headed by a woman, that has been around for centuries. It is strictly hierarchical: one boss, one clear successor-in-waiting. No questions about how you join; you are born to it for the most part, marry into it sometimes. Power goes down through the generations and so does money. (There's plenty of that.) Members are tight-knit and protective of each other. They trust other "blood" members totally, trust the in-laws mostly, and view the rest of the world with deep and permanent suspicion. They call it "the firm."

No, the boss isn't Don Corleone and this isn't a Mafia family. As British readers may have guessed, it's a family, but a royal one, headed since 1952 by Her Majesty the Queen. The royals call it "the firm" because it is, indeed, a classic family firm. And while family firms with female heads were pretty unusual at the time of the queen's coronation, they aren't at all unusual today.

The radicals of the 1960s believed in feminism and free love but also in communal living. They set their faces against all long-established institutions, and both they and appalled conservative onlookers saw their movement as an attack on the traditional family. It is ironic, therefore, that one result of the genuine and profound revolution in women's lives is that, in some classes and some spheres, the family is stronger than ever before.

Most of the world's enterprises, now as throughout history, are family firms: little workshops in the teeming streets of third-world cities, small farms, construction workers with a son or nephew in tow, shops, dry cleaners, local restaurants. New companies almost always begin as family concerns. Entrepreneurs tap their families for money; they mortgage their homes, they work in the garage or the spare bedroom; family members supply cheap and committed labor.

In Western societies, we tend to think of the economy as having moved on—"progressed"—from being a family-dominated affair. Capitalism allows a company to grow by tapping and harnessing money from large numbers of people, who then own a small part of it. A majority of Americans work not in family businesses, but either for large companies whose shares are traded, and which are run by senior employees, or for the public and not-for-profit sector.[17]

And yet, even in the US, around 90 percent of registered businesses are family ones. Over three-quarters of private sector employees work in firms that are family-controlled, some of them huge. At the start of the twenty-first century, well over half of private sector GDP in the US was generated by family-owned or family-controlled concerns.[18]

In most developed countries, family businesses are more important than in America. In Germany, for example, it is the small and medium-sized companies (the *Mittelstand*), mostly family-controlled, that power Germany's export success and domination of machine tools and precision engineering.[19] The Swedish economy is dominated by large entrepreneurial family firms, and its family firms have a considerably longer life, on average, than nonfamily firms. The most important is the Wallenberg group, now controlled by the fifth generation of the family. Over the industrialized world as a whole, between 45 and 75 percent of a country's GNP is generated by family-controlled firms.[20]

Succession planning is what decides a family business's fate. This has always been a problem—"clogs to clogs in three generations" is the English version of a pretty universal tag.[21] But today the would-be dynast has some new options. You can pass control to your daughter, and not just to your son or the ambitious son-in-law who targeted the boss's daughter.

My own family illustrates the benefits. My great-grandfather was a baker, with a small shop and embryonic delivery business; and the child who took that over was not a son but his eldest, unmarried daughter. Ruby had been the bookkeeper, the commercial brains, the manager. She duly grew the business, passing it on to a family member from the next generation.

But in another part of my family, at much the same time, the entrepreneurial paterfamilias—decidedly richer than Great-Aunt Ruby ever became—thought business was for men, not women. He left the whole thing to his sons. His daughters had no involvement with the business; his eldest daughter, who later made her own tidy fortune, wasn't even considered as a successor. The sons—predictably, or so I'm told—ran the business into the ground.

Mary Myers Kauppila is someone who illustrates perfectly the benefits of female succession. She is a serial entrepreneur and set up her own first company in her freshman year at Harvard. She is also the CEO of the privately held business founded by her father: a business that started with one small mortgaged ranch in California and then went a long way up.

I interviewed her on a wet, dark Boston afternoon in the company's East Coast headquarters. It is a small, elegant suite overlooking Commonwealth Avenue, a street of classic brownstones and an occasional mansion, which is now largely commercial but was once the heartland of the Boston Brahmins. Mary herself, behind a large desk in a noncorporate office full of books and pictures, is smart, unflashy, distinctively and, I'm pretty sure, very expensively dressed.

It was, she says, always obvious that the second CEO would be her. "My brother works in the agriculture part of the business, and he's certainly a partner and part of decision-making. But I manage most of the assets, and most all of the functions of the enterprise at large. Someone's got to rise to the occasion. I'm older. I'm bossy. And, as my mother used to say, I was my father's clone."

She took over after decades at the helm of companies she had set up herself, selling out the last and largest of these in 1996, and going back to the family business "because my father's health was starting to fail and it was just time for a succession plan to be implemented. And I spent a year on almost a private equity due diligence process: very interesting actually. What was profitable? What wasn't? Where were all these assets in the nooks and crannies of our balance sheet?

"We're very efficient because we can make decisions quickly. I do have a whole advisory structure and lots of wonderful colleagues. And should something happen to me—since I'm sort of keeper of the works— they would be my contingency plan, with a succession plan that I hope extends for a long time to come."

Developing economies have already produced privately held companies of impressive size. Many highly successful Chinese companies involve a partnership between husband and wife: they started it together and run it together. Family businesses can make long-term investment decisions without worrying about shareholders hunting for short-term profits. And the people at the top have a common interest in the firm's long-term survival, rather than in extracting a huge bonus before they cut and run to manage some other company. This makes established family businesses rather more risk-averse on average than the top management teams of listed corporations.[22] But looking at where risk-taking recently took banks, financial services and the world economy, that's not obviously a disadvantage.

It's impossible to know how many family businesses are promoting their daughters but easy to find high-profile examples. Ana Patricia Botín, for example, is CEO of Santander UK, one of the UK's biggest banks.[23] She is one of six children of the billionaire executive chairman of the Spanish Santander Group, a member of the fifth generation of the family that built the business, and the one tapped to succeed her father.

In mining, that apparently most macho of industries,[24] Georgina Rinehart is Australia's richest individual (not just its richest woman) and currently a good bet to become the richest individual in the world. She became executive chairman of the HPPL mining giant on her father's death: it was on the skids by the time she inherited, since when she has transformed its fortunes.[25] And for a real sign of change it is hard to beat Saudi Arabia's Lubna Olayan. She—and not her brother—is CEO of the Olayan Financing Company, the holding group for the vast privately held conglomerate that was founded by her father and is still based—as she is—in Saudi Arabia.

Children brought up with a business know about it deeply and instinctively. Mary Myers Kauppila was seven when her father lost his job and borrowed money to buy a ranch in California. "So at that point I went to work with him. My first job was at about age seven as an irrigator; you did whatever was necessary. It was called survival with very limited resources. But we got lucky. I mean, we did use leverage, and by about eleven years old I was upgraded from physical labor to be in the office, helping to do the financial analysis and planning, and was running manual spreadsheets at that point.

"I learned all about borrowing money and buying the next ranch. I also learned about the investment business, because we had operating companies and a developing investment portfolio. This was my childhood. And looking back, it was just the richest and most fabulous environment in which to grow . . ."

And one that made a big difference to her ability to think entrepreneurially.

"It's instinctive. It's instinctive what risk is about, it's instinctive about how you muster resources. Just living it and seeing it . . . sure, it's a whole bunch easier. If my father had been a banker would I have had the same drives? Maybe, maybe not, I don't know. My father loved what he did and that is what I aspired to."

Substantive day-to-day involvement breeds expertise and, in the past, it was denied to daughters. The arrival of emancipated, educated females is therefore great for family businesses; in a single move, you double the available talent. Some of that female talent will be creative, some of it financial, some good at human relations and some aggressive and risk-taking. But all of it is in the family.

UPSIDE, DOWNSIDE

So far, this chapter has given most attention to the positive aspects of family ties. But as feuding concubines and abusive stepfathers make clear, there is a darker side to family favoritism. And at state level, the victory of nepotism over "universalist" values is destructive.

Radicals in the 1960s were not the first to declare war on the family. A century before, Marx and Engels had argued that the traditional patriarchal family oppresses women and "contains in germ not only slavery but also serfdom."[26] In the official dogma of Communist states, advancing the interests of your kin was duly anathema.

In practice, nepotism and favoritism thrived, with little in the political system and nothing in the legal one to stop it. In the years before they collapsed, the Communist states of the USSR and Eastern Europe were increasingly run by a *nomenklatura* dominated by the children of officials and house-trained intellectuals.[27] Cuba and North Korea are as family-dominated as any princely state. And in today's capitalist-but-Communist China, the "princelings"—children of senior Communist Party officials and politicians—are increasingly prominent in politics and business.

Li Changchun was ranked fifth in the Politburo in 2012 with responsibility for media and propaganda; his daughter Li Tong runs a huge investment fund focusing on media industries. Wen Jiabao, former Chinese premier and a vocal critic of official corruption, has a son, Winston, who founded one of the most successful private equity funds in China. A well-connected Chinese investor told the *Financial Times*, "If Winston is bidding for a deal, we wouldn't even try—we try to avoid competing with the big princelings."[28]

As Professor Victor Shih explained to the *FT*, "Private equity is a very good area for princelings . . . It is an easy way to make money because everyone will be willing to back them because of their connections."[29]

It is not that Communist officials are more prone to nepotism than anyone else. Rather, as flesh-and-blood people, the powerful look out for their families exactly as others do; and the fewer the constraints on officials' and politicians' power, the more easily they can do so. At its worst, this brings us the "family state," exemplified by modern Central Asia.

The five "stans" of the region—Kazakhstan, Kyrgyzstan, Uzbekistan, Turkmenistan and Tajikistan—became independent when the Soviet Union disintegrated in 1991. They are all Muslim. They were all, also, once at the heart of Genghis Khan's empire; and Genghis Khan always vested great power and responsibility in his daughters, whom he (no doubt rightly) trusted far more than he ever did those potential rivals, his sons.

Today, these countries vary in their degree of wealth. Kazakhstan has enormous mineral, gas and petroleum deposits, Uzbekistan has mineral and gas potential and Turkmenistan has vast gas fields, whereas Kyrgyzstan is very poor and Tajikistan even poorer, though with hydroelectric potential. Politically, they vary in the degree to which their leaders allow any degree of political opposition at all. But they are all corrupt. They all have women in positions of real power and influence. And these women are, almost uniformly, powerful because they are part of the ruling family.

This does not mean that the women hold nominal positions, as tokens or fronts for men. On the contrary, in every case daughters are as prominent and powerful as sons, let alone sons-in-law. Kazakhstan, for example, with its huge mineral and energy resources, is the archetype of what one academic from the region describes as the Central Asian "family-state, where the president's son controls the business sphere and the daughter leads the mass media."[30] Its president has been reelected with repeated landslide votes, supported by a coalition of pro-government parties including one founded by his daughter, Dariga Nazarbayeva. She is slated to be his heir, while over in Uzbekistan the most likely successor to the president is his eldest daughter, Gulnara.

"Family states" are an extreme, and unstable to boot. But they highlight a more general point. Female emancipation changes family dynamics and increases the number of people on whom family leaders can rely totally. It does so when families' activities are legal and productive. It also does so when they are corrosive and dysfunctional.

More generally, across the world, the rise of families headed by two well-paid, successful and highly educated adults is creating a phalanx of male and female parents ready to devote both money and intensive parenting to furthering their children's interests. The success with which they do so creates, as we will see, a formidable obstacle to social mobility.

PRIMED FOR THE TOP

In most developed countries, the last few decades have brought growing income inequality. The change is much more extreme in some countries than others, and one or two countries have seen little or no change.[31] But the basic trend is international. And as we saw in Chapter 6, it is true among women, not only among men.

But that is individual inequality. Our attention is focused in large part on individuals who, at the top end, are part of the "1 percent," or indeed among the "one in 1,000," averaging well over $1 million a year.[32] It is about middle-class individuals doing jobs where real incomes have stagnated for years. What happens when we look not at individuals but at households? And especially at households with two working-age adults, one female and one male?

The answer isn't automatic or obvious. As we saw in Chapter 1, more and more women entered the workforce between 1950 and 2000. And their average earnings have been catching up with men's: for example, in the US, while middle-income male salaries have grown little over the past few decades, women's have grown quite fast.[33] So in many middle- and lower-income families, women's increased earnings will tend to offset the results of growing inequality among men.

However, many women are now earning sums that are large in absolute terms and these high earners are drawing away from the female average. This group, the focus of this book, is usually highly educated, and they earn more on an hourly basis, work longer hours and take fewer breaks from employment than other women. Indeed, many take no breaks at all—either because they do not have children or because their earnings are high enough, in absolute and relative terms, to pay for good full-time childcare.

And these women are rarely found in households where men are mid-level earners with stagnating incomes. Rather, they are overwhelmingly dating, cohabiting with and marrying men like themselves. In the first months of the Obama administration, Anna Fifield of the *Financial Times* was able to identify at least fifteen couples, both of whom were given senior appointments—with a fairly 50/50 split in terms of whether the men or women were receiving the more senior one.[34] They are the most visible examples of a sizeable new phenomenon.

Households with two high-earning adults do very nicely indeed. And in the US, where the women who have most increased their working hours are the graduates, the growth in women's employment has tended to make households more unequal overall. Gøsta Esping-Andersen, one of the world's leading analysts of the welfare state, calculates that the US would be significantly less unequal than it is today if women in the top 20 percent of couples had stuck to their old 1980 working patterns.[35]

. However, it is important to recognize that women's employment doesn't always increase household inequality. That is basically an empirical question, a function of what else is going on across the labor market.[36]

Take Italy. More Italian women are employed than a few years ago, but their employment rate is still lower than in most developed countries, especially among the less well educated and less well-off; the wives of the lowest-earning husbands are only half as likely to be at work as those with the best-off husbands. Even so, women's employment serves to reduce rather than increase overall household inequality. That is because male employment rates have actually been declining, at the same time as wage gaps among Italian men widened. Women's wages have stopped things from becoming even more unequal than they are.[37]

Either way, families with two high earners are doing very nicely everywhere. They earn a lot relative to others. They also earn a lot in absolute terms. Both matter.[38]

Take as an example a married couple, British this time, both full-time professionals and each earning at the 90th percentile—that is, making more than nine-tenths of other full-time female and male employees respectively. There are a large number of people in this position, and they are all earning twice the median UK full-time wage.[39] Pooled, that means that they have a pre-tax income of roughly four times that of a full-time middle-class middle-income worker, let alone someone who is low-paid. Further down the educational scale, not only are incomes lower, but two full-timers are less likely: one full-time, one part-time job is a lot more common.

If you're part of a two-career, two-full-time-incomes household, then fixed-cost items—cars, computers, holidays—take up a much smaller proportion of your income than they do for the less well-off. As for relative wealth, when you are relatively richer than other people, hiring them becomes a possibility. As we've seen, alongside female professional success, servants have returned. But it is not just nannies, hairdressers and personal trainers that relative wealth makes available. It is also good teachers.

The broadest road to success, in modern societies, leads through elite education. Affluent families use their money to promote their children's chances and cushion them against falls; their single most important purchase is education. Not just college education, but preschool, high school, home tuition and a lot of CV-relevant extras. And the money involved is serious. Especially in the cities.

SCHOOL'S IN

Cities are rich. Cities are growing. They are the seat of political power, the epicenters of media influence and the natural habitat of today's best-educated two-career families. It is much easier to find two well-paid jobs with prospects in a city than in a country town. So all around the world, professionals juggling family and work live in the city. And gasp over the school fees.

School fees are the downside of city life. In the US overall, 11 percent of students attend private schools, and in the Chicago suburbs the figure is dead on the national average: 11 percent exactly. But in the city of Chicago, about 50 percent of non-Hispanic white children are in private schools with the associated fees.[40] In the UK, just 7 percent of five- to eighteen–year-olds overall attend private schools. But in the affluent boroughs of inner London, the figure can rise to over 40 percent.[41]

Many of these schools are seriously expensive. Sidwell Friends School in Washington, DC, a favorite with American presidents, charges tuition of $30,000 a year. Some of the most academically selective private schools in Britain pride themselves on keeping costs—and fancy facilities—down. They still charge upwards of £10,000. Harry Potter's Hogwarts is free; but with Eton, you are looking at well over £30,000 a year.

All this is before one ever gets to the cost of college; and there are no economies of scale. One child, one fee; two children, two fees. No wonder that, as we saw earlier, only the very rich have three children. Amy Wax, a University of Pennsylvania law professor married to an eminent cancer researcher, bucks the trend, but only, she suspects, because of the years the family spent in Charlottesville at the University of Virginia.

"In Charlottesville we had a huge house and we had a live-in nanny. Life was easy there; it's sort of a small town and everything's close in. I think in part we had three children because we were there.

"It really meant a lot to me to have a good traditional family life and to have kids. I would have had four. What stopped me was the logistics, but also financially it was prohibitive."

In Charlottesville, lots of professional people saw the public (i.e., state) schools as a real option. In Philadelphia, says Amy, two of her three are still "in public school. Which is equivalent to child abuse. The irony is that I am one of the most conservative people on my faculty, and one of the only ones that has their kids in public school.

"On one level I'm a little puzzled that more women don't have larger families. On the other hand I see very clearly why they don't. There are two trends that are on a collision course with each other. One is the desire of women to have it all, and for the first time the real possibility of having it all. But on the other hand there is this code of intensive mothering that goes with a whole sort of class anxiety."

Certainly in my interviews I was struck by how many of the people I talked to had been to private schools themselves; even more by the numbers who were sending their own children there. This was entirely regardless of their political opinions. It is, however, consistent with the way today's highly educated parents approach childcare, which, as we saw in Chapter 3, is not about being at home with kids around the place, running in and out, but about time spent in dedicated, attention-giving, tiger-mother mode.

One of my graduate students, talented but struggling, came to see me recently. Her undergraduate education was at a large and nonprestigious institution: she had great grades but no proper training in the analytic writing skills her degree with us requires. She chose her undergraduate course, she told me, "because they said they were in the top twenty. I can see now, that must have been the top twenty for something totally different from academics. But what did I know? No one in my family had anything to go on."

No two-degree all-professional family would have made that mistake. Amy Wax notes that, for many modern parents, "getting your kid into Harvard or whatever is a full-time job. It's building that résumé, taking the kids to activities, making sure that they have the enrichment.

You're doing everything for them. And you're afraid not to because if you just let them do it for themselves they'll screw up, and other people's parents are doing it for them."

In the big cities, this process starts very early. Publishing executive Vanessa Mobley, contemplating modern America, sees the world of "advantaged" children as competitive to "a degree that's almost hard to imagine. In a lot of ways, you know, your adulthood begins in middle school, because your fortunes as an adult are determined by the college that you attend. It's like the seventh grade is your transcript for college. But then the big question is—how do you get your kid into that school? I mean, if the kid doesn't go to a good elementary school first, then they're never going to get in.

"I'll give you an example. I have friends who moved here recently from Chicago. And so schools—finding a school—took over their lives. The way it works in New York City private schools is that if you can get your eldest child into the school the others have preference; so a lot rests on the older child. And in this case, the older child is shy. Very shy. Shy is hard, shy doesn't do well. Because at these schools, it's a minimal amount of real cognitive analytical testing, it's truly the interview . . .

"And because they have the means, they applied to, and I kid you not, nearly every private school in New York City. Can you imagine the pain of this child who is shy and has to attend interviews at, I think, seventeen schools? He was admitted to none of them. Not a one. His mother was catatonic."

As we all would have been. And eventually he was admitted somewhere, in August for a September start, and, says Vanessa, "is thriving." But this child was five. Not eighteen, not even eleven. Kindergarten is just the start.

London is slightly less high-stress, but only slightly. I remember the day when my daughter took the entrance exam for a particular fee-paying high school, the only one she positively wanted to attend. I looked, in near-hysteria, at a sea of children. There seemed to be thousands of them, obviously far more than could possibly be accepted. How could I have been so careless? Why wasn't she down for two dozen entrance exams? A friend, that same month, found her small son fighting back tears as he struggled with practice entrance papers. "What will happen to me if no one, anywhere, wants me?" he asked.

These two stories had happy endings. Not all do. Tokyo is up there with New York and has been for decades longer. Examinations dominate any Chinese middle-class childhood. And the stress is equal, the anxiety and the expenditures the same, whether the children are boys or girls. The upside of a meritocratic society is that girls can compete equally. On the downside are the consequences for everyone's childhood of a society built around exams and certificates.[42]

Among the elites of developing countries the International Baccalaureate is a highly favored upper secondary certificate. It is a demanding and prestigious examination, taken at age seventeen or eighteen in a variety of subjects and recognized for entry by top universities around the world. It is offered, for the most part, in private schools around the world, including many in Asia and the Gulf; and the majority of entrants are girls.[43] Gone are the days when the future Princess Diana attended a girls' private school that, typically, gave her no serious academic instruction at all, while her brother's school tutored him for Oxford.

And the ultimate point of all this effort? Securing your child's entry to the right college or university. Professional and wealthy parents around the world are fixated with this. And as we saw in Chapter 5, they are quite right to care.

SEVERAL STEPS AHEAD

As higher education has expanded, the biggest change has been in middle- and upper-middle-class behavior. Once, affluent families sent only their academically able kids to college. Today, once your family income tops a certain level, getting a degree is pretty much automatic. The issue isn't whether you go, but merely where.

Clever kids do still come through from nowhere. There are rags-to-riches stories not just in the workplace, but also when schools and teachers spot and nurture talent. However, among poorer families, college-going is still very closely tied to academic talent. As college enrollments have soared, more poor kids enroll; but it isn't automatic and their parents haven't been surveying the college terrain since they were five years old.

The result? Family income actually has a stronger influence on college attendance than it did a few decades ago. And that influence is even stronger and more obvious when you look at who goes to the "top" institutions. Universities in the US Ivy League boast that they provide "needs blind" admission, with scholarships to help anyone whose family income is too low to cover full costs. True. But not only do a large proportion of students come from families with no need of help; even those who gain scholarships have median family incomes that put them in the top income quartile. Entry patterns at top UK universities are similar.[44]

The most dramatic example of family influence is the favored access that American private colleges give to "legacy students." These are the children of alumni, who are, in turn, a source of major support for any private institution. At Harvard, for example, it is estimated that your chances of getting admitted as an undergraduate are four times higher if your father or mother went there.[45] At Princeton, a 1998 study found that "legacies" were offered admission at more than three times the rate of other applicants and that their relative advantage had actually increased over the decade.[46]

Europeans, when they hear about this, are shocked; and it is true that Europe has no "legacy" students at its top institutions.[47] But the substance of European advantage is not so different. France was the continent's leader in insisting, from the nineteenth century on, that entry to elite institutions should be based on purely academic criteria and open competition. The state set up a country-wide network of academic high schools (*lycées*), and professional and elite families for the most part still send their children to these "public high schools" rather than to fee-paying private schools. But not just to any old one.

Entry to the top positions in French society is normally via a degree from one of the highly selective *Grandes Écoles* rather than the regular universities.[48] As we saw in Chapter 5, the gender balance in the *Grandes Écoles* has equalized rapidly in recent years. But the class balance has not. On the contrary, success in the exams has become more and more concentrated among the children of upper-middle-class families, many of whom attend just a few elite Paris high schools in wealthy and privileged neighborhoods.[49]

And what about families in countries without either top world universities or elite institutions of the French type? In Germany, for example, the quality of higher education has been flattened and equalized by allowing anyone with an academic high-school leaving certificate to enroll pretty much where, and for whatever degree, they like. Italy is similar. Does this free professional parents and their children from the relentless educational race?

To a degree. Mid-level professional couples, successful, but locally based rather than part of the national elite, will have their children schooled near home, both at high school and at university. But this simply opens up another gulf, because in these countries the top families, the seriously wealthy, simply walk away from their home universities. They send their children abroad.

Chancellor Helmut Kohl, for example, was leader of Germany for over fifteen years. He was the architect of German reunification, the personification of German tastes in food, drink, holidays. He also sent one son to Harvard and one to MIT. In November 2011, as the Greek economic crisis deepened, you could see a photo of two young men next to each other: one the current beleaguered prime minister, the other the leader of the opposition. And where had they been photographed? As classmates and freshmen at Amherst College, Massachusetts, USA.

FAMILY FIRST

In this early part of the twenty-first century, we are highly occupied, especially in the West, with the growth of inequality, the rise of the new plutocrats and the "1 percent" who are profiting at a time of economic fragility and fear.

This book has documented a rather different divide. It is between the professional elites and the rest of society. Changes within this group have been massive and indeed revolutionary, because for the first time in human history its men and women lead lives that are in most essentials the same. They study together, work together, make careers and compete with each other. They also marry each other, have children together and pool their incomes to their daughters' and sons' benefit.

Caroline Marcus, working in museums and galleries, describes her work as "an absolute passion. It's more than a job, it's about passion for collections. [But] the pay is low and it's very difficult . . . unless there is a dual family income, to sustain a certain quality of life. Whether I was male or female, I wouldn't be able to give my kids the quality of life that they're experiencing if my salary was the solo income."

In developed societies, the top 20 percent of earners pretty much equates with the professional elite. And when you look at that group, and at its children, things seem remarkably the same the developed world over. Families are doing a pretty good job at keeping their children in that top quintile and stopping them from sliding down the job or income scale.

The tendency for children born into the "top fifth" of the developed world to stay there is both high and surprisingly uniform. Precisely the same proportion stay there currently, generation to generation, in Denmark as in the US, and slightly more stay put in Sweden than in Britain.[50]

It isn't everyone. We are not becoming closed, caste societies. Nor are we all the same in terms of social mobility generally.[51] But the differences are at the bottom and in the middle. On this measure, the Scandinavians, for example, do very well, offering far more opportunity for upward mobility from the bottom of the income distribution than other countries for which we have data. But at the top, they look like everyone else.

Most people sign up willingly to the idea that social mobility is a good thing. The reality is that we all believe in social mobility if it means more people moving up.[52] We are nothing like so keen when it is our own children traveling downward. And so, all over the world, the upper middle classes work very hard to help their young. They don't run to trust funds, but they can pay the school fees. They can devote time to helping with homework and working their contacts. Married couples who both sit in the cabinet are still a rarity.[53] But a doctor and a lawyer? A professor and a banker? A school head teacher and a company director? There are plenty of those. Among the elites, the family hasn't disintegrated as a result of women's new workplace opportunities. It has morphed into something as formidable as ever before.

CONCLUSION

For ambitious, educated women, the 1960s were the portal to a golden age. On this side, full access to elite colleges, employment choices, sexual freedom; on the other, casual sexism, restricted opportunities and the kitchen sink. Yes, today also has rising divorce, low fertility and hard choices between family and career. But go back?

Until just the other day, prosperous men and women led utterly different lives. Family histories, gravestones, memorial plaques confirm it. Capable eighteenth-century Rebecca Mather is typical; her "conduct in the various relations of Domestic Life had been uniformly such that, when She exchanged this World for a better, her Loss was most sincerely regretted by her Family, her Friends and her Acquaintances." How else could she be remembered? Her husband, memorialized alongside, discharged "great Public Trusts."[1]

We have abandoned this once taken-for-granted world and, having stepped into the present, find past attitudes receding into an unreachable distance. This is not just true for the developed West. Across most of our interconnected globe, recently unquestioned beliefs about women's capacities and intelligence, about daughters compared to sons, have become quite simply inconceivable.

But is our new world what anyone expected?

Along the route, myriad reformers and revolutionaries campaigned for women's education, rights and opportunities. Some focused entirely on women; others on change to the whole social order. The world we now inhabit contains much to which they aspired—but the revolution in women's education and employment has not delivered the sort of society that many imagined. There is still inequality. There is still class. There is still family. And there is not much sisterhood.

So what next? "Never make forecasts, especially about the future," cautioned Hollywood's Samuel Goldwyn; and there will certainly be surprises to come. Nonetheless, by looking at how we arrived at today, we can tell quite a lot about the immediate future, and whether our new social order is a stable one.

PROPHECIES UNFULFILLED

The twentieth century was friendly to utopian visionaries. It bred people who believed one could create a new society and new sorts of people, and do so deliberately, to a plan. Reality taught otherwise; at its worst— under Lenin, Hitler, Mao—ideas-driven revolution brought not just upheaval but suffering and death to millions. But revolution was born, for the most part, out of idealism and outrage.

The iconic feminists of the 1960s and 1970s were of their century. They believed passionately in female equality and in sisterhood, and were also deeply opposed to traditional family life.

"Women's liberation, if it abolishes the patriarchal family, will abolish a necessary substructure of the authoritarian state, and once that withers away, Marx will have come true willy-nilly, so let's get on with it," wrote Germaine Greer in *The Female Eunuch*; while the "Declaration of Feminism" (1971) argued that "[m]arriage has existed for the benefit of men . . . We must work to destroy it."[2]

Mid-century feminism was like utopian socialism in its desire to end the traditional family. That family is indeed in retreat. Women can increasingly often support themselves. Record numbers of adults live alone. Divorce rates are high in all developed societies. Large numbers of graduates, male and female, neither marry nor have children. In the West, high and rising proportions of children are born out of wedlock and single parenthood has reached levels that previous centuries never imagined possible.

And yet, the result is hardly what feminism's prophets foretold. Marriage and the "intact" nuclear family are now strongest among the educated, the direct successors of those 1960s and 1970s college generations who burned bras and were first to embrace the sexual revolution. It is one of the respects in which elite women have become so different from other, contemporary women, and more like elite men.

THE XX FACTOR

Today, it is graduate couples, men and women, who dedicate the most time to their children, and who devote huge amounts of money, as well as time and worry, to their education. They do so because they are fully aware of the role that formal education plays in the modern labor market. They believe that getting the "best" and the most prestigious education possible will help all their children, female and male, succeed in an unforgiving world. And, as we have seen, they are right.

Utopian visions dwell on equality; peace; brotherhood; sisterhood. What we actually have today is a world in which boom and bust continue to follow hard on each other's heels, different regions and industries thrive and decline, emerging economies figure ever larger in the global economy and skilled manufacturing jobs are vanishing. It is a world in which, notoriously, the top 1 percent, and 0.1 percent, are capturing ever higher shares of national income. But the top 15 or 20 percent—the graduates and professionals that this book examined—are also drawing away from the flatlining middle. No wonder people want good jobs, graduate jobs, for themselves and for all their children.

As this book has emphasized, among the elites occupational change has been genuinely revolutionary. In the developed world, half of professional and higher management jobs are held by women. Women not only make up a majority of university students, but are taking a good half of places in the top universities, and actually outnumber men in America's Ivy League. There is no reason to suppose that this process has peaked. There will surely be more and more penetration of top jobs by women, as younger cohorts come through and developing countries become richer.

But this does not mean that elite men and women will become totally identical and interchangeable. And it is certainly not the end of, or for, successful men.

A FEMALE IDENTITY

When I ask my undergraduate students to describe the three characteristics that define them, the men and women are equally and highly unlikely to include their gender. But among working adults, most women still see being female as central to their lives. They do so at all levels of education, and much more often than men.

We know this from national data. Asked to pick their top three from a list of self-descriptors that include being a woman, or man, more than half of all graduate women choose "being a woman." For graduate men, the figure is just over a third—and they are much less likely than women to make it their first choice. Moreover, these figures are very similar at all educational levels.[3]

Given all the changes this book has outlined, why do graduate women still feel so female? The reason must, surely, be children.

Male and female graduates may be equally likely or unlikely to have children. But, as we've seen, the women think about children more and from much earlier on. Graduate women are far more likely to work continuously, post-birth, than other women, and far more likely to work full-time. But it is nonetheless graduate mothers, not fathers, who are most likely to cut back their hours at work. In spite of all those articles about alpha women needing "him indoors," the numbers of highly successful women with stay-at-home mates remain tiny.

This is why my own prediction is that, at the very top of a profession, 30 or 40 percent female is going to be common, and a 50/50 split will stay rare. In some places, the current dearth of females is temporary. For example, in the UK, the independent Monetary Policy Committee sets interest rates. Every time there is a vacancy, there is a desperate search for a suitable woman, which often fails. Ten or twenty years from now, I am sure that will be far less of a problem. The key change is not that women are the majority of college students: this statistic reflects, as much as anything, the way in which "female" jobs (like nursing) have become college-based faster than "male" ones. What really matters, and has happened, is that women are half the student population in the world's top universities.

But investment banks, top law firms, multinationals where CEOs live on planes: these are not going to hit gender equality. At a recent big stock exchange meeting on mechanisms for investing in public infrastructure, I counted eighteen women to 103 men. The women were just as senior, but that is fewer than one in six. In other professions— publishing, museums, veterinary science, medical general practice—it is and will be the reverse.

You can't just explain these patterns away as "socialization" and amenable to wholesale change. The Israeli kibbutz, which tried, is one of the most studied utopian experiments ever. The socialist founders set out to create communities in which everything was shared, and which also broke down the traditional male/female stereotypes. So children lived in dormitories, rather than individual family homes, everyone ate in the cafeteria and every effort was made to allocate jobs in a gender-blind way.

It didn't last. Women with new babies gravitated to jobs close to the nursery, so they could feed their babies easily; very quickly, the "caring" jobs became female-dominated. By the second generation, separate family homes were replacing the children's dormitories, as parents reclaimed their children. The kibbutzim, by adapting, have survived. But the radical recasting of childcare has not.[4]

Why did this happen? Arguments rage about whether any of it is biological and about how much of it is social conditioning. Like a number of my interviewees, I think that, since it's normal for the mother to be the prime parent, a good many highly educated women seize the role happily without offering their partner the option. More women will also have thought about it ahead of time and will therefore be in relatively child-friendly careers. But a lot of it is surely what academics call "path dependence": take one step in a given direction and things just go on from there.

Women get pregnant. Women give birth. And women breastfeed. Even with formula and breast pumps, it is much simpler if mothers provide most of the care for newborns. And once you have started down that path, where mothers have the larger childcare role, why upend things for the sake of it?

Of course, it is also true that most mothers *like* being with their babies. Given how much work babies involve, there wouldn't be many humans around otherwise. But in explaining why so many high-achieving mothers, and so few fathers, are the prime parent, even in a dual-career age, "path dependence" surely matters.

So, I would suggest, does another factor. Successful women don't like to marry down.

OUR CHILDREN'S FATHERS

Women have always wanted high-quality males as fathers for their children and their grandchildren. Once, their lifetime opportunities were concentrated around success in "landing a catch" within the marriage market. This is no longer true, but paternity still matters. Women's ambitions, coupled to the modern labor market, drain women from poor areas and create a female surplus in the city haunts of desirable, marriageable men.[5] In the preceding chapters, we have also seen the power of modern assortative mating. Men, after all, care deeply about the quality of their children's mothers too.

Among the poorly educated, with few prospects, women today often opt for single motherhood: better a baby fathered by an unsatisfactory and absent male than no baby at all. But very few professional women make such a choice.

And what about the broad middle of the job pyramid? This book has concentrated on the top, on what sociologists used to call "Class 1," but social change goes well beyond there. As late as the mid-1980s close to half the adult women in major Western societies thought that "[a] man's job is to earn money; a woman's is to look after the home and family."[6] Today, most adult women are employed, while breadwinner jobs are in decline. Among married couples and cohabitees, two incomes are now the general rule. Nonprofessional women mostly work in "female" jobs, often with low average pay; but across the occupational spectrum, women's pay has been increasing at a faster average rate than men's, and has been critical in maintaining household incomes. And while among the elites two professional careers have heralded the return of the servant classes, it is "tag-team" babysitting by parents balancing shifts, and not the high-paid nanny, that is most representative of modern family life.

None of these changes presages a future in which women no longer care about the quality of their children's fathers or leave the men to do all the housework. The old norm of breadwinner salaries has gone. Increasingly and finally employers pay men and women the same when what they are doing is the same work. Add in recessions and job losses, economic change and all the "ills that flesh is heir to," and in many households, in a given year, the result is that the woman will earn more. But in many others, the man will. Indeed, you'd expect the latter still to be the majority; and they are.[7]

Moreover, men are very likely indeed to be the higher earner in top-quintile families with babies. Among highly educated new mothers, almost none provides the sole or even the main support for their child.[8] Before they bring anything so precious into the world, they want it to have a good, dependable and solvent father. There is no reason why that should change.

THE HAPPINESS STAKES

Ours is not, on the whole, a utopian age. But it is one in which educated women have opportunities and achievements to their names that nineteenth-century pioneers would not have believed possible. It is therefore a little surprising to find so many elite women still arguing passionately for directed, top-down social change—change designed to improve things for female elites.

Within Europe, campaigns for female quotas for company boards have been gathering strength.[9] More generally, advocates of reform argue that companies should—indeed "must"—change the way they operate, creating flexible arrangements especially to help women with children, and a world of "re-imagined work lives" and "flexibility without marginalization."[10] As one recent proponent of wholesale change explained, "I still strongly believe that women can 'have it all' (and that men can too). I believe that we can 'have it all at the same time.' But not today, not with the way America's economy and society are currently structured."[11]

The writer in this case was Anne-Marie Slaughter, a one-percenter who moved to Washington to become director of policy planning at the State Department, a "foreign-policy dream job," while her husband, a Princeton University professor, stayed in New Jersey with their teenage boys. She then left the job two years later, in large part because of concerns about one of her sons.

The focus of these contemporary female manifestos is almost entirely elite women, not the tens and hundreds of millions who staff nursing homes, restaurants, back offices and retail parks worldwide. No matter. The likelihood of an economy structured for the convenience of mothers with children is vanishingly small, whether at the pinnacle of the job pyramid or down below.

Today's reality, as we have seen, is that professionals now work longer hours than other occupational groups, whereas in the past they worked fewer; and operate in a world where the economy is increasingly globalized. Employers can and do accommodate employees they want to keep, as best they can. Work that can be done part-time largely is. But any firm that decides to be highly family-friendly when its competitors are not is demonstrably adopting an extremely high-risk strategy.[12] And top-grade firms get that way by "being able to provide more service, more quickly, round the clock than your competitor."[13]

The reality of the professional workplace and the fact that we can't, actually, have it all probably explains why one recent news item got such enormous coverage. It concerned a research finding that women have been combining ever greater career success with falling levels of happiness.[14] It was much reported, much repeated, and is not really true. Or rather, it is true only in the US. American adults have moved from a situation where women were noticeably more likely than men to report themselves very happy to one of rough equality between the sexes, at a somewhat lower level.

Across Europe, in contrast, both men and women report increases in happiness over the last forty years; but men have been getting happier faster, right across the continent.[15] In the UK, the most recent large survey found very little difference between men's and women's happiness, and pretty high levels everywhere, though higher at the top of the occupational ladder than further down; and divorced fathers were pretty glum.[16]

However, women do generally report being more stressed and feeling more short of time than men. This isn't class- or occupation-specific. It shows up in developed country after developed country—Germany, Israel, Sweden, Australia, the Netherlands—with the largest differences found in the US. Mothers feel much more stressed than fathers when working equivalent numbers of hours in total. And wives also report doing more different things than husbands in a given period of time.

It's not clear why women "juggle" so much more than their male partners, rather than dividing tasks up more equally. I would guess it is a bit like holding the baby: it seems the simplest way to proceed. As we saw in Chapter 4, in most families men still do more of the paid hours and women more of the unpaid; and if women are at home more, they will tend to become the organizers at the household end. But home multitasking and home organizing will be on top of whatever crashed in on them at work, so they end up with more balls in play.[17] Juggling is correlated with higher stress and also a pretty plausible explanation for it.

Still, one needs a sense of proportion. The shore of Utopia is a hard place to reach; but today's educated women, in developing and developed countries, are surely much closer to it than the overwhelming majority of their female ancestors. We live in households where work time and tasks and, indeed, power are shared more equally between men and women than ever before.[18] As we live and work longer, the years in which anyone juggles small children and career shrink proportionately. Work through your sixties, as more and more do and will, have one child, and the result is that only 10 percent of your working life involves little children. Have no children, as happens for many professionals, male and female, and while it may be a source of regret, life will also offer enormous freedoms.

Choices, for today's women, have become far less consequential and determining than they once were. For Jane Austen, with whom we started, to marry or not was a once and for all decision. Everything else about her life would follow from it; and her control over her own fate was, either way, deeply limited. No educated female in the developed world today stands where she stood. If the future is anything remotely like our contemporary world, none will. And that, certainly, is progress.

APPENDIX

SUPPLEMENTARY TABLES ON REPORTED SEXUAL BEHAVIOR

Note: Where the tables shown here are based on existing publications, fuller details (including sample size, confidence intervals), will be found in the original texts. Some tables are based on original analyses of Natsal data and appear here for the first time. Fuller versions can be found at: www.kcl.ac.uk/sspp/departments/management/people/academic/wolf .aspx.

Table 1 **Median Age at First Intercourse of British Men and Women Reported in 1990**

a. Respondents aged 25–34 and born 1956–65 (for the vast majority of whom education was complete)

	degree	A level	O level/CSE	other	none
Males	18	17	17	17	16
Females	19	18	17	18	17

b. Respondents aged 45–59 (born 1930–45)

	degree	A level	O level/CSE	other	none
Males	21	19	19	18	18
Females	21	21	20	20	20

Source: Natsal

Table 2 **Males: Reported Underage and 21+ First Sex**

Graduate men in Britain are three times less likely than non-graduate men to report having underage sex; they are also almost as likely as graduate women to have had their first sexual experience at age twenty-one or older.

	Graduate males 25–34: 1990	Non-graduate males 25–34: 1990	Graduate males 25–34: 2000	Non-graduate males 25–34: 2000
% reporting first sex at under 16	9	26	11	36
% reporting first sex at 21+	23	9	14	6

Source: Natsal

Table 3 **Reported Sexual Activity by British Women, by Education, in 1990 and 2000 Respectively (Natsal Data Using the Same Groupings as the 1990 US Analyses)**

a. Number of male sexual partners reported, lifetime to date: Britain, 1990, women aged 25–44 (percentages)

	0/1	2	3–4	5–9	10–20	21+
Degree	25	14	21	20	15	5
A levels	36	18	18	17	8	2
GCSEs/O levels	38	18	22	14	7	1
No formal qualifications	41	20	21	13	5	Less than ½

b. Number of male sexual partners reported, lifetime to date: Britain, 2000, women aged 25–44 (percentages)

	0/1	2	3–4	5–9	10–20	21+
Degree	20	11	17	26	20	6
A levels	20	11	15	30	18	6
GCSEs/O levels	19	11	24	28	14	4
No formal qualifications	20	12	25	28	11	3

c. Number of other-sex sexual partners reported for the last five years (percentages) Natsal (Britain).

Females 1990	Non-graduate, 25–34	Graduate 25–34	Non-graduate, 35–44	Graduate 35–44
0	3	4	3	3
1	69	56	83	78
2	14	14	9	10
3–4	9	17	4	8
5+	4	10	1	2

Numbers rounded and may not sum to 100. For the 25–34 age group, differences by education are highly significant (p<0.0001); for 35–44 year olds, differences by education are not statistically significant.

d. Number of other-sex sexual partners reported for the last five years (percentages) by British males

Males 1990	Non-graduate, 25–34	Graduate 25–34	Non-graduate, 35–44	Graduate 35–44
0	3	5	4	3
1	53	46	73	68
2	12	16	9	12
3–4	16	16	8	5
5+	16	19	5	11

For 25–34 year olds, differences by education are non-significant ; for 35–44 year olds they are highly significant (p <0.001).
Source: Natsal

Table 4a **Percentage of British Adults Reporting No Sexual Partners in the Last Year, 1990 and 2000**

	Age 25–34	Age 35–44	Age 45–54
Females 1990	7	7	19
Males 1990	9	9	11
Females 2000	5	8	n/a
Males 2000	9	8	n/a

Source: Natsal

Table 4b **Percentage of American Adults Reporting No Opposite-Sex Sexual Partners in the Last Year: 22–44 Year Olds by Education**

	<HS	HS	Some college	Bachelor's +
Females	8	7	12	10
Males	8	9	14	11

Source: National Survey of Family Growth 2006–8

Table 4c **Number of Opposite-Sex Partners in the Last Five Years: Britain (Percentages)**

Females 2000	Non-graduate, 25–34	Graduate 25–34	Non-graduate, 35–44	Graduate 35–44
0	2	2	3	3
1	61	52	76	75
2	16	15	12	12
3–4	13	16	6	8
5+	9	16	3	3

For 25–34 group, $p<0.0001$. For 35–44 group, non-significant

Males 2000	Non-graduate, 25–34	Graduate 25–34	Non-graduate, 35–44	Graduate 35–44
0	2	4	3	2
1	41	36	65	66
2	14	14	12	9
3–4	17	18	11	10
5+	25	28	9	13

Source: Natsal
For 25–34 graduate/non-graduate differences non-significant; for 35–44. $p< 0.05$

Table 4d Percentage Reporting More than One Sexual Partner in the Last Twelve Months, American Adults Age 22–44, 2006–2008

% males reporting:	2 partners	3 partners	4 or more partners
<High school	7.2	3.4	5.9
High school diploma	7.5	3.7	6.7
Some college, no bachelor's	7.2	3.8	5.5
Bachelor's and above	7.9	2.4	3.4
% females reporting:			
<High school	8.7	2.5	1.4
High school diploma	6.7	2	3.1
Some college, no bachelor's	7.6	2.3	2.9
Bachelor's and above	4.3	1.2	1.3

Source: Chandra et al. 2011

Table 5 Reported Sexual Activity of British Females, 1990

%s	Non-graduate females 25–34	Graduate females 25–34	All females 35–44
No sex reported in previous four weeks	16	22	17
5–8 occasions	28	24	27
>8 occasions	24	18	19

(No significant differences by education in either age group)
Source: Natsal

Table 6 Reported Sexual Activity of Young Adult British Males, 1990 and 2000

%s	Non-graduate males 25–34: 1990	Graduate males 25–34 1990	Non-graduate males 25–34: 2000	Graduate males 25–34 2000
No sex reported in previous four weeks	18	25	16	20
5–8 occasions	27	22	23	19
>8 occasions	27	20	25	26

The difference between graduate and non-graduate men is significant ($p<0.0001$) for 1990: non-significant in 2000. Younger graduate men report an increase in sexual activity between 1990 and 2000, whereas their non-graduate peers do not (see above) but the differences are non-significant. For the older group (men 35–44: not shown), there were no significant differences by education in 1990 or 2000.
Source: Natsal

Table 7 **Data on Median Reported Number of Sex Occasions in Last 4 Weeks for Women: Britain 1990 and 2000 by Marital Status (in Brackets, 75th Centile)**

	1990: age 16–59	2000: age 16–44
Married	4 (8)	4 (8)
Cohabiting	6 (10)	6 (11)
Single	0 (5)	1 (6)

Source: Natsal reference tables.

Table 8 **USA: Reported Frequency of Sex in Past 12 Months—Women, 1990**

	Not at all	Few times a year	Few times a month	2 or 3 times a week	4 or more times a week
< HS	19	15	36	23	8
HS graduate	11	16	38	30	6
Any college	14	17	37	26	7

Note: Female US 1990 data do not show linear differences by education
Source: Michael et al. (1994)

Table 9 **Median Number of Times American Women Report Sex with a Male in the Last 4 Weeks, by Education: 2006–2008**

	Married women 25–44
< HS	4
HS	3
Some college	5
Bachelor's	5
Graduate school +	3
All	4

Source: Survey of Family Growth 2006–8

Table 10 **Percentage of British Women Reporting No Sex in the Past Four Weeks, 1990**

%	Non-graduates	Graduates
Full sample	16	22
Women who reported being in a partnership during the last year	10	15

Differences by education: p<0.05 for full sample, p<0.005 for "partnership" sub-sample.
Source: Natsal

Table 11 Median Number of Sex Occasions in Last Four Weeks: British Women Age 25–44, 2000

	Median	% reporting > 8
No quals.	3	20
Good GCSEs	4	23
Some higher education post–A level	4	23
Degree	3	20
All	4	22

Differences by education, while statistically significant for median number of occasions, had declined compared to 1990, and were not large or linear (p<0.05). There were no significant differences by education in the percentages reporting 8 or more.
Source: Natsal

Table 12 Reported Frequency of Female Sexual Intercourse, Averaged over the Last Twelve Months: American Females, 1990

	Not at all	Few times a year	Few times a month	2 or 3 times a week	4 or more times a week	Total % reporting 2 or more times a week
Non-cohabiting	**32**	23	24	15	5	20
Co-habiting	**1**	8	35	42	14	56
Married	**3**	12	47	32	7	39

Source: Michael et al. (1994) Note the differences in proportions reporting zero (in **bold**).

Table 13 Attitudes of Young Female British Adults to One-Night Stands, 2000

% saying one-night stands are:	Always wrong	Rarely or never wrong
Graduate females age 25–34	17	32
Non-graduate females age 25–34	32	24

Source: Natsal

Table 14 **Attitudes of Adult British Males (25–44) to One-Night Stands, 1990 and 2000**

% saying one-night stands are:	Non-graduate men 1990	Graduate men 1990	Non-graduate men 2000	Graduate men 2000
Always wrong	32	28	19	15
Rarely/never wrong	29	24	42	37

Difference between graduates and non-graduates is highly significant (p<0.001) in both cohorts.
Source: Natsal

Table 15 **Attitudes of British Males to Homosexuality, 1990 and 2000**

% aged 25–44 who think:	Male non-graduates 1990	Male graduates 1990	Male non-graduates 2000	Male graduates 2000
Male homosexuality is always wrong	59	28	45	21
Female homosexuality is always wrong	47	25	29	16
Male homosexuality is rarely/never wrong	27	47	41	62
Female homosexuality is rarely/never wrong	30	49	47	65

Highly significant (p<0.0001) differences on all graduate/non-graduate comparisons.
Source: Natsal

Table 16 **Enjoyment of Sex: Male and Female Responses, Britain, 2000**

How much do you enjoy sex? (%s)	All men	Graduate men	Non-graduate men
Always	55	51	56
Most of the time	36	41	34
Sum of the above	91	92	90
	All women	Graduate women	Non-graduate women
Always	35	32	35
Most of the time	51	57	50
Sum of the above	86	89	85

Note: This table includes all sexually active Natsal respondents (ie age 16–44) and not just 25–44 year olds.
Source: Natsal 2000

Table 17 **Desire for Sex: Male and Female Adults Age 25–44, Britain, 2000**

(Responses to the question: How much sex would you like compared to the present?)

	All men	Graduate men	Non-graduate men
Much more	15	14	15
More	38	44	36
Sum of the above	53	58	51
	All women	Graduate women	Non-graduate women
Much more	11	11	10
More	29	40	27
Sum of the above	40	52	37

Differences between graduate men and all other categories were highly significant (p<0.01). However, for young graduate men compared to young graduate women, no statistically significant differences were found.
Source : Natsal

Table 18 **Male and Female Views on Orgasm for Women: Britain, 1990 and 2000**

"Sex without orgasm or climax cannot be satisfying for a woman"	Non-graduate males 1990	Graduate males 1990	Non-graduate females 1990	Graduate females 1990
% agreeing	38	31	30	17
% disagreeing	42	46	54	69
	Non-graduate males 2000	Graduate males 2000	Non-graduate females 2000	Graduate females 2000
% agreeing	40	31	32	27
% disagreeing	32	44	41	52

Source: Natsal 1990, 2000.

Table 19 **Percentage of Men Reporting Two or More Sexual Partners in the Previous Year: Britain, 1990 and 2000**

25–34 year olds	Graduate males 25–34: 1990	Non-graduate males 25–34 1990	Graduate males 25–34 : 2000	Non-graduate males 25–34 2000
% reporting 2+ sexual partners in the last year	17	15	23	23

Differences between graduates and non-graduates are non-significant.

35–44 year olds	Graduate males 35–44: 1990	Non-graduate males 35–44 1990	Graduate males 35–44: 2000	Non-graduate males 35–44 1990
% reporting 2+ sexual partners in the last year	13	9	17	12

Differences between graduates and non-graduates are non-significant.
Source: Natsal

Table 20 **Percentage of Women Aged 20–44 Who Have Had Two or More Partners in the Past Year: USA**

	Single	Married	Cohabiting
Less than high school	17.5	1.6	9.1
High school diploma	22.2	1.6	6.0
College	15.5	1.2	8.3

2006–8 Survey of Family Growth data.
Source: Chandra et al. 2011

Appendix: Supplementary Tables on Reported Sexual Behavior

Figure A1 **Median Number of Times American Women Report Sex with a Male in Last 4 Weeks by Educational Group, 2006–2008**

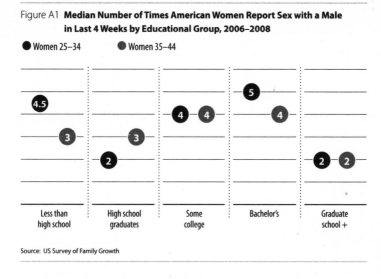

⬤ Women 25–34 ⬤ Women 35–44

Source: US Survey of Family Growth

Figure A2 **Percentage of British Women Age 25–44 With a Sexual Partner Reporting Oral Sex in the Last Year**

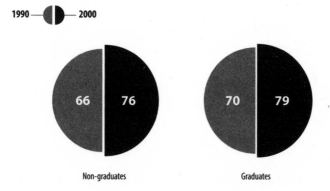

1990 —◖◗— 2000

Source: Natsal

Figure A3 **Percentage of British Women Age 25–44, with a Sexual Partner Reporting Anal Sex in the Last Year**

1990 ——◖—— 2000

6 | 11 — Non-graduates

4 | 12 — Graduates

Source: Natsal

Figure A4 **Percentage British Women Reporting That They Had Underage Sexual Intercourse**

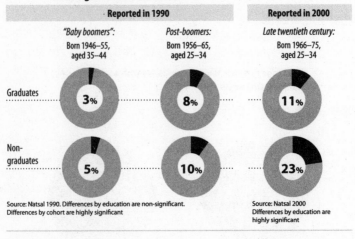

Reported in 1990		Reported in 2000
"Baby boomers": Born 1946–55, aged 35–44	*Post-boomers:* Born 1956–65, aged 25–34	*Late twentieth century:* Born 1966–75, aged 25–34

Graduates — 3% — 8% — 11%

Non-graduates — 5% — 10% — 23%

Source: Natsal 1990. Differences by education are non-significant. Differences by cohort are highly significant

Source: Natsal 2000 Differences by education are highly significant

---

Figure A5 **Median Number of Male Sexual Partners Reported by Non-Graduate and Graduate Women, Age 25–44, Britain (Lifetime to Date)**

All non-graduates

Graduates

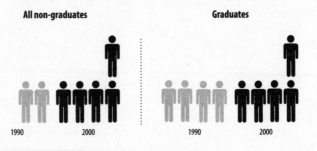

1990   2000   1990   2000

Source: Natsal 1990, Natsal 2000

NOTES

INTRODUCTION

1. In Jane Austen's case, her brothers'. Nineteenth-century novels are full of "poor relations," whose ubiquity was taken for granted by contemporaries and whom we, as
modern readers, barely register.
2. Nor is it the case that educated men are increasingly choosing to be "deadbeats" or
"playboys." (The labels are from Kate Bolick's 2011 article "All the single ladies"
[*The Atlantic*, November 2011].)
3. In estimating the size of the new female elite, I have calculated the overall average size of the rich + the upper middle classes in (a) all developed societies, (b) all
middle-income countries and (c) all developing countries. In developed societies—
where males and females now level-peg almost completely up to age 30 and to a
large degree up to age 40—I have then taken women to be about 40 percent of the
group: this is consistent with detailed recent estimates for the US and the UK. In
middle-income and developing countries I estimate women to form about 20 percent of the (much smaller) total numbers in this rich + upper-middle-class group.
Analysts of the class structure of modern developed societies consistently identify
two groups at the top of the class structure: namely, the very rich (less than 1 percent) and the "upper middle class" or "highly educated professionals and salaried,"
making up about 15 percent or a little more of the employed population. In poorer
countries these groups make up somewhere between 2 and 7 percent of the total.
See, for example, Thompson and Hickey, 2005.
4. Nancy Astor, the MP in question, was elected in 1919. The year before, the Irish
nationalist Countess Constance Markievicz had been elected to a Dublin constituency while in prison for political activities. However, she refused to take the seat.
The Irish Republic declared independence a few months later. Markievicz became
a member of the first Dáil, the Irish Republic's Parliament (initially while still in
prison), served as a minister and followed a political career in the Irish Republic
until her death in 1927.

Notes

1: GOODBYE TO ALL THAT

1. Fox, 2000: 48.
2. Ibid.: 52.
3. Irene herself married the artist Charles Dana Gibson, creator, in his drawings, of the "Gibson Girl": tall, slender and specifically "American," and the ideal female type for a good twenty years. The oldest Langhorne daughter, Lizzie, never made the transition, instead remaining in Virginia, married to a Virginian.
4. Cline, 2009.
5. See Introduction, note 3.
6. In pre-agricultural societies, there was little waged labor, and even in agricultural ones, many people worked in subsistence agriculture and used money very little; but the general point holds.
7. She is played by Christina Hendricks—possessor of a fantastic hourglass figure, *Esquire*'s Best Looking American Woman of 2010 and supposedly responsible for a direct increase in the number of women opting for breast-augmentation surgery. See http://www.telegraph.co.uk/health/healthnews/8290407/Mad-Men-star-Christina-Hendricks-sparks-rush-for-breast-implants.html.
8. For the exchange between Joan and Peggy see http://leethomson.myzen.co.uk/Mad_Men/Mad_Men_1x01_-_Smoke_Gets_in_Your_Eyes.pdf: 11.
9. Goldin, 1991.
10. Sheridan and Stretton, 2004.
11. Vinovskis, 1990: 7.
12. The post–Civil War South offered far fewer alternatives to marriage and motherhood than the world of the 1920s and had experienced a rate of slaughter, in the young white male population, that was at least as great as that for the Western European powers in 1914–18; but in the North the period after the Civil War was one of enormous immigration, on top of generally lower losses, and there was no such dramatic impact on women's lives.
13. Nicholson, 2008: 71.
14. Quoted ibid.: 22–3.
15. Quoted ibid.: 24.
16. Hakim, 2004 and 2011a; Esping-Andersen, 2009.
17. The International Labour Organization (ILO) is a UN agency based in Geneva that has carried out an extensive program of research on gender and the labor market. ILO senior researchers argue that "a gender-segregated labor market is not something which should be taken as inevitable or natural, especially in the long run." See Melkas and Anker, 1997; see also Anker, Melkas and Korten, 2003.
18. OECD 2002: Table 2.10. Women in 2000 totaled 48 percent of professionals, 54 percent of technicians and associate professionals, and 30 percent of the "legislators, senior officials and corporate managers" group.
19. When it comes to their highly educated women, Scandinavian countries are right on trend. In Sweden, for example, 44 percent of production managers, 52 percent of lawyers and 39 percent of senior civil servants are now women. See Statistics Sweden: "Employees 16–64 years old, 2009."

20. In Germany, for example, where women are increasing their share of the "top" jobs, occupations across the labor market as a whole have become markedly more segregated by gender. Figures are for (old) West Germany. See Blossfeld, 1987, cited in Hakim, 2004: 156. The figures given by Blossfeld are for the states that were part of West Germany pre-reunification.

21. Hakim, 2004: 155. Hakim classified the UK workforce in the 1990s into jobs that were "mixed," "male" and "female": mixed if they were between 25 and 55 percent female, female if more than 55 percent female, male if less than 25 percent female (and so more than 75 percent male). Less than 20 percent of the workforce was found in mixed occupations; the rest was more or less evenly divided between occupations that were predominantly male and occupations that were predominantly female. Moreover, she established that it was the small group of "mixed" occupations that had the highest incidence of "higher-status and higher-paid" occupations.

22. Table n1 **Top 20 Female Occupations in the USA, 2009**

Occupation	Number of women employed	Proportion (%) who are female
Secretaries and administrative assistants	3,074,000	97
Registered nurses	2,612,000	92
Elementary and middle school teachers	2,343,000	82
Cashiers	2,273,000	74
Nursing, psychiatric and home health aides	1,770,000	89
Retail salespersons	1,650,000	52
First-line supervisors/managers of retail sales workers	1,459,000	44
Waiters and waitresses	1,434,000	72
Maids and housekeeping cleaners	1,282,000	90
Customer service representatives	1,263,000	68
Childcare workers	1,228,000	95
Bookkeeping, accounting and auditing clerks	1,205,000	92
Receptionists and information clerks	1,168,000	92
First-line supervisors/managers of office and administrative support workers	1,163,000	71
Managers, all other (i.e. managers not in specified and separately enumerated sectors)	1,106,000	34
Accountants and auditors	1,084,000	62
Teacher assistants	921,000	92
Cooks	831,000	42
Office clerks, general	821,000	82
Personal and home care aides	789,000	85

Source: US Department of Labor Women's Bureau Fact Sheets: 20 Leading occupations of employed women (2009 figures)

23. See, for example, Goldin and Katz, 2008a; College Board, 2008; Leitch, 2006.

24. Table n2 **Number of Full-Time Walmart Employees**

	Walmart: Number of Full-Time Employees
1975	21,000
1987	200,000

Notes

Walmart: Number of Full-Time Employees	
1996	675,000
2000	1,140,000
2005	1,700,000
2006	1,900,000
2007	1,900,000
2008	2,055,000
2009	2,100,000
2010	2,100,000

Sources: CNN Money; Fortune 500; Walmartstores.com

25. The baseline is only 16,000, giving a grand total of 11,500 more jobs. In a workforce of 150 million that barely registers.

26. US Department of Labor, 2009. In the UK, the fastest-growing occupation of the twenty-first century is conservation officer: there are 15,000 more of them than when the twenty-first century began. Care assistants, meanwhile, are up by 156,000. UK Commission for Employment and Skills, 2010. In contrast, manufacturing, though it still demands highly skilled workers, is also, outside China's assembly plants, ever more capital-intensive, with constant productivity increases and corresponding decreases in numbers employed. See, for example, Michaels, Natraj and Van Reenan, 2010.

27. Among the major industrial sectors of England and Wales, for example, construction employees are 90 percent male and manufacturing 73 percent. Education, meanwhile, is 73 percent female and, in the health and social work sector, 80 percent of employees are women. See Census 2001: Table S035. If you compare the UK in 1901 and in 1991, there is a clear decline in the number of men working in jobs that are more than 60 percent male, from 92 percent in 1901 to 77 percent in 1991. But there is almost no such decline for women. In 1901 74 percent of British women worked in jobs that were more than 60 percent female. In 1991, with a much larger female workforce, the figure was 70 percent. See Gallie, n.d. Meanwhile, across the "rich country" club of the OECD, at the dawn of the twenty-first century, women were half the professionals—but just 4 percent—less than one in 20—of drivers and 3 percent of building trades workers, compared to 77 percent of health sector employees and 73 percent of "salespersons." See Hakim, 2004: 151.

28. In 1900 half the UK male workforce was working in occupations where there was not a single female employee.

29. Just 22 percent of female workers in fourteen other OECD countries examined by the ILO were working in occupations with such overwhelmingly female recruitment. See Melkas and Anker, 1997: 352.

30. The percentage of men working in male-dominated occupations is similar to that for the rest of the OECD. Among mechanics and construction workers, women hover around the 2 percent mark, just as they do elsewhere. It is the women who are much more concentrated in occupations that are extremely female. See Melkas and Anker, 1997.

31. Haataja, 2009.

Notes

32. In 1910 the US Census counted 558 practicing female lawyers—roughly one for every 200 men—and no female judges or magistrates. See http://www.law.harvard .edu/news/bulletin/backissues/spring99/article2.html.

33. US Bureau of the Census: 1970 Census of Population.

34. The table below provides detailed figures on changes in female representation.

Table n3 **Percentage of Females in Major Professional and Senior Managerial Occupations in the UK**

Occupation	1971	1981	1990	1999	2009
Lawyers and judges	4	14	27	35	43
Teachers in higher education	25	27	37	43	50
Doctors and dentists	18	23	30	38	42
Scientists	7	20	26	34	39
Economists, statisticians, system analysts and computer programmers	15	19	19	26	39

Sources: Hakim, 2004; Labour Force Survey, 2009

Note: Occupational classifications changed to a very significant degree in the early 2000s. Occupations are only shown if there were no major alterations to their particular definition. Scientists include mathematicians as well as biologists, chemists, physicists and "other scientists."

35. Women make up over 60 percent of British medical school graduates and residents, and 43 percent and rising of all those practicing medicine. Of UK management consultants 39 percent are women—70,000 of them—as are 44 percent of insurance underwriters. Source: Labour Force Survey, 2009. In the US 50 percent of purchasing managers are women, as are 56 percent of loan officers and 43 percent of news reporters; and the majority of insurance underwriters are, unlike in the UK, female. Of US insurance underwriters 63 percent are female. Source: US Current Population Survey, 2009, US Department of Labor 2010. In France women make up 47 percent of those employed in scientific and technical activities, 58 percent of finance and insurance executives and 44 percent of those in the publishing and audiovisual sector. See Table 203, Emploi salarié selon les secteurs d'activité: Insée, Estimations d'emploi at http://www.insee.fr/fr/themes/detail.asp ?reg_id=0&ref_id=ir-martra10&page=ir.

36. UK Labour Force Survey (data analysis carried out for this publication by Scott Blevins).

37. The very first female partner was Jeanette Loeb in 1986; Fitt was the first on the equity side.

38. Steinem, 2008.

39. Goldin, 2006: 11.

40. Dench, 2010: 2. Dench is referring to an episode in a memoir by Toby Young called *How to Lose Friends and Alienate People*.

41. Figure n1 overleaf summarizes a century of change for the US, including that post-1940s takeoff.

42. Rattigan, 1953: 119–20. Rattigan was himself a Bomber Command rear-gunner.

43. In the US, as recently as 1970, the gap between women's and men's participation rates was 36 percentage points, three times as great as it is today. See US Census Bureau, 2010b: Tables 586, 598. Since 1970, the proportion of all women over 16

Figure n1 **Trends in US Female Employment**

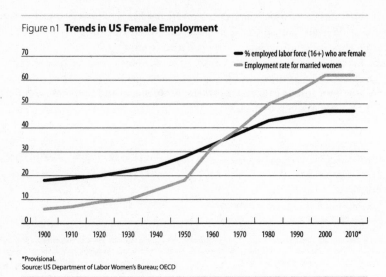

● % employed labor force (16+) who are female
● Employment rate for married women

*Provisional.
Source: US Department of Labor Women's Bureau; OECD

who are in the labor force has increased from four to nearly six in every ten. See Lee and Mather, 2008. This is still somewhat lower than for men: in 2009 just over seven in ten American men over 16 were in the labor force. Male employment rates in developed countries are typically between ten percentage points higher than women's (in countries with generally high participation rates) and 20 percentage points higher (in the lower-participation rate ones). See OECD, 2010: Table B. The highest female rates are for Scandinavia, but include many individuals who are absent from the workplace on maternity, family or other leave but still counted in the statistics as employed. Countries vary enormously in both the maternity and the family leave benefits they offer, and in whether women absent on official forms of leave are counted as employed. Christina Jonung and Inga Persson carried out a detailed comparison of Swedish work patterns with those of the US, France, Norway and Finland. They concluded that, once adjusted for differences of this type, and differences in actual hours worked, Sweden is "not that exceptional" (p.271) in the relationship between its male and female working patterns. See Jonung and Persson, 1993.

44. See previous note. With lengthening time spent in education, few developed societies get much above 80 percent "gainfully employed" among adult men, let alone women, as shown below.

Table n4 **Labor Force Participation Rates (%): Selected OECD Countries, 2009**

	Men 15–64	Women 15–64
Australia	82.6	70.1
Canada	81.8	74.4
Denmark	84.0	77.3
France	74.7	65.9
Germany	82.2	70.4

Notes

	Men 15–64	Women 15–64
Israel (2008)	68.1	59.5
Italy	73.7	51.1
Japan	84.8	62.9
Korea	76.9	53.9
Netherlands	84.1	73.5
UK	83.2	70.2
US	80.4	69.0
OECD weighted average	80.2	67.9

Sources: OECD Employment Outlook, 2010; Statistical Annex Table B Paris
Note: Figures for the UK and US are for 16–64-year-olds.

In all OECD countries, females are close to half the labor force: for example, 48 percent in Sweden, 46 percent in the UK, 43 percent in Japan and 41 percent even in Italy.

45. I have used OECD figures and definitions: absolute numbers vary depending on how "part-time" is defined, but the general pattern is the same whatever definitions are used. For example, the US Department of Labor says 26 percent of American women work part-time in its "Quick Stats on Women Workers 2009," compared to the 19 percent in the OECD statistics for the US. (All OECD statistics are provided by member governments, but to standard OECD-wide definitions.)

46. Moreover, male and female part-timers are also different sorts of people. Men who work part-time tend to be young or old, either students and job-market entrants, or people nearing (or in) retirement. Women, on the other hand, are very often in their thirties, forties and fifties, the prime working years.

47. See, for example, Cousins and Tang, 2004; Hakim, 2004; Crompton and Lyonette, 2007, especially pp. 61–3.

48. This does not mean that there are no part-time female professionals; there is a male–female difference here too, which largely reflects female working patterns related to motherhood. In the 2001 UK Census, for example, 3 percent of the male corporate managers were working part-time, compared to 15 percent of the women. And among health professionals—doctors and dentists—30 percent of women were working part-time, more than three times the proportion of men who were part-timers. However, in most nonprofessional occupations, the male–female differences are far greater, as are the absolute percentages of women who are part-time. In the UK, for example, 70 percent of female sales staff work part-time. See UK Census 2001: Table S035.

49. This holds when controlling for other factors. Bosch et al. estimate the probability that, in 2000, a "prototypical" marrried childless woman of 40 would be employed, depending on her education, as follows (Table n5):

Table n5 **Probability of Employment for Dutch Women**

	0 hours	1–11	12–24	25–34	35+
Primary education	43	2	19	15	21
Lower secondary	18	4	27	21	30
Upper secondary	8	6	31	23	32
Tertiary	0	6	30	26	38

Source: Bosch, Deelen and Euwals, 2008: Table 4.2

50. Four in five (80 percent) are working full-time, compared to just one in five part-time, whereas among the least qualified, it falls to two in three. See American Time Use Survey data for 2003, analyzed by Anne-Marie Jeannet. Chapter 4 discusses time use data in detail.

51. The results of this are very clear when one looks at labor market statistics broken down by age. In the US, for example, there are more women than men, in total, in the labor force among 16- to 19-year-olds and 20- to 24-year–olds. (NB: Absolute numbers of men and women in the labor market are also affected by differences in the percentages of men and women who are in the military or incarcerated.) Among 25- to 34-year-olds and 35- to 44-year-olds, the pattern reverses itself; and then, post-45, flips back to a female majority. In the US the shift from a female majority among the young and the old to a minority in middle age is big enough to mean that, for the over-25 population as a whole, men's participation rates are higher. In the UK full-time employment rates for women are highest at age 25–9; then fall; they rise at age 45+ and among those in their fifties reach equality with men's. See Office for National Statistics, 2010: Chapter 4.

52. See Table n5 above for Dutch patterns. US figures are as follows:

Table n6 **Rate of Participation in the Labor Market (%): Population 25 and Over (Civilian, Non-Institutional), 2009: USA**

	Less than high-school diploma	High-school graduate, no college	Less than a bachelor's degree	College graduate
Males	59.2	72.1	77.5	81.8
Females	33.8	52.8	65.9	73.3

Source: US Bureau of the Census, Statistical Abstract of the United States: Table 592

53. Examples include the following:

Table n7 **Labor Market Participation: Population Aged 25–64, 2008**

	Male participation rate (%): Less than upper-secondary education	Male participation rate (%): Tertiary education	Female participation rate (%): Less than upper-secondary education	Female participation rate (%): Tertiary education
Australia	81	93	60	82
Canada	74	90	51	83
Germany	81	92	56	84
Italy	75	89	38	80
Japan (upper secondary vs. tertiary)	92	96	64	68
Korea	81	92	59	63
Netherlands	81	92	53	87
UK	79	92	58	86

Source: OECD Employment Outlook, 2010: Table D

54. Bennetts, 2007.

55. Goodwin, 2010; see also Walter, 2010.

56. Prince William inherited a large amount from his mother, over and above his expectations as a future Prince of Wales and monarch.

57. A quarter of those without children work 20 or fewer hours a week; only 34 percent of the childless work more than 35 hours. Bosch, Deelen and Euwals, 2008.

58. Cousins and Tang, 2004: 536.

59. Bosch, van der Klaauw and van Ours, 2009.

60. Bosch, Deelen and Euwals, 2008: 22. Dutch women are not completely indifferent to money (which would be very odd). But they have a strong positive taste for part-time work, which seems to have increased rather than decreased in recent cohorts.

61. See "Five Books Interview" with Ellen de Bruin on http://fivebooks.com/interview/ellen-de-bruin-on-women-and-happiness.

62. Rumbelow, 2011.

63. From the 1990s on, part-time workers have had the same benefits (for example, holiday entitlements) as full-timers. Tax reforms have been designed to encourage participation by lowering the marginal tax burden on a second worker in a household, but have not been designed to favor part-time work over full-time work. There are generous childcare subsidies. See Bosch, Deelen and Euwals, 2008.

64. Bosch, van der Klaauw and van Ours, 2009.

65. For example, the Dutch spend below the EU average on health, but run a system that is generally recognized as high quality.

66. See, for example, Dench, 2010; Hakim, 2011a; Pinker, 2008; Fawcett Society, 2005.

67. Strandh and Nordenmark, 2006: 609.

68. Cousins and Tang, 2004: 542. It is also the case that, among fathers and mothers, Swedish data are more "symmetrical": fathers and mothers report levels and patterns of conflict that are much more similar to each other than is the case with Dutch fathers and mothers, or British fathers and mothers.

69. One of the surprising things I have discovered, in a life of academic research, is that low-paid workers in routine jobs are often far more satisfied with their jobs than professionals. They expect less and compare what they have with what they might realistically find, not with the gold at the end of the rainbow. See Wolf and Evans, 2010; Clark, 1997.

70. City and Guilds Career Happiness Index, 2009; see www.cityandguilds.com; Crawford, 2010.

71. Aubenas, 2011: 58.

72. See, for example, Shackleton, 2008; Bertrand, Goldin and Katz, 2009; Gudrais, 2010.

73. See, for example, Wax, 2004.

74. In many parts of the world, labor regulations and employer-linked insurance and pension payments have a major impact on whether, and how far, part-time workers are more or less expensive per hour than full-timers. However, the enormous growth of part-time work at lower levels in most developed countries—a development that is often criticized for creating a mass of largely female, insecure, "prospect-less" jobs—further suggests that if employers are not creating lots of part-time openings at the top, they have good reason not to.

75. The UK civil service encourages job-sharing for women who are "fast-track" and tapped for promotion; and does so as part of a commitment to equal opportunity,

Notes

as well as retention of high-quality staff. But it is definitely more expensive (and inconvenient) short-term than having a single person in the job. Whether this pays off long-term, by making more female higher-quality full-timers available down the line, is not something that anybody has any realistic chance of quantifying.

76. Research by Bertrand, Goldin and Katz shows that women with Harvard MBAs are far less likely to combine employment and children fifteen years after graduation than are female medical graduates from Harvard; and that MBAs in the corporate and finance sector incur a severe wage penalty for any career interruptions. See Gudrais, 2010; Bertrand, Goldin and Katz, 2009.

77. In the US, less-skilled men (high-school graduates and high-school dropouts) saw real wage declines from 1979 to the mid-1990s, and though average real wages for this group then moved up again, in 2004 they were still 15 percent below the 1979 level. For women, in contrast, real wages for high-school dropouts rose 5 percent over the same period, and those of high-school graduates rose 17 percent. Meanwhile, for women with more than high school (some time spent in college or a full degree), earnings rose an average of 31 percent, compared to just 12 percent for comparable men. See Blank and Shierholz, 2006.

78. Female employment rates are now largely flatlining, with one major exception: employment for older people—men and women—is increasing, in belated response to rising longevity.

2: THE RICH GET RICH AND THE POOR GET CHILDREN

1. "Ain't We Got Fun?" (vaudeville song, 1921; music by Richard A. Whiting, lyrics by Raymond B. Egan and Gus Kahn).

2. A favorite candidate is the Toba volcanic eruption. There is no unanimity over either the existence of a bottleneck at all or its date, but the balance of opinion is in favor both of such an event, and of the survivors being based in Africa. See, for example, Huff et al., 2010; Goldstein and Chikhi, 2002.

3. The table below provides examples for some of the world's largest developing countries

Table n8 **Average Numbers of Births per Woman, 1960–2010: Selected Developing Countries**

	South Africa	India	China
1960	6.45	5.87	5.47
1980	4.79	4.69	2.63
2000	2.87	3.21	1.76
2010	2.46	2.63	1.60

Source: Gapminder.org

4. In Japan, the average number of births per woman was over five in the 1920s; it was down to 1.4 by 2000. See Date and Shimizutani, 2007. A fall in population was expected by 2012, but population levels have been stabilized by large numbers of Japanese returning from abroad and low levels of out-migration. In other developed countries, high levels of immigration are also currently counterbalancing the impact of low birth rates.

Notes

5. In 1976 10 percent of US women aged 40–44 were childless. In 2006 it was 20 percent. National Surveys of Family Growth, as cited in Preston and Hartnett, 2008, and Dye, 2008.
6. It is around 30 percent in the UK, for example: see Smith and Ratcliffe, 2009. In France, among women born in the 1950s, those with "long" education, at least two years more than the average for their cohort, were twice as likely to be childless as those with "short" education (two years less than the average). The figures are 17 percent and 8 percent respectively: see Touleman, Pailhé and Rossier, 2008.
7. If women with associate degrees are added in, the proportion of graduates rises to just short of 40 percent. However, women with associate degrees are generally more like those with "some college" in their fertility and labor market engagement than like those with bachelor's (or above).
8. Figures based on 2010 Census data: 40–44-year-old women are 7.4 percent of the female population and 11.32 million in number. The cohorts that were aged 40–44 in 2006 had rather higher childlessness, estimated at 25 percent.
9. Many women with less than high school are foreign-born.
10. Table n9 **Proportion of Women (%) Who Are Childless in the UK**

Percent childless at age 45: Women born in the UK in 1958		Percent childless at age 40: Women resident in the UK, born in 1965	
Obtained some form of post high-school qualification	24	College-educated	30
No formal qualifications	11	Left school at 16 (qualified and unqualified combined)	15

Sources: Kneale and Joshi, 2008; Ratcliffe and Smith, 2007

For women born 1960–63 in England and Wales, the Office of National Statistics estimates that 19–20 percent in total are childless at the age of 45. See ONS Birth Statistics 2008: Table 10.

11. *The Economist*, 2011: 20.
12. See Date and Shimizutani, 2007: 25, 28.
13. In 1970 female fertility rates for high-school dropouts were 1.35 as large as those for graduates; in 2006, 1.5 times higher (data as shown in Figure 2.2).
14. For all US white women aged 35–44 with five+ years of college, US Census Bureau figures show a 30.3 percent childlessness rate in 1982 (figures for other ethnic groups are not broken out into four years/five years+). See US Bureau of the Census Current Population Reports Series P-20 no. 387.
15. There is a vast literature on the subject of male/female differences, some of which is addressed directly in Chapter 10. Many feminist writers of the 1960s and 1970s argued that there were no important biological influences on the different ways men and women lived and behaved, and that these were entirely socially constructed. Since then there has been growing acceptance that biology plays some part, though continuing arguments about how much and in what ways. See Rhoads, 2004, and Pinker, 2008, for recent overviews that argue that gender differences are fundamental

and far-reaching. Prominent authors who argue that social factors remain critical in explaining women's lives—and continued lack of equal opportunity—include Dorothy Smith (see especially Smith, 1990) and Carol Gilligan (see Gilligan, 1997).

16. Hrdy,1999: 8. Hrdy bases her calculations on the !Kung hunter-gatherers, who lived in an arid and demanding environment, but one that was nonetheless largely disease-free.

17. Hrdy, 1999; Pinker, 2011.

18. See, for example, Ní Bhrolcháin, Beaujouan and Berrington, 2010. The proportion of childless women who state that they do not expect to have a child does increase significantly among those in their mid-thirties. For a discussion of the gap between Japanese expectations/intentions and actual fertility, see Date and Shimizutani, 2007.

19. Sleebos, 2003.

20. Back in the 1980s, sociologist Kathleen Gerson studied, in detail, a group of American women who graduated successfully from high school in the 1960s and 1970s. Those who went to college were, predictably, more likely to end up childless than those who did not; but that was where any obvious explanations end. Some of the determined high-school careerists instead settled down to be primarily wives and mothers, while teenagers who expected to follow conventional "domestic" lives, much as their mothers were doing, often ended up in their thirties unmarried and very career-oriented. But these women were not irrational or thoughtless. On the contrary, they made their choices for very good reasons, in the light of their particular choices, relationships and circumstances. See Gerson, 1985: 94, 79.

21. Betts, Rose and Vernon, 2011. The article was written in response to a survey suggesting that 43 percent of "generation X" graduate women, born between 1965 and 1978, would have no children. These numbers are higher than for any previous generation that has completed child-bearing; but the survey very probably exaggerates the final level of childlessness, since many respondents were between 33 and 40 at the time of responding, and, as this chapter discusses, 30+ is now the prime child-bearing age for graduate women. It is reported by the Center for Work-Life Policy: http://www.worklifepolicy.org/index.php/section/research_pubs. See also Table n9 above for UK women born in 1965.

22. Zerjal et al., 2003.

23. Goldin and Katz, 2008b. The 1970 cohort covers those graduating 1969–72; the 1980 one, 1979–82; and the 1990 one, 1989–92. Information was collected fifteen years after graduation, when alumni were in their mid- to late thirties.

Table n10 **Birth Rates Among Harvard/Radcliffe Graduates, from 1970**

	1970 cohort M	1970 cohort F	1980 cohort M	1980 cohort F	1990 cohort M	1990 cohort F
% with at least one child ever born	65.70	62.5	66.0	60.8	64.9	62.0
Average number of children	1.28	1.17	1.42	1.35	1.41	1.31
Number of cases	1453	672	1363	858	1195	1013

Source: Goldin and Katz 2008b

24. Adrian, 2007.

25. See the Centre for Longitudinal Studies website for details of the birth cohort studies and their research outputs: http://www.cls.ioe.ac.uk/.

26. Table n11 **Percentage of UK-Born Men and Women, Born 1958, with No Children Born by Age 46**

UK-born men Bachelor's degree	UK-born men Higher degree	UK-born women Bachelor's degree	UK-born women Higher degree
28.5	29.7	25.7	30.0

Source: unpublished data from NCDS (2004 sweep)

27. Figures from the British Cohort Survey 1970 show that 48 percent of all 1970-born men are childless at age 34 (unpublished data). For those with some tertiary qualifications (including sub-degree) this increases to 56 percent; for comparable women at that age the figure is 42 percent, but the gap can be expected to close given that men are, on average, a few years older at first parenthood. See Kneale and Joshi, 2008: the authors predict identical rates of eventual childlessness for college-educated men and women.

28. The Natsal surveys (discussed in detail in Chapter 8) collected data on representative samples of British adults in 1990 and 2000, including the age of respondents at the birth of their first child. As shown below, the proportions of men aged 35–44 reporting that they had not yet had a child was significantly higher for graduates in both years (p <0 .0001).

Table n12 **Percentages of British Men Reporting No Children to Date**

	Percentage of childless male respondents aged 35–44 (confidence intervals)
Graduate men 1990	28 (23, 34)
Non-graduate men 1990	22 (19, 23)
Graduate men 2000	31 (27, 36)
Non-graduate men 2000	24 (21, 26)

Source: Natsal 1990 and 2000: unpublished data: tables generated by Dr. Cath Mercer for this study. Among fathers, larger proportions of non-graduates reported a first birth at age 20–24 and larger proportions of graduates reported a first birth at age 30–44. Average age at first birth increased for both groups of men between 1990 and 2000.

29. Martinez et al., 2006.

30. We know that among American graduate men born in the 1930s and 1940s, almost everyone who was going to be a father was one already by the age of 40: see below.

Table n13 **Percentages of US Men Reporting No Children**

	Men born 1933–52 at age 39	Men born 1933–52 at age 57	Men born 1953–74 at age 39
<High school	25	24	30
High school	13	11	33
College +	18	18	40

Source: Laumann et al., 1994: 468–69

31. *Sunday Times* (London), February 2, 2005: 8. Moreover, the figures showed that 82 percent of the cleverest women in the sample got married and 88 percent of the cleverest men did: hardly a yawning divide.

32. Rindfuss, Morgan and Swicegood, 1988, as quoted in Martin, 2000. Looking at 1975 birth rates and patterns, we find that two-thirds of those American women

who were childless at age 30 in that year could expect still to be childless at age 45. That was also the case in 1900, 1920 and on through the century. This figure has now fallen to less than half for childless 30-year-old graduates, though it remains much the same level for non-graduates.

33. Smith and Ratcliffe, 2009. Of those leaving school by or at age 16, 70 percent had their first child by age 30 in the 1944–48 and 1964–68 birth cohorts. For those leaving education at 21 or later the proportion fell from 60 to 30 percent (data from the Family Expenditure Survey and the Family Resources Survey). Among British women born in 1958, only around 2 percent of the most poorly educated group had their first child after age 33, compared to 10 percent of graduates. See Kneale and Joshi, 2008. Meanwhile, their early thirties have become the most common time for graduate mothers to start a family.

34. For example, within Europe, France is seen as having a "successful" population policy, because its birth rate has increased recently. But its demographers point out that much of that increase simply consists of a one-time boost, as many women move from having children in their twenties to their thirties. See Pison, 2009.

35. In the US, almost 80 percent of them are mothers by the age of 25. See Ellwood and Jencks, 2004; Wu, Bumpass and Musick, 2001, as quoted in Edin and Kefalas, 2005; Martin, 2000.

36. Ellwood and Jencks, 2004: Table 2.2; Kneale and Joshi, 2008: Table 1.

37. Post-30, child-bearing plummets exactly as it did throughout the twentieth century. See Dye, 2008.

38. Figure n2 shows the different current patterns, by education, for American women.

39. By the 1990s, half of the female graduates who were childless at 30 could expect to have at least one child before they were 45, rather than only a third as in the earlier

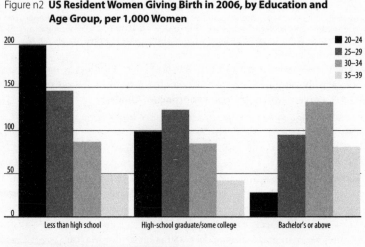

Figure n2 **US Resident Women Giving Birth in 2006, by Education and Age Group, per 1,000 Women**

Source: US Census Bureau, American Community Survey, 2006

part of the century. The proportion of graduates who were childless at 30, and then had two children by their mid-forties, doubled between the 1970s and the 1990s (from 15 percent to 31 percent); and the proportion who were childless at 30 and went on to have at least one child rose from 35 percent to just over half. See Martin, 2000: Figure 1.

40. Edin and Kefalas, 2005: 172–73.
41. Ibid.: 183–84.
42. Ibid.: 176–81.
43. Because family income fluctuates greatly over a lifetime, one cannot compare completed fertility across income in the same way as is possible for the more and less educated. However, in 2006 the fertility rate for women with a family income of $10,000 to $14,999 was twice that for women with family incomes of $200,000. See Dye, 2008.
44. Edin and Kefalas, 2005.
45. Nicholson, 2008; Abbott, 2003.
46. Milligan, 2005; Laroque and Salanie, 2008; Whittington, 1992.
47. Ilan, 2008. The reforms reduced benefits for fifth and later children, if born after the change. Birth rates in Arab families also decreased post-reform.
48. Between 1999 and 2003, real spending per child on these benefits rose by more than 50 percent, unprecedented over the previous 30 years.
49. Brewer, Ratcliffe and Smith 2008b: 12. See also Brewer, Ratcliffe and Smith 2008a. The research team concluded that, among parents who did not complete high school, the probability of having a birth increased by 1.3 percentage points, equivalent to a 15 percent increase. Some of this is, of course, likely to involve changed timing rather than changed final family size.
50. Burggraf, 1997: 65.
51. Because the changes directly altered people's incomes—and because incomes' net of the reforms could not be calculated easily, especially for those receiving tax credits—you cannot compare "before" and "after" fertility using income groups. Less-educated parents almost all became better off; the more educated mostly did not.
52. Smith and Ratcliffe, 2009. The authors report some unpublished Norwegian data that indicate that the gap between less- and highly educated women has shrunk in Norway because of a rapid decline in fertility among the former, but otherwise the pattern appears to be general.
53. For example, among British women in their early forties in 2000, one-child families were more common among the highly educated: half of this group had either one child or none. See Sigle-Rushton, 2008. Among British women born in 1965, comparing those who left school at 16 (the earliest possible) with the college-educated, about 20 percent of both groups had a completed family of one child; and about 40 percent of the former and about a third of the latter had two children. Families of three+ were almost twice as common among the early leavers (roughly 30 percent and 15 percent respectively). Among women in France, there is no marked difference in the proportions with two-child families but the same relationships as elsewhere between education and childlessness and large families. See Ratcliffe and Smith, 2007, and Touleman, Pailhé and Rossier, 2008.

54. See, for example, Touleman, Pailhé and Rossier, 2008. Natsal 2000 survey data show that in contemporary Britain about one non-graduate woman in ten and about one graduate woman in 20 has more than three children (unpublished data analyzed for this publication by Dr. Cath Mercer).
55. Kiser and Schacter, 1949.
56. Dye, 2008; Martin, 2008. In 2004 households earning over $400,000 a year—which means people in the top 1.3 percent of household earnings—had significantly more children than those in the top 5 percent, top 10 percent or top half of the income distribution as a whole. By the time the woman in the household was in her mid-forties, 41 percent had three or more children. Nationally only 28 percent of women that age had three or more children. Fertility rose significantly for families in the top 1.3 percent between 1996 and 2004, but not for those in the top 5 percent or 10 percent.
57. Adsera, 2004.
58. Academics conclude that such policies generally have more influence on the timing of births than they do on completed family size; and where professionals are concerned, it is unclear whether governments anywhere are having any influence at all. See Lundberg and Pollak, 2007. The one possible exception to the rule that birth rates are very hard to influence other than for the poor is Canadian. When Quebec introduced a payment for new births (and a large payment for third births) and the rest of Canada did not, fertility in the province rose markedly. It went up a remarkable 25 percent for third and later births, although it is impossible to know how much of this was timing—people having the babies they had been thinking of for a while, before the payment vanished again.
59. Dixon and Margo, 2006.
60. Korea's fertility rate is also currently below that of Japan. Singapore has an unusually high proportion of professionals in its workforce (male and female). Total fertility rates are available on a regularly updated basis for Japan and Korea from the OECD database (www.oecd.org) and for Singapore from the Department of Statistics Singapore (www.singstat.gov.sg).
61. See page 29.

3: THE RETURN OF THE SERVANT CLASSES

1. Blessings on the hand of women!
   Angels guard its strength and grace
   In the palace, cottage, hovel,
   Oh, no matter where the place:
   Would that never storms assailed it,
   Rainbows ever gently curled;
   For the hand that rocks the cradle
   Is the hand that rules the world.
   Woman, how divine your mission
   Here upon our natal sod!
   Keep, oh, keep the young heart open

Always to the breath of God!
All true trophies of the ages
Are from mother-love impearled;
For the hand that rocks the cradle
Is the hand that rules the world

William Ross Wallace, "What rules the world" (excerpt), 1865

Wikipedia, the online encyclopedia, comments (2009) that "[w]hile some feminists would claim that the poem leads to gendered essentialism, recent trends in third wave feminism, with its reclamation of the significance of maternity, have used the poem as a type of heralding of maternal contributions."

2. Joshi, 2003.

3. Bureau of Applied Social Research (BASR), Columbia University, 1957. Although criticisms relating to the college's failure to provide more preparation for "life" were the more frequent, some of the most vehement criticisms reflected a perceived movement by Barnard toward doing just this. The authors comment that, although such critics "are not a large group [they] include a disproportionate number of PhDs, persons close to 'inner' academic circles, and some of Barnard's most distinguished or famous graduates" (p. 33). Overall, alumnae were very positive, but only a minority would reenter if choosing "today" (that is, 1956), largely because they wanted a co-ed school, or because they would not want to be in New York.

4. Ibid.: 11, Alumna, class of '29.

5. Ibid.: 12, Alumna, class of '35.

6. Female graduates in the inter-war and wartime period married far more often than their predecessors. For example, a 1951 survey of alumnae at Vassar, another of the top US women's colleges, indicated that 89 percent of Vassar graduates from the 1930s and 1940s were married or engaged (Miscellany News, Vassar Alumna Association: report on 1950 decennial questionnaire).

7. BASR, 1957: Alumna, class of '37.

8. In the UK in 1980, 27 percent of mothers with a child under five were employed; the figure was 54 percent in 2001.

9. Joshi, 2003. See also Macran, Joshi and Dex, 1996. The gap for graduate mothers in the 1950s was very slightly higher than for non-qualified mothers.

10. The usual rule is that a job must be held open until the end of the maternity-leave period. Women have no obligation, or indeed incentive, to state whether they will return until the last minute.

11. Schönberg and Ludsteck, 2007. The evidence here suggests that maternity leave is not a very effective way to promote equality. Overall, lack of disruption to employment is what matters and women are only protected during the statutory leave period.

12. Joshi, 2003: Table 1. She calculates that the median interruption—the number of years after which at least half of first-birth mothers return to work—was five years for the least-educated group of British mothers born in 1958 and around four for their counterparts born in 1970, whereas the most educated, in both groups, had a median interruption of less than a year. Data for 2010 for American mothers of

newborns show that, overall, just over half (55 percent) reentered the labor force within a year; but the figures were 76 percent (and 60 percent full-time) for those with graduate or professional degrees, 30 percent (10 percent full-time) for high-school dropouts and 52 percent (28 percent full-time) for high-school graduates. See US Census Bureau Current Population Survey, June 2010: Detailed Table 6: Labor force participation among mothers 15 to 44 years old.

13. In Scandinavia, maternity leave tends to be long and generous, but labor market policies and childcare facilities are organized on the assumption that people will work full-time. In the US, the pressure to get health insurance from your employer drives a lot of women to work full-time in situations where their European counterparts would probably not do so.

14. Goldin, 2004.

15. Boushey, 2005. For 2004, Boushey calculates labor force participation for all mothers as 28.8 percent for dropouts, 60.2 percent for high-school graduates and 77 percent for those with graduate degrees. For mothers with children under six, the figures for these groups are 18.2 percent, 55.6 percent and 73.2 percent (Table 5). All figures are for the 25–44 age group.

16. Ibid.: 10.

17. Ibid.: 12. The difference between mothers and non-mothers has been shrinking in the US, but remains significant for all other educational groups. For those with less than a high-school diploma, the "child penalty"—the drop in the likelihood of being in the labor market if you have a child compared to being childless—fell from 30.5 percentage points in 1984 to 21.7 percentage points in 2004 for women aged 25–44. For college graduates it fell from 12.6 to 4.6.

18. Joshi, 2002.

19. For less-educated British mothers, things barely changed: see note 12 above.

20. In the West, "employment continuity is invariably lowest among low-educated women with children, with the notable exception of Portugal, a long-standing outlier that has never been properly explained." See Hakim, 2004: 131.

21. Dex, Hawkes, Joshi and Ward, 2005: 207–36. Of those with higher-level qualifications 90 percent were working by the time their child was five (even if other siblings had been born in the meantime). See also Dex and Ward, 2010. Among graduates, over half were continuously employed from the end of maternity leave onward.

22. See OECD, 2001. Table 4.1 provides data on employment rates by education where available (only a minority of countries have this information available over time). Sometimes graduate mothers of children under six are twice as likely to be working as the poorly educated, sometimes half as likely again, but the differences are large and in many cases have grown. Countries where the gap between high- and low-education mothers is very large and has grown include Ireland, Greece, Belgium and Germany. In only two countries—Portugal and Austria—is the participation gap between high-education and low-education mothers less than 30 percentage points.

23. See, for example, Budig and England, 2001; Anderson, Binder and Krause, 2002.

24. Slaughter, 2012.

25. Hewlett, 2007: 2.

26. Shackleton, 2008; Bertrand, Goldin and Katz, 2009; Office for National Statistics 2009b, 2010.

27. Among less-skilled women in the US, although having children still has a negative effect on wages, this is far smaller than in previous generations: see Blank and Shierholz, 2006. The declining impact of children may be partly because of welfare-to-work policies, which have reduced the time low-income US women—especially single mothers—spend out of the labor market. Blau and Kahn, 2006, discuss female–male wage convergence in the 1980s and 1990s (faster in the 1980s, slower in the 1990s) and the underlying factors.

28. Many women work in highly feminized occupations, such as childcare and cleaning, where wages are relatively low, but which are also—and non-coincidentally—likely to offer shift work and part-time employment that fit in with family responsibilities. See Shackleton, 2008.

29. Sandberg, 2013, loc. 91/4237.

30. Weinberger and Kuhn, 2006; Smith and Ratcliffe, 2009.

31. Dex and Joshi, 2005.

32. Amuedo-Dorantes and Kimmel, 2005.

33. In terms of pay/income per hour.

34. Joshi, 2002: 455–6.

35. See, for example, Smith and Ratcliffe, 2009: Figures 3.6 and 3.7.

36. The relevant literature is reviewed in Wilde, Batchelder and Ellwood, 2010. The authors' own analysis, looking at women in their forties at the start of the twenty-first century, found that graduate mothers continued to pay a penalty in terms of future career and earnings. However, their sample seems rather odd, in that the most educated were no more likely to be working full-time with an under-five than lower-skilled women. This is not the normal picture for mothers of young children. (See, for example, the most recent US Census Bureau Current Population Survey data, discussed above.)

37. These women had been aged 14–21 in 1979, when they were sampled as part of the National Longitudinal Survey of Youth (NLSY79).

38. Amuedo-Dorantes and Kimmel, 2005.

39. Chevalier, 2007. Overall, male–female wage gaps among graduates are very largely accounted for by occupation chosen and workplace characteristics.

40. Wilde, Batchelder and Ellwood, 2010.

41. In 2005 and 2004 respectively.

42. Belkin, 2003.

43. Boushey, 2005.

44. Ibid.: 12. She also points out that as a general rule, any such economic changes tend to "disproportionately hurt less-educated mothers," not those with graduate or indeed bachelor's degrees.

45. Time Use Survey data are discussed in detail in Chapter 4.

46. It is also why, when you *do* find women with graduate degrees who are in their thirties and out of the workforce, this small minority are overwhelmingly likely to be mothers of young children. That is not true for out-of-work women in general. See Boushey, 2006: 11. Among less-educated groups, a combination of limited job

Notes

opportunities, low pay, ill-health and extended-family demands means that having children is much less important, either way, in determining whether or not they are employed.

47. For example, in the US, over half of mothers with husbands earning at the 95th percentile or above are employed when they have children under seven, compared to nearly three-quarters when the husband earns at the 75th–95th percentile. In the UK, there is a 10 percentage point drop in participation between those whose husbands are at the 95th percentile or above, and those who are at the 90th or above. However, it is still true that the more highly educated the wife the less likely she is to stay home. See Ebell, 2012.

48. Dye, 2008; Martin, 2008. Martin reports that in 2004, households with incomes of over $400,000 amounted to the top 1.3 percent of households, and fertility rose significantly for families in this top 1.3 percent between 1996 and 2004. It did not do so for those in the top 5 percent or 10 percent. In the US population as a whole, in 2004, only 28 percent of women aged mid-forties+ had had three or more children by the time they reached this age.

49. Among British women born in 1958, only around 2 percent of the most poorly educated group had their first child after the age of 33, compared to 10 percent of graduates. See Kneale and Joshi, 2008.

50. Controlling for pretty much anything you can think of, men do earn more as "pre-fathers" in the year or two before a birth than men who are just like them in every other way. See Koslowski, 2011.

51. Sarti, 2008: 86–7.

52. Milkman, Reese and Roth, 1998: 484. Domestics made up just 0.05 percent of workers—one in 2,000—in 1980. The researchers report that when they asked the government statistical agency (Statistics Sweden) "whether the 1990 data . . . could possibly be accurate, our correspondent agreed that there were probably more than two servants in the country, but added, 'It is very seldom that a family have domestic servants because it is very expensive to pay them a fair salary . . . It is just a few families in the very high upper class that have such help these days. I know, for instance, no family in my neighborhood or of my relatives or of my colleagues who have or have had any domestic servants in the last 10 years. That was much more common in the 1960s and 1970s' " (p.503).

53. "Thou shalt not covet thy neighbor's house; thou shalt not covet thy neighbor's wife, nor his manservant, nor his maidservant, nor his ox, nor his ass, nor anything that is thy neighbor's," Exodus 20.17 (King James Bible).

54. Homans, 1984: 14, 70.

55. See Light, 2008.

56. "The meaning of home for wealthy white women is a completely different one than for their employees for whom it is social alienation and a site of exploitation," quoted in Lutz, 2008: 43.

57. Milkman, Reese and Roth, 1998: 484; Coser, 1973.

58. Schwenken and Heimeshoff, 2011: 47.

59. The German statistical office estimates that 4 million families employ some domestic help (though not, mostly, full-time). See Lutz, 2008: 45, 47. Ehrenreich, 1999,

estimates that 14–18 percent of US households employed servants in the late 1990s. The British Social Attitudes survey in 2007–2008 found that 7 percent of adult British respondents admitted to employing someone to do housework; and in an ONS survey in 2001 less than 1 percent of UK couples stated that they employed people for anything other than childcare. See Park et al., 2008.

60. O'Connor, 2011.
61. Flanagan, 2006: 73–4.
62. Short, Goldscheider and Torr, 2006.
63. Folbre, 2008: 65. Folbre uses USDA figures; my figures are updated (roughly) using the Consumer Price Index.
64. Folbre, 2008 (2002 figures updated using the CPI).
65. Boushey, 2006: 8.
66. O'Connor, 2011. All the maids in the local London street that she studied were born in England or Wales.
67. Ehrenreich and Hochschild, 2003.
68. Parreñas, 2005: 23. Americans see the change largely in relation to immigration over the southern border, altering the nature of the labor force, but theirs is simply one example of a much more general pattern: "Just as it is now rare to find African American women employed in private domestic work in Los Angeles, so too have Chinese women vanished from the occupation in Hong Kong" to be replaced by Filipinos. See Lutz, 2008: 198. It is impossible to count today's servant numbers accurately, but in Spain—one of the few countries with reasonably good statistics—half of domestic workers are immigrants, while in the US estimates are far higher. Spain had a series of amnesties in the 2000s, and so "informal" (unregistered) labor declined. There are—or were before the current recession—at least

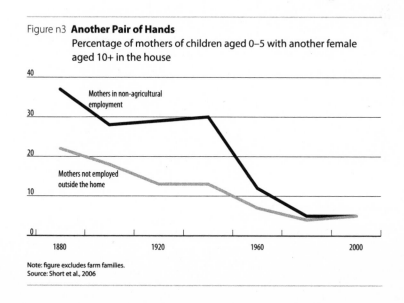

Figure n3 **Another Pair of Hands**
Percentage of mothers of children aged 0–5 with another female aged 10+ in the house

Note: figure excludes farm families.
Source: Short et al., 2006

three-quarters of a million people working in domestic service in Spain out of a total population of 45 million. See Schwenken and Heimeshoff, 2011: 46.

69. Lutz, 2008: Introduction.

70. Non-standard work (irregular shifts, late hours) is growing in importance in the US workplace—among full-timers it rose from 14 to 18 percent of jobs between 1980 and 2010, but it is especially important for part-timers. Of "non-standard" employed mothers 37 percent pay for childcare as compared to 68 percent of those working standard hours. Those working non-standard hours don't spend less time with children but more (*ceteris paribus*); the things that drop are time with spouse and own personal time. Childcare used to accommodate non-standard work by mothers is overwhelmingly fathers/other relatives. See Connelly and Kimmel, 2010: 97–101.

71. Boushey, 2006: 3, 4.

72. Large-scale nurseries, free for everyone, were pioneered in Scandinavia explicitly to promote gender equality in the workplace. Although they are very high-quality and greatly valued domestically, they do not seem to have achieved this aim (see Chapter 1).

73. Dex and Ward, 2004. See Figure n3.

74. Among those British non-graduate mothers who work—and fewer do—the least educated/most disadvantaged use formal settings rather more than middle groups, reflecting, one assumes, recent UK government policies and subsidies, which have been designed to encourage single mothers in particular back into the labor market. See Ward and Dex, 2007: Chapter 9, Sweep 2. Use of paid formal childcare, as opposed to informal/family arrangements, is roughly twice as common among graduate mothers as among those with just high school. See Ward and Dex, 2007; Smith and Ratcliffe, 2009.

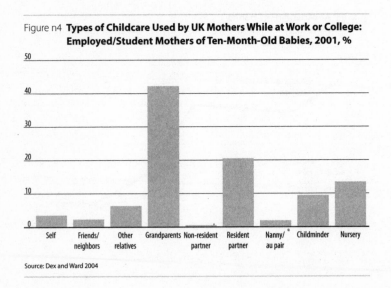

Figure n4 **Types of Childcare Used by UK Mothers While at Work or College: Employed/Student Mothers of Ten-Month-Old Babies, 2001, %**

Source: Dex and Ward 2004

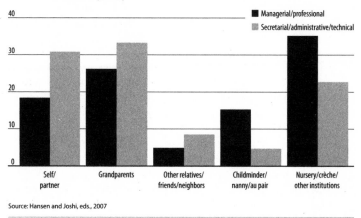

Figure n5 **Percentages of Professional and White-Collar Working Mothers of Three-Year-Olds Using Different Childcare Arrangements in the UK (2003)**

Source: Hansen and Joshi, eds., 2007

75. Brown-Lyons, Robertson and Layzer, 2001. American two-earner families with incomes in the upper quartile are more than twice as likely to use formal arrangements as those in the bottom quartile.

76. We know, from time-use data, that lower-income parents will very often arrange work times that allow one or other to babysit. This saves money at the expense of time spent together: Hamermesh, 2008.

77. Boushey, 2006.

78. Matsui, 2010.

79. See Chapter 11 for further discussion.

4: PIZZA AND PARTNERS

1. The cases described here are all real, although the names are not. US time-use data cited in this chapter come from the American Heritage Time Use Study (AHTUS) and other data from the Multi-national Time Use Study (MTUS). The MTUS was begun in the 1980s by Professor Jonathan Gershuny, the founding director of Oxford University's Centre for Time Use Research (http://www.timeuse.org/). It now brings together data from 22 countries and has made access to a range of national data sets, over time, much simpler than in the past. The AHTUS is a database of national time-diary samples spread over five decades, which is maintained and has been expanded by the Centre: http://www.timeuse.org/ahtus. Analyses of time-use data were carried out directly for this book by Anne-Marie Jeannet except where otherwise stated and referenced; and the assistance of Oxford University's Centre for Time Use Research staff is gratefully acknowledged.

2. Chapter 1 pointed out that Scandinavia, generally regarded as the most sexually egalitarian region of the world, has record levels of occupational segregation, with women concentrated in overwhelmingly female jobs. It is also the region that

hollowed out the home most enthusiastically, and looked at in this light, the statistics no longer surprise. Scandinavians moved furthest, fastest, soonest to free women from domestic labor in the home, including childcare, and instead paid people to carry out these tasks in government-funded settings. Large numbers of women duly moved to paid employment in these home-replacing jobs. The result was an occupationally segregated labor market to replace the segregation of work and home.

3. The kibbutz movement introduced communal dining (as well as children's dormitories) in order to break down traditional gender roles, seeing this as central to genuine socialism. Kibbutzim never accounted for more than a small proportion of the Israeli population. Currently, about 106,000 people—just over 1 percent of the total population, a little under 2 percent of the Jewish population—live on kibbutzim, and there has been a movement away from the early communal patterns, with children now living with their parents rather than in dormitories.

There is, however, a movement that campaigns for recognition of the economic contribution of unpaid home-based care and housework through payment of wages for these services by governments. The International Wages for Housework Campaign was founded by Selma James and began organizing in a number of countries in the 1970s.

4. It is a sign of how wealthy our societies have become that in the developed world we spend, on average, only about 10 percent of our incomes on food, compared to almost half—sometimes even more—in developing countries. The US Bureau of Statistics Consumer Expenditure Survey calculates that, for a US family of 2.5, 10 percent of gross income is on average spent on food. Food Freedom estimates that 40 percent of disposable income (on average) is spent on food in India, 48 percent in the Philippines and 50–60 percent in some sub-Saharan African countries.

5. In the UK, from 1992 to 2004, household spending on food products grew 75 percent but expenditure on catering products consumed outside the home grew 102 percent, and in 2004 overtook (in total value) spending on food and drink eaten in the home. See *United Kingdom Input-Output Analyses*, 2006 edition. ISSN 1741–7155. Available as a Web-only publication on www.statistics.gov.uk/inputoutput.

6. US trends are shown below:

Table n14 **Percentage of Food Expenditure on Food at Home and Away from Home**

Year	Food at home (%)	Food away %
1960	73.7	26.3
1961	73.2	26.8
1969	66.7	33.3
1979	61.0	39.0
1989	54.8	45.2
1999	53.0	47.0
2009	51.4	48.6

Definition

| At home | Food-at-home expenditures include food sales from (1) Food stores; (2) Other stores; (3) Home delivery and mail order; (4) Farmers, manufacturers, and wholesalers; and (5) Home production and donations. |
| Away from home | Food-away-from-home expenditures include food sales from (1) Eating and drinking places, (2) Hotels and motels, (3) Retail stores and direct selling, (4) Recreational places, (5) Schools and colleges, and (6) All other. |

Source: http://www.ers.usda.gov/Briefing/CPIFoodAndExpenditures/measuringtheersfoodexpendituresseries

7. Department for Environment, Food and Rural Affairs, 2010: 24; Blow, Leicester and Oldfield, 2004: 21. Actual "eating out"—full meals—was 22 percent of food spending in the UK in 2001, compared to 14 percent in 1969. Also expenditure on catering grew very fast between the mid-1970s and late 1990s—from 3 percent to 7.5 percent of average weekly expenditure. See Family Expenditure Survey data.

8. See website of the French Ministry of Foreign Affairs, 2007.

9. Ramey, 2008, 2006.

10. A 1913 home economist quoted in Ramey, 2008.

11. Shaw, *Pygmalion*, Act II.

12. Ramey, 2008: 18–23.

13. Fisher et al. note that "[u]npaid work declined significantly across the period essentially offsetting their increased time in paid work . . . the average number of episodes of unpaid work for women of all ages dropped from 5 in 1965–66 . . . to 3 in the 1990s and in 2003" (Fisher et al. 2007 12–13). Episodes are per day.

14. Hamrick and Shelley, 2005. Figures are from the 2003–2004 American Time Use Survey. For women with children under 18, the average time on food preparation and cleaning up is 52.8 minutes; for employed women 37.8 minutes; for all women 47.4 minutes a day.

15. The first commercial countertop microwave oven for household use went on sale in 1967.

16. Ephron, 1983: 81.

17. Hewlett, 2002. Hewlett argues that "the price women pay for their children . . . seems to have gone up . . . working women are still stuck with most family responsibilities and this severely limits how well they can do in their careers" (pp. 133–36).

18. Oriel Sullivan, Oxford University Centre for Time Use Research: personal communication.

19. Daniel Hamermesh is one of the leading time-use scholars in the US, and he and colleagues surveyed people, male and female, who might be expected to know their facts: labor economists, public finance economists (both largely male groups), plus faculty and graduate students in an elite American sociology department. See Burda, Hamermesh and Weil, 2007: 8–9.

20. Sullivan, 2011; Sullivan and Gershuny, 2012.

21. See especially Hochschild and Machung, 1989, and Greenstein, 2000. Sociologist Arlie Hochschild's highly influential "second shift" study, back in 1989, was based on a study of 50 American dual-earner couples. She and co-author Machung claimed that men who earned more than their wives never did any housework; while among couples where the wife earned more than the husband, she still did by far the largest share rather than threaten her husband's male identity. The argument seemed to be borne out by some later statistical analysis of American data: American men were doing far less and women far more than their share of housework, in relation to their relative earnings. Men who were economically dependent—unemployed or low-earning compared to their wives—were, apparently, avoiding housework, as a way of asserting masculinity.

22. Sullivan, 2011.
23. Sullivan, 2006; Sullivan, 2010a and 2010b. British and US data indicate that by the 1990s, men with manual and clerical jobs had assumed as much responsibility for household tasks as had professional ones.
24. Even in countries with very high female employment rates, the female population as a whole devotes more than half its total working hours to unpaid, non-market work.
25. Sullivan, 2010b and 2011, notes that, in the quantitative studies (note 22 above) that appeared to show "gender deviance neutralization"—women doing more work to protect men's egos—reanalysis has shown this to be restricted to the most extreme cases—basically 2–3 percent of men with particularly low incomes/insecure labor market positions. Some of them would have been unemployed at the time of interview, but not necessarily so long- or even short-term. "When absolute income is added to the models, the gender deviance neutralization effect disappears," she notes. She also notes that, in qualitative interviews, there may well be a tendency among some groups of men to under-report rather than over-report housework, hence the differences between the evidence from qualitative studies and that found in detailed diary-based time-use analyses. "Whether or not such under-reporting itself constitutes a kind of gender deviance neutralization, it is not the same behavioral effect as is frequently quoted and referred to," she argues. Finally, much of this evidence is now quite old: men's and women's behavior may have changed since the 1980s.
26. The time-use diaries kept by Americans show that, since 1985, men of all ages have been involved in an average of two episodes of unpaid domestic work every day (not counting childcare), and that between 85 and 90 percent of men participated in such work on any given day. Fisher et al., 2007: 4.
27. See Gershuny and Robinson, 1988, for a first longitudinal analysis of change.
28. Sullivan and Gershuny, 2012.
29. Gerson, 2010.
30. Sullivan, n.d.: 8. Oriel Sullivan and Jonathan Gershuny have shown that the way couples behave, in dividing up the housework, is driven by how many hours of paid work each is currently doing *but also by their potential wage-earning capacity;* and that this is true across countries and cultures: Sullivan and Gershuny, 2012. (The analysis here used British Household Panel Survey data.) More and more families involve two working adults, and it is now equally common across all social groups for couples to share unpaid household work, at least to some degree.
31. Sullivan and Gershuny, 2012: 34. Generally, including the unemployed in an analysis of who does the housework, rather than just looking at employed men, makes a big difference to the picture. In this analysis, 46 percent of men in the group with the lowest qualifications relative to their wives were not in employment.
32. Burda, Hamermesh and Weil, 2007. Countries studied were the US, Germany, the Netherlands, Italy, Spain, the UK, Belgium, Denmark, Finland, Norway, Sweden, Australia, Israel, Canada, Japan, France, Mexico, New Zealand, Estonia, Slovenia,

Hungary, South Africa, Benin, Madagascar and Mauritius. Germany, the Netherlands and the US have particularly detailed information for the early 2000s, and "there is essentially no difference by gender in total work. Men work more in the market, women engage in more home production, but these balance out" (p. 4).

33. It's also true that less-educated Italian women work less than most Westerners. (Educated Italian women, meanwhile, work in a "typical" Western way: with the result that Italy looks very gender-equal in terms of average pay.)

34. Table n15 **Total Work (All Early 2000s): Minutes per Representative Day**

	Germany F	Germany M	Italy F	Italy M	Netherlands F	Netherlands M	US F	US M
Total work	444	436	480	405	392	399	472	476
Tertiary	676	654	593	595	659	634	641	616
Leisure	320	349	367	440	388	407	327	348

Source: Adapted from Burda, Hamermesh and Weil, 2007: Table 1

(Burda, Hamermesh and Weil use a more inclusive definition of "total work" than some authors, to include tertiary activities—things that we cannot pay others to do and must do some of, such as sleeping or eating.)

35. Partly because they put in longer hours of paid employment than most other developed countries. See Hamermesh, 2008.

36. Caitlin Flanagan, growing up in 1970s California, went to her first psychotherapist when she was sixteen; a psychotherapist who suddenly, one day, "sat up straight in her chair and began discussing . . . in the most heated terms imaginable . . . marriage—specifically her own. 'I mean, who's going to do the shit work?' she asked angrily. 'Who's going to make the pancakes?' I stared at her uncomprehendingly. . . But in 1978 shit work was becoming a real problem." Flanagan also notes that to understand the different attitudes to housekeeping of her mother and herself "you have to understand the attitudes of the women who came between us, many of whom thought that the simple tasks such as making beds and washing dishes could potentially ensnare them in a millennia-old trap of patriarchy and dashed ambition." See Flanagan, 2006: 166.

37. One incredibly detailed study, involving minute-by-minute videoing of 32 dual-earner families, was carried out between 2002 and 2005—UCLA/Sloan Center on Everyday Lives of Families (CELF). The researchers measured stress by having participants spit into a vial, from which they could measure the stress hormone cortisol on a regular basis (Carey, 2010). Couples demonstrating the least stress tended to have the least need to negotiate over tasks constantly. See Saxbe et al., 2011; Izquierdo and Klein, 2010.

38. We know that couples coordinate their leisure time (Oriel Sullivan: personal communication) and leisure is rated as the most enjoyable of all combined activities.

39. And seem either to have concentrated on some rather atypical cases or to have misinterpreted key statistics. See note 26.

40. Fisher et al., 2007: 4. Compare housework recollected in tranquility with the precise measurements of diary-keepers and you find that, at least in the US, both men

Notes

and women overestimate their contributions by about 50 percent. More generally, in cases where it has been possible to compare "remembered" contributions with detailed same-day diary-keeping, it turns out that both men and women exaggerate the time they spend on housework—but men tend to do it by a larger margin. See also Sullivan, 2010a; Kan, 2008; Arnold et al., 2012.

41. Data are from the Millennium Cohort study, which tracks a large sample of British children born in 2000. See Kanji and Schober, 2012; Hansen and Joshi, 2007, especially Chapter 9. The figures on mothers as main earner do not differentiate by education, and numbers are too small to allow for robust estimates at this level of detail.

42. Joyti De-Laurey was convicted in 2004 of stealing from three managing directors of Goldman Sachs: Jennifer Moses, her husband, Ron Beller, and Scott Mead.

43. See, for example, Fisher et al., 2007.

44. Costa, 2000. Figures for waged and salaried men with a single job.

45. Ibid.: 162. "In the 1890s, hours worked were 11 for men in the bottom decile but fell to 9 for men in the top decile . . . men in the top decile began work an hour later than men in the bottom decile (8:00 a.m. rather than 7:00 a.m.) and took an hour for lunch rather than a half hour. By 1973 . . . men in the bottom decile worked close to 9 hours and those in the top decile close to 8 hours. By 1991, daily hours worked increase with the wage decile, from 8 for those in the bottom to almost 9 for those in the top." There are similar patterns for women but they are harder to interpret because of the major changes that took place in married women's employment. By 1991 for unmarried women, the usual length of a workday ranges from 6.23 hours in the bottom decile to 8.23 in the top. See ibid.: 163.

46. Vickery, 2003: 115.

47. Ibid.

48. Hamermesh and Lee, 2003.

49. In the US, for example, the American Time Use Survey data show that, on average, men spent 360 minutes, on a weekday, in paid work plus commuting to it. For women, the average for paid work plus commuting was about 260 minutes per day.

50. Overall, "the men of 2003 still look like the men of 1965, [but] the profile of a woman's day in 2003 resembles the men's 2003 daily profile more than it does the women's day-profile in 1965." See Fisher et al., 2007: 16.

51. Ibid.: 14. In the US, most of the change took place between 1965 and 1985.

52. See below, adapted from Table V, p.992, of Aguiar and Hurst, 2007. In 1965, the total of market and non-market work, excluding childcare, was on average 61 hours a week for men and 55 for women.

Table n16 **Changes in Average Working Hours per Week**

A. Men—USA

Change, 1965–2003	HS dropout	HS graduate	Some college	Bachelor's and postgraduate
Total market work	–18	–14	–13	–4
Total non-market	3	4	4	3
Leisure : recreation + sleep/personal care	12	7	6	0

Notes

B. Women—USA

Change, 1965–2003	HS dropout	HS graduate	Some college	Bachelor's and postgraduate
Total market work	−2	2	7	4
Total non-market	−10	−11	−11	−9
Leisure: recreation + sleep/personal care	8	6	3	1

53. Aguiar and Hurst, 2007. Divergence becomes marked from the 1980s on.

54. Ibid. Data from American Time Use Survey.

55. Kanji, 2010. Kanji also estimates that in 26 percent of couples aged 20–60 both are employed for about 40 hours a week, but no more.

56. Source: ATUS.

57. Nothing else outside work comes close to TV-watching in the time it takes up. But in data for the early 2000s there are clear differences around healthy living—sport, exercise—even though most of us, it turns out, don't do very much of either. In the US, women with post-college qualifications spent on average 13 minutes per day on sports or exercise. This is over three times as much as women with less than high-school qualifications, whose average is four minutes and twice as much as those with some college. In the UK, women with higher than secondary education qualifications spent on average ten minutes per day on exercise, which is double the five minutes averaged by those who left school unqualified.

58. AHTUS and MTUS data show that:

- In the US, women who are employed sleep on average 488 minutes; 3 percent less than those who work part-time (504 minutes) and 9 percent less than their non-employed (532 minutes) counterparts. Within each category, there is quite a large range of values.

- When considering education, the differences in amount of sleep are more striking. A typical non-employed woman with less than high-school qualifications sleeps on average 575 minutes, which is 19.5 percent more than a woman who has achieved post-college qualifications and is working full time, and sleeping 481 minutes.

These differences are also visible in the United Kingdom.

- Women who were non-employed with "secondary or less" academic qualifications slept on average for 523 minutes, 10 percent more than women who had achieved above secondary education and were working full-time, who slept on average for 475 minutes.

- The male counterparts of the latter group, full-time employed with "above secondary education," slept a similar amount of time per night at an average of 473 minutes.

(Sources: AHTUS, 2003; MTUS, 2005.)

Data on sleep for France are older (MTUS, 1997) and show the same pattern but less markedly. In France, women with less than secondary education spent on average 545 minutes sleeping, whereas women with more than secondary education spent on average 513 minutes. Non-working women with less than secondary education slept for 552 minutes on average; this is 9 percent more than women with

Notes

more than secondary education and in full-time employment, who sleep an average of 509 minutes.

59. And while many of us claim (to ourselves and others) that we don't need much sleep, we're mostly wrong: "out of every 100 people who believe they only need five or six hours of sleep a night, only about five people really do," according to a past president of the American Academy of Sleep Medicine, Dr. Daniel D. Buysse of the University of Pittsburgh Medical Center, quoted in Beck, 2011.

60. ATUS, 2003: Survey 7. The amount of time spent watching TV increased for all Americans between the 1980s and 2003 but far less for highly educated groups than others.

61. In France, women with a less than secondary education, on average, spent 143 minutes per day watching TV. This is about 40 percent more than those with a secondary education, who watched an average of 103 minutes per day. Women with above secondary qualifications spent 69 minutes on average. (The standard deviation is approximately 70 for each of these categories.) Women not in employment with less than secondary education spent the most time watching television (compared to any other employment/educational category), an average of 166 minutes per day. Their male counterparts spent an average of 198 minutes. Women in full-time employment with more than a secondary education spent the least time watching television (compared to any other employment/educational category), an average of 58 minutes. Their male counterparts spent notably more time watching television, with an average of 90 minutes per day. Thus in the French data the difference between men and women is greater at higher levels of education (MTUS, 1998).

62. In 2005 UK women who had less than secondary education qualifications watched 190 minutes on average. Women with secondary education achievement watched 114 minutes on average. Women with greater than secondary education qualifications averaged 90 minutes. Women with less than full secondary education and not employed spent an average amount of 275 minutes per day—that's four and a half hours—watching television. (Their male counterparts watch even more, with an average of 310 minutes per day.) This is more than three times as much as full-time working women with more than a bachelor's degree, who spent an average of 88 minutes.

63. Much of the difference is accounted for by the fact that women who are at home, or part-time, tend to spend more time on housework; and the highly educated are the least likely to be non-employed, or part-time. UK 2005 data for 25–44-year-olds (MTUS) show that women with tertiary education averaged 51 minutes a day on household tasks, those with upper secondary 73 minutes and those with less than upper secondary (GCSE only or less) 98 minutes. But this does not control for children or employment. In 2003, American women with less than high school spent on average slightly over 26 hours per week (225 minutes per day) in "total nonmarket work" excluding childcare, whereas those with a bachelor's or above averaged just under 21 hours (183 minutes). See Aguiar and Hurst, 2007: Table V, p.992. In Australia, holding other things constant, mothers with bachelor's or postgraduate degrees spend on average about half an hour a day less on housework

than those with no qualifications or only vocational ones. See Craig, 2006. Among Australian men, university-educated men are averaging 20 minutes a day more on childcare than the least qualified, although the absolute amounts of time involved are smaller. (Australian men spend around a third as many minutes in total on childcare as women.) Ibid.: 567.

64. Hamermesh, 2008: 25–26.

65. Actual figures are as follows—based on Table 6: Burda, Hamermesh and Weil, 2007, plus original analysis of UK data from the MTUS. The analysis of US and German data uses different education and work categories from those used in the UK analysis.

Table n17 **Average Working Time (Minutes per Day) by Education**

	Highest education	Second highest	Third highest	Lowest
US male	524	470	468	366
German male	455	456	448	416
US female	518	474	455	386
German female	475	465	456	406

	Most educated (some college through postgraduate)	Least educated (no formal qualifications at upper secondary level)
UK male	345	263
UK female	358	243

66. In the UK, women with less than secondary education working full-time spent an average of 43 minutes per day on housework. Those not working spent more than twice as much time, or 88 minutes per day on housework. In the Netherlands, women with less than secondary education on average spent 72 minutes per day on housework in the early 2000s. Women with secondary education spent 64 minutes per day on average and women with more than secondary education spent 46 minutes on average per day on housework, which is significantly less than women with fewer educational qualifications. In the US (data are for 25–44-year-olds only) women who in 2003 worked full-time and were high-school dropouts averaged 196 minutes a day on all forms of unpaid work combined, compared to 172 for those with postgraduate education and 176 for those with a bachelor's only. For part-timers the comparable figures were 259, 268 and 279 minutes.

67. With one single exception! Among adult men (25–59) in France, in the year 2000, time-use data show self-employed men with no children putting in more hours than other groups of French men. Otherwise the pattern is totally consistent for men and women. (The self-employed in France generally report much longer hours of paid work than do the employed.) Figures from ATUS and MTUS.

68. Zelizer, 1994.

69. Parents are often ambivalent about filing suits for damages, on the grounds that it implied that money could be an adequate compensation; many hand them over to charity. Equally a token or small award can sacralize the death in a way that a large one cannot. Ibid.: 163.

70. Ibid.

71. In the last quarter-century men generally have reported "large increases in the time they spend with children," and especially men with the highest level of educational

attainment. See Sullivan, 2010: 20; Connelly and Kimmel, 2010. Internationally, the only activities that modern mothers are doing less of than their 1960s forebears are reading to children and talking to them—and the latter probably doesn't allow for all those conversations in the car, which will fall under "travel" in the time-use diaries. Craig and Mullan, 2011, confirm that this finding holds also for Australia, Denmark, Italy and France.

72. Kuper, 2010.

73. For children under 18, it is nearing two hours a day in the US. And for children under 13, college-educated married American women—most of them working—put in an average of two and a half hours of primary care plus four hours more "with" the child though doing something else as well.

74. Craig, 2006: 568. For men, the pattern is the same: university-educated fathers spend an average of 20 minutes a day more on childcare than the least qualified. (Total childcare time is less for men.) Ibid.: 567. The Australian analyses relate to households with at least one child under 12; the US and UK data are for households with at least one resident child under 18.

75. Namely that higher-earning, more-educated fathers are increasing their time commitment faster than others. See Koslowski, 2011.

76. "Higher-wage married mothers spend more time on caregiving and . . . the more time they spend on caregiving, the more time their husbands spend on caregiving, leading to a substantial time gap between time devoted to young children across wage groups." See Connelly and Kimmel, 2010: 91. Married US mothers average 154 minutes in "primary" caregiving on weekdays and 107 on weekend days, but also 259 minutes additional "time with child," and 423 minutes like this on weekends. Single mothers average 129, 87, 230 and 386 minutes respectively. Ibid.: 26.

77. Flanagan, 2006: 46.

78. Ibid.

79. Ibid.: 69–70.

80. Warner, 2006: 63.

81. Warner, in particular, seems to think this is an American issue and that the French, for example, have none of these issues and problems. We do not have the time-use data with which to compare France and the US directly over the last decades in terms of childcare, but as Chapter 5 shows, France enjoys just as much of an educational arms-race as the US (or the UK or Japan).

82. Ibid.: 64.

83. Personal communication.

5: MAKING IT

1. Story from BBC News website, December 1, 2009, using Department for Education official figures and press release: http://news.bbc.co.uk/go/pr/fr/-/2/hi/uk_news/education/8353257.stm.

2. Office for National Statistics, 2012: Table 6. Health employment was 13 percent of the total.

3. For a full analysis of world trends, see Barro and Lee, 2010. For example, in 1950, females aged 15+ in the Middle East and North Africa averaged less than half a

year of education; they now average almost six and a half, and the female–male ratio for average length of education has doubled from 0.41 to 0.82. In Europe and Central Asia, women's average length of schooling is now higher than men's (9.89 years completed versus 9.36 years). Even in South Asia, the region where the ratio is the lowest, the male–female gap has shrunk enormously, from 0.26 to 0.69, and average schooling for females has risen from less than six months to over four years.

4. De Waal, 2011: 184.

5. In 1900 there were almost 1,500 women studying full-time, though in my own institution, King's College London, there were still only 12 full-time women in 1900 compared to 262 men. See Board of Education, 1900; Windolf, 1997.

6. By 2010 total US enrollments in degree-granting institutions numbered over 20 million.

Table n18 **USA: Numbers in Higher Education (Degree-Granting Institutions)**

	Males (2000s)	Females (2000s)
1970	5,044	3,537
1980	5,874	6,223
1990	6,284	7,535
2000	6,722	8,591
2010	8,770	11,658

Source: NCES, 2011: Table 199

7. Canada in 1979 had slightly more females than males at university (12 percent females, 10 percent males). By 2005, universities were 41 percent female, 26 percent male. (Gender breakdown in Canadian colleges is roughly equal.) See Christofides, Hoy and Yang, 2009. Australia has a clear majority of women in both mainstream universities and higher vocational (college) education (UNESCO World Education Indicators), as do France (Guionnet and Neveu, 2009) and the UK, where 57 percent of undergraduates are female (Higher Education Statistics Agency).

8. For a fuller discussion of trends in developing countries see Wolf, 2012.

9. In the US, the numbers of male and female undergraduates were roughly equal from 1900 to 1930, but this reflects in large part the fact that American teachers trained in higher education institutions, whereas in much of Europe they were in "normal schools" or training colleges, which were not included in the higher education statistics. See Goldin, Katz and Kuziemko, 2006.

10. Most primary school teachers are female and graduates; a century ago, in Europe, they were already mostly women, but they were not university students. The colleges and "normal schools" where they trained were often all-female and safely secluded in the country, away from bright lights, temptation and men.

11. National Center for Education Statistics, *The Condition of Education*: Indicator 7.

12. LSAT. In the UK, the LNAT (National Admissions Test for Law) is becoming comparably important.

13. The peak, so far, was 49.6 percent in 2003–2004; in 2010–2011 it was 46.9 percent. See Association of American Medical Colleges, 2011.

14. Letters from Patricia Burgess (*The Times*, November 17, 2011) and Helen Alexander-Brown (November 18, 2011). Burgess's letter was a response to claims that judicial appointments in the UK were not being made on the basis of merit, as evidenced by

the small number of women at very senior levels. She stated that "strict criteria are laid down, and if the candidates, of whatever gender, do not score a minimum of points against these they are deemed ineligible for appointment" and that the current gender imbalance reflected instead the small numbers of women graduating in law in the 1960s and 1970s.

15. The *CPGE* (*Classes Préparatoires pour les Grandes Écoles*, preparing post-*baccalauréat* pupils for the *Grandes Écoles* entrance examinations) are 57 percent male, reflecting this. See Hilal, 2010. Students who want to take those exams do an extra two years of grinding academic study after graduating from upper secondary school, before taking the exam, and, depending on their performance, gain entry to one or other of the *écoles*—which are themselves strictly ranked.

16. Hilal, 2010.

17. OECD, 2009a: Appendix B, Table 3.

18. OECD, 2009a.

19. Ibid. In general, girls are now as likely to outscore boys in math as vice versa on national and international measures, although the differences in the international studies are not very large. The OECD PISA studies find that boys are more likely to find math interesting. As students get older, math and science become increasingly male-dominated in high school and beyond.

20. Pinker, 2008: Chapter 8; Rhoads, 2004: Chapter 6.

21. See, for example, Spender, 1982; Brophy, 1985; Streitmatter, 1994, especially pp. 126–29; Keddie and Mills, 2007; Altermatt et al., 1998.

22. A number of UK studies have found differences between men and women in the distribution of degree results, with men more highly represented at the top and bottom extremes in a way that cannot be accounted for by subject studied or prior attainment. See, for example, McNabb, Pal and Sloane, 2002.

23. http://nsse.iub.edu/html/about.cfm. Figures given are for 2010.

24. Coleman, 2010: 67. The Arabic-language (and now also English-language) TV news station, broadcasting from Qatar, is enormously popular and influential throughout the region.

25. Ibid.: 93, 120.

26. Women studied at Cambridge in a number of women's colleges but were not granted full degrees until 1947 (when the reform passed with no dissenting votes); this was much later than in any other British university (including Oxford). For a full discussion of the 1897 events see, for example, Sutherland, 2006: Chapter 7; Tullberg, 1998.

27. For example, the US government has supported it for particular ethnic groups, and the Indian government for particular castes.

28. There may be a few jobs where gender is clearly relevant to the ability to carry out the tasks and where gender discrimination is still allowed, but the number is small and shrinking. Countries that operate with strict laws and regulations in this area include all the OECD countries in Europe, North America and Australasia.

29. Figures for the Millennium Cohort babies born in 2000. See Hansen et al., 2010: 129–31.

30. Until quite recently, a good many European countries allowed lawyers to qualify by an apprenticeship route, working in a lawyer's office and taking examinations.

31. See, for example, Keats, 1967; Dore, 1976; Brown and Hesketh, 2004; Goldin and Katz, 2008a; Wolf and McNally, 2011.

32. Wolf, 2002; Wolf, 2009; Brown and Hesketh, 2004.

33. His deputy, in a coalition government, is the Cambridge-educated leader of the Liberal Democrats.

34. Ed Miliband, educated at Oxford, was the victor. One of the other candidates was his brother, David, another Oxford graduate. The other three were Ed Balls (Oxford), Diane Abbott (Cambridge) and Andy Burnham (Cambridge). In one of the most celebrated TV sitcoms in recent British history, *Yes Minister*, a leading character, the manipulative and highly competent top civil servant Sir Humphrey, famously talks about the need for "a system to preserve the important things of life . . . like the opera, the countryside, the universities—both of them." "Oxbridge" graduates are less dominant in Parliament as a whole than on the front benches, but still mammothly over-represented: in the 2010 Parliament, just under 30 percent of MPs were educated at Oxford or Cambridge. See Sutton Trust, 2010.

35. The *Grandes Écoles*, as explained above, are small teaching institutions from which the overwhelming majority of the French elite graduate.

36. Of course, some people do succeed differently, such as Nicolas Sarkozy, the victor in the 2007 French presidential election, who did not attend a *Grande École* and who lost to Hollande in 2012. Edith Cresson, France's first female prime minister, graduated from a super-selective *Grande École*, the École des Hautes Études Commerciales in Paris, in the 1950s.

37. It is a sign of just how self-confident a top university can be that, when the world moved over to a new way of writing Chinese-character words, and "Beijing" appeared on the scene, Peking University saw no reason whatsoever to change its practices.

38. We have particularly good data for the UK. See, for example, Hussain, McNally and Telhaj, 2009; they conclude that the relationship between wage returns and university quality is highly nonlinear, with a much higher return to degrees from the very "top" institutions.

39. Frank and Cook, 1995: 11, 12, 148.

40. Hoxby, 2009: 95.

41. Kyoto is almost as good academically but has nothing like as many powerful political alumni.

42. Original analyses. Data for Figures 5.3a and 5.3b were provided for this chapter by the Admissions Offices at institutions concerned.

43. The picture would look a little more uneven if I included all-female Pembroke College, Brown's "sister" institution, but it did not have the prestige of Vassar, Bryn Mawr or the other sisters, so I have omitted it. I have also had to omit Columbia from the 1950 count, because the university was unable to supply us with undergraduate numbers separately. Including it would certainly have wiped out any redressing of the balance introduced by Pembroke's female students. The colleges

Notes

included are, for 1950, Mount Holyoke, Barnard, Vassar, Bryn Mawr, Wellesley, Smith, Radcliffe—the Seven Sisters—Harvard, Yale, Princeton, Dartmouth,
Brown and University of Pennsylvania. For 2010, Columbia is added; Radcliffe has
been merged with Harvard and does not enroll its own students anymore.

44. *University of Oxford Gazette*, 2011: 46 percent of students at undergraduate
level—which is the key group for elite entry—were female in 2010. Cambridge
averaged 49 percent female undergraduates over the decade to 2010: *Cambridge
University Reporter*, 2010.

45. Opening to Chapter 15.

46. In Austen's day this meant either Oxford or Cambridge.

47. Wesleyan, Amherst and Williams are all highly selective private liberal arts colleges, which, unlike the main Ivy League universities, have remained undergraduate institutions. They are consequently less well known outside the US.

48. As Michael Young pointed out in *The Rise of the Meritocracy*, it is not actually
obvious why being born—by chance—with a relatively high IQ should mean that
you "deserve" success in a way that being born—by chance—upper class, or good-
looking, or indeed male does not. But that is how our societies today operate.

49. Dore, 2000; Bakker and Wolf, 2001.

50. Karabel, 2005.

51. Oxford by 2011 had no single-sex colleges and Cambridge no all-male ones.

52. Vickery, 2003.

53. See, for example, Doepke and Tertilt, 2008. Religion, especially Protestantism, also
played some role in encouraging high levels of literacy for both women and men.

6: THE WAY WE LIVE NOW

1. Analysts of the class structure of modern developed societies (see, for example,
Thompson and Hickey, 2005; Hakim, 2004) estimate the very rich to number less
than 1 percent, with the "upper middle class" or "highly educated professionals
and salaried" making up about 15 percent of the employed population. See Introduction note 3 for an explanation of how the 70 million estimate was derived using
these figures. Given Chinese and Indian growth rates, and population, it will soon
be considerably more.

2. See, for example, *The Times*, Thursday, November 10, 2011: 33.

3. As quoted in *Financial Times*, 2009: 38.

4. Ibid.: 19, 36.

5. Floud and Johnson, 2004. Even in the outer fringes of the British Isles, such as the
Scottish Highlands, agriculture was part of a market economy, based around raising cattle for sale in the Lowlands.

6. Until the Married Women's Property Acts of 1870 and 1882 (and their Scottish
equivalents), the property of a British woman came under the control of her husband at marriage.

7. By 1891 there were still only 101 female doctors in the whole of the UK (1891 Census figures).

8. If you take £100 million today as the equivalent of £1 million in 1900, there still
are not very many. In the British "rich list," about 75 women are individually worth

£100 million or more. A good half of these have simply inherited the money or obtained it in a divorce settlement, and have no active involvement in business, while many of the others are involved in running a successful family business but did not create it. There are, however, some genuine female entrepreneurs in the list (for example, Mary Perkins and Jacqueline Gold).

9. In purchasing power, Chinese income per head in 2012 was slightly over a fifth of American (and Indian less than a tenth).

10. Grant Thornton, 2009.

11. Desai, 2012: 51.

12. Ibid.: 43.

13. See, for example, Wong, 1950.

14. Xinran, 2011.

15. Yukongdi, 2009.

16. Grant Thornton, 2009.

17. Wolf, 2004; Chevalier and Lindley, 2009.

18. Coleman, 2010.

19. She was widowed, like so many, as a young First World War bride.

20. A number of associations and websites keep count of female politicians' success: see, for example, http://www.guide2womenleaders.com/; http://womenshistory.about.com; http://theonlinegk.wordpress.com. Before Margaret Thatcher became prime minister of Britain in 1979, there had only ever been four female prime ministers anywhere in the world. Between 1980 and 2011, there were another fifty.

21. Originally part of Pakistan, it became independent in 1971.

22. Mrs. Bandaranaike, Sheikh Hasina and Khaleda Zia all had assassinated fathers or husbands; Indira Gandhi was the daughter of India's first prime minister and was assassinated herself. So was Benazir Bhutto, who was the first female prime minister of Pakistan, the first elected female head of a Muslim state and also the daughter of a former prime minister who had been executed in what many regarded as a political act by the then-military ruler of the country. She was also assassinated.

23. She lost the 2012 election and is currently a member of the Rajya Sabha, the upper house of the Parliament of India.

24. http://news.bbc.co.uk/1/hi/8625337.stm, consulted January 22, 2012.

25. "Follow the money" is the advice given to the investigative journalists Woodward and Bernstein by their main source, "Deep Throat," in the film *All the President's Men*, about the Watergate scandal, which led to the resignation of President Nixon in 1974.

26. Atkinson, 2008; Kopczuk, Saez and Song, 2010. There has been a great deal of discussion and analysis of the increasing inequality in earnings and the emergence, notably in the US and UK, of a small group of individuals earning enormous amounts of money in absolute and relative terms. A discussion of why this has occurred lies outside the scope of this book, but it seems clear that while countries vary in the degree to which inequality is increasing, the pattern is a general one. It is also clear that we are returning to patterns more like those of the first half of the twentieth century, in terms of both inequality per se and the greater role played, among the super-rich, by earned money rather than inherited wealth and dividends. See

Atkinson, 2008; Saez, 2012. The huge increases in inequality reported in recent decades are largely in income; wealth distribution, at least in the US, has been much more stable. See Kopczuk and Saez, 2004, and also Esping-Andersen, 2009.

27. The 1930s, 1940s and early 1950s, during which inequality fell across the whole developed world. See Atkinson, 2008.

28. For example, between 1979 and 1989 full-time average pay for US men dropped 4 percent and women's rose 12 percent. Male and female wages converged especially fast in the US during the 1980s; in the 1990s they continued to do so but at a slower rate. See Blau and Kahn, 2006.

29. By 2007, the US Department of Labor Women's Bureau estimated that women accounted for 51 percent of persons employed in the high-paying management, professional and related occupations in the US labor market; the figure for the UK is similar. US Department of Labor, 2007; Hakim, 2004. See also OECD, 2002.

30. In some countries there are more women in this group; in most, more men, but even in the most extreme case (Canada) the difference is only 4 percentage points.

31. Statisticians in North America and Western Europe find no evidence of pay discrimination among young men and women in comparable jobs, and gaps in average and median pay, across the workforce, have been shrinking throughout the developed world. The median hourly pay of men and women in their twenties is now the same in the UK. (Office for National Statistics Annual Survey of Hours and Earnings. Average pay is still higher for men.) See also Weinberger and Kuhn, 2006; Carlsson and Rooth, 2008. The same applies to wealth as compared to income. Among younger Americans—those aged 25–39—there is no gender effect. Any apparent "gender gaps" in wealth holdings at this age are a function of whether people are working and of their education levels. See Schmidt and Sevak, 2006.

32. In the US, median male wages have stagnated since the 1970s but women's have not. See Blau and Kahn, 2006; Weinberger and Kuhn, 2006.

33. Kopczuk, Saez and Song, 2010: see especially Table 1 and Figures VI and X. For the population as a whole, the earnings share going to the top percentile rose from 7.21 in 1980 to 12.28 in 2004; and for men, from 6.85 to 13.44. The increase in inequality among men has been much sharper, but from a less unequal base: in 1960 inequality among men was markedly lower than among women. Ibid. (The authors calculate that the share of earnings going to the top 20 percent in 2004 was 51 percent for all workers, 52 percent for men, 47 percent for women. Note that this calculation excludes self-employment and very low-paid workers earning less than $2575 a year in 2004.) Inequality among women has been increasing, even though they have also been catching up on men. In 1980, women in the top 1 percent of female earners were paid just over 4 percent of total female earnings. By 2004, that figure had almost doubled: the top 1 percent of women were pulling in 8 percent of total female earnings. This reflects the fact that, among high-earning professionals, women have been catching up with men especially fast. See Kopczuk, Saez and Song, 2007: 13–14. Meanwhile, the proportion of women in the top 5 percent of UK earners has doubled in the last decade. Women made up roughly one in ten of the "top 5 percent" of earners in the UK in 1999. Ten years later, in 2009, it had

Notes

doubled to one in five. Data from the UK Labour Force Survey analyzed for this book by Scott Blevins.

34. Kopczuk, Saez and Song, 2010. Their panel is "Commerce and Industry," which excludes government employees, agriculture, hospitals, education, social services, religious and membership organizations.

35. Fourteen percent = one in seven in the US. In the UK, as in the US, males remain much more highly overrepresented at the very pinnacle of the income distribution, the top 1.0 and 0.1 percent. See Blau and Kahn, 2006. Males in 2004–2005 constituted 84 percent of the top 1–0.1 percent taxpayers in the UK and 91 percent of the top 0.1 percent. The same analyses show that 85 percent and 84 percent respectively of these groups were working-age adults (under 65) and 24 percent and 35 percent respectively were company directors. See Brewer, Sibieta and Wren-Lewis, 2008: Appendix B, Tables 2 and 4.

36. Table n19 **Income Trends for High Earners, UK**

	Annual income £s (rounded): Full-time women at this level	Income as % male equivalent
1999		
90th percentile	26,000	73
95th percentile	31,500	70
Mean	16,000	75
Median	14,000	76
2009		
90th percentile	44,000	77
95th percentile	48,000	77
Mean	24,000	78
Median	21,000	81

Source: UK Labour Force Survey: Q4 1999 and Q4 2009 compared (analyses carried out for this book by Scott Blevins)

37. Kopczuk and Saez, 2004, estimate that the percentage of females in the top 2 percent for wealth rose from 32 percent in 1948 and 30 percent in 1958 to 50 percent in 2000. These are sizeable numbers. A move from 30 percent to 50 percent of this "rich group" involves 300,000 more women, and 300,000 fewer men. If you take those falling just below the top 1 percent—those in the 98th percentile/the top 2–1 percent—the change is even more marked: from 29 percent female in 1958 to 56 percent in 2000. These figures include inheritance, and as discussed below there has always been a large number of heiresses among the super-rich. But the top 2 percent, and the top 2–1 percent, encompass large numbers of people, and the changes reflect the growing earnings and wealth of women in their own right.

38. Kopczuk, Saez and Song, 2007 and 2010, estimate that for the top 1 percent of US earners, annual earnings doubled from 6.5 percent in 1978 to 13 percent of total US earnings in 2004. In the top 1 percent, the proportion of women grew from 2 percent in 1980 to 14 percent in 2004; in the top decile (top 10 percent) of earners, the proportion of women went from about 2 percent in 1970 to 8 percent in 1980 to 22 percent by 2004. And among the next 10 percent (those earning between the 80th and 90th percentiles) it has gone from, again, a tiny 3 or 4 percent just forty years ago to about 30 percent in the early 2000s.

Notes

39. Edlund and Kopczuk, 2007, 2009.
40. This is a tiny fraction of the population (about 0.0002 percent of adults in 2000)—much smaller than the top 0.01 percent (one in 10,000 or about 20,000 people in the US case) whom statisticians typically identify as a super-elite.
41. Table n20 **Percentage of the Forbes 400 (USA) Who Were Women, 1982–2010**

Year	% women	Year	% women
1982	18	1998	15
1986	19	2002	12
1990	16	2006	13
1994	17	2010	11

Source: Table is based on and updates Edlund and Kopczuk, 2007

42. Bach, Corneo and Steiner, 2009. Compared to the US, Germany is characterized by large numbers of unincorporated firms, and its economic elite draw a larger share of income from income as compared to interest and dividends. The average income of the German economic super-elite, as defined by the authors, was 16 million euros in 2003.
43. See, for example, Atkinson, 2008; Kopczuk and Saez, 2004; Piketty and Saez, 2006; Atkinson, Piketty and Saez, 2011.
44. Edlund and Kopczuk, 2007: Table 5. Women have generally owned a half or more of those fortunes owned by heirs or heiresses, rather than by economically active individuals.
45. 2009 remuneration. Underlining how males' and females' experiences at the top converge, Rosenfeld could draw the same sort of astronomical salary as her male counterparts and gets bonuses for missing her financial targets in just the same way too. See Kellaway, 2011: 14. In a review of companies' annual reports, and their accompanying drivel, Kellaway writes, "My favorite statement this year is Kraft's which seeks to explain why Irene Rosenfeld got a bonus of $2.1m in return for missing her financial targets."
46. Among American men in 2008, 1,329,000 made >$250,000; the mean was $441,949—that is, slightly lower than for females in this bracket. Of women, 173,000 made between $200,000 and $250,000.
47. The mean for full-time males in 2008 was $64,000 and full-time females $45,000. The mean for all men in employment was $48,000 and for all women in employment $29,000. Far more men than women earned $250,000 or more, as one would expect from these figures. But the point of note here is the sheer number of high-earning females, not the continuing existence of a gender gap in the population as a whole.
48. Milne-Tyte, 2010.
49. Almost as many were unmarried men; married couples were less than two-thirds of purchasers. Almost half of the single female purchasers lived alone; the rest were largely mothers. See Drew, 2006. In terms of purchases, numbers are almost identical for men and women: 258,000 men and 248,000 women bought houses worth $200,000 to $300,000. For houses worth over $300,000, purchases were made by 141,000 single women and 192,000 single men between 2000 and 2003.
50. See Klinenberg, 2012, on the rise in single living generally.

7: SOMETHING TO REGRET?

1. See Vickery, 2003.
2. Lakdawalla, 2001: 47. As noted earlier, the US was unusual in locating teacher training in the universities from early on. Many of these graduate teachers would, in Europe, have studied in specialist non-university teacher training colleges.
3. Van Kleeck, 1918. Figures are all as a percentage of those employed at any point.
4. Alcott, 1908: 32–33.
5. Hughes, 1993: 167. The proposed curriculum included "Writing, Arithmetic, History, Grammar, Geography, and Needle Work." French, German, Latin, Music and Drawing were also offered for an extra fee.
6. Brandon, 2008: 42.
7. Ibid.: Eliza's story is particularly tragic. She married, but after the birth of a daughter fell into what sounds like extreme postnatal depression, and was persuaded by Mary to leave her husband, which in those days also meant relinquishing her child.
8. Census figures: sum of all female teachers (including art and music teachers). Professionals comprised 7 percent of the employed female workforce in 1880. Between 1880 and 1910, England's professional women quadrupled in number and women began to penetrate medicine, the law, journalism and the clergy. By 1890, 313,000 English women were classified as professionals, compared to 343,000 men: they included 217,000 teachers and 53,000 nurses. The US Census groups all "professions and personal services" together, so the category includes chimney sweeps and barbers as well as lawyers and clergymen, and is not comparable.
9. The attitude of affluent families to employment in elementary and grade schools is brilliantly captured by Arnold Bennett in his novel *The Old Wives' Tale*, set in provincial England of the 1860s:

    "Yes," said Sophia, "I should like to be a teacher. That's what I want to be."

    "A school-teacher?" inquired Mrs Baines.

    "Of course. What other kind is there?" said Sophia sharply . . .

    "I don't think your father would like that," Mrs Baines replied. "I'm sure he wouldn't like it." . . .

    What startled and surprised Mrs Baines was the perfect and unthinkable madness of Sophia's infantile scheme . . . Orphans, widows and spinsters of a certain age, suddenly thrown on the world—these were the women who, naturally, became teachers, because they had to become something. But that daughters of comfortable parents, surrounded by love and the pleasures of an excellent home, should wish to teach in a school was beyond the horizons of Mrs Baines's common sense. Comfortable parents of today who have a difficulty sympathising with Mrs Baines should picture what their feelings would be if their Sophias showed a rude desire to adopt the vocation of chauffeur.

    Bennett 1995: 50–51.
10. Glenday and Price, 1974: 57–58.
11. Paterson and Fewell, 1990: 93.
12. The census included all living graduates to 1915—response rates were high and

ranged from 91 percent at Barnard to 46 percent for Cornell; others were between 55 and 85 percent. Results are reported in Van Kleeck, 1915, and the data underlying Figure 7.1 are shown below:

Table n21 **Occupations of Alumnae of Elite US Colleges, to 1915**

	Number	Teaching only	Other only	Teaching + other	Never worked
Barnard	1,267	591	164	191	321
Bryn Mawr	971	375	121	117	358
Cornell	782	503	92	59	128
Mount Holyoke	1,895	1,213	192	252	238
Radcliffe	1,188	664	159	139	226
Smith	3,605	1,441	425	383	1,356
Vassar	2,363	891	286	236	950
Wellesley	4,256	2,029	440	489	1,298
Wells	412	142	45	24	201

13. They married more often than earlier cohorts, mostly to fellow graduates of top northeastern colleges, though they still married far less often than their contemporaries.

14. Barnard College archives. Author's own analysis of unpublished data from alumnae survey. Of the class of 1918, 73 percent married; 85 percent were or had been employed. Of this group, 42 percent had worked entirely as teachers, or had taught as well as doing other jobs; another 17 percent were or had been employed as librarians, school administrators or social workers. The Vassar alumnae magazine of 1937 reports very similar occupations for the Vassar class of 1912. Of those who were ever employed, 47 percent taught school (*Vassar: The Alumnae Magazine*, XXII, 1, October 15, 1937).

15. Somerville College Report, 1987: 64 and 1996: 106.

16. British Cohort Study, 1970: unpublished analysis of data by Andrew Jenkins. Using reading scores at age 11, 10 percent of the top decile of women and 8 percent of the second decile became teachers. Using math scores at age 11, the figures are 9 percent and 8 percent. Around two-thirds of female teachers from the 1970 birth cohort were in the eighth decile or below at age 11.

17. Entering students used to register high grade point averages and SAT scores, but today the average for freshmen in education faculties is near the bottom. In the 1960s, 20–25 percent of elementary and secondary female teachers scored in the top decile on SATs/ACT scores. By 1992, only 10 percent did so. The sharp decline in average quality is in large part because teaching has lost the brightest female students. See Lakdawalla, 2001.

18. Chapoulie, 1987: 117, Table 23. The figures are for *agrégés*. See below for men and women:

Table n22 **Education of French Teachers (Academic *Lycées*)**

Date of qualifying	% female agrégés who completed classes préparatoires	% male agrégés who completed classes préparatoires
Pre-1955	63	54
1955–65	36	49
1966 on	23	53

19. For example, in the US, graduates of top colleges are recruited to teach in disadvantaged areas by "Teach For America" and in the UK by "Teach First." Most of the people who participate in these programs then go on to other careers, although a few do decide to make a career in education.

20. In the US, the majority of schoolteachers were women by 1860. And as late as 1940 teachers still accounted for half the active US female graduate workforce overall. See Lakdawalla, 2001: 56.

21. In the half-century from 1945, the pay of elementary school teachers dropped in most Western countries by about 10–20 percent compared to the graduate average. Ibid.

22. Glenday and Price, 1974: 39.

23. Margadant, 1990: 73.

24. Ibid.: 77, 78.

25. Wolf, 2002: Chapter 2.

26. Figures vary by source and phrasing of the question. The US Current Population Survey for 2010 reports that just over a quarter of adult Americans volunteered in the last 12 months, whereas in the large "Giving and Volunteering in the US" survey (Independent Sector, 2001), 44 percent report that they did so.

27. Home Office, 2001.

28. Gordon Brown, celebrating Volunteers' Week, 2009 : http://volunteerindy.livejournal.com/352.html.

29. Ruston, 2003. Using 2000 Time Use data, Ruston finds that average time spent volunteering (age 16 up) is four minutes a day. An average eight minutes a day is spent helping others (family, neighbors). In interviews 11 percent of men and 13 percent of women say they have volunteered at some point in the past four weeks. On a diary day, it is 3 percent and 3 percent.

30. Carlin, 2001: 801. Having children increases the participation rate but reduces the number of hours *ceteris paribus*.

31. Egerton and Mullan, 2008. Full-time employed women record an average three minutes a day on formal volunteering, compared to five minutes for the part-time employed and six minutes for the retired; for men it is two minutes, seven minutes and seven minutes respectively.

32. A minority has maintained and even increased their contributions. In all the countries for which we have data, the more educated remain more likely to volunteer. For many of them, the time commitment is very small; but for a few it is still large. Meanwhile, among the less well-off and less educated, the people who do volunteer tend to give a larger amount of time than the average donated by graduates. See Carlin, 2001: 817; Statistics Canada 71–542-X: Table 2.2, Volunteer rate, mean and median volunteer hours.

33. Time-use data from France show that the average time spent on volunteering/civic activities (which includes trade unions and professional organizations) is quite a bit lower than in the Netherlands or the US. However, college graduates who are not in paid employment average 15 minutes a day, twice as much as anyone else, and three times more than non-employed people with only high-school educations.

34. In the mid-1960s, college graduates averaged 15 minutes a day, twice the level of high-school graduates with no college (women with some college were in between).

In the 1970s, absolute levels dropped off sharply, although the overall averages pick up somewhat in the time-use surveys of 2003–2010. In the latest surveys, the gap between graduate women and those with a high-school diploma and no or some college is much reduced compared to the 1960s, although high-school dropouts still report much less volunteer activity. American Time Use Survey data analyzed by A.-M. Jeannet.

35. Moreover, the general expectation in America was that married women would stop working—something that was far less true of the French École Normale graduates preparing to teach in the *lycées*—and some of these women married straight from college. See Margadant, 1990.

36. Almost a third had held some sort of office in their church, but almost every one of these had also been involved at a serious level with other nonreligious charities and community activities as well. Author's own analysis of Barnard College records.

37. Penelope Jessel, died 1996, Somerville College Oxford Report, 1996: 137–38.

38. Nancy Wassbrough, died 1997, Somerville College Oxford Report, 1996: 156–58.

39. Egerton and Mullan, 2008: 148.

40. People who give substantial amounts of their time are also, whatever their income and education, likely to be religious. In the Netherlands, for example, fewer people go to church than in the 1970s, but those who do are even more likely to volunteer than churchgoers were in the past (25 percent went to church on a weekly basis in 1975, down to 11 percent in 2005; 52 percent of this group volunteered compared to 18 percent for those not attending—in 1975 it was 41 percent and 19 percent). Some but not all of the volunteering was for church purposes. See van Ingen and Dekker, 2011; see also Bekkers, 2004. In the US, female volunteering is disproportionately found among women who are active in their religion. And their volunteering is not just for faith-related causes. In a large recent survey of American religion and faith, Putnam and Campbell, 2010, found that about overall half their respondents, male and female, reported volunteering for a nonreligious cause. They also compared adults who were in the top and the bottom quartiles nationally in terms of having lives bound up with religious institutions, and striking differences emerged. Almost two-thirds of the most religious reported volunteering for nonreligious causes. Among the least religious it was about one-third (62 percent of those with "top quartile" in religiously based social networks controlling for other factors, and 35 percent for the lowest quartile). Nor is this a class phenomenon. Religious attendance tends to be somewhat higher among college-educated Americans than among non-graduates (very markedly so in the case of African Americans), but it is nothing like as important an influence on religiosity as age, ethnicity and where you live. "Who personifies the most religious type of American? An older African American woman who lives in a Southern small town. And the least religious? A younger Asian American man who lives in a large Northeastern city": ibid.: 28. Even in a country like England, where churchgoing has declined rapidly in recent decades, churches and religious groups remain the dominant source of new charitable activities and campaigning, including some of the most important and best-known "general" charities founded in the last fifty years (Oxfam, Crisis, Fairtrade). See Wolf, 2008.

Notes

41. Prochaska, 2006: 63.
42. L. M. Hubbard, "Statistics of Women's Work," in A. Burdett-Coutts (ed.), *Women's Mission*, 1993: quoted in Prochaska, 1980: 224.
43. W. Booth, *In Darkest England and the Way Out*, 1890, p. 191: quoted ibid.: 16.
44. Lillian Wald case notes, quoted in *Reform Synagogues*, 1985: 488.
45. McCarthy, 2003.
46. McCarthy, 2003b: 84. Using the Consumer Price Index, $1 in 1863 was equivalent to $18.88 in 2012.
47. Notably the Anti–Corn Law League, the huge campaign that led to the repeal of the Corn Laws in 1846 and ushered in a century of free trade and cheap food for the UK. The Ladies' Committee of the League had 360 members covering the entire country, with links to their communities and responsibility for organizing and fund-raising there. See Prochaska, 1980: 63.
48. Prochaska, 2006: 85; McCarthy, 2003a: 185.
49. Prochaska, 1980: 222.
50. Skocpol, 1992: 2002.
51. Sutherland, 2006.
52. Ibid.: 129.
53. Ibid.: 132.
54. ATUS data for 2003–2010.
55. Some people have argued that the time not donated during a working life is made up for by large-scale volunteering among pensioners. Figure n6 gives the lie to this claim.
56. The national body responsible for regulating and overseeing charities.
57. Templeton, 2006: 23.
58. Quoted in Prochaska, 2006: 73.

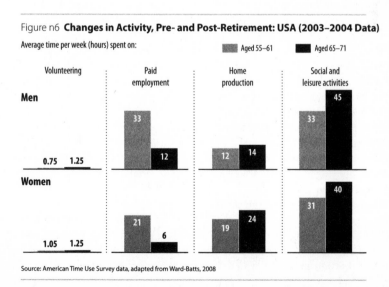

Figure n6 **Changes in Activity, Pre- and Post-Retirement: USA (2003–2004 Data)**

Average time per week (hours) spent on: ▪ Aged 55–61 ▪ Aged 65–71

Source: American Time Use Survey data, adapted from Ward-Batts, 2008

59. Lundström, 1996: 132.

60. Dutch figures, which provide detailed breakdowns by age, education and employment status, show no significant differences by gender. See, for example, Bekkers, 2004. In the US, working-age women are somewhat more likely to volunteer than men: over a full year, 23 percent of men and 29 percent of women report doing so. See US Bureau of Labor Statistics, 2011.

61. Lipsky, 1980: 29

62. Skocpol, 2003; see also, Skocpol, 2000.

63. Theda Skocpol also points out that a lot of the leaders of the populist right-wing "Tea Party" movement are women. For example, the Massachusetts leader in 2010 was a woman who had a job but had spent time at home and is a long-standing volunteer. As Skocpol notes, this is much more like the older pattern of female activity (personal communication).

64. These changes are compounded by the fact that many (still) come from WASP (White Anglo-Saxon Protestant) backgrounds, and it is the WASP denominations— the Episcopalians, the Methodists—who have lost ground in recent decades. See Putnam and Campbell, 2010.

65. Williams, 2006: 23.

66. *Analysis*, BBC Radio 4, December 13, 2006.

67. See, for example, Walter, 2005, who marshaled the usual employment statistics (average salary, number of female senior judges) to argue that "full equality is still a distant promise."

68. Wolf, 2006.

8: SEX AND THE SINGLE GRADUATE

1. Extract from Jane Austen's *Emma*, chapter 10.

2. We know this because we know how primitive contraception was and because we have good data on the percentage of children born out of wedlock for a range of Western societies. In England and Wales, for example, the percentage hovered around or a little above 5 percent from the late 1500s to the mid-twentieth century (since when it has shot up to 47 percent in 2010). Patterns for the rest of Western Europe are very similar. See Fernandez-Villaverde, Greenwood and Guner, 2010.

3. See Chapter 11, pp. 214.

4. The first contraceptive pill was authorized by the FDA for prescription, in the US, in 1960 and first marketed actively in 1961; but it was not available in all states to married women until 1965 and unmarried women till 1971. It was authorized and prescribed in Australia, West Germany and the UK from 1961. Japan, because of heavy lobbying from the Japanese Medical Association, was unusual in only authorizing its use in 1999.

5. The dramatic fall in births in Japan, where Japanese doctors kept the Pill out for forty years, shows how effectively families can control births without oral contraceptives, especially if other techniques are available. Japan was one of the first countries to have a clear twentieth-century abortion law—the "Eugenic Protection Law": abortion has in theory to be justified in terms of hereditary illness etc. but in

practice the law legalized abortion. Otherwise, until 1999, when the Pill was finally authorized, condoms were the main form of birth control. But the Pill—like high-quality IUDs—hands control to women.

6. For obvious reasons we have no reliable figures on the frequency of illegal abortions. In Soviet-era Russia, and a number of other Communist states, abortion was both legal and very common because of the unavailability of oral contraceptives and unreliability of other methods. For example, in the 1960s USSR, almost three abortions were recorded for every live birth.

7. Greenwood and Guner, 2010.

8. See Chandra et al., 2011, for the US; British figures for 2000 are found in Natsal, 2000, Reference Tables, Table 3.1 (National Survey of Sexual Attitudes and Life-styles II, 2000–2001). The Natsal survey encompassed mainland Britain, not the UK (so England, Scotland and Wales but not Northern Ireland).

9. See Appendix.

10. Figures for 2009. Median age at first marriage was two years higher in 2009 than in 1999. See Office of National Statistics (Population Statistics): http://www.ons.gov.uk/ons/taxonomy/index.html?nscl=Marriages%2C+Cohabitations%2C+Civil+Partnerships+and+Divorces.

11. Online shopping and social networks may have pushed porn down the list of most-visited sites since the early days of the Web, but in terms of searches, it is still huge. Porn-related keywords are the ones people search for most; and mainstream sites are happy to encourage and capitalize on hits from sex-related searches. See Kelly, 2011.

12. See, for example, *Woman and Home*, September 2010, Advertisements Directory.

13. Levy, 2005: 7–8.

14. Ibid.: 9.

15. Walter, 2010.

16. Ibid.: 35.

17. Ibid.: 23–24.

18. Levy, 2005: 13.

19. Walter, 2010, 123.

20. Ibid.

21. Ibid.: 35–36.

22. 2006–2008 Survey of Family Growth figures.

23. For a discussion of the "natural" alliances between women, with few or no formal powers, and childless eunuchs, which characterize imperial courts—not just in China but in Rome, Byzantium, Persia and the Ottoman Empire—see Dettenhofer, 2009. Dettenhofer notes that, in periods when organized eunuch power was very important, women's ambitions were typically responsible for this state of affairs: with no children of their own, eunuch officials made natural allies who could promote the dynastic claim of a particular woman's son.

24. Herrin, 2001: 170ff.

25. See, for example, Vickery, 2003.

26. See, for example, Herman, 2004; Abbott, 2007; Seigle, 1993.

27. Ruth Rosen notes that, in the late nineteenth century, with the growth of large cities, men moved into a business that, in the US, had been largely female-owned. See Rosen, 1983: 71.
28. Ibid.: 89. The figure of $40,000 for building Mahogany Hall is from http://en.wikipedia.org/wiki/Lulu_White.
29. Abbott, 2007.
30. Gottlieb, 2010.
31. Ibid.
32. As they did, for example, in Byzantium. Empress Theodora, wife of Justinian and enormously powerful and influential in her own right, was an actress and (more or less automatically) a courtesan.
33. Quoted in Gottlieb, 2010: 33.
34. Ibid.
35. The anonymous verses "She was poor but she was honest" catch this perfectly:

> In the rich man's arms she flutters
> Like a bird with broken wing
> First he loved her, then he left her
> And she hasn't got a ring
> See him in the splendid mansion
> Entertaining with the best
> While the girl that he has ruined
> Entertains a sordid guest . . .
> . . . It's the same the whole world over
> It's the poor that gets the blame
> It's the rich that gets the pleasure
> Isn't it a blooming shame?

36. Hefner graduated from Brandeis, an elite private university in Massachusetts.
37. Arrowsmith did not win but increased her party's share of the vote.
38. The median age was 17.
39. The median age at first intercourse for female dropouts in the 2006–2008 Survey of Family Growth was 16 among both 25–34 and 35–44-year-olds. However, the average was just under 17 for the older group and 16 years, 2 months for the younger group. The average for those with higher degrees—just over 19—did not change statistically between the two cohorts, but it (and the median) fell for those with some college or a bachelor's only.
40. 2006–2008 Survey of Family Growth: data analysis carried out for this book by Anne-Marie Jeannet.
41. British data here and throughout this chapter are from the Natsal survey, which covers England, Scotland and Wales (though not Northern Ireland) and is the largest scientific study of sexual behavior to date. The 1990 survey (18,876 people) was followed by another ten years later (12,110 people), which asked many of the same questions. Results from the third, 2010–2011, survey of around 15,000 people will, unfortunately, appear too late for this book. Many of the figures reported here are previously unpublished and were produced especially for this book by Dr. Cath Mercer. The Appendix summarizes key results from these new analyses that are

not reported in detail in the text. See the Natsal sites for details of publications and of the remit and schedule for the latest survey: http://www.ucl.ac.uk/iph/research/sexualhealthandhiv/natsal: http://www.natcen.ac.uk/study/natsal.

42. In 1990, the difference in age at first intercourse between those born 1946–55 and those born 1956–65 is highly significant (p<0.0001), but in neither group is there a statistically significant difference between graduates and non-graduates. However, the differences between graduates and non-graduates, for the 1966–75-born cohort, in the percentage reporting a first experience under 16, are highly significant (p<0.0001). The *least* educated women (a subset of the non-graduates) were already significantly more likely to have underage sex than their contemporaries by the 1970s. Adjusting for age, in the 1990 sample underage sex was almost twice as likely if a woman had no qualifications at all than if she had a degree. See Johnson et al., 1994: Chapter 4. To summarize, in a comparison between graduate women and (all) non-graduate women, there are no significant differences by education in 1990, but highly significant ones in 2000.

43. Because, in absolute terms, most girls in the latter part of the twentieth century had their first sexual experience in their late teens, differences by education group are less obvious from "median age" statistics than from more fine-grained analyses looking at, for example, proportions reporting underage sex. (The median is the age at which half the group has had sex and half haven't yet.) That median number was 17 in both 1990 and 2000 for non-graduate British women aged 25–44, and 19 and 18 respectively for graduates. But underlying these numbers there is not merely a major rise in early experience, but a dramatic difference between graduate and non-graduate women in these two cohorts. See Appendix Table 1 for male and female median figures.

44. See Appendix Table 1.

45. In contrast to age at first intercourse, the differences between graduate and non-graduate women in the percentage reporting a late first experience, at 21 or more, are highly significant for all cohorts surveyed (p<0.0001). Of "baby boom" female graduates (born 1946–55) 40 percent had their first sexual experience at age 21 or later, compared to 20 percent of their non-graduate female contemporaries. This latter difference reflects in part a very different average age at first marriage for women with different education levels. See Appendix Table 2 for male graduate/non-graduate differences in reports of underage and 21+ first sex.

46. Fernandez-Villaverde, Greenwood and Guner, 2010.

47. Researchers have developed very good ways of encouraging honest responses and checking on consistency and reliability. However, obtaining funding for the pioneering surveys was very difficult: many of the surveys had to be scaled back, or rely on foundation funding as politicians backed off nervously.

48. The results of the major American survey carried out in 1990 are reported in Michael et al., 1994: see pp. 106–107. The sample was 3,432 adults, aged 18–59, who appeared to be representative of the population on all standard demographic variables. Other countries that carried out surveys at roughly the same time included Britain, France, Sweden, Finland and Australia.

49. Researchers refer to the problem of "social desirability bias" to describe cases

where responses are affected by what is considered acceptable. See, for example, Martinelli and Parker, 2009.

50. Unlike the published US data, the 1990 British results generally separate out women from men. In addition, for this chapter, Dr. Cath Mercer carried out a range of additional education-related analyses of Natsal data for both 1990 and 2000.

51. Even then there are some problems: a shift from writing an answer on paper and handing it over to entering it on a laptop, as happened between 1990 and 2000, seems to make some people more willing to report certain types of behavior. But the effects do not seem to be very large or indeed consistent. See Copas et al., 2002; Johnson et al., 2001.

52. Medved and Wallechinsky, 1976: 168.

53. Ibid.: 27.

54. Around 30 percent of 55–59-year-olds reported five or more lifetime partners (though they had been adult for longer than other interviewees). For college graduates a bare majority—52 percent—reported fewer than five to date. Note: Male and female reponses are merged. The categories used in Figure 8.1 are those used and reported by Michael et al., 1994.

55. Among those a decade younger, born 1956–65, 25 percent of British graduates report first sex at age 21+; this falls a little, but not much, to 19 percent, for those a decade younger still. In contrast, among non-graduate British women, only 11 percent of those born 1956–65, and only 6 percent of those born 1966–75 (and age 25–34 in 2000) report that their first sexual experience was at age 21 or later. See Natsal.

56. The same pattern holds among "boomer" generation men (aged 35+). The 2000 figures for Britain show median number of partners in the last five years as remaining higher for graduate women under 35 but the gap has shrunk. Otherwise there are no major differences between graduates and non-graduates. Between 1990 and 2000, the proportion of 25–34-year-olds reporting three+ partners also increases for all groups. See Appendix, Table 4c. See also Johnson et al., 2001.

57. Beaujouan and Ní Bhroicháin, 2011: Table 1, p. 42. In the 1960s, when most people married in their twenties, less than 10 percent of either men or women cohabited before marriage. Today, it is over 70 percent for those marrying in their late twenties, over 80 percent for those marrying in their thirties.

58. Michael et al., 1994; Johnson et al., 1994. While it is theoretically possible that a sizeable number of the multiple partners reported in the US 1990 data were—for male respondents—prostitutes, data on numbers paying for sex make this extremely unlikely. See Michael et al., 1994: 196; Ward et al., 2005: 467–71. In Natsal data, 2 percent of men report paying for sex at some point in 1990, and 4 percent report doing so in 2000.

59. Holtby's "Are Spinsters Frustrated?" is quoted in Nicholson, 2008: 32. See also p. 177 for estimates of how many unmarried women were virgins in the inter-war period.

60. In 2000, there were no significant education-related differences among British men for median reported opposite-sex lifetime partner numbers. All figures quoted in this and the previous paragraph from unpublished analyses carried out by Dr. Cath

Mercer, Natsal/UCL plus Natsal 2000 Reference Tables, available at http://www
.ucl.ac.uk/iph/research/sexualhealthandhiv/natsal; http://www.natcen.ac.uk/study/
natsal.

61. See Chandra et al., 2011: Tables 3 and 4. In the 2006–2008 survey, graduates
(male and female) tend to report rather fewer lifetime partners than some other
educational groups, but the trend is not strong or linear.

62. When the variable of interest is the number who have ever had five or more partners, there is a nonlinear relationship with education for British men aged 25–44:
graduates and the least educated report lower numbers than in-between groups, but
the absolute differences are not huge (p<.01). For women, again there is a strong
but nonlinear relationship between education and the percentage who have ever
had five+ partners. It is definitely higher for the least educated, but lower for "some
college" than for graduates. Unpublished Natsal data.

63. The figure was 35 out of 617 female graduates aged 25–44 (5.7 percent), compared
to 1.3 percent for non-graduates in 1990.

64. See Appendix Tables 3a and 3b.

65. Natsal, 2000.

66. In the 2000 Natsal survey, 15 graduates—about 1 percent—reported more than 50
male partners to date. Of these, 10 were single and had never been married, two
had previously been married and three were cohabiting; six had at least one child.
Median age was 32. (Interquartile range 29–40.)

67. Defined as reporting one partner or more in the past year. British figures from Natsal Reference Tables: Table 3.17. US figures: Chandra et al., 2011.

68. See Appendix Tables 4a and 4b.

69. The Reference Tables for Natsal 1990 and 2000 show that, in 1990, 3 percent of
women aged 25–34 and 35–44 and 11 percent aged 45–54 reported no sex in the
last five years. See Johnson et al., 1994: Table 5.1. In 2000, 2 percent of women
aged 25–34 and 4 percent of those aged 35–44 report no opposite-sex partners
in the last five years (Table 3.9). There are no significant differences by education
level.

70. In 2000 differences in the number of partners (including a count of zero) were non-
significant for graduate and non-graduate British women. In 1990, the differences
between the distributions reached significance (p=0.0138), but actual differences in
the proportion reporting no partner in the last year were not very large: the figures
were 12 percent for non-graduates, 9 percent for graduates.

71. There is also evidence that, during the 1980s, high-risk practices declined, as indicated by a fall in diagnoses of sexually transmitted diseases such as gonorrhea. For
example, in England, Wales and Northern Ireland, Health Protection Agency statistics show a sharp fall during the period 1980–95. There was then a rise (1998–
2003), though not to anything like 1980 levels, and a further falling off. Male and
female incidence follow parallel tracks.

72. Even when you leave out the people who report no sex at all in the last four weeks,
the median number of occasions only goes up from about once to one and a half
times a week.

73. See Appendix Tables 5, 6 and 7.

74. See Appendix Table 12. In 1990, the US, Britain, France, Finland and Sweden had very similar responses to a question about how many times people had had sex in the last year (rather than the last four weeks, which was not asked). And while a year is a long time to remember accurately, it is not obvious why people would remember more or less accurately depending on their marital status.

75. Back in 1990, there were no major differences by education in how often American women reported sex, whereas in Britain there were. By 2000, the British differences have declined and the American ones increased. Among unmarried cohabiting American women—who report significantly more sexual intercourse than married women do, as is the case in all other well-conducted sex surveys—the average is just over eight times in the last four weeks for the most sexually active subgroup, the high-school graduates. It is six and a half on average for cohabitees with higher degrees. See 2006–2008 Survey of Family Growth data. Original analyses by A.-M. Jeannet.

76. See Appendix Table 9. Among single Americans, there are no education-related differences in the numbers reporting a whole year without a partner, but there are in the number of months for which single women report sexual activity. Single high-school dropouts are the most active (at eight months of the year on average) and college women least (at six). See Lindberg and Singh, 2008: Table 2.

77. British data do not distinguish between graduates with higher degrees and those with bachelor's only. There is some difference by education in 1990, with average activity statistically but not enormously lower for graduates; by 2000, differences had declined and although still statistically significant were small and nonlinear. See Appendix Tables 10 and 11.

78. Among the quarter of 22–44-year-old female Americans reporting multiple partners in the course of a single year, as opposed to five years or a lifetime, non-graduates are, today, more likely to feature than graduates. But a female high-school graduate is currently more likely than someone with a bachelor's degree to be in the group reporting frequent changes of partner in the last 12 months. Men generally report multiple partners in one year more often than women. (This does not mean they are all lying! See note 80 below and Chandra et al., 2011: Table 1 and Lindberg and Singh, 2008: Table 3.)

79. In 1990, 7 percent of 25–34-year-olds and 4 percent of 35–44-year-old British women reported two or more sexual partners in the last year. In 2000, the figures were 12 percent and 7 percent respectively: Johnson et al., 2001. Unlike the US data there is no significant difference between graduate and non-graduate women on this measure. See Appendix Table 19 for British males and Table 20 for US female figures.

80. For all 25–44-year-olds taken together, the comparable numbers are 5.5 percent (1990) and 9.8 percent (2000). See Natsal, 1990 and 2000.

81. British women aged 25–34: it was up from about 1 percent of young adult women overall in 1990. See Natsal Reference Tables: Table 3.17. There are no major differences between graduate and non-graduate women on this measure. Among British men, numbers reporting multiple partners also rose between 1990 and 2000, by a smaller percentage but from a larger base; as is common, men are more likely to

report multiple partnerships. This may be because different values result in under-reporting and/or over-reporting by women and men respectively. But it may also reflect the existence of a few highly promiscuous women, and of prostitutes.

82. Analysis by A.-M. Jeannet of Family Growth Survey data.

83. See Appendix Table 20. See also Lindberg and Singh, 2008.

84. A San Francisco intersection that became famous as the center of 1960s counter-culture and "flower power."

85. Michael et al., 1994: 156–57; Hakim, 2011b; Rhoads, 2004.

86. Specifically, 35 to 21 percent among graduates and 59 to 35 percent among non-graduates. Natsal, 1990 and 2000.

87. Major differences between British graduate and non-graduate women (p<0.0001) are evident for each separate age group, from both surveys. There are also major differences (though rather different ones) between male graduates and non-graduates. See Appendix Table 13 and Table 14. Overall, the shift in values is very clear. Women remain consistently less likely than men to view one-night stands as never or almost never wrong; but younger women in 2000 are considerably more positive (or less negative) about them than those a decade older—who are, in turn, more positive than their own cohort was a decade before.

88. See Appendix Table 15.

89. In 1990, 16 percent of British female graduates aged 25–44 thought male homosexuality to be always wrong and 42 percent of non-graduates.

90. British figures for female attitudes to female homosexuality are virtually identical for all groups/both periods. Among younger female graduates in 2000 only 8 percent think male homosexuality is always wrong, and 77 percent that it is never or rarely so. These figures are consistently very different from those for men, who, while much more tolerant in 2000 than 1990, nonetheless remain significantly less accepting of male homosexuality than women are. (Male graduates are more tolerant than non-graduates; nonetheless, in 2000, 21 percent considered male homosexuality to be always wrong, twice the female graduate level.) Males' tolerance of female homosexuality is as high as that of females.

91. *Cosmopolitan* UK, Sex tips, December 2011. Retrieved from http://www.cosmo politan.co.uk/love-sex/tips/.

92. Results are only reported here for variables where the difference between graduates and non-graduates reached conventional levels of statistical significance. Unless reported otherwise, these are significant at the 0.01 level (p < 0.01).

93. This question was only asked in 2000. Every sub-group of men (graduate/non-graduate, by age group of under 25, 25–34 and 35–44) showed total levels of 90 percent or more except for the youngest non-graduates; and every sub-group of women registered 85 percent or above except, again, for the youngest non-graduates. See Appendix Table 16.

94. See Appendix Table 17.

95. See Appendix Table 18.

96. Laumann et al., 1994. The mean number of practices found "appealing" was 1.27 (out of a maximum of 12) for those with less than a high school diploma and 2.13 for those with a graduate degree—a linear relationship. Since one of the options

offered—and by far the most popular—was vaginal intercourse, the main implication is that, in 1990, the vast majority of American women were not attracted by anything else, whether it was vibrator use, anal stimulation, anal sex, sex with a stranger or forced sex.

97. Michael et al., 1994: Chapter 7, Table 12.
98. British data, which ask about oral and anal sex in the last year, not a lifetime, show no major differences between graduates and non-graduates in either 1990 or 2000. See Appendix.
99. Michael et al., 1994: Chapter 7, Table 11 (figures for passive oral sex used) and Chandra et al., 2011: Table 5.

9: WORKING GIRLS

1. Belle de Jour, 2005: 10.
2. This refers to 25–34-year-olds. See Chapter 8 and Appendix.
3. See, for example, the story of Rahab the harlot in the Book of Joshua, Chapter 2.
4. Abbott, 2007: 262.
5. See Davies, 2009. Davies carried out an extensive investigation of the data, the origin of inflated claims and the way in which these became current and treated as factual. See also Sanders, 2005 and 2008. The most serious problem in contemporary Britain, and in some other European countries, was not even touched upon in the trafficking panic: namely the "grooming" of very young girls by local men who flatter, seduce and then pimp them. In the UK this phenomenon is concentrated in certain cities and most commonly involves men from ethnic communities that strictly control the behavior of their own young women. See, for example, Norfolk, 2011a and 2011b.
6. Rosen, 1983: xvii.
7. Rosen states that the capitalized value of earnings for a professional prostitute was more than four times that of a hardworking industrial worker in the first decade of the twentieth century. See ibid.: 71–86.
8. Stead, 1964: 255, quoted in Rosen and Davidson, 1977. Stead was a campaigning journalist, spiritualist and peace activist who drowned in the sinking of the *Titanic*.
9. Rosen and Davidson, 1977: xxvii–xxviii.
10. Ibid.: 193.
11. The two were put in contact by a Philadelphia social worker, Herbert Welsh, after Maimie was hospitalized for morphine addiction, and corresponded from 1910 to 1922.
12. Rosen and Davidson, 1977: 52.
13. Edlund and Korn, 2002, report data suggesting that, in the 1990s, nearly 10 percent of Thai women worked as prostitutes at some point in the decade. Estimates for nineteenth-century US and UK cities vary enormously: statistical sources are very poor (see Slater, 2010) and many of the estimates were produced by campaigners who wished to influence public opinion. During the "white slavery" panic of the 1900s, newspapers estimated that there were more than 10,000 professional prostitutes in Chicago, out of a population of about 2 million (Abbott, 2007).

14. Sanders, 2008: 64.
15. Ibid.: 66.
16. Brents, Jackson and Hausbeck, 2009: 153–55.
17. Sanders, 2008: 52.
18. Ibid.
19. The study by Sudhir Venkatesh is described in detail in Levitt and Dubner, 2009: Chapter 1.
20. The empirical evidence is summarized in Edlund and Korn, 2002; Edlund, Engelberg and Parsons, 2009; and Levitt and Dubner, 2009. In the early 1990s, street prostitutes seem to have averaged about $25–$30 an hour, and typically were paid for about 13 hours a week. Their hourly rate was roughly four times what they could earn at other low-wage jobs. Estimates of yearly earnings vary from about $19,000 to $24,000 a year, compared to an average for all working women of a little above $20,000 at that time.
21. Turner, 2012.
22. Edlund, Engelberg and Parsons, 2009.
23. Levitt and Dubner, 2009: 55.
24. Maimie Pinzer's family cut her off.
25. Edlund and Korn, 2002: 185–86.
26. Edlund, Engelberg and Parsons, 2009, note that escorts charge most when they are at "prime" marriage age (26–30) rather than younger, suggesting that this is offsetting the higher price incurred by undertaking sex work at this age rather than before or later. It may also, however, reflect the best combination of youth and skill.
27. Belle de Jour, 2005: 11.
28. Ibid.: 47.
29. Brents, Jackson and Hausbeck, 2009: 272.

10: PRETTY GIRLS AND PEACOCKS' TAILS

1. Leslie Wexner, quoted in Silverstein and Fiske, 2005: 154.
2. In the most recent National Survey of Family Growth, 92 percent of American males aged 18–44 said they were sexually attracted only to the opposite sex; 4 percent said they were attracted mostly to the opposite sex; and 1 percent that they were attracted equally to both. See Chandra et al., 2011.
3. Buss, 2003: 51.
4. Ibid.
5. Ibid.: 100–101.
6. Ibid.: 111.
7. Ibid.; Hamermesh, 2011.
8. But conversely, photos of really good-looking people of our own sex, against whom our own looks suffer in comparison, generally make us feel worse. See Kenrick et al., 1993. Generally, people's self-image suffers when they see that someone else is better than they are at something; the more strongly, the more it is something central to their self-image. The relationship is not simple, though: if it were, advertisers would show clothes and cosmetics on ugly girls, not beautiful ones. (The

advertisements imply that we might look like that, with that product, although obviously we know—rationally—that this isn't the case.)

9. Rhode, 2010: 23.

10. See, for example, Lemley, 2000; Hamermesh, 2011. See also the "Faceprints" site: http://web.mac.com/vicjohn/FacePrints/Welcome.html.

11. Rhode, 2010: 23. Quite a lot of the evidence is from the increasingly ingenious experiments that university psychologists devise (usually with undergraduates as subjects) and in which participants are invited to play games or make judgments under carefully varied conditions (see, for example, Hosoda, Stone-Romero and Coats, 2003). This makes it unwise to place too much weight on specific findings about the level and nature of preferences, but the consistency of findings is impressive.

12. See especially Hamermesh, 2011.

13. Ibid.: 173, 180.

14. Hamermesh and Biddle, 1994; Hamermesh, 2011: 45–52. The "other things" held constant include factors such as education, family background and IQ. One possible explanation for the rather surprising finding that women's salaries are not affected more than men's may be that the least attractive women appear more likely, in the data sets Hamermesh examines, not to be working at all. In general, women's ratings are more dispersed (ibid.: 30).

15. Hamermesh, 2011: 46. Most of the large-scale data sets identified by Hamermesh date back to the 1970s, but smaller recent studies (for example, of young US adults in 2000) confirm the general pattern (ibid.: 49, 52).

16. Ibid.: 118, 130.

17. Ibid.: 77–80. Data are from Germany, Finland and Australia.

18. China—the world's largest labor market—has almost no anti-discrimination laws of any sort. Peter Kuhn and Kailing Shen analyzed a large sample of Chinese top-end job advertisements posted on a big Internet site over a five-month period: using a Web crawler they were able to collect and analyze data on 633,664 job ads in total, 70 percent of them requiring at least some post-secondary education. They report that "34 percent of firms that advertised . . . placed at least one ad stipulating a preferred gender" and "47, 29 and 10 percent respectively expressed a preference for age, physical attractiveness and height respectively. Ninety percent of firms who placed 50 or more ads expressed a preference for at least one of these characteristics" (Kuhn and Shen, 2009: 1). They found that 10 percent of ads had a gender preference (male or female); 8 percent specified that the applicant should be physically attractive. There was relatively little overlap between the two categories, so most ads calling for physical attractiveness did not specify gender. But of the ads that were aimed specifically at women, a third also required applicants to be physically attractive, compared to 7 percent of ads aimed at men. Ads requiring beauty also tended to be less demanding than average (for this site) in terms of the levels of employment and experience required. The jobs most likely to ask for women and for good looks were concentrated in occupations with a lot of customer contact—tourism and entertainment, retail, beauty and fitness—plus "administration."

19. Hamermesh, 2006.

20. Hamermesh, 2011: 80. Data are available for the US and Germany. The effects are largest for introductory classes.

21. Presumably because they have built up larger practices among clients who prefer their attorneys to look good. See Biddle and Hamermesh, 1998. The analysis is based on graduates of a large prestigious law firm, which conducts regular follow-up surveys: ratings were based on photos for entering classes. Over 4,400 ratings were obtained.

22. In concrete terms, an attorney whose appearance in a photo taken on average nearly 20 years earlier placed him one standard deviation below the mean of looks was earning around 12 percent less per annum than one whose looks at that time put him one standard deviation above the mean. See Biddle and Hamermesh, 1998: 187. The "beauty effect" seems to be even stronger for self-employed attorneys than for those employed by large firms.

23. Pfann et al., 2000.

24. Buss, 2003: Chapter 4.

25. Hakim, 2011b.

26. Ibid.: 228.

27. They are also more interested in "non-standard" forms of intercourse, and masturbate more. See, for example, Laumann et al., 1994; Michael et al., 1994.

28. Landry et al., 2005. The raw data show that a one-standard-deviation increase in personal beauty for the person soliciting increases hourly returns from approximately $6 to more than $12, or about 100 percent, almost entirely because more people in total give (as opposed to individuals giving more money).

29. Hamermesh, 2011: 91.

30. American Psychological Association, 2007.

31. Men and women also seem both to take greater risks in the presence of the opposite sex. See McAlvanah, 2009.

32. Gladwell, 2005.

33. Babcock and Laschever, 2003.

34. See, for example, Booth, 2009; Booth and Nolen, 2009; Niederle and Vesterlund, 2007. The Booth and Nolen study reports on an experiment involving students from mixed- as well as single-sex schools and reports that girls from single-sex schools behave much the same as boys even when in mixed-sex groups.

35. Coates and Herbert, 2008; Apicella et al., 2008.

36. Pinker, 2008.

37. See, for example, Hewlett, 2007.

38. See, for example, Christine Lagarde, former French finance minister and head of the IMF, in Lagarde, 2010.

39. The birds are natives of India; most birds in England are in captivity, but there are also now some small wild populations.

40. As quoted in Buss, 2003: 105. The quotation is from Margulis and Sagan, 1991: 103. A related point is made by Trivers, 1985: 395, quoted in Buss.

41. Griskevicius et al., 2007.

42. Korda, 1979: 58.

43. Ibid.: 59.
44. He also advised, "If you must ask for money, ask for twice what you need. Your request . . . will then go up to a much more intelligent man for approval" (ibid.: 100).
45. Harper, 2000. Tall women do not enjoy advantages; though very small ones seem to.
46. Caruso, Rahnev and Banaji, 2009. People discriminate by weight even when choosing team members for a sedentary activity.
47. Loh, 1993; Gortmaker et al., 1993; Averett and Korenman, 1996. The main sources of data are longitudinal studies tracking cohorts of young people over time, such as the UK's National Child Development Study and the USA's National Longitudinal Study of Youth. Although obesity is associated with poverty and low education levels, it continues to have a negative effect on earnings and marriage rates even after controlling for these and other factors; and the "killer period" seems to be between ages 16 and 24. Women who become obese after this do not experience the same effects. The "raw" data for American women in the NLSY (reported by Averett and Korenman, 1996: 313) show that obese women earned an average hourly wage that was three-quarters of the average for women their age. However, the data find this effect only for women, not men, and not for African American women either. English data suggest that, with multiple controls, young obese women earn around 10 percent less an hour; again, there is no effect for men. See Sargent and Blanchflower, 1994; Harper, 2000.
48. Bovey, 1989: 13.
49. Rhode, 2010: 79.
50. Buss, 2003.
51. Jones, 2010. The industry was itself a product of industrialization and an explosion in the number of young women with substantial amounts of money left over after food and lodging were covered.
52. The UK figure includes noninvasive treatments—peels, fillers, etc.
53. Source: American Association of Plastic Surgeons.
54. Susan Brownmiller (an influential early feminist) quoted in Rhode, 2010: ix.
55. The eminent primatologist Susan Hrdy is one of the people who insist that there is little to be gained from myths "that emphasize woman's natural innocence from lust for power, her cooperativeness and solidarity with other women. Such a woman never evolved among the other primates. Even under those conditions most favorable to high status for females—monogamy and closely banded 'sisterhood'— competition among females remains a fact of primate existence" (Hrdy, 1981: 190). Researchers have spent months and years observing the way other primates interact: in every such case competition among females is clearly documented. Ours is the sole exception, because no primatologists have sat in corners recording, scientifically, how women do or don't compete over the things they want. But is it really plausible that we are the only primate species to be different? Hrdy doesn't think so. Primate females compete for high-status mates and to be high status themselves. (The two go together.) Primate females also compete for resources for their offspring and for themselves. It sounds, as Hrdy remarks, like any human society: it is certainly hard to think of a single good and convincing novel (let alone a great one)

in which women don't compete, and don't behave like full-fledged adult primates. And, of course, in which men don't too.

56. Friedman, 2010 and 2012.

11: ONE OF YOUR OWN KIND

1. The first sentence of *Pride and Prejudice*.

2. Schwartz and Mare, 2005; Esping-Andersen, 2009: 68. Research on assortative mating compares actual patterns to what would happen if mating was random in terms of education (or any other variable), and thus takes into account changes in underlying distributions of any particular characteristic.

3. A high-school graduate and a college graduate were 25 percent less likely to marry each other in the late 1980s than they had been in 1940. See Schwartz and Mare, 2005. Although very few female graduates were married to men with no college, about a third were married to men with some college but not a full bachelor's. The percentage of US graduate husbands with graduate wives was 37 percent in 1970, 71 percent in 2007 (30–44-year-olds). See Fry and Cohn, 2010.

4. Whelan, 2006.

5. Blossfeld and Timm, 2003: 333. This major research project on "who marries whom" in Western countries confirms that, in the past, many men married "down" in educational terms and many women married "up" simply because so many fewer women obtained a good education. (The alternative would have been for many educated men not to marry at all.) But marrying someone with the same education as yourself is also much more common than if people married randomly in this respect given current high and more equal education levels.

6. In the very recent past, there has been a decrease in the percentage of married American female graduates aged 30–44 whose husbands have a full bachelor's degree (from 70 percent in 1970 to 64 percent in 2007). This reflects the huge increase in female college enrollments not just absolutely but relative to men, and the growth of predominantly female occupations, especially in the health field, which require a college degree. (This is an international development: nursing, for example, has become a graduate profession in a number of countries where this was not historically the case.) There has been no parallel development for men: skilled, heavily male jobs such as electricians remain non-graduate. See Fry and Cohn, 2010.

7. Goux and Maurin, 2003: 64, 57. For example, among men born in the 1930s, "random" marriage with respect to education would have produced 50 percent homogamous marriages, and it was actually 57 percent; for those born 1964–78, the comparable figures are 26 percent and 40 percent. For the equivalent female cohorts the percentages are 50 percent and 56 percent; and 29 percent and 43 percent. The German data for the same research project (Blossfeld and Timm, 2003) also show that, when compared to contemporaries who have the same level of education as their parents, children who have higher education levels than their parents are more likely than others to marry "down," and children who have less education than their parents are somewhat more likely to marry back "up."

8. Chan and Halpin, 2003: see especially 191–93.

9. Tony Blair (ex–prime minister and ex-leader of Labour Party), Nick Clegg (leader

of Liberal Democrat Party, deputy prime minister from 2010) and Ed Miliband (leader of Labour Party) are all married to successful lawyers. Gordon Brown (ex–prime minister and ex-leader of Labour Party) is married to a founding partner of a leading PR consultancy; David Cameron (prime minister from 2010 and leader of Conservative Party) to a leading designer and company director.

10. Steir and Shavit, 2003.

11. For example, one very eminent female colleague of mine, a leading academic psychologist, has been married for decades to a man who left school at 17—but who runs a highly successful and profitable landscaping company.

12. Blossfeld and Timm, 2003.

13. The researchers (Sweeny and Cancian, 2004a) interpreted their results as probably showing that men emphasized wives' future earnings more than in the past, and more generally as showing an increase in the importance of women's economic prospects in determining how they fare in the marriage market. Their work was the subject of a debate. Julie Press argued that the results were perfectly consistent with women placing *less* emphasis on men's earnings than in the past. However, this is not true. As Paula England pointed out, that would only be the case if "men's noneconomic characteristics are perfectly positively correlated with their earning power, but this is an unrealistic assumption." See England, 2004, and Press, 2004. See also Sweeny and Cancian, 2004b. The researchers concentrated on white women because the marriage rate is much lower among American black women, and because other research indicates significantly different patterns of mating/assortative mating among blacks. See also Fry and Cohn, 2010: 14. Between 1970 and 2007, graduate husbands became increasingly likely, and high-school dropouts much less likely, to have wives whose earnings put them in the top 50 percent for women aged 30–44.

14. Women in the bottom parental wealth category, for example, were only half as likely to marry men in the "top" category as they would be if wealth played no direct role, but twice as likely to marry men with zero expectations like their own. And it is the same in reverse for women from the top of the parental wealth pyramid. See Charles, Hurst and Killewald, 2011. The wealth categories used are quite broad, with 39 percent of the sample falling into the top category. The US is unusual in having data available with which to examine parental wealth of spouses.

15. Brooks, 2000: 19, 13–14.

16. Fry, 2010.

17. See Wax, 2011, and Edin and Kefalas, 2005, for why this is the case, and the extent to which it reflects economics, socialization, or both.

18. *Vassar,* XXIII.1,1937; XXIV.5, 1939. Among highly successful women, such as those listed in the 1948–49 edition of *Who's Who in America,* almost half of those over 55 and 36 percent of those aged 45–54 had never married, compared to 9 percent of women of their ages in the US population as a whole. See Kiser and Schacter, 1949. See also Nicholson, 2008: 265.

19. Fry, 2010.

20. Fernandez, Fogli and Olivetti, 2002: Figure 1.

21. The "crude marriage rate"—the proportion of the population getting married in

a given year—fell between 1960 and 2009 in every European country: halving in Spain, more than halving in Hungary, almost halving in France. Eurostat: Population/Marriage and Divorce Statistics, Table 1: crude marriage rate per 1,000 inhabitants. Some of the fall reflects changes in the age structure of the population; but much reflects falls in the percentage ever married and an ongoing increase (year on year) in age at first marriage. The probability of ever marrying has fallen quite rapidly—typically by ten or more percentage points for those born after 1960, compared to mid-century babies. For example, between 1986 and 2007, the proportion ever married fell from 79 to 69 percent for Australian males and 86 to 74 percent for Australian females. See Australian Bureau of Statistics, 2007. In England and Wales, 88 percent of men born in 1951 and 93 percent of women born that year had married at least once by the time they were 45. Among those born ten years later, in 1961, the comparable numbers were 79 percent and 85 percent. See Demey et al., 2011.

22. Table n23 **Percentage of US Women Never Married in 1986 and 2009**

	25–29 years	40–44 years	55 years plus
White non-Hispanic: 1986	24.0	3.8	4.8
White non-Hispanic: 2009	43.4	10.3	4.7
Black women: 1986	44.3	13.3	3.5
Black women: 2009	70.5	33.1	13.0

Source: Kreider and Ellis, 2011. The data are from Table 1, p.3.

23. Kreider and Ellis, 2011. Among those born 1940–44, 91 percent of men and of women were married by age 40, 83 percent and 87 percent respectively by age 30. For the 1960–64 born, the figures are 81 percent and 64 percent (for both sexes).

24. Overall, across the EU, 37 percent of births were out of wedlock in 2009. Source: Eurostat.

25. Black women in the US have uniformly lower rates of marriage and higher rates of out-of-wedlock birth, overall and for each level of education, than do white women. However, the basic patterns within-group are exactly the same. Among black American women who gave birth in 2006–2007, less than 10 percent of the high-school dropouts were married, compared to just over 20 percent of high-school graduates, 30 percent of those with some college and almost 70 percent of college graduates. There has also been a rapid increase in extramarital births among Hispanics, currently averaging 45 percent overall. See Wax, 2011.

26. Ibid.: 23.

27. Goodman and Greaves, 2010. Figures derived from Chapter 3. By age five, the number living with a single parent has risen to about a quarter.

28. This compares with 35 percent of those with no formal qualifications and 28 percent of mothers with only the most basic formal qualifications. See Kiernan and Smith, 2003. For "level 5" mothers (with degrees or equivalent qualifications) they report 3 percent single, 14 percent cohabiting and 83 percent married. For level 4 (some post-secondary qualifications) the figures are 5 percent, 18 percent, 77 percent. Overall, about 60 percent of UK Millennium babies were born to married parents, another quarter to cohabiting but unmarried parents and the final 15 percent to single, non-cohabiting mothers. See Dex and Joshi, 2005: 26.

29. Other major primate families include the apes and the monkeys.

30. Genghis Khan probably holds the record for the number of identified descendants—16 million of them—but plenty of other rulers had more recorded children than he did. See Zerjal et al., 2003.

31. Suckling was the necessary practice for mothers throughout the whole of human history until a very short time ago, when modern formula was invented. Suckling—breastfeeding—inhibits ovulation and acts as quite an effective contraceptive, further spacing births and reducing the number of babies a female human can bear.

32. For example, Buss argues that "[h]umans were not designed by natural selection to coexist in niceness and matrimonial bliss. They were designed for individual survival and genetic reproduction" (2003: 15).

33. Monarchs and the very rich could father large numbers of illegitimate children *and* provide for them.

34. Titi monkeys are certainly more monogamous than we are; the father spends far more time than the mother does on the heavy task of carrying and holding a newborn. Adult male orangutans, by contrast, don't live in bands, but rather alone most of the time, although they will typically have a "home range" that covers the ranges of several adult females with whom they mate. Hamadryas baboon troops are made up of a collection of harems, where one male jealously guards "his" females.

35. Chimpanzees, with whom we share 98 percent of our DNA, live in bands and the males patrol its boundaries to protect food resources, prevent "foreign" males from impregnating the band's females, and also, it seems, to try to stop these same females from sneaking out. A female chimp mates on average 138 times, and with 13 different males, for every infant born to her (which puts humans' contemporary activities in perspective). One detailed study of a chimp band found that half the babies born in the study period had been sired by males from outside the band. "Undetected . . . female chimps were slipping away to solicit outsiders" (Hrdy, 1999: 85). If you are not relying on your babies' fathers to provide significant help—as chimps are not—then female promiscuity is perfectly viable.

36. Ibid.: 82, italics mine. In this case, Hrdy's example case is baboons. However, in every single primate species—chimps, monkeys, humans—status matters. It brings resources directly, and also gives access to resources through high-status kin. When the identity of the father is clear, his status matters as well as the status of the mother.

37. Among British women who married in the last half of the nineteenth century, the average number of live births was greater among middle-income and poorer families than among the professional and managerial classes; declining child mortality meant that this translated into larger completed families, even though, relatively speaking, infant and child mortality remained much higher among families working in mining and manufacturing. The children of agricultural workers had relatively low mortality. See Garrett et al., 2006.

38. Logically, since "males who invested in infants not their own would be genetically out-competed by males whose priority was seeking additional mates" (Hrdy, 1999: p. 227ff.). For an extensive discussion of the evidence on male/female differences in nurturing behavior in humans, and the extent that these are biologically based, see Pinker, 2008, and Rhoads, 2004.

39. For obvious reasons, across the animal kingdom, "only monogamously mated males . . . with a high probability of being the father provide *direct* and *extensive* care." If a male thinks the baby is someone else's, his incentive to look after it falls off sharply. See Hrdy, 1999: 226.

40. In Florence, between 1500 and 1700, the proportion of baptisms involving abandoned babies never fell below 10 percent; in some terrible years of the nineteenth century, it rose to over 40 percent. See ibid.: 304.

41. Margaret Mead's 1928 classic, *Coming of Age in Samoa,* was especially influential in arguing that Samoan society allowed widespread sexual experimentation by adolescents and did not treat adultery seriously; but its conclusions have been widely criticized as incorrect and based on inadequate fieldwork.

42. Humans have always practiced birth and population control extensively, although until very recently birth control was terrifyingly unreliable. Earlier societies practiced infanticide, often widely, as a way of controlling population in the absence of effective birth control.

43. In 2009, the shares of live births out of wedlock were Denmark 46.8, Finland 40.9, Iceland 64.4, Norway 55.1, Sweden 54.4.

44. Stevenson and Wolfers, 2007.

45. Esping-Andersen, 2009: 26. In the big study of assortative marriage discussed earlier in the chapter, the Swedish researchers, alone in the study, chose to *define* marriage as cohabitation and examine partnerships, not marriages. See Henz and Jonsson, 2003.

46. "The flight from marriage: briefing on Asian demography," *The Economist,* August 20–26, 2011: 20.

47. Ohlsson-Wijk, 2011. Among 18–28-year-old Swedes, the highly educated are more than twice as likely to marry as those with relatively low education. However, very few Swedes marry young.

48. Number of marriages per 1,000 population. Source: OECD Family database, SF3.1.

49. Sweden's overall marriage rate has actually increased in the last few years, although it is not clear why. One possible reason is changes in the composition of the Swedish population. Ohlsson-Wijk, 2011, who has analyzed the change, concluded that it was not accounted for by an increase in the number of foreign-born Swedish citizens, although the fact that Sweden now has many native-born citizens whose parents are foreign-born may have generated different attitudes to marriage and cohabitation. The importance of population changes is consistent with the fact that the proportion of marriages taking place in the established Church has continued to decline.

50. But the desire for companionship is constant across class. The more mundane benefits of living together—shared rent, shared expenses, shared housework—also apply across the board. Living with someone in a stable partnership is also, as we saw in Chapter 8, the best way to have a regular sex life, and a particular type of sex life. That point was encapsulated, poignantly, by a laborer in a modest New Orleans brothel, early in the twentieth century, talking to a social reformer surveying the vice scene: "I'd say that the whole thing, from the time you got in the room until the time you came, didn't take three minutes . . . But a man keeps

looking for somebody he can just feel—well, like he isn't always alone." Abbott, 2007: 45.

51. Wax, 2011.

52. Kanji and Schober, 2012: 17, 18. Married couples in which the mother is the only earner face more than twice the risk of divorce faced by other couples in the early years of a child's life. After that, for the few who are still in that situation, the chances do not seem to be any higher than for other "earner types."

53. "Equal earner" and "mother main earner" couples do not seem to be more unstable than average, however, and indeed equal-earning seems to make relationships more stable among cohabiting couples. (For married couples the link is less clear, varying with model specifications.) However, as the researchers point out, "selection effects are probably operating, with couples who could not sustain equal earning or whose relationship may have dissolved . . . leaving the group of equal earners with only the couples who were able to manage . . . remaining" (ibid.: 19).

54. They may not know the exact statistics for partnership and marital breakups, but a combination of press coverage and experience is likely to have told them that marriages tend to last longer, and they want the most security they can get. The evidence that marriages last longer than partnerships is extensive. For example, among the parents of UK-born babies born in 2000 (the Millennium Cohort), 27 percent of unmarried couples who were living together at the time of the child's birth no longer are by the time he or she is five. For married couples the figure is 9 percent. However, it is not at all clear whether being married has any causal effects: the characteristics of married and unmarried couples are quite different. See Goodman and Greaves, 2010.

55. Though Goldsmith made the remark famous, he did not coin it.

56. For successful men, as for successful women, having children within marriage is generally a far more attractive proposition than the opposite. But the balance of advantage is, on the whole, more obvious and more pressing for women. I would bet that, holding everything else constant, successful women become more willing to have children in a partnership, but outside marriage, the closer to 40 they get. That is certainly consistent with my personal experience, but I don't have the data to prove it.

57. The fertility of men is generally related to their education, in the same way as it is for women. See Jones and Tertilt, 2006.

58. Natsal, 2000: Reference Table 8.3. Married men in general are much more likely to report this as an ideal than married women—9 percent compared to 3 percent—and the proportion of married men and women who report that they have had more than one partner in the last year mirrors this. (Reference Table 3.18): 8 percent and 4 percent, respectively.

59. Ward et al., 2005.

60. In the US, the typical (median) age at first marriage was 28 in 2008 for both the college and the non-college educated, whereas in 1960 it had been 23 for the college-educated and 21 for everyone else. See Fry, 2010. In 1950, the median US age for (all) men was 22.8 and for women 20.3; in 1890, it was 26.1 and 22.0. Source: US Census Bureau, Current Population Survey, Table MS-2. In Australia,

the median age at first marriage rose from 25.9 to 29.6 for men in the space of just 20 years (1987–2007); for women it was 23.8 and 27.6. See Australian Bureau of Statistics, 2009: Australian Social Trends 2007 4102.0 Couples in Australia: http://www.abs.gov.au/AUSSTATS/abs@.nsf. In the UK, the median age at first marriage in 2007 was 31.9 for men and 29.8 for women; in 1991, 27.5 and 25.5. See ONS, 2009: Population Trends No. 135: England and Wales Marriage rates: http://www.ons.gov.uk/ons/publications. In Japan in 1950, the median age at first marriage was 25.9 for men, 23 for women; in 2010, 30.5 for men and 28.8 for women. See Statistics Bureau, 2011: Statistical Handbook of Japan 2011, Table 2.6 (Tokyo: Ministry of Internal Affairs and Communications).

61. Gould, Moav and Simhon argue that "male inequality generates inequality in the number of wives per man in traditional societies, but manifests itself as inequality in the quality of wives in developed societies" (2008: 333).

62. See, for example, Goux and Maurin, 2003.

63. In 2009. Source: Eurostat.

64. Isen and Stevenson, 2010: 22.

65. Fry, 2010. Figures for 2008. For 35–39-year-olds, the likelihood of divorce during the year was 1.6 percent for graduates; for non-graduates, it was 2.9 percent. For 25–29-year-olds, it was 1.8 percent and 3.6 percent respectively. In America, divorce rates have fallen somewhat from their 1970s highs in recent years, as fewer people marry and those who do, marry later. But this fall is by far the most marked among college graduates. Taking the period from 1970 on, and looking at divorce after ten or twenty years of marriage, there has been almost no change in rates among those with some college; and only a very recent fall among high-school graduates. See Isen and Stevenson, 2010.

66. Dronkers and Härkönen, 2008. This is partly, but by no means entirely, because education is closely associated with current income, which also has a major impact on whether couples split: hard times increase the risk, just as financial improvements reduce them. See Boheim and Ermisch, 2001.

67. Clarke and Berrington, n.d.

68. Overall, divorce rates in Sweden have fallen (along with the propensity to marry in the first place); but for women with the lowest levels of education they have actually increased. See Hoem, 1997.

69. Edin and Kefalas, 2005: 112.

70. Ibid.: 127.

71. Ibid.: 130.

72. Wax, 2011.

73. Among American women aged 30–44 in 2007, 69 percent of graduate women were currently married; but only 56 percent of all non-graduate women, far lower than a half-century before. In 1970, 83 percent of non-graduate and 82 percent of graduate women 30–44 were currently married. The figures for males in 1970 were 86 percent and 88 percent respectively. See Fry and Cohn, 2010. See also Stevenson and Wolfers, 2007.

74. Pre-war only 2 percent of Japanese men and women never married; as recently as 1970, only 4 percent of women in their forties and 2 percent of men were single. See

Retherford, Ogawa and Matsukura, 2001. Today, almost 20 percent of Japanese women in their late thirties are unmarried. Among older Japanese, the proportion of men never married is markedly higher than the proportion for women that age though both have been rising sharply. In 2010, 20 percent of men aged 50 and over had never married compared to a little over 10 percent of women aged 50+. Source: National Institute of Population and Social Security Research, Japan.

75. The only European country where the rate remained below 10 percent in 2009 was Greece. Source: Eurostat.

76. It is apparently from a toast given at a Holy Cross College alumni dinner in 1910 by John Collins Bossidy. The full verse is: "And this is good old Boston / The home of the bean and the cod / Where the Lowells . . ." etc.

77. For two hundred years, the Adams family produced a succession of politicians and eminent officeholders and writers, including two leading figures on the American Revolution, one of whom (John) became the country's second president. His son, John Quincy Adams, was the sixth president, and the author of the eponymous classic *The Education of Henry Adams* was John Quincy Adams's grandson.

78. Homans, 1985: 13, 15. Homans's own research showed clearly that people's opinions and tastes are created and strongly reinforced by the people they mix with, and that they like to be with people they agree with and understand. So opposites don't usually attract, even if they meet. See Homans, 1974. See also Bishop, 2008.

79. England, 2004: 1036.

80. See Bishop, 2008, for a discussion of how people's choices of residence in the US have created neighborhoods that are increasingly segregated by culture and politics as well as income. This tends to be less true in more crowded countries with a higher proportion of older and public housing, although the centers of "desirable" cities such as Paris or Amsterdam have become much less socially mixed over the past few decades.

81. Quoted in *The Times* magazine, September 1, 2012: 29–30.

82. Edlund, 2005.

12: FAMILIES UNLIMITED

1. There were periodic breakdowns in order, when one dynasty was replaced by another; but new imperial families would then take over the bureaucracy and rule, and collect taxes, through it in the same way as their predecessors.

2. Dettenhofer, 2009.

3. Daly and Wilson, 1996, 2005; Hrdy, 1999, for the frequency of infanticide by primate males.

4. Weatherford, 2010.

5. Stone, 1995.

6. The evidence is reviewed in Washington, 2008.

7. Oswald and Powdthavee, 2010. The voting shift isn't huge, but it is clear and statistically significant. Data are for the UK and Germany.

8. Campbell, 2004, 2006; Kaufmann, Petrick and Shaw, 2008. The arguments were also treated in depth in *Analysis* (Radio 4), March 14, 2010 ("Babies and Biscuits": http://www.bbc.co.uk/programmes/b006r4vz/broadcasts/2010/03).

9. The men who promoted the development of women's education in the nineteenth century were close to, and influenced by, the women in their own families; whether someone was an "early adopter" of the idea that women should be educated was not random.

10. Putnam and Campbell, 2010.

11. Washington, 2008. We are all influenced by the people we know. Our opinions are changed by the people we live next to in student housing (Homans, 1974), never mind our families and the people we love. A clear example from outside "feminist" politics is former US senator Pete Domenici. Domenici was a fiscal and social conservative. Yet in the 1980s, he built a cross-party coalition supporting health insurance parity for mental illness. He became a champion of the cause when his daughter was diagnosed with schizophrenia. His major allies were similar: mental illness had touched their families too.

12. *The Economist*, 2010.

13. Hrdy, 1999.

14. Barcellos, Carvalho and Lleras-Muney, 2011. Sources of data include time-use studies as well as health, nutrition and vaccination statistics.

15. *The Economist*, 2010.

16. Solomon and Sirimavo Bandaranaike. Solomon Bandaranaike was assassinated in 1959; his widow was the first female head of government in the world and served as prime minister three times, for a total of eighteen years.

17. US Census Bureau figures.

18. Figures from US Small Business Administration statistics and Bureau of the Census statistical brief 93–10, "Who Owns America's Farmland?" Moreover, one-third of the Fortune 500 companies were family-controlled. See Poza, 2007. Not all family-controlled and family-owned firms are family-*run*, though many will combine family members and non-family, especially at board level. (Walmart, currently the single largest private sector employer in the world, is an example.)

19. The largest family-managed German businesses with a stock market listing have outperformed the leading index by a wide margin for many years. See Linnemann, 2007. The 50 largest family businesses employ about 1.5 million people; 95 percent of German businesses are family ones.

20. Neubauer and Lank, 1998. Countries vary substantially in how far they offer legal protection and advantages to minority shareholders, which families often become when a company grows large enough. And historically, cultures have varied in how far they welcome outsiders (including those who marry into a family) and give them a real say in a family concern: Francis Fukuyama argues that these cultural differences explain why Japan has developed very large companies more widely than Chinese cultures, including Taiwan. But these are variations around a high average level of family enterprise. See Seabright, 2010: Chapter 13; Fukuyama, 1995.

21. See, for example, Bloom and Van Reenen, 2006.

22. Barba Navaretti, Faini and Tucci, 2008. "On average" is also the operative phrase. Germany's huge Schaeffler engineering company, owned by Maria-Elisabeth Schaeffler and her son George, nearly lost its independence a few years ago as a result of a hugely ambitious takeover of car-parts manufacturer Continental.

23. In 2011, it was second largest in terms of mortgages held and third largest in terms of deposits.

24. Apparently; but the giant mining company Anglo American appointed a female CEO in 2006, one of only three in the FTSE-100 at the time.

25. She managed to wrest total control only after fourteen years of litigation with her stepmother. She has four children, is reported to see three of them as lazy and unsuited to business, and is grooming the fourth, a daughter, to succeed her.

26. Engels, 1972: 121.

27. See Djilas, 1957; Konrad and Szelényi, 1979.

28. *Financial Times*, July 11, 2012.

29. "To the money born," *Financial Times*, March 30, 2010.

30. Kydyralieva, 2010.

31. See especially Atkinson, 2008.

32. For example, in 2008, about one in 100 US males had an income of over $250,000. The mean income for this group ($440,000) was over ten times the mean male income that year. Current Population Survey figures: Table PINC-11. Piketty and Saez, 2006, estimate that the top 0.1 percent—one in 1,000—earn almost 8 percent of US income, which gives an average of over $3 million apiece, using 2008 PINC-11 figures. Female figures are somewhat lower.

33. See, for example, Atkinson, 2008; New Strategist Publications, 2007.

34. In many cases, one or other left their position within the next few years, and as far as I know, there has been no comprehensive tracking of "couples" in the meantime. Two of the 15 couples counted by Anna Fifield were gay: she notes that the list was not exhaustive. In the UK, nine of the new MPs elected for the first time in 2010 were the sons or daughters of politicians—current and former MPs and members of the House of Lords. Nine doesn't sound like much. But it meant that the chances of becoming an MP were, quite literally, several hundred thousand times as great if your parent was a politician than if election was randomly distributed throughout the population. Analysis by Jim Pickard: *Financial Times*, May 13, 2010.

35. And it would be significantly less unequal again if women in the "bottom quintile" couples worked as often, and for as many hours, as those at the top. See Esping-Andersen, 2009: 59–71. Analyses of changing inequality over time are complicated by the growing numbers of single mothers, who tend to be poor. In the case of couples, who are the focus of Esping-Andersen's analysis, the lowest-earning 20 percent of couples are also far and away the least likely to be dual-earning—which is, of course, one reason why they are low-earning. In the US, low-earners are also the group where the woman's earnings, when she is in work, are likely to be the most important. As average unskilled male earnings have fallen, women's earnings have become increasingly important in maintaining household incomes. See ibid.: 64–69. Individuals—typically men—with a stay-at-home spouse earn slightly more than those with working spouses, but the differences do not come close to the levels of a second salary. See Bardasi and Taylor, 2005; Blackaby, Carlin and Murphy, 1998.

36. The conventional way of measuring inequality is by the "Gini coefficient," but this is a summary statistic that can incorporate very different distributions and movements over time. For example, in the US, there has been a big increase in the

coefficient (indicating greater inequality) since 1980 because of a surge in income at the top, but the ratio of earnings between the 80th and 50th percentiles (for both sexes combined) has hardly changed. Kopczuk, Saez and Song, 2010.

37. Del Boca and Pasqua, 2003.

38. Figure n7 below shows what happened to US household incomes in the period 1970–2000 and how different things look if you compare percentage changes with absolute ones. The percentage increase for the bottom quintile was almost half as large as for the top quintile. The absolute increase in earnings was only about a twentieth as much.

39. There are still more men than women overall at the 90th and 95th percentiles, so it is more realistic to visualize a couple each of whom is at or above the 90th percentile for their own gender. They will then, pooled, earn a combined income of more than four times the median full-time female wage plus rather less than four times the median male one.

40. Sander, 2006.

41. Department for Education Performance Tables (School Details). For example, 43 percent of secondary pupils in Kensington and Chelsea attend independent schools.

42. See, especially, Young, 1958; Dore, 2000.

43. Figure n8 shows International Baccalaureate entries.

44. Karabel, 2005: especially 512–13; Belley and Lochner, 2007; Wolf, 2002. In England, Oxford and Cambridge entrance is based on academic portfolios, exams and subject-related interviews, and the student body has moved to rough male/female balance. But in spite of constant criticism and direct pressure from central government, the proportion of students from private (independent) secondary schools has been stuck at around half for years; and state school entrants are overwhelmingly from the affluent middle class.

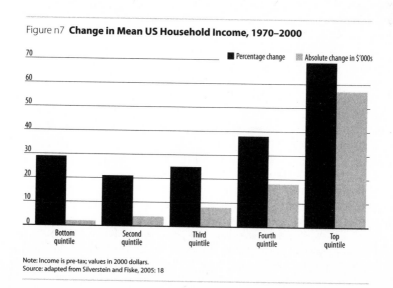

Figure n7 **Change in Mean US Household Income, 1970–2000**

Note: Income is pre-tax; values in 2000 dollars.
Source: adapted from Silverstein and Fiske, 2005: 18

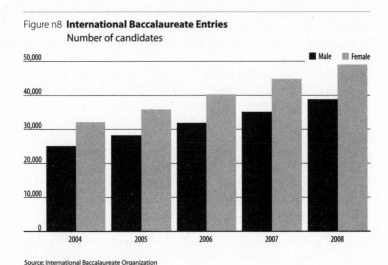

Figure n8 **International Baccalaureate Entries**
Number of candidates

Source: International Baccalaureate Organization

45. http://www.thecrimson.com/article/2011/5/11/admissions-fitzsimmons-legacy-legacies/.
46. Karabel, 2005: 550.
47. All of which receive substantial contributions from the state.
48. Entry to these *"classes préparatoires"* is itself competitive; they recruit across schools and not just from the one where they are based. But, of course, the quality of the school you attend affects performance at this point too.
49. Bourdieu, 1989; Wolf, 2002; Brezis and Crouzet, 2004. Around 2 percent of a cohort enters one of the *Grandes Écoles*, slightly fewer than the proportion entering one of the top 50 US colleges. ENA (École Normale d'Administration) is a postgraduate *école* with an especially tight link to elite positions. It recruits about 100 students a year and was explicitly intended to recruit from across French society on the basis of talent; to that end, it has a two-stream entry, direct from a first degree and from serving civil servants. By 1993 almost half of the heads of the 200 largest French companies came via ENA. Even with this second stream, families from top cadres—about 8 percent of the population—supply 63 percent of ENA students. See Brezis and Crouzet, 2004: 10–122.
50. Esping-Andersen, 2009: 73. The proportion is just over a third in every case, highlighting the fact that there is still considerable mobility, even at the top. The children of the rich also do not, on the whole, slide into penury—not in one generation anyway. See Björklund, 2008.
51. Blanden and Machin, 2007; Sutton Trust, 2010.
52. If you are worried about social mobility, you should probably be highly relieved that so many of today's top-fifth are not marrying, not having babies, having just one child and generally leaving plenty of vacancies at the top! Some people believe

that social mobility has fallen because hot-housed daughters are taking the jobs that less fortunate boys would otherwise obtain. See, for example, Willetts, 2011. However, this implies that the size of the professional workforce is fixed, which is implausible. The growth in the proportion of professional jobs has leveled off across the world, but this is as a *proportion* of the labor force, not absolutely. Other things being equal, as the number of people in employment grows, so does the number of jobs of any type. It is true that for the very top jobs, which are fixed in number—like being a cabinet minister—men's opportunities have indeed declined as women compete alongside them. But any change in general mobility is more likely to be class- than gender-related, as elite families become (even) better at protecting the position of sons and daughters alike.

53. The most prominent recent example is British: Ed Balls and Yvette Cooper, both cabinet ministers in the last Labour government and now leading members of the opposition front bench.

CONCLUSION

1. The memorial plaque to the Mathers is in the cloisters of Corpus Christi College, Oxford.

2. Greer, 1980: 326. The "Declaration of Feminism" was a 1973 manifesto distributed by Helen Sullinger and Nancy Lehmann and important in early 1970s American feminism.

3. British Social Attitudes data 2007–2008; see Park et al., 2008. Respondents were asked to choose the three "identities" that best described them from a list, with the option of adding something else or saying "None of these." The other options were being a spouse or partner; being a parent; religion; race; being young/middle-aged/old; being a working person/retired/unemployed; being a city or country person. Among graduates, 29 percent of women and 15 percent of men made being a man/woman their first choice, and 55 and 35 percent respectively made it one of their three. Among those with A levels or equivalent (high-school graduates) the figures were 18 percent and 56 percent for women, 11 percent and 33 percent for men. (Unpublished analyses carried out for this volume.)

4. See, for example, Blumberg, 1989, Tiger and Shepher, 1975.

5. See the discussion at the end of chapter 11 and Edlund, 2005.

6. By 2006, UK agreement levels for that selfsame statement were down to around 1 in 7. (British Social Attitudes survey data.) See Dench, 2010: 8. West Germans showed a similar shift (although Americans, curiously, did not: substantial numbers of them retained traditional attitudes to this question into the 2000s). See Adler and Brayfield, 2006.

7. You find, as you would expect, that average hourly wages for men and women become unequal as people get older and start families, and many women go part-time. Mundy, 2012, extrapolates current trends to predict that women will become the majority breadwinners of the future. In fact, in families where both husband and wife are earning, the percentage of wives who earn more than their husbands was still well under a third in 2009, although it had increased sharply since 2006,

reflecting the recession and the rapid loss of male manufacturing and construction jobs. (The percentage increased from 19.2 in 1990 to 23.3 in 2000, 25.9 in 2007 and 28.9 in 2009. Source: US Department of Labor, Women in the Labor Force: A Databook. Table 25.)

8. See Chapter 3.
9. See, for example, http://www.30percentclub.org.uk/. The European Commission is proposing legally binding rules including quotas to increase the representation of women on corporate boards as well as sanctions applied to companies that do not meet the proposed objectives.
10. Authors arguing that companies have to change to accommodate women's desire to meet family commitments and, especially, raise children without sacrificing career progression include Hewlett, 2007, Roth, 2006, and Williams, 2000.
11. Slaughter, 2012.
12. Wax, 2004, discusses at length the possible impact of introducing family-friendly practices (such as no overtime expectations/right to flexible hours), including the risk that companies that are first-movers will attract very large numbers of employees with a need for family benefits, thus driving up their costs compared to competitors; and that policies that, on introduction, benefit workers unequally will reduce the level of effort of other workers. She also discusses the way in which anti-discrimination laws may affect employers' willingness or ability to trade benefits for pay even when workers desire this. She demonstrates that if you get the "worker mix" right, a family-friendly workplace may indeed work efficiently (and that there is certainly no reason to assume that current arrangements are optimal), but that this will be very hard to achieve.
13. Merit Janow, chairwoman of the NASDAQ Stock Market, Columbia University professor and former Wall Street lawyer.
14. Stevenson and Wolfers, 2009. The decline it documents began at exactly the same time as housework hours plummeted!
15. Ibid.: 213. In America there seems actually to have been a decline in women's (self-reported) happiness. The percentage changes are not enormous in absolute terms but, on a national scale, imply changes for a large number of people. In the 1970s American women typically "outscored" men by six percentage points in the proportions reporting themselves to be very happy. Among US twelfth-graders, young men have since then become increasingly happy and young women slightly less so; Stevenson and Wolfers do not have a clear explanation since the shift does not seem to be associated with education, marital status or income. They do, however, note that young women in twelfth grade seem to be increasingly busy, increasingly ambitious and dissatisfied with their lack of leisure.
16. Office for National Statistics, 2012b.
17. Craig and Mullan, 2011; Offer and Scheider, 2011. The high-stress US has high levels of female full-time working. Swedish women, as we saw in Chapter 1, report more stress than other Europeans, and are also largely full-time. Korea, the one country where women don't report more stress, also has relatively low female employment. Hamermesh, 2008.

18. Blood and Wolfe, 1960, first delineated the relationship between husbands' and wives' earnings and their relative influence on decisions made within the family. See also Kulik, 2011, for recent work confirming the relatively egalitarian decision-making prevalent in contemporary families where both partners are likely to have comparable potential lifetime earnings.

BIBLIOGRAPHY

Abbott, K., 2007. *Sin in the Second City: Madams, Ministers, Playboys and the Battle for America's Soul*. New York: Random House.

Abbott, M., 2003. *Family Affairs: A History of the Family in 20th Century England*. London: Routledge.

Adler, M.A. and Brayfield, A., 2006. Gender regimes and cultures of care: Public support for maternal employment in Germany and the United States. *Marriage and Family Review*, 39(3/4), pp. 229–53.

Adrian, H., 2007. *Implications of Long-Lasting Birth Deficits on the Wealth of Nations*. Mainz: Johannes Gutenberg–Universität Mainz.

Adsera, A., 2004. Changing fertility rates in developed countries: The impact of labor market institutions. *Journal of Population Economics*, 17(1), pp. 17–43.

Aguiar, M. and Hurst, E., 2007. Measuring trends in leisure: The allocation of time over five decades. *Quarterly Journal of Economics*, 122(3), pp. 969–1006.

Alcott, L.M., 1908. *Little Women* (Everyman Library edition). London: J. M. Dent and Sons.

Altermatt, E.R., Jovanovic, J., and Perry, M., 1998. Bias or Responsivity? Sex and Achievement-Level Effects on Teachers' Classroom Questioning Practices. *Journal of Education Psychology*, 90(3), pp. 516–27.

American Heritage Time Use Study, release 4, 2011. Oxford: Centre for Time Use Research, Oxford University.

American National Survey of Student Engagement, 2010. Bloomington, IN: Indiana University Center for Postsecondary Research. [online] Available at: http://nsse.iub .edu/html/summary_tables.cfm.

American Psychological Association (APA), 2007. Report of the APA Task Force on the Sexualization of Girls. Washington, DC: American Psychological Association. [online] Available at: http://www.apa.org/ pi/women/programs/girls/report-full.pdf.

Amuedo-Dorantes, C. and Kimmel, J., 2005. The motherhood wage gap for women in the United States: The importance of college and fertility delay. *Review of Economics of the Household*, 3(1), pp. 17–48.

Andersen, R., Curtis, J. and Grabb, E., 2006. Trends in civic association activity in four democracies: The special case of women in the United States. *American Sociological Review*, 71(3), pp. 376–400.

Anderson, D.J., Binder, M. and Krause, K., 2002. The motherhood wage penalty: Which mothers pay it and why? *American Economic Review, Papers and Proceedings*, 92(2), pp. 354–58.

Anker, R., Melkas, H. and Korten, A., 2003. Gender-based occupational segregation in the 1990s. ILO working paper 16. Geneva: International Labour Office.

Apicella, C.L., Dreber, A., Campbell, B., Gray, P.B., Hoffman, M. and Little, A.C., 2008. Testosterone and financial risk preferences. *Evolution and Human Behavior*, 29, pp. 384–90.

Archambault, E., 2001. Historical roots of the nonprofit sector in France. *Nonprofit and Voluntary Sector Quarterly*, 30(2), pp. 204–20.

Arnold, J.E., Graesch, A.P., Ragazzini, E. and Ochs, E., *Life at Home in the Twenty-First Century: 32 Families Open Their Doors*. Los Angeles: UCLA, Cotsen Institute of Archaeology Press.

Associated Press, 2008. Text of Spitzer resignation statement, March 12.

Association of American Medical Colleges (AAMC), 2011. U.S. medical school applicants and students. [online] Available at: http: //www.aamc.org/publications.

Atkinson, A.B., 2008. *The Changing Distribution of Earnings in OECD Countries*. New York: Oxford University Press.

Atkinson, A.B., Piketty, T. and Saez, E., 2011. Top incomes in the long run of history. *Journal of Economic Literature*, 49(1), pp. 3–71.

Attwood, C. et al., 2003. 2001 Home Office Citizenship Survey: People, families and communities. [online] Available at: http://www.communities.gov.uk/documents/communities/pdf/452422.pdf.

Aubenas, F. (trans. A. Brown), 2011. *The Night Cleaner*. Cambridge: Polity.

Australian Bureau of Statistics, 2007. Australian social trends, 2007: Lifetime marriage and divorce trends. ABS catalogue no. 4102.0. Canberra: ABS. [online] Available at: www.abs.gov.au/ausstats/abs@.nsf/mf/4102.0.

Averett, S. and Korenman, S., 1996. The economic reality of the beauty myth. *Journal of Human Resources*, 31(2), pp. 304–30.

Babcock, L. and Laschever, S., 2003. *Women Don't Ask: Negotiation and the Gender Divide*. Princeton, NJ: Princeton University Press.

Bach, S., Corneo, G. and Steiner, V., 2009. From bottom to top: The entire income distribution in Germany 1992–2003. *Review of Income and Wealth*, 55(2), pp. 303–30.

Bakker, S. and Wolf, A. (eds.), 2001. *Assessment in Education*, 8(3). Special Issue: Examinations and entry to higher education: Pressure and change in a mass system.

Barba Navaretti, G., Faini, R. and Tucci, A., 2008. Does family control affect trade performance? Evidence for Italian firms. CEP discussion paper 0896. London: Centre for Economic Performance, LSE.

Barcellos, S.H., Carvalho, L. and Lleras-Muney, A., 2011. Parental investment in India: Are boys and girls treated differently? *Research in Public Policy*, 12, pp. 11–12.

Bardesi, E. and Taylor, M., 2005. Marriage and wages. ISER working paper 2005-1. Colchester: Institute for Social and Economic Research, University of Essex.

Barro, R.J. and Lee, J.-W., 2010. A new data set of educational attainment in the world, 1950–2010. NBER working paper 15902. Cambridge, MA: National Bureau of Economic Research.

BBC News, 2011. US Iraqi jailed for killing daughter in Arizona. [online] Available at: http://www.bbc.co.uk/news/world-us-canada-13101536.

Beaujouan, E. and Ní Bhrolcháin, M., 2011. Cohabitation and marriage in Britain since the 1970s. *Population Trends*, 145 (Autumn). London: Office for National Statistics.

Beck, M., 2011. The sleepless elite: Why some people can run on little sleep and get so much done. *Wall Street Journal. Health Journal*, April 5. [online] Available at: http://online.wsj.com/article/ SB10001424052748703712504576242701752957910.html.

Bekkers, R.H.F.P., 2004. Giving and volunteering in the Netherlands: Sociological and psychological perspectives. PhD thesis, University of Utrecht. [online] Available at: http://igitur-archive.library.uu.nl/dissertations/2006-0329-200032/index.htm.

Belkin, L., 2003. The opt-out revolution. *New York Times Magazine*, October 26.

Belle de Jour, 2005. *The Intimate Adventures of a London Call Girl*. London: Phoenix Books.

Belley, P. and Lochner, L., 2007. The changing role of family income and ability in determining educational achievement. NBER working paper 13527. Cambridge, MA: National Bureau of Economic Research.

Bennett, A., 1995. *The Old Wives' Tale* (World Classic edition). Oxford: Oxford University Press.

Bennetts, L., 2007. *The Feminine Mistake: Are We Giving Up Too Much?* New York: Voice.

Bertrand, M., Goldin, C. and Katz, L.F., 2009. Dynamics of the gender gap for young professionals in the corporate and financial sectors. NBER working paper 14681. Cambridge, MA: National Bureau of Economic Research.

Betts, H., Rose, H. and Vernon, P., 2011. Why generation X women aren't having kids. *The Times Magazine*, July 2.

Biddle, J.E. and Hamermesh, D.S., 1998. Beauty, productivity and discrimination: Lawyers' looks and lucre. *Journal of Labor Economics*, 16(1), pp. 172–201.

Bishop, B., 2008. *The Big Sort*. Boston: Houghton Mifflin.

Björklund, A., 2008. Intergeneration top income mobility in Sweden: A combination of equal opportunity and capitalistic dynasties. IZA discussion paper 3801. Bonn: Institute for the Study of Labor (IZA).

Blackaby, D.H., Carlin, P.S. and Murphy, P.D., 1998. What a difference a wife makes: The effect of women's hours of work on husbands' hourly earnings. *Bulletin of Economic Research*, 50(1), pp. 1–18.

Blanden, J. and Machin, S., 2007. Recent changes in intergenerational mobility in Britain. London: Centre for Economic Performance, LSE.

Blank, R.M. and Shierholz, H., 2006. Exploring gender differences in employment and wage trends among less-skilled workers. NBER working paper 12494. Cambridge, MA: National Bureau of Economic Research.

Blau, F.D. and Kahn, L.M., 2006. The US gender pay gap in the 1990s: Slowing convergence. Working Paper 508. Princeton University: Industrial Relations Section.

Bibliography

Blood, R.O. and Wolfe, D.M., 1960. *Husbands and Wives: The Dynamics of Married Living.* New York: Free Press.

Bloom, N. and Van Reenen, J., 2006. Measuring and explaining management practices across firms and countries. CEP discussion paper 0716. London: Centre for Economic Performance, LSE.

Blossfeld, H.-P., 1987. Labor market entry and the sexual segregation of careers in the Federal Republic of Germany. *American Journal of Sociology*, 93(1), pp. 89–118.

Blossfeld, H.-P. and Timm, A., 2003. Who marries whom in West Germany? In: H.-P. Blossfeld and A. Timm (eds.), 2003. *Who Marries Whom? Educational Systems as Marriage Markets in Modern Societies.* Dordrecht: Kluwer Academic, pp. 19–36.

Blossfeld, H.-P. and Timm, A. (eds.), 2003. *Who Marries Whom? Educational Systems as Marriage Markets in Modern Societies.* Dordrecht: Kluwer Academic.

Blow, L., Leicester, A. and Oldfield, Z., 2004. Consumption trends in the UK 1975–99. London: Institute of Fiscal Studies.

Blumberg, R.L., 1989. Toward a feminist theory of development. In Wallace, R.A. (ed.), *Feminism and Sociological Theory* Newbury Park, CA: Sage

Board of Education, 1900. *Report of the Board of Education.* London: HMSO.

Boheim, R. and Ermisch, J., 2001. Partnership dissolution in the UK—the role of economic circumstances. *Oxford Bulletin of Economics and Statistics*, 63(2), pp. 197–208.

Bolick, K., 2011. All the single ladies. *The Atlantic*, November.

Booth, A.L., 2009. Gender and competition. IZA discussion paper 4300. Bonn: Institute for the Study of Labor (IZA).

Booth, A. L. and Nolen, P.J., 2009. Choosing to compete: How different are girls and boys? IZA discussion paper 4027. Bonn: Institute for the Study of Labor (IZA).

Bosch, N., Deelen, A. and Euwals, R., 2008. Is part-time employment here to stay? Evidence from the Dutch Labour Force Survey 1992–2005. IZA discussion paper 3367. Bonn: Institute for the Study of Labor (IZA).

Bosch, N., van der Klaauw, B. and van Ours, J., 2009. Female part-time work in the Netherlands. [online] Available at: http://www.voxeu.org/index.php?q=node/3946.

Bourdieu, P., 1989. *La noblesse d'état: Grandes écoles et esprit de corps.* Paris: Les Editions de Minuit.

Boushey, H., 2005. Are women opting out? Debunking the myth. CEPR reports and issue briefs 2005–36. Washington, DC: Center for Economic and Policy Research.

Boushey, H., 2006. Tag-team parenting. CEPR reports and issue briefs 2006–20. Washington, DC: Center for Economic and Policy Research.

Bovey, S., 1989. *Being Fat Is Not a Sin.* Boston: Pandora Press.

Brandon, R., 2008. *Other People's Daughters: The Life and Times of the Governess.* London: Weidenfeld and Nicolson.

Brents, B.G., Jackson, C.A. and Hausbeck, K., 2009. *The State of Sex: Tourism, Sex and Sin in the New American Heartland.* New York: Routledge.

Brewer, M., Ratcliffe, A. and Smith, S., 2008a. Does welfare reform affect fertility? Evidence from the UK. IFS working paper W08/09. London: Institute of Fiscal Studies.

Brewer, M., Ratcliffe, A. and Smith, S., 2008b. Welfare reform: The impact on fertility. *Research in Public Policy*, 7 (Autumn), pp. 10–12.

Brewer, M., Sibieta, L. and Wren-Lewis, L., 2008. Racing away? Income inequality and the evolution of high incomes. IFS briefing note 74. London: Institute of Fiscal Studies.

Brezis, E.S. and Crouzet, F., 2004. The role of higher education institutions: Recruitment of elites and economic growth. CESifo working paper 1360. Munich: CESifo Group.

British Cohort Survey 1970 (unpublished data).

Brooks, D., 2000. *Bobos in Paradise: The New Upper Class and How They Got There*. New York: Simon & Schuster.

Brophy, J., 1985. Interactions of male and female students with male and female teachers. In: L.C. Wilkinson and C.B. Marrett (eds.), 1985. *Influences on Classroom Interaction*. Orlando, FL: Academic Press, pp. 115–42.

Brown-Lyons, M., Robertson, A. and Layzer, J., 2001. *Kith and Kin-Informal Child Care: Highlights from Recent Research*. New York: National Center for Children in Poverty.

Budig, M.J. and England, P., 2001. The wage penalty for motherhood. *American Sociological Review*, 66(2), pp. 204–25.

Burda, M., Hamermesh, D. and Weil, P., 2007. Total work, gender and social norms. IZA discussion paper 2705. Bonn: Institute for the Study of Labor (IZA).

Bureau of Applied Social Research (BASR), Columbia University, 1957. Comments and criticisms on Barnard: A survey of alumnae opinions prepared for associate alumnae of Barnard College. New York: Columbia University/Barnard College archives.

Burggraf, S.P., 1997. *The Feminine Economy and Economic Man: Reviving the Role of Family in the Post-Industrial Age*. Reading, MA: Addison-Wesley.

Buss, D.M., 2003. *The Evolution of Desire: Strategies of Human Mating* (4th edition). New York: Basic Books.

Caldwell, C., 2008. The ideology of teen pregnancy. *Financial Times*, June 28, p. 13.

Cambridge University Reporter, 2010. Special Issue 4, 141, October.

Campbell, R., 2004. Gender, ideology and issue preference: Is there such a thing as a political women's interest in Britain? *British Journal of Politics and International Relations*, 6(1), 20–44.

Campbell, R., 2006. *Gender and the Vote in Britain: Beyond the Gender Gap*. Colchester: ecpr monographs.

Cancedda, A., 2001. Employment in household services. Dublin: European Foundation for the Improvement of Living and Working Conditions.

Carey, B., 2010. Families' every fuss, archived and analyzed. *New York Times*, May 22. [online] Available at: http://www.nytimes.com/2010/05/23/science/23family.html.

Carlin, P.S., 2001. Evidence on the volunteer labor supply of married women. *Southern Economic Journal*, 67(4), pp. 801–24.

Carlsson, M. and Rooth, D.-O., 2008. An experimental study of sex segregation in the Swedish labor market: Is discrimination the explanation? IZA discussion paper 3811. Bonn: Institute for the Study of Labor (IZA).

Caruso, E.M., Rahnev, D.A. and Banaji, M.R., 2009. Using conjoint analysis to detect discrimination: Revealing covert preferences from overt choices. *Social Cognition*, 27(1), pp. 128–37.

Chan, T.W. and Halpin, B., 2003. Who marries whom in Great Britain? In: H.-P. Blossfeld and A. Timm (eds.), 2003. *Who Marries Whom? Educational Systems as Marriage Markets in Modern Societies*. Dordrecht: Kluwer Academic, pp. 171–94.

Chandra, A., Mosher, W.D., Copen, C. and Sionean, C., 2011. *Sexual Behavior, Sexual Attraction and Sexual Identity in the United States: Data from the 2006–2008 National Survey of Family Growth*. National Health Statistics Reports, 36. Hyattsville, MD: National Center for Health Statistics.

Chang, H.-J., 2010. *23 Things They Don't Tell You about Capitalism*. London: Allen Lane.

Chapoulie, J.-M., 1987. *Les professeurs de l'enseignement secondaire: Un métier de classe moyenne*. Paris: Editions de la Maison des Sciences de l'Homme.

Charles, K.K., Hurst, E. and Killewald, A., 2011. Marital sorting and parental wealth. NBER working paper 16748. Cambridge, MA: National Bureau of Economic Research.

Chaucer, G. *The Canterbury Tales*. Modern English version available online at Googlebooks: http://classiclit.about.com/library/bl-etexts/gchaucer/bl-gchau-can-collected.htm.

Chevalier, A., 2007. Education, occupation and career expectations: Determinants of the gender pay gap for UK graduates. *Oxford Bulletin of Economics and Statistics*, 69(6), pp. 819–42.

Chevalier, A. and Lindley, J., 2009. Overeducation and the skills of UK graduates. *Journal of the Royal Statistical Society*, Series A, 172(2), pp. 307–37.

Christofides, L.N., Hoy, M. and Yang, L., 2009. The gender imbalance in participation in Canadian universities, 1977–2005. CESifo WP 2791. Munich: CESifo Group.

Clark, A.E., 1997. Job satisfaction and gender: Why are women so happy at work? *Labour Economics*, 4(4), pp. 341–72.

Clarke, L. and Berrington, A., n.d. Socio-economic predictors of divorce. Mimeo: London School of Hygiene and Tropical Medicine.

Cline, E., 2009. Why college women favor Obama. *New Republic*, September 22.

CNN Money, 2010. Fortune 500, Walmartstores.com. [online] Available at: http://money.cnn.com/magazines/fortune/fortune500.

Coates, J.M. and Herbert, J., 2008. Endogenous steroids and financial risk taking on a London trading floor. *Proceedings of the National Academy of Science*, 105(16), pp. 6167–72.

Cohen, W.B., 2003. The European comparison. In: L.J. Friedman and M.D. McGarvie (eds.), 2003. *Charity, Philanthropy and Civility in American Society*. Cambridge: Cambridge University Press, pp. 385–412.

Coleman, I., 2010. *Paradise Beneath Her Feet: How Women Are Transforming the Middle East*. New York: Random House.

College Board, 2008. *Coming to Our Senses: Education and the American Future*. New York: The College Board.

Combs, M.B., 2006. *Cui bono*? The 1870 British Married Women's Property Act, bargaining power and the distribution of resources within marriage. *Feminist Economics*, 12(1–2), pp. 51–83.

Community Business, Hong Kong, 2009. Gender diversity in Asia. [online] Available at: www.communitybusiness.org.

Connelly, R. and Kimmel, J., 2010. *The Time Use of Mothers in the United States at the Beginning of the 21st Century*. Kalamazoo, MI: W. E. Upjohn Institute.

Copas, A.J., Wellings, K., Erens, B., Mercer, C.H., McManus, S., Fenton, K.A., Korovessis, C., Macdowell, W., Nanchahal, K. and Johnson, A.M., 2002. The accuracy of reported sensitive sexual behavior in Britain: Exploring the extent of change 1990–2000. *Sexually Transmitted Infections*, 78, pp. 26–30.

Corcoran, S.P., Evans, W.N. and Schwab, R.S., 2002. Changing labor market opportunities for women and the quality of teachers 1957–1992. NBER working paper 9180. Cambridge, MA: National Bureau of Economic Research.

Coser, L., 1973. Servants: The obsolescence of an occupational role. *Social Forces*, 52(1), pp. 31–40.

Cosmopolitan UK, 2011. Sex tips. *Cosmopolitan UK*, December. [online] Available at: http://www.cosmopolitan.co.uk/love-sex/tips.

Costa, D.L., 2000. The wage and the length of the work day: From the 1890s to 1991. *Journal of Labor Economics*, 18(1), pp. 156–81.

Cousins, C.R. and Tang, N., 2004. Working time and work and family conflict in the Netherlands, Sweden and the UK. *Work Employment and Society*, 18(3), pp. 531–49.

Cowley, E., McKenzie, T., Pharoah, C. and Smith, S., 2011. The new state of donation: Three decades of household giving to charity 1978–2008. Cass Business School, City University London, and CMPO, University of Bristol.

Craig, L., 2006. Parental education, time in paid work and time with children: An Australian time-diary analysis. *British Journal of Sociology*, 57(4), pp. 553–75.

Craig, L. and Mullan, K., 2011. How mothers and fathers share childcare: A cross-national time-use comparison. *American Sociological Review*, 76(6), pp. 834–61.

Crawford, M., 2010. *The Case for Working with Your Hands: Or Why Office Work Is Bad for Us and Fixing Things Feels Good*. London: Penguin.

Crompton, R. and Lyonette, C., 2007. Are we all working too hard? Women, men and changing attitudes to employment. In: A. Park, J. Curtice, K. Thomson, M. Phillips and M. Johnson (eds.), 2007. *British Social Attitudes 2006–2007: The 23rd Report*. London: Sage, Chapter 3.

Crompton, R. and Lyonette, C., 2008. Who does the housework? In A. Park, J. Curtice, K. Thomson, M. Phillips, M. Johnson and E. Clery (eds.), 2008. *British Social Attitudes 2007–2008: The 24th Report*. London: Sage, pp. 53–80.

Daly, M. and Wilson, M., 1996. Violence against stepchildren. *Current Directions in Psychological Science*, 5(3), 77–81.

Daly, M. and Wilson, M., 2005. The "Cinderella effect" is no fairy tale. *Trends in Cognitive Science*, 9(11), 507–8.

Date, Y. and Shimizutani, S., 2007. Why has Japan's fertility rate declined? *The Japanese Economy*, 34(1), pp. 4–45.

Davies, N., 2009. Prostitution and trafficking—the anatomy of a moral panic. *Guardian*, October 20.

Bibliography

De Waal, E., 2011. *The Hare with Amber Eyes*. London: Vintage.

Deere, C.D. and Doss, C.R., 2006. The gender asset gap: What do we know and why does it matter? *Feminist Economics*, 12(1–2), pp. 1–50.

Del Boca, D. and Pasqua, S., 2003. Employment patterns of husbands and wives and family income distribution in Italy (1977–98). *Review of Income and Wealth*, 49(2), pp. 221–45.

Demey, D., Berrington, A., Evandrou, M. and Falkingham, J., 2011. The changing demography of mid-life from the 1980s to the 2000s. *Population Trends*, 145(Autumn), pp. 16–34.

Dench, G., 2010. *What Women Want: Evidence from British Social Attitudes*. London: Hera Trust.

Department for Environment, Food and Rural Affairs (Defra), 2010. Food statistics pocketbook 2010. [online] Available at: http:// www.defra.gov.uk/statistics/files/ defra-stats-foodfarm-food-pocketbook-2010.

Desai, P., 2012. *Breaking Out: An Indian Woman's American Journey*. New Delhi: Penguin.

Dettenhofer, M.H., 2009. Eunuchs, women and imperial courts. In: W. Scheidel (ed.), 2009. *Rome and China. Comparative Perspectives on Ancient World Empires*. New York: Oxford University Press, Chapter 4.

Deviren, F. and Babb, P., 2005. *Young People and Social Capital*. Office for National Statistics. [online] Available at: www.ons.gov.uk/ons/guide-method/user-guidance/ social-capital-guide/the-social-capital-project/young-people-and-social-capitalphase -2.pdf.

Dex, S. and Joshi, H. (eds.), 2005. *Children of the 21st Century: From Birth to Nine Months*. Bristol: Policy Press.

Dex, S. and Ward, K., 2004. Child care. In: S. Dex and H. Joshi (eds.), 2004. *Millennium Cohort Study First Survey: A User's Guide to Initial Findings*. London: Centre for Longitudinal Studies, Chapter 11.

Dex, S. and Ward, K., 2010. Employment trajectories and ethnic diversity. In: K. Hansen, H. Joshi and S. Dex (eds.), 2010. *Children of the 21st Century: The First Five Years*. Bristol: Policy Press, pp. 95–114.

Dex, S., Hawkes, D., Joshi, H. and Ward, K., 2005. Parents' employment and childcare. In: S. Dex and H. Joshi (eds.), 2005. *Children of the 21st Century: From Birth to Nine Months*. Bristol: Policy Press, pp. 207–36.

Dex, S., Ward, K. and Joshi, H., 2006. Changes in women's occupations and occupational mobility over 25 years. Paper presented to the 25th Anniversary Conference, Department of Trade and Industry Working paper 2006/1. Centre for Longitudinal Studies, Institute of Education, University of London.

Dixon, M. and Margo, J., 2006. *Population Politics*. London: IPPR.

Djilas, M., 1957. *The New Class: An Analysis of the Communist System*. New York: Praeger.

Doepke, M. and Tertilt, M., 2008. Women's liberation: What's in it for men? CEPR discussion paper 6771. London: Centre for Economic Policy Research.

Dore, R., 1976, 2000. *The Diploma Disease*. London: Allen and Unwin/Institute of Education.

Drew, R.B., 2006. Buying for themselves: An analysis of unmarried female home buyers. Harvard University: Joint Center for Housing Studies No. 6–3.

Dronkers, J. and Härkönen, J., 2008. The intergenerational transmission of divorce in cross-national perspective: Results from the Fertility and Family Surveys. *Population Studies*, 62(3), pp. 273–88.

Dye, J.L., 2008. Fertility of American women: 2006. Current population reports P20–558. US Census Bureau.

Ebell, M., 2012. The parent trap: Dual income households and the cycle. Unpublished paper. London: CEP/LSE.

The Economist, 2010. Gendercide: The world-wide war on baby girls. March 4. [online] Available at: http://www.economist.com/node/15636231.

The Economist, 2011. The flight from marriage: Briefing on Asian demography. August 20–26, pp. 19–22.

Edin, K. and Kefalas, M., 2005. *Promises I Can Keep: Why Poor Women Put Motherhood Before Marriage*. Berkeley: University of California Press.

Edlund, L., 2005. Sex and the city. *Scandinavian Journal of Economics*, 107(1), pp. 25–44.

Edlund, L. and Kopczuk, W., 2007. Women, wealth and mobility. NBER working paper 13162. Cambridge, MA: National Bureau of Economic Research.

Edlund, L. and Kopczuk, W., 2009. Women, wealth and mobility. *American Economic Review*, 99(1), pp. 146–78.

Edlund, L. and Korn, E., 2002. A theory of prostitution. *Journal of Political Economy*, 110(1), pp. 181–214.

Edlund, L., Engelberg, J. and Parsons, C.A., 2009. The wages of sin. Columbia University Economics discussion paper 0809–16. New York: Columbia University.

Egan, R.B. and Kahn, G. (lyrics); Whiting, R.A. (music), 1921. "Ain't we got fun?"

Egerton, M. and Mullan, K., 2008. Being a pretty good citizen: An analysis and monetary valuation of formal and informal voluntary work by gender and educational attainment. *British Journal of Sociology*, 59(1), pp. 145–63.

Ehrenreich, B., 2000. Maid to order. The politics of other women's work. *Harper's Magazine*, April 2000. Available at http://www.barbaraehrenreich.com/maidtoorder.htm.

Ehrenreich, B. and Hochschild, A.R. (eds.), 2003. *Global Woman: Nannies, Maids, and Sex Workers in the New Economy*. London: Granta.

Ellwood, D.T. and Jencks, C., 2004. The spread of single-parent families in the United States since 1960. John F. Kennedy School of Government RWP04–008: Harvard University, Cambridge, MA.

Engels, F., 1972 (originally published 1884). *The Origin of the Family, Private Property and the State*. London: Lawrence and Wishart.

England, P., 2004. More mercenary mate selection? Comment on Sweeney and Cancian (2004) and Press (2004). *Journal of Marriage and Family*, 66(4), pp. 1034–37.

Ephron, N., 1983. *Heartburn*. New York: Pocket Books.

Esping-Andersen, G., 2009. *The Incomplete Revolution: Adapting to Women's New Roles*. Cambridge: Polity.

Eurostat, 2011. *Europe in Figures—Eurostat Yearbook 2011: Population*. European

Commission. [online] Available at: http://epp.eurostat.ec.europa.eu/cache/ITY
_OFFPUB/CH_02_2011/EN/ CH_02_2011-EN.PDF.

Fawcett Society, 2005. *Are We There Yet? 30 Years of Closing the Gap Between
Women and Men*. London: Fawcett Society.

Fernandez, R., Fogli, A. and Olivetti, C., 2002. Marrying your mom: Preference
transmissions and women's labor and education choices. NBER working paper
9234. Cambridge, MA: National Bureau of Economic Research.

Fernandez-Villaverde, J., Greenwood, J. and Guner, N., 2010. From shame to game in
one hundred years: An economic model of the rise in premarital sex and its
de-stigmatization. NBER working paper 15677. Cambridge, MA: National Bureau
of Economic Research.

Financial Times, 2009. The top women in world business. Weekend Magazine,
September 26.

Financial Times, 2010. To the money born. March 30.

Financial Times, 2012. The family fortunes of Beijing's new few. July 11: 10.

Fisher, K., Egerton, M., Gershuny, J.I. and Robinson, J.P., 2007. Gender convergence
in the American Heritage Time Use Study (AHTUS). *Social Indicators Research*, 82,
pp. 1–33.

Flanagan, C., 2006. *To Hell with All That: Loving and Loathing Our Inner
Housewife*. New York: Little, Brown.

Floud, R. and Johnson, P. (eds.), 2004. *The Cambridge Economic History of Modern
Britain, Volume 1*. Cambridge: Cambridge University Press.

Folbre, N., 2008. *Valuing Children: Rethinking the Economics of the Family*.
Cambridge, MA: Harvard University Press.

Fox, J., 2000. *Five Sisters: The Langhornes of Virginia*. New York: Simon & Schuster.

Frank, R.H. and Cook, P.J., 1995. *The Winner-Take-All Society*. New York: Free Press.

Frazis, H. and Stewart, J., 2006. How does household production affect earnings
inequality? Evidence from the American Time Use Survey. Working paper 393.
Washington, DC: US Bureau of Labor Statistics.

Frederickson, B.L., Roberts, T.-A., Noll, S.M., Quinn, D.M. and Twenge, J.M., 1998.
That swimsuit becomes you: Sex differences in self-objectification, restrained eating
and math performance. *Journal of Personality and Social Psychology*, 75(1), pp.
269–84.

Freeland, C., 2012. *Plutocrats: The Rise of the New Global Super-Rich*. New York:
Allen Lane.

Frejka, T., Jones, G.W. and Sardon, J.-P., 2010. East Asian childbearing patterns and
policy developments. *Population and Development Review*, 36(3), pp. 579–606.

Friedman, V., 2010. What suits George Osborne. Material World blog, *Financial
Times*, October 20. [online] Available at: http://blogs.ft.com/material-world/
2010/10/20/what-suits-george-osborne/.

Friedman, V., 2012. Tied to the election. *Financial Times*, August 24. [online] Available
at: http://blogs.ft.com/material-world/.

Fry, R., 2010. *The Reversal of the College Marriage Gap*. Washington, DC: Pew
Research Center.

Fry, R. and Cohn, D.'V., 2010. *Women, Men and the New Economics of Marriage*. Washington, DC: Pew Research Center.

Fukuyama, F., 1995. *Trust: The Social Virtues and the Creation of Prosperity*. London: Penguin.

Gallie, D. Skill change and the labor market: Gender, class and unemployment. Unpublished manuscript.

Garrett, E., Reid, A., Schürer, K. and Szreter, S., 2006. *Changing Family Size in England and Wales: Place, Class and Demography, 1891–1911*. Cambridge: Cambridge University Press.

Gershuny, J. and Robinson, J.P., 1988. Historical change in the household division of labour. *Demography*, 25(4), pp. 537–52.

Gerson, K., 1985. *Hard Choices: How Women Decide About Work, Career and Motherhood*. Berkeley: University of California Press.

Gerson, K., 2010. Falling back on Plan B: The children of the gender revolution face uncharted territory. In: B.J. Risman (ed.), 2010. *Families as They Really Are*. New York: Norton.

Gilligan, C., 1997. *Between Voice and Silence: Women and Girls, Race and Relationships*. Cambridge, MA: Harvard University Press.

Gladwell, M., 2005. *Blink: The Power of Thinking Without Thinking*. New York: Little, Brown.

Glenday, N. and Price, M., 1974. *Reluctant Revolutionaries: A Century of Head Mistresses, 1874–1974*. London: Pitman Press.

Goldin, C., 1991. Marriage bars: Discrimination against married women workers from the 1920s to the 1950s. NBER working paper 2747. Cambridge, MA: National Bureau of Economic Research.

Goldin, C., 2004. The long road to the fast track: Career and family. NBER working paper 10331. Cambridge, MA: National Bureau of Economic Research.

Goldin, C., 2006. The quiet revolution that transformed women's employment, education and family. NBER working paper 11953. Cambridge, MA: National Bureau of Economic Research.

Goldin, C. and Katz, L.F., 2003. The "virtues" of the past: Education in the first hundred years of the new republic. NBER working paper 9958. Cambridge, MA: National Bureau of Economic Research.

Goldin, C. and Katz, L.F., 2008a. *The Race Between Education and Technology*. Cambridge, MA: Belknap Press.

Goldin, C. and Katz, L.F., 2008b. Transitions: Career and family life cycles of the educational elite. *American Economic Review: Papers and Proceedings*, 98(2), pp. 363–9.

Goldin, C., Katz, L.F. and Kuziemko, I., 2006. The homecoming of American college women: The reversal of the college gender gap. NBER working paper 12139. Cambridge, MA: National Bureau of Economic Research.

Goldstein, D.B. and Chikhi, L., 2002. Human migrations and population structure: What we know and why it matters. *Annual Review of Genomics and Human Genetics*, 3, pp. 129–52.

Goodman, A. and Greaves, E., 2010. Cohabitation, marriage and child outcomes. IFS Commentary C114. London: Institute for Fiscal Studies.

Goodwin, D., 2010. Scrub up and strike gold. *Sunday Times*, July 4 (Supplement).

Gortmaker, S.L., Must, A., Perrin, J., Sobol, A.M. and Dietz, W.H., 1993. Social and economic consequences of overweight in adolescence and young adulthood. *New England Journal of Medicine*, 329(14), pp. 1008–12.

Gottlieb, R., 2010. *Sarah: The Life of Sarah Bernhardt*. New Haven: Yale University Press.

Gould, E.D., Moav, O. and Simhon, A., 2008. The mystery of monogamy. *American Economic Review*, 98(1), pp. 333–57.

Goux, D. and Maurin, E., 2003. Who marries whom in France? An analysis of the cohorts born between 1934 and 1978. In: H-P. Blossfeld and A. Timm (eds.), 2003. *Who Marries Whom? Educational Systems as Marriage Markets in Modern Societies*. Dordrecht: Kluwer Academic, pp. 57–78.

Grand, C., 1992. Explaining the male–female wage gap: Job segregation and solidarity wage bargaining in Sweden. *Acta Sociologica*, 34(4), pp. 261–78.

Grant Thornton, 2009. International business report 2009—global overview. Privately held businesses: The lifeblood of the global economy. [online] Available at: http://www.internationalbusinessreport.com/Reports/2009/Reports/global-overview/index.asp.

Greenstein, T.N., 2000. Economic dependence, gender and the division of labor in the home: A replication and extension. *Journal of Marriage and the Family*, 62(2), pp. 322–35.

Greenwood, J. and Guner, N., 2010. Social change: The sexual revolution. *International Economic Review*, 51(4), pp. 893–923.

Greer, G., 1980. *The Female Eunuch*. New York: McGraw-Hill.

Griskevicius, V., Tybur, J.M., Sundic, J.M., Cialdini, R.B., Miller, G.F. and Kenrick, D.T., 2007. Blatant benevolence and conspicuous consumption: When romantic motives elicit strategic costly signals. *Journal of Personality and Social Psychology*, 93(1), pp. 85–102.

Gudrais, E., 2010. Family or fortune: A quant's quandary. *Harvard Magazine*, January–February.

Haataja. A., 2009. Fathers' use of paternity and parental leave in the Nordic countries. On-line working papers 2/2009 KELA—the Social Insurance Institution of Finland.

Hackl, F., Halla, M. and Pruckner, G.J., 2009. Volunteering and the state. IZA discussion paper 4016. Bonn: Institute for the Study of Labor (IZA).

Haidinger, B., 2008. Contingencies among households: Gendered division of labor and transnational household organization—the case of Ukrainians in Austria. In: H. Lutz (ed.), 2008. *Migration and Domestic Work: A European Perspective on a Global Theme*. Aldershot: Ashgate, pp. 127–44.

Hakim, C., 2004. *Key Issues in Women's Work: Female Diversity and the Polarisation of Women's Employment* (2nd edition). London: Glass House Press.

Hakim, C., 2011a. *Feminist Myths and Magic Medicine: The Flawed Thinking Behind Calls for Further Equality Legislation*. London: Centre for Policy Studies.

Hakim, C., 2011b. *Honey Money: The Power of Erotic Capital*. London: Allen Lane.

Hamermesh, D.S., 2006. Changing looks and changing "discrimination": The beauty of economists. *Economics Letters*, 93(3), pp. 405–12.

Hamermesh, D.S., 2008. The time of our lives. In: J. Kimmel (ed.), 2008. *How Do We Spend Our Time? Evidence from the American Time Use Survey*. Kalamazoo, MI: W. E. Upjohn Institute, pp. 11–30.

Hamermesh, D.S., 2011. *Beauty Pays: Why Attractive People Are More Successful*. Princeton, NJ: Princeton University Press.

Hamermesh, D.S. and Biddle, J.E., 1994. Beauty and the labor market. *American Economic Review*, 84(5), pp. 1174–94.

Hamermesh, D.S. and Lee, J., 2003. Stressed out on four continents: Time crunch or yuppie kvetch? NBER working paper 10186. Cambridge, MA: National Bureau of Economic Research.

Hamrick, K. and Shelley, K.J., 2005. *How Much Time Do Americans Spend Preparing and Eating Food?* Washington, DC: USDA.

Hanlon, M., 2011. The alpha woman is bending our brains for the beta. *Sunday Times*, November 13, pp. 2–3.

Hansen, K., Jones, E., Joshi, H. and Budge, D., 2010. *Millennium Cohort Study Fourth Survey: A User's Guide to Initial Findings* (2nd edition). London: Centre for Longitudinal Studies.

Hansen, K. and Joshi, H. (eds.), 2007. *Millennium Cohort Study Second Survey: A User's Guide to Initial Findings*. London: Centre for Longitudinal Studies.

Hardill, I. and Baines, S., 2003. Doing one's duty? Voluntary work and the "New Economy." *Local Economy*, 18(2), pp. 102–8.

Harper, B., 2000. Beauty, stature and the labor market: A British cohort study. *Oxford Bulletin on Economics and Statistics*, 62 (issue supplement s1), pp. 771–800.

Harvard Law Bulletin, 1999. 1871 to 1950: Waiting for the HLS door to open. *Harvard Law Bulletin* (Spring). [online] Available at: http://www.law.harvard.edu/news/bulletin/backissues/spring99/article2.html.

Heer, D.M., 1963. The measurement and bases of family power: An overview. *Marriage and Family Living*, 25, pp. 133–9.

Henz, U. and Jonsson, J.O., 2003. Who marries whom in Sweden? In: H-P. Blossfeld and A. Timm (eds.), 2003. *Who Marries Whom? Educational Systems as Marriage Markets in Modern Societies*. Dordrecht: Kluwer Academic, pp. 235–65.

Herman, E., 2004. *Sex with Kings*. London: HarperCollins.

Herrin, J., 2001. *Women in Purple: Rulers of Medieval Byzantium*. London: Weidenfeld and Nicolson.

Hewlett, S.A., 2002. *Baby Hunger: The New Battle for Motherhood*. London: Atlantic Books.

Hewlett, S.A., 2007. *Off-Ramps and On-Ramps: Keeping Talented Women on the Road to Success*. Cambridge, MA: Harvard Business School Press.

Hilal, N., 2010. *Les femmes dans l'enseignement supérieur*. Paris: INSEE (FOCUS).

Hochschild, A.R. and Machung, A., 1989. *The Second Shift: Working Parents and the Revolution at Home*. Berkeley: University of California Press.

Hoem, J., 1997. Educational gradients in divorce risks in Sweden in recent decades. *Population Studies*, 51(1), pp. 19–27.

Homans, G.C., 1974. *Social Behavior: Its Elementary Forms* (revised edition). New York: Harcourt Brace Jovanovich.

Homans, G.C., 1984. *Coming to My Senses: The Autobiography of a Sociologist*. New Brunswick, NJ: Transaction Books.

Home Office, 2001. *Citizenship Survey: People, Families and Communities*. London: Home Office.

Hosoda, M., Stone-Romero, E.F. and Coats, G., 2003. The effects of physical attractiveness on job-related outcomes: A meta-analysis of experimental studies. *Personnel Psychology*, 56(2), pp. 431–62.

Hoxby, C.A., 2009. The changing selectivity of American colleges. *Journal of Economic Perspectives*, 23(4), pp. 95–118.

Hrdy, S.B., 1981. *The Woman That Never Evolved*. Cambridge, MA: Harvard University Press.

Hrdy, S.B., 1999. *Mother Nature: Natural Selection and the Female of the Species*. New York: Pantheon.

Huff, C.D., Xing, J., Rogers, A.R., Witherspoon, D. and Jorde, L.B., 2010. Mobile elements reveal small population size in the ancient ancestors of *Homo sapiens*. *Proceedings of the National Academy of Sciences of the United States of America*, 107(5), pp. 2147–52.

Hughes, K., 1993. *The Victorian Governess*. London: Hambledon Press.

Hussain, A., McNally, S. and Telhaj, J., 2009. University quality and graduate wages in the UK. CEE discussion paper no. 0099. London: LSE Centre for the Economics of Education.

Ilan, S., 2008. Child welfare doesn't benefit society. *Ha'aretz*, July 2. [online] Available at: http://www.haaretz.com/print-edition/opinion/child-welfare-doesn-t-benefit-society-1.247053.

Independent Sector, 2001. Giving and volunteering in the United States 2001: Findings from a national survey. Washington, DC: Independent Sector.

International Baccalaureate Organization, 2008. The IB diploma program statistical bulletin, May. Examination Session. Cardiff: International Baccalaureate Organization. [online] Available at: http://www.ibo.org/facts/statbulletin/dpstats/documents/May2008StatisticalBulletin.pdf.

Inter-Parliamentary Union, 2009. Women in national parliaments. [online] Available at: http://www.ipu.org/wmn-e/arc/classif310509.htm.

Isen, A. and Stevenson, B., 2010. Women's education and family behavior: Trends in marriage, divorce and fertility. NBER working paper 15725. Cambridge, MA: National Bureau of Economic Research.

Izquierdo, C. and Klein, W., 2010. Family Commitments at Home: The Work of Negotiating Responsibilities. Paper presented at the CELF Conference "Reconsidering the American Dream," Los Angeles, CA, April 28–29.

Johnson, A.M., Copas, A.J., Erens, B., Mandalia, S., Fenton, K., Korovessis, C., Wellings, K. and Field, J., 2001. Effect of computer-assisted self-interviews on reporting of sexual HIV risk behaviors in a general population sample: A methodological experiment. *AIDS*, 15(1), pp. 111–15.

Johnson, A.M. , Mercer, C. M., Erens, B., Copas. A.J. et al., 2001. Sexual behavior in Britain: Partnerships, practices and HIV risk behaviors. *The Lancet*, 358, pp. 1835–42.

Johnson, A.M., Wadsworth, J., Wellings, K. and Field, J., with Bradshaw, S., 1994. *The National Survey of Sexual Attitudes and Lifestyles*. Oxford: Blackwell Scientific Press.

Jones, G., 2010. *Beauty Imagined: A History of the Global Beauty Industry*. New York: Oxford University Press.

Jones, L.E. and Tertilt, M., 2006. An economic history of fertility in the US: 1826–1960. NBER working paper 12796. Cambridge, MA: National Bureau of Economic Research.

Jonung, C. and Persson, I., 1993. Women and market work: The misleading tale of participation rates in international comparisons. *Work, Employment and Society*, 7(2), pp. 259–74.

Joshi, H., 2002. Production, reproduction and education: Women, children and work in a British perspective. *Population and Development Review*, 28(3), pp. 445–74.

Joshi, H., 2003. Men's and women's lifetime earnings: Some more equal than others. In: Evidence to House of Lords Session 2002–03, 4th Report: Select Committee on Economic Affairs, Aspects of the Economics of an Ageing Population, Vol. II, pp. 137–41, HL Paper 179-II. London: House of Lords.

Kan, M.Y., 2008. Measuring housework participation: The gap between "stylised" questionnaire estimates and diary-based estimates. *Social Indicators Research*, 86(3), pp. 381–400.

Kanji, S., 2010. Do fathers work less when mothers earn more? Mimeo: Sociology Department, University of Cambridge.

Kanji, S., 2011. What keeps mothers in full-time employment? *European Sociological Review*, 27(4), pp. 509–35.

Kanji, S. and Schober, P., 2012. Can couples survive when the mother is the main or an equal earner? Unpublished working paper. Basle: Department of Sociology.

Karabel, J., 2005. *The Chosen: The Hidden History of Admission and Exclusion at Harvard, Yale and Princeton*. Boston: Houghton Mifflin.

Kaufmann, K.M., Petrocik, J.R. and Shaw D.R., 2008. *Unconventional Wisdom: Facts and Myths about American Voters*. Oxford: Oxford University Press.

Keats, J., 1967. *The Sheepskin Psychosis*. New York: Dell.

Keddie, A. and Mills, M., 2007. *Teaching Boys: Developing Classroom Practices That Work*. Crows Nest, NSW: Allen and Unwin.

Kellaway, L., 2011. The drivel is in the details with CEO pay deals. *Financial Times*, April 18, p. 14.

Kelly, J., 2011. 13 "mainstream" sites powered by porn. *This or That*, January 25. [online] Available at: http://thisorthat.com/blog/13-mainstream-sites-powered-by-porn.

Bibliography

Kenrick, D.T., Montello, D.R., Gutierres, S.E. and Trost, M.R., 1993. Effects of physical attractiveness on affect and perceptual judgments: When social comparison overrides social reinforcement. *Personality and Social Psychology Bulletin*, 19(2), pp. 195–9.

Kiernan, K. and Smith, K., 2003. Unmarried parenthood: New insights from the Millennium Cohort Study. *Population Trends*, 114 (Winter), pp. 26–33.

Kimmel, J. (ed.), 2008. *How Do We Spend Our Time? Evidence from the American Time Use Survey.* Kalamazoo, MI: W. E. Upjohn Institute.

Kipling, R., The ladies. Available at http://www.poemhunter.com/poem/the-ladies/.

Kiser, C.V. and Schacter, N.I., 1949. Demographic characteristics of women in "Who's Who." *Milbank Memorial Fund Quarterly*, 27(4), pp. 392–433.

Klinenberg, E., 2012. *Going Solo: The Extraordinary Rise and Surprising Appeal of Living Alone.* New York: Penguin.

Kneale, D. and Joshi, H., 2008. Postponement and childlessness: Evidence from two British cohorts. *Demographic Research*, 19(58), pp. 1935–68.

Knijn, T. and Komter, A. (eds.), 2004. *Solidarity Between the Sexes and the Generations.* Cheltenham: Edward Elgar.

Kolesnikova, N. and Yang Liu, 2011. The gender wage gap may be much smaller than most think. *The Regional Economist*, October, pp. 14–15. St. Louis: Federal Reserve Bank.

Konrad, G. and Szelényi, I., 1979. *The Intellectuals on the Road to Class Power.* New York: Harcourt Brace Jovanovich.

Kopczuk, W. and Saez, E., 2004. Top wealth shares in the United States 1916–2000: Evidence from estate tax returns. NBER working paper 10399. Cambridge, MA: National Bureau of Economic Research.

Kopczuk, W., Saez, E. and Song, J., 2007. Earnings inequality and mobility in the United States: Evidence from Social Security data since 1937. NBER working paper 13345. Cambridge, MA: National Bureau of Economic Research.

Kopczuk, W., Saez, E. and Song, J., 2010. Earnings inequality and mobility in the United States: Evidence from Social Security data since 1937. *Quarterly Journal of Economics*, 125(1), pp. 91–128.

Korda, M., 1979. *Charmed Lives: A Family Romance.* New York: Avon.

Koslowski, A.S., 2011. Working fathers in Europe: Earning and caring. *European Sociological Review*, 27(2), pp. 230–45.

Kreider, R.M. and Ellis, R., 2011. Number, timing and duration of marriages and divorces: 2009. Washington, DC: Household Economic Studies, US Census Bureau. [online] Available at: http://www.census.gov/prod/2011pubs/p70-125.pdf.

Kuhn, P. and Shen, K., 2009. Employers' preferences for gender, age, height and beauty: Direct evidence. NBER working paper 15564. Cambridge, MA: National Bureau of Economic Research.

Kulik, L., 2011. Developments in spousal power relations: Are we moving toward equality? *Marriage and Family Review*, 47(7), pp. 419–35.

Kuper, S., 2010. I am a negative role model. *Financial Times*, December 11.

Kydyralieva, S., 2010. Elites of Central Asia and economic development. Paper presented to the WIDER Conference on elites and development: Helsinki.

Bibliography

Lacey, T.A. and Wright, B., 2009. Occupational employment projections to 2018. *Monthly Labor Review*, 132(11), pp. 82–123. Washington, DC: US Department of Labor.

Lagarde, C., 2010. What if it had been Lehman Sisters? *Herald Tribune*, May 11.

Lakdawalla, D., 2001. The declining quality of teachers. NBER working paper 8263. Cambridge, MA: National Bureau of Economic Research.

Landry, C., Lange, A., List, J.A., Price, M.K., Rupp, N.G., 2005. Toward an understanding of the economics of charity: Evidence from a field experiment. NBER working paper 11611. Cambridge, MA: National Bureau of Economic Research.

Laroque, G. and Salanie, B., 2008. Does fertility respond to financial incentives? CESifo working paper 2339. Munich: CESifo Group.

Laumann, E.O., Gagnon, J.H., Michael, R.T. and Michaels, S., 1994. *The Social Organization of Sexuality: Sexual Practices in the United States*. Chicago: University of Chicago Press.

Le Grand, C., 1992. Explaining the male–female wage gap: Job segregation and solidarity wage bargaining in Sweden. *Acta Sociologica*, 34, pp. 261–78.

Lee, M.A. and Mather, M., 2008. *US Labor Force Trends*. Population Bulletin 63 No.2. Washington, DC: Population Reference Bureau.

Leitch, S., 2006. Prosperity for all in the global economy—world-class skills: Final report (Leitch Review of Skills). London: Stationery Office for HM Treasury.

Lemley, B., 2000. Isn't she lovely? *Discover Magazine*, February, pp. 42–9.

Levitt, S.D. and Dubner, S.J., 2009. *Superfreakonomics: Global Cooling, Patriotic Prostitutes, and Why Suicide Bombers Should Buy Life Insurance*. New York: William Morrow/HarperCollins.

Levy, A., 2005. *Female Chauvinist Pigs: Women and the Rise of Raunch Culture*. New York: Simon & Schuster.

Light, A., 2008. *Mrs. Woolf and the Servants*. London: Penguin.

Lindberg, L.D. and Singh, S., 2008. Sexual behavior of single adult American women. *Perspectives on Sexual and Reproductive Health*, 40(1), pp. 27–33.

Lindgren, H., 2002. Succession strategies in a large family business group: The case of the Swedish Wallenberg family. Paper presented to the 6th European Business History Association Congress, August, Helsinki.

Linnemann, C., 2007. *Germany's Mittelstand—an Endangered Species?* Frankfurt am Main: Deutsche Bank Research.

Lipsky, M. 1980. Street-level bureaucracy: Dilemmas of the individual in public services. New York: Russell Sage Foundation.

Loh, E.S., 1993. The economic effects of physical appearance. *Social Science Quarterly*, 74(2), pp. 420–38.

Lundberg, S. and Pollak, R.A., 2007. The American family and family economics. IZA discussion paper 2715. Bonn: Institute for the Study of Labor (IZA).

Lundström, T., 1996. The state and voluntary social work in Sweden. *Nonprofit and Voluntary Sector Quarterly*, 7(2), pp. 123–46.

Lutz, H., 2008. When home becomes a workplace: Domestic work as an ordinary job in Germany? In: H. Lutz (ed.), 2008. *Migration and Domestic Work: A European Perspective on a Global Theme*. Aldershot: Ashgate, pp. 43–60.

McAlvanah, P., 2009. Are people more risk-taking in the presence of the opposite sex? *Journal of Economic Psychology*, 30(2), pp. 136–46.

McCarthy, K.D., 2003a. Women and political culture. In: L.J. Friedman and M.D. McGarvie (eds.), 2003. *Charity, Philanthropy and Civility in American Society*. Cambridge: Cambridge University Press, pp. 179–98.

McCarthy, K.D., 2003b. *American Creed: Philanthropy and the Rise of Civil Society, 1700–1865*. Chicago: University of Chicago Press.

McLean Taylor, J., Gilligan, C. and Sullivan, A.M., 1997. *Between Voice and Silence: Women and Girls, Race and Relationships*. Cambridge, MA: Harvard University Press.

McNabb, R., Pal, S. and Sloane, P., 2002. Gender differences in student attainment: The case of university students in England and Wales. *Economica*, 69, pp. 481–503.

Macran, S., Joshi, H. and Dex, S., 1996. Employment after childbearing: A survival analysis. *Work, Employment and Society*, 10(2), pp. 273–96.

Maitland, A. and Halls, S., 2009. FT top women in world business. *Financial Times, Weekend Magazine*, September 26.

Margadant, J.B., 1990. *Madame le Professeur: Women Educators in the Third Republic*. Princeton, NJ: Princeton University Press.

Margulis, L. and Sagan, D., 1991. *Mystery Dance: On the Evolution of Human Sexuality*. New York: Summit Books.

Martin, S., 2008. Recent changes in fertility rates in the United States: What do they tell us about Americans' changing families. Briefing paper for the Council on Contemporary Families. [online] Available at: http://www.contemporaryfamilies. org/gender-sexuality/fertility.html.

Martin, S.P., 2000. Diverging fertility among U.S. women who delay childbearing past age 30. *Demography*, 37(4), pp. 523–33.

Martinelli, C. and Parker, S., 2009. Deception and misreporting in a social program. *Journal of the European Economic Association*, 7(4), pp. 886–908.

Martinez, G.M., Chandra, A., Abma, J.C., Jones, J. and Mosher, W.D., 2006. Fertility, contraception and fatherhood: Data on men and women from Cycle 6 (2002) of the National Survey of Family Growth. *Vital Health Statistics*, 23(26). Hyattsville, MD: National Center for Health Statistics.

Matsui, K., 2010. Womenomics: The time is now. Tokyo: Goldman Sachs. [online] Available at: http://www2.goldmansachs.com/our-thinking/women-and-economics/ womenomics-2011/index.html.

Mead, M., 1928. *Coming of Age in Samoa: A Psychological Study of Primitive Youth for Western Civilization*. New York: HarperCollins.

Medved, M. and Wallechinsky, D., 1976. *What Really Happened to the Class of '65?* New York: Random House.

Mees, H., 2007. *Weg met het deeltijdfeminisme!* Amsterdam: Nieuw Amsterdam. Quoted in: R. Wilson, 2008. The three degrees of feminism. *Amsterdam Weekly*, December 2008.

Melkas, H. and Anker, R., 1997. Occupational segregation by sex in Nordic countries: An empirical investigation. *International Labour Review*, 136(3), pp. 341–63.

Michael, R.T., Gagnon. J.H., Laumann, E.O. and Kolata, G., 1994. *Sex in America: A Definitive Survey*. New York: Little, Brown.

Michaels, G., Natraj, A. and Van Reenan, J., 2010. Has ICT polarised skill demand? Evidence from eleven countries over 25 years. CEP discussion paper 987. London: Centre for Economic Performance, LSE.

Milkman, R., Reese, E. and Roth, B., 1998. The macrosociology of paid domestic labor. *Work and Occupations*, 25(4), pp. 483–510.

Milligan, K., 2005. Subsidizing the stork: New evidence on tax incentives and fertility. *Review of Economics and Statistics*, 87(3), pp. 539–55.

Milne-Tyte, A., 2010. No advertising love for single women. *Marketplace Morning Report*, radio broadcast, March 25. Available at http://www.marketplace.org/topics/business/no-advertising-love-single-women.

Mount, F., 2010. *Full Circle: How the Classical World Came Back to Us*. New York: Simon & Schuster.

Multinational Time Use Study, 2011. Versions World 5.5.3, 5.80 and 6.0. Oxford: Centre for Time Use Research, Oxford University. [online] Available at: http://www.timeuse.org/mtus/.

Mundy, L., 2012. *The Richer Sex*. New York: Simon & Schuster.

National Center for Education Statistics (NCES), various. *The Condition of Education*. Washington, DC: NCES.

National Center for Education Statistics (NCES), 2011. *Digest of Education Statistics*. Washington, DC: NCES.

National Survey of Sexual Attitudes and Lifestyles, 1990–1991 (Natsal I). London: NatCen/UCL/LSHTM. [online] Available at: http://www.ucl.ac.uk/iph/research/sexualhealthandhiv/natsal and http://www.natcen.ac.uk/study/natsal.

National Survey of Sexual Attitudes and Lifestyles, 2000–2001 (Natsal II). London: NatCen/UCL/LSHTM. [online] Available at: http://www.ucl.ac.uk/iph/research/sexualhealthandhiv/natsal.

Neubauer, F. and Lank, A., 1998. *The Family Business: Its Governance for Sustainability*. Routledge: London.

New Strategist Publications, 2007. *American Incomes: Demographics of Who Has Money* (6th edition). Ithaca, NY: New Strategist.

Ní Bhrolcháin, M., Beaujouan, E. and Berrington, A., 2010. Stability and change in fertility intentions in Britain, 1991–2007. *Population Trends*, 141, pp. 13–35.

Nicholson, V., 2008. *Singled Out: How Two Million Women Survived Without Men After the First World War*. London: Penguin.

Niederle, M. and Vesterlund, L., 2007. Do women shy away from competition? Do men compete too much? *Quarterly Journal of Economics*, 122(3), pp. 1067–101.

Norfolk, A., 2011a. Revealed: Conspiracy of silence on UK sex gangs. *The Times*, January 5.

Norfolk, A., 2011b. Action on the gangs who groom girls for sex. *The Times*, November 21.

O'Connor, S., 2011. Acacia Grove: Who lived in a street like this? *The Dulwich Society Journal*, 169 (Summer), pp. 28–31.

Odone, C., 2009. *What Women Want . . . and How They Can Get It*. London: Centre for Policy Studies.

OECD, 2001. Balancing work and family life: Helping parents into paid employment. *Employment Outlook 2001*. Paris: OECD, Chapter 4.

OECD, 2002. Women at work: Who are they and how are they faring? Employment Outlook 2002. Paris: OECD, Chapter 2.

OECD, 2008. To Which Fields of Education Are Students Attracted? (Indicator A4). Paris: OECD Available at: [online] www.oecd.org/edu/highereducationandadult learning/48630719.pdf.

OECD, 2009a. *Equally Prepared for Life? How 15-Year-Old Boys and Girls Perform in School*. Paris: OECD.

OECD, 2009b. *Employment Outlook 2009: Tackling the Jobs Crisis*. Paris: OECD. [online] Available at: http://www.oecd-ilibrary.org/employment/oecd-employment -outlook-2009_empl_outlook-2009-en.

OECD, 2010. *Employment Outlook 2010: Moving Beyond the Jobs Crisis*. Paris: OECD. [online] Available at: http://www.oecd-ilibrary.org/employment/oecd -employment-outlook-2010_empl_outlook-2010-en.

OECD, 2011. *Education at a Glance*. Paris: OECD.

OECD family database. SF3.1: Marriage and divorce rates. [online] Available at: http:// www.oecd.org/dataoecd/4/19/40321815.pdf.

Offer, S. and Scheider, B., 2011. Revisiting the gender gap in time-use patterns: Multitasking and well-being among mothers and fathers in dual-earner families. *American Sociological Review*, 76(6), pp. 809–33.

Office for National Statistics (ONS), 2003. Census 2001: National report for England and Wales, part 1. London: ONS. [online] Available at: http://www.ons.gov.uk/ons/ rel/census/census-2001-national-report-for-england-and-wales/national-report-for -england-and-wales-part-1/index.html.

Office for National Statistics (ONS), 2006. *United Kingdom Input-Output Analyses, 2006 Edition*. [online] Available at: www.statistics.gov.uk/inputoutput.

Office for National Statistics (ONS), 2008. *Birth Statistics Series FM1*. Available at: http://www.ons.gov.uk/ons/rel/vsob1/birth-statistics--england-and-wales--series -fm1-/no—37—2008/index.html.

Office for National Statistics (ONS), 2009. Population trends—age at marriage by sex and previous marital status, 1991, 1997, 2001, 2003–2007. *Population Trends*, No. 135 (Spring). [online] Available at: http://www.ons.gov.uk (Population Trends Archive) or download directly as Population_trends_135_tcm77–161412.pdf.

Office for National Statistics (ONS), 2010a. Labour market. *Social Trends 40, 2010 edition*. Chapter 4. [online] Available at: http://www.ons.gov.uk/ons/rel/social -trends-rd/social-trends/social-trends-40/social-trends-40---labour-market-chapter .pdf.

Office for National Statistics (ONS), 2010b. Income and wealth in *Social Trends 41*. Full report available from www.ons.gov.uk (ISSN 2040–1620): chapter on income and wealth (authored by S. Carrera and J. Beaumont) downloadable separately as income201_tcm77–248505.pdf

Office for National Statistics (ONS), 2011. Statistical bulletin: Marriages in England

and Wales, 2009. [online] Available at: http://www.ons.gov.uk/ons/rel/vsob1/marriages-in-england-and-wales--provisional-/2009/index.html.

Office for National Statistics (ONS), 2012a. *Labour Market Statistics: Workforce Jobs by Industry*. Swansea: ONS.

Office for National Statistics, 2012b. *First ONS Annual Experimental Subjective Well-being Results*. Swansea: ONS.

Office for National Statistics (various). *Annual Survey of Hours and Earnings*. [online] Available at: http://www.ons.gov.uk/ons/about-ons/surveys/a-z-of-surveys/annual-survey-of-hours-and-earnings—ashe-/index.html.

Ohlsson-Wijk, S., 2011. Sweden's marriage revival: An analysis of the new-millennium switch from long term decline to increasing popularity. *Population Studies*, 65(2), pp. 183–200.

Oswald, A.J. and Powdthavee, N., 2010. Daughters and left-wing voting. *Review of Economics and Statistics*, 92(2), pp. 213–27.

Owen, J., 2006. Evolution less accepted in U.S. than other Western countries, study finds. *National Geographic News*, August 10 [online] Available at: http://www.news.nationalgeographic.com/ news/2006/08/060810-evolution.html.

Park, A., Curtice, J., Thomson, K., Phillips, M., Johnson, M. and Clery, E. (eds.), 2008. *British Social Attitudes 2007–2008: The 24th Report*. London: Sage.

Parreñas, R.S., 2005. *Children of Global Migration: Transnational Families and Gendered Woes*. Palo Alto, CA: Stanford University Press.

Paterson, F.M.S. and Fewell, J. (eds.), 1990. *Girls in Their Prime: Scottish Education Revisited*. Edinburgh: Scottish Academic Press.

Pfann, G.A., Biddle, J.E., Hamermesh, D.S. and Bosman, C.M., 2000. Business success and businesses' beauty capital. *Economics Letters*, 67(2), pp. 201–207.

Piketty, T. and Saez, E., 2006. The evolution of top incomes: A historical and international perspective. NBER working paper 11955. Cambridge, MA: National Bureau of Economic Research.

Pinker, S., 2008. *The Sexual Paradox: Men, Women and the Real Gender Gap*. New York: Scribner.

Pinker, S., 2011. *The Better Angels of Our Nature: The Decline of Violence in History and Its Causes*. London: Allen Lane.

Pison, G., 2009. France 2008: Pourquoi le nombre de naissances continue-t-il d'augmenter? *Population et Sociétés*, 454 (March). Paris: INED.

Poza, E.J., 2007. *Family Business* (2nd edition). Mason, OH: Thomson South-Western.

Press, J.E., 2004. Cute butts and housework: A gynocentric theory of assortative mating. *Journal of Marriage and Family*, 66(4), pp. 1029–33.

Preston, S.H. and Hartnett, C.S., 2008. The future of American fertility. NBER working paper 14498. Cambridge, MA: National Bureau of Economic Research.

Prochaska, F., 1980. *Women and Philanthropy in 19th Century England*. Oxford: Oxford University Press.

Prochaska, F., 2006. *Christianity and Social Service in Modern Britain*. Oxford: Oxford University Press.

Putnam, R.D. and Campbell, D.E., 2010. *American Grace: How Religion Divides and Unites Us*. New York: Simon & Schuster.

Ramey, V., 2006. A century of work and leisure. NBER working paper 12264. Cambridge, MA: National Bureau of Economic Research.

Ramey, V., 2008. Time spent in home production in the 20th century: New estimates from old data. NBER working paper 13985. Cambridge, MA: National Bureau of Economic Research.

Ratcliffe, A. and Smith, S., 2007. Fertility and women's education in the UK: A cohort analysis. CMPO working paper 07/165. Bristol: Centre for Market and Public Organisation, University of Bristol.

Rattigan, T., 1953. *Collected Plays Volume 1*. London: Hamish Hamilton.

Raymo, J.M. and Iwasawa, M., 2005. Marriage market mismatches in Japan: An alternative view of the relationship between women's education and marriage. *American Sociological Review*, 70, pp. 801–22.

Reform Synagogues of Great Britain (1985). *Forms of Prayer for Jewish Worship III: Prayers for the High Holydays*. London: Reform Synagogues of Great Britain.

Retherford, R.D., Ogawa, N. and Matsukura, R., 2001. Late marriage and less marriage in Japan. *Population and Development Review*, 27(1), pp. 65–102.

Rhoads, S., 2004. *Taking Sex Differences Seriously*. San Francisco: Encounter Books.

Rhode, D., 2010. *The Beauty Bias: The Injustice of Appearance in Life and Law*. New York: Oxford University Press.

Rindfuss, R.R., Morgan, S.P. and Swicegood, G., 1988. *First Births in America*. Berkeley: University of California Press.

Rosen, R., 1982. *The Lost Sisterhood: Prostitution in America, 1900–1918*. Baltimore: Johns Hopkins University Press.

Rosen, R. and Davidson, S. (eds.), 1977. *The Maimie Papers*. New York: Feminist Press.

Roth, L.-M., 2006. *Selling Women Short: Gender and Money on Wall Street*. Princeton, NJ: Princeton University Press.

Rumbelow, H., 2011. Happiness is working part time. *The Times*, February 28.

Ruston, D., 2003. *Volunteers, Helpers and Socialisers: Social Capital and Time Use*. London: Office for National Statistics. [online] Available at: http://www.statistics. gov.uk/articles/nojournal/Time_Use_Volunteers_helpers_socialisers.pdf.

Saez, E., Striking it richer: The evolution of top incomes in the United States. University of California. [online] Available at: http://elsa.berkeley.edu/~saez.

Sandberg, S. with Scovell, N. 2013. *Lean In: Women, Work and the Will to Lead*. London: W. H. Allen.

Sander, W., 2006. Private schools and school enrollment in Chicago. Chicago Fed Letter 231: Chicago Federal Reserve, October 1.

Sanders, T., 2005. *Sex Work: A Risky Business*. Abingdon: Willan.

Sanders, T., 2008. *Paying for Pleasure: Men Who Buy Sex*. Abingdon: Willan.

Sargent, J.D. and Blanchflower, D.G., 1994. Obesity and stature in adolescence and earnings in young adulthood: Analysis of a British birth cohort. *Archives of Pediatrics and Adolescent Medicine*, 148(7), pp. 681–7.

Sarti, R., 2008. The globalisation of domestic service—an historical perspective. In: H. Lutz (ed.), 2008. *Migration and Domestic Work: A European Perspective on a Global Theme*. Aldershot: Ashgate, pp. 77–98.

Saxbe, D.E., Repetti, R.L. and Graesch, A.P., 2011. Time spent in housework and leisure: Links with parents' physiological recovery from work. *Journal of Family Psychology*, 25(2) 271–281.

Schmidt, L. and Sevak, P., 2006. Gender, marriage and asset accumulation in the United States. *Feminist Economics*, 12(1–2), pp. 139–66.

Schönberg, U. and Ludsteck, J., 2007. Maternity leave legislation, female labor supply, and the family wage gap. IZA discussion paper 2699. Bonn: Institute for the Study of Labor (IZA).

Schuyt, T.N.M., Gouwenberg, B.M. and Bekkers, R.H.F.P. (eds.), 2011. *Giving in the Netherlands: Donations, Bequests, Sponsorship and Volunteering*. Amsterdam: Reed Business.

Schwartz, C.R. and Mare, R.D., 2005. Trends in educational assortative marriage from 1940 to 2003. *Demography*, 42(4), pp. 621–46.

Schwenken, H. and Heimeshoff, L.-M. (eds.), 2011. *Domestic Workers Count: Global Data on an Often Invisible Sector*. Kassel, Germany: Kassel University Press.

Scrinzi, F., 2008. Migrations and the restructuring of the welfare state in Italy: Change and continuity in the domestic work sector. In: H. Lutz (ed.), 2008. *Migration and Domestic Work: A European Perspective on a Global Theme*. Aldershot: Ashgate, pp. 29–42.

Seabright, P., 2010. *The Company of Strangers: A Natural History of Economic Life* (revised edition). Princeton, NJ: Princeton University Press.

Seigle, C.S., 1993. *Yoshiwara: The Glittering World of the Japanese Courtesan*. Honolulu: University of Hawaii Press.

Shackleton, J.R., 2008. *Should We Mind the Gap? Gender Pay Differentials and Public Policy*. London: IEA.

Shaw, G.B., 1916. *Pygmalion* (first performed 1912). Multiple editions and downloadable from Project Gutenberg.

Sheridan, T. and Stretton, P., 2004. Mandarins, ministers and the bar on married women. *Journal of Industrial Relations*, 46(1), pp. 84–101.

Short, S.E., Goldscheider, F.K. and Torr, B.M., 2006. Less help for mother: The decline in coresidential female support for the mothers of young children, 1880–2000. *Demography*, 43(4), pp. 617–29.

Sigle-Rushton, W., 2008. England and Wales: Stable fertility and pronounced social status differences. *Demographic Research*, 19, pp. 455–502.

Silverstein, M.J. and Fiske, N., 2005. *Trading Up: Why Consumers Want New Luxury Goods and How Companies Create Them*. New York: Portfolio.

Skocpol, T., 1992. *Protecting Soldiers and Mothers: The Political Origins of Social Policy in the United States*. Cambridge, MA: Belknap Press of Harvard University Press.

Skocpol, T., 2000. Religion, civil society and social provision in the U.S. In: M.J. Bane, B. Coffin and R. Thiemann (eds.), 2000. *Who Will Provide? The Changing Role of Religion in American Social Welfare*. Boulder, CO: Westview Press, pp. 21–50.

Skocpol, T., 2002. The institutional foundations of democratic civil society in America—and beyond. Stein Rokkan Lecture, September 27, Bergen, Norway.

Bibliography

Skocpol, T., 2003. *Diminished Democracy: From Membership to Management in American Civic Life.* Norman: University of Oklahoma Press.

Slater, S.A. 2010. Containment: Managing street prostitution in London 1918–1959. *Journal of British Studies,* 49(2), 332–57.

Slaughter, A.-M., 2012. Why women still can't have it all. *The Atlantic,* July/August.

Sleebos, J., 2003. Low fertility rates in OECD countries: Facts and policy responses. OECD Social, employment and migration working papers No. 15. Paris: OECD.

Smith, D.E., 1990. *The Conceptual Practices of Power: A Feminist Sociology of Knowledge.* Toronto: University of Toronto Press.

Smith, S. and Ratcliffe, A., 2009. Women's education and childbearing: A growing divide. In: J. Stillwell, E. Coast and D. Kneale (eds.), 2009. *Fertility, Living Arrangements, Care and Mobility: Understanding Population Trends and Processes—Volume 1.* Dordrecht: Springer, Chapter 3.

Spender, D., 1982. *Invisible Women: The Schooling Scandal.* London: Writers and Readers Publishing Cooperative Society.

Statistics Bureau, Japan, 2011. *Statistical Handbook of Japan 2011.* Tokyo: Ministry of Internal Affairs and Communications.

Statistics Canada. *Caring Canadians, Involved Canadians* (annual publication).

Statistics Sweden (various). Economic and Employment statistics. Available at: http://www.scb.se/Pages/List____259594.aspx.

Stead, W., 1964 (originally published in 1894). If Christ came to Chicago. Quoted in: R. Rosen and S. Davidson (eds.), 1977. *The Maimie Papers.* New York: Feminist Press.

Steinem, G., 2008. Women are never front runners. *New York Times,* January 8. [online] Available at: http://www.nytimes.com/2008/01/08/opinion/08steinem.html?_r=0.

Steir, H. and Shavit, Y., 2003. Two decades of educational intermarriage in Israel. In: H-P. Blossfeld and A. Timm (eds.), 2003. *Who Marries Whom? Educational Systems as Marriage Markets in Modern Societies.* Dordrecht: Kluwer Academic, pp. 315–30.

Stevenson, B. and Wolfers, J., 2007. Marriage and divorce: Changes and their driving forces. NBER working paper 12944. Cambridge, MA: National Bureau of Economic Research.

Stevenson, B. and Wolfers, J., 2009. The paradox of declining female happiness. *American Economic Journal: Economic Policy,* 1(2), pp. 190–225.

Stone, L., 1995. *Uncertain Unions and Broken Lives: Marriage and Divorce in England, 1660–1857.* Oxford: Oxford University Press.

Storvik, A.E. and Schøne, P., 2010. In search of the glass ceiling: Gender and recruitment to management in Norway's state bureaucracy. *British Journal of Sociology,* 59(4), pp. 729–55.

Strandh, M. and Nordenmark, M., 2006. The interference of paid work with household demands in different social policy contexts: Perceived work-household conflicts in Sweden, the UK, the Netherlands, Hungary and the Czech Republic. *British Journal of Sociology,* 57(4), pp. 597–617.

Streitmatter, J., 1994. *Toward Gender Equity in the Classroom State.* Albany: State University of New York Press.

Sullivan, O., 2006. *Changing Gender Relations, Changing Families: Tracing the Pace of Change Over Time*. New York: Rowman and Littlefield.

Sullivan, O., 2010a. Changing men's contribution to family work. In: B.J. Risman, *Families as They Really Are*. New York: Norton.

Sullivan, O., 2010b. Changing differences by educational attainment in fathers' domestic labour and child care. *Sociology*, 44(4), pp. 716–33.

Sullivan, O., 2011. An end to gender deviance neutralization through the performance of housework? A review and reassessment of the quantitative literature using insights from the qualitative literature. *Journal of Family Theory and Review*, 3, pp. 11–13.

Sullivan, O., n.d. Changing differences in the division of domestic labour: The case of childcare. Mimeo: Oxford University Centre for Time Use.

Sullivan, O. and Gershuny, J., 2012. Relative human capital resources and housework: A longitudinal analysis. DP 2012–04, Department of Sociology, University of Oxford.

Sunday Times (Chittenden, M. and Dobson, R.), 2005. Clever devils get the bird. *Sunday Times*, February 2, p. 8.

Sutherland, G., 2006. *Faith, Duty and the Power of Mind: The Cloughs and Their Circle*. Cambridge: Cambridge University Press.

Sutton Trust, 2010. *The Educational Backgrounds of Members of Parliament in 2010*. London: Sutton Trust.

Sweeny, M.M. and Cancian, M., 2004a. The changing importance of white women's economic prospects for assortative mating. *Journal of Marriage and Family*, 66(4), pp. 1015–28.

Sweeny, M.M. and Cancian, M., 2004b. Placing patterns of economic assortative mating in context: A reply to Press (2004) and England (2004). *Journal of Marriage and Family*, 66(4), pp. 1038–42.

Templeton, T. 2006. The Guardian Angels. *The Observer Magazine* (London). February 19, 2006, pp. 23–28.

Thompson, W. and Hickey, J., 2005. *Society in Focus*. Boston: Pearson, Allyn & Bacon.

Tiger, L. and Shepher, J. 1975. *Women in the Kibbutz*. New York and London: Harcourt Brace Jovanovich.

Touleman, L., Pailhé, A. and Rossier, C., 2008. France: High and stable fertility. *Demographic Research*, 19 (article 16), pp. 503–56.

Trivers, R., 1985. *Social Evolution*. Menlo Park, CA: Benjamin/Cummings.

Tullberg, R.M., 1998. *Women at Cambridge*. Cambridge: Cambridge University Press.

Turner, J., 2012. A question of cybersex. *The Times*, February 21, pp. 4–5.

UK Commission for Employment and Skills, 2010. Skills for jobs: Today and tomorrow—the national strategic skills audit for England 2010—Volume 1: Key findings. [online] Available at: http://www.ukces.org.uk/assets/bispartners/ukces/docs/publications/national-strategic-skills-audit-for-england-2010-volume-1-key-findings.pdf.

University of Oxford Gazette, 2011. Supplement 2 to No.4945, Vol. 141.

US Bureau of Labor Statistics, 2003. *American Time Use Survey*. [online] Available at: http://www.bls.gov/tus/.

US Bureau of Labor Statistics. *Consumer Expenditure Survey.* [online] Available at: http://www.bls.gov/cex/.

US Bureau of Labor Statistics, 2011. *Volunteering in the United States—2010.* USDL-11–0084. Washington, DC: US Department of Labor. [online] Available at: http://www.bls.gov/news.release/archives/volun_01262011.htm.

US Census Bureau, 1982. *Current Population Reports.* Population Characteristics: P20–387.

US Census Bureau, 2008. *American Community Survey 2006. Fertility of American Women: 2006.* [online] Available at: http://www.census.gov/prod/2008pubs/p20-558.pdf.

US Census Bureau, 2009. *Current Population Survey, 2009. Annual Social and Economic Supplement.* Table PINC-11. Income distribution to $250,000 or more for males and females: 2008. [online] Available at: http://www.census.gov/hhes/www/cpstables/032009/perinc/new11_001.htm.

US Census Bureau, 2010a. *Current Population Survey, June 2010. Fertility of American Women: 2010.* [online] Available at: http://www.census.gov/hhes/fertility/data/cps/2010.html.

US Census Bureau, 2010b. *Statistical Abstract of the United States.* [online] Available at: http://www.census.gov/prod/2009pubs/10statab/labor.pdf.

US Census Bureau, 2011. *Statistical Abstract of the United States.* [online] Available at: http://www.census.gov/prod/2011pubs/11statab/labor.pdf.

US Census Bureau, 2011. *Statistical Abstract of the United States* (Labor Force Status section). Available at: http://www.census.gov/compendia/statab/cats/labor_force_employment_earnings.html.

US Department of Agriculture, Economic Research Service. *Food CPI and Expenditures: Measuring the ERS Food Expenditure Series.* [online] Available at: http://www.ers.usda.gov/Briefing/CPIFoodAndExpenditures/Data/Expenditures_tables/.

US Department of Labor, 2009. *Monthly Labor Review*, November.

US Department of Labor and US Bureau of Labor Statistics, 2010. *Women in the Labor Force: A Databook.*

US Department of Labor Women's Bureau, 2007. *Employment Status of Women and Men in 2007.* [online] Available at: http://www.dol.gov/wb/factsheets/Qf-ESWM07.htm.

US Department of Labor Women's Bureau, 2009. *Quick Stats on Women Workers, 2009.* [online] Available at: www.dol.gov/wb/stats/stats_data.htm.

Van Ingen, E. and Dekker, P., 2011. Changes in the determinants of volunteering: Participation and time investment between 1975 and 2005 in the Netherlands. *Nonprofit and Voluntary Sector Quarterly*, 40(4), pp. 682–702.

Van Kleeck, M., 1918. A census of college women. *Journal of the Association of Collegiate Alumnae*, 40(9), pp. 557–91.

Vassar: The Alumnae Magazine (various). Poughkeepsie, NY: Vassar College.

Vickery, A., 2003. *The Gentleman's Daughter: Women's Lives in Georgian England.* New Haven: Yale University Press.

Vinovskis, M., 1990. Have social historians lost the Civil War? Some preliminary demographic speculations. In: M. Vinovskis (ed.), *Towards a Social History of the American Civil War*. Cambridge: Cambridge University Press.

Wallace, W.R., 1865. What rules the world (excerpt).

Walter, N., 2005. Prejudice and evolution. *Prospect*, 111.

Walter, N., 2010. *Living Dolls: The Return of Sexism*. London: Virago.

Ward, H., Mercer, C.H., Wellings, K., Fenton, K., Erens, B., Copas, A. and Johnson, A.M., 2005. Who pays for sex? An analysis of the increasing prevalence of female commercial sex contacts among men in Britain. *Sexually Transmitted Infections*, 81(6), pp. 467–71.

Ward, K. and Dex, S., 2007. Parental employment. In: K. Hansen and H. Joshi (eds.), 2007. *Millennium Cohort Study Second Survey: A User's Guide to Initial Findings*. London: Centre for Longitudinal Studies, Chapter 9.

Ward-Batts, J., 2008. Household production, consumption and retirement. In: J. Kimmel (ed.), 2008. *How Do We Spend Our Time? Evidence from the American Time Use Survey*. Kalamazoo, MI: W. E. Upjohn Institute.

Warner, J., 2006. *Perfect Madness: Motherhood in the Age of Anxiety*. New York: Riverhead Books.

Washington, E.L., 2008. Female socialization: How daughters affect their legislator fathers' voting on women's issues. *American Economic Review*, 98(1), pp. 311–32.

Wax, A.L., 2004. Family-friendly workplace reform: Prospects for change. *Annals of the American Academy*, 596, pp. 36–61.

Wax, A.L., 2011. Diverging family structure and "rational" behavior: The decline in marriage as a disorder of choice. In: L.R. Cohen and J.D. Wright (eds.), 2011. *Research Handbook on the Economics of Family Law*. Cheltenham: Edward Elgar, pp. 15–71.

Weatherford. J. 2010. *The Secret History of the Mongol Queens: How the Daughters of Genghis Khan Saved His Empire*. New York: Crown.

Webb, N.J. and Abzug, R., 2008. Do occupational group members vary in volunteering activity? *Nonprofit and Voluntary Sector Quarterly*, 37(4), pp. 689–708.

Weinberger, C. and Kuhn, P., 2006. The narrowing of the US gender earnings gap 1959–1999: A cohort-based analysis. NBER working paper 12115. Cambridge, MA: National Bureau of Economic Research.

Whelan, C.B., 2006. *Why Smart Men Marry Smart Women*. New York: Simon & Schuster.

Whittington, L.A., 1992. Taxes and the family: The impact of the tax exemption for dependents on marital fertility. *Demography*, 29(2), pp. 215–26.

Wilde, E.T., Batchelder, L. and Ellwood, D.T., 2010. The mommy track divides: The impact of childbearing on wages of women of differing skill levels. NBER working paper 16582. Cambridge, MA: National Bureau of Economic Research.

Willetts, D., 2011. *The Pinch: How the Baby Boomers Took Their Children's Future— and Why They Should Give It Back*. London: Atlantic Books.

Williams, F., 2004. Trends in women's employment, domestic service, and female migration: Changing and competing patterns of solidarity. In: T. Knijn and A. Komter (eds.), 2004. *Solidarity Between the Sexes and the Generations*. Cheltenham: Edward Elgar, Chapter 12.

Williams, F. and Gavanas, A., 2008. The intersection of childcare regimes and migration regimes: A three country study. In: H. Lutz (ed.), 2008. *Migration and Domestic Work: A European Perspective on a Global Theme*. Aldershot: Ashgate, pp. 13–28.

Williams, J., 2000. *Unbending Gender: Why Family and Work Conflict and What to Do About It*. New York: Oxford University Press.

Williams, S., 2006. Shuffling the pack. *Telegraph Magazine*, London: 23–27.

Windolf, P., 1997. *Expansion and Structural Change: Higher Education in Germany, the US, and Japan, 1870–1990*. Boulder, CO: Westview Press.

Wolf, A., 2002. *Does Education Matter?: Myths About Education and Economic Growth*. London: Penguin.

Wolf, A., 2004. Education and economic performance: Simplistic theories and their policy consequences. *Oxford Review of Economic Policy*, 20(2), pp. 315–33.

Wolf, A., 2006. Working girls. *Prospect*, 121, pp. 28–33.

Wolf, A., 2008. Why Britons are turning their backs on charity. *Observer*, Comment, May 25.

Wolf, A., 2009. Why more enrollments don't mean a better economy. *Change: The Magazine of Higher Learning*, 41(4), pp. 10–17.

Wolf, A., 2012. Two for the price of one? The contribution to development of the new female elites. In: A. Amsden, A. DiCaprio and J. Robinson (eds.), 2012. *The Role of Elites in Economic Development*. Oxford: Oxford University Press.

Wolf, A. and Evans, K., 2010. *Improving Literacy at Work*. London: Routledge.

Wolf, A. and McNally, S. (eds.), 2011. *Education and Growth*. Cheltenham: Edward Elgar.

Wong, J.S., 1950. *Fifth Chinese Daughter*. Seattle: University of Washington Press.

Worland, J.C., 2011. Legacy admit rate at 30 percent. *The Harvard Crimson*, May 11. [online] Available at: http://www.thecrimson.com/article/2011/5/11/admissions-fitzsimmons-legacy-legacies/.

Wu, L., Bumpass, L. and Musick, K., 2001. Historical and life course trajectories of nonmarital childbearing. In: L. Wu and B. Wolfe (eds.), 2001. *Out of Wedlock: Causes and Consequences of Nonmarital Fertility*. New York: Russell Sage, pp. 3–48.

Xinran, 2011. *Message from an Unknown Chinese Mother*. London: Vintage Books.

Young, M., 1958. *The Rise of the Meritocracy*. London: Thames and Hudson.

Yukongdi, V., 2009. The changing face of women managers in Thailand. In: C. Rowkey and V. Yukongdi (eds.), 2009. *The Changing Face of Women Managers in Asia*. Abingdon: Taylor and Francis (Routledge), pp. 199–223.

Zelizer, V.A., 1994. *Pricing the Priceless Child: The Changing Social Value of Children*. Princeton, NJ: Princeton University Press.

Zerjal, T. et al., 2003. The genetic legacy of the Mongols. *American Journal of Human Genetics*, 72(3), pp. 717–21.

ACKNOWLEDGMENTS

*T*here are many people without whom this book could not have been completed; but without David Goodhart, the founder of *Prospect* magazine, it would never have been started either. It was David who, way back in 2005, persuaded me to ponder the wider consequences of a world in which many millions of women pursue professional careers, the state provides universal benefits, but the financial burden of raising a middle-class child falls almost entirely on the parents. The article on "Working Girls" that I duly wrote for *Prospect* attracted enormous attention in the UK, and also made me ever more aware of how fundamental a social change we are living through. This book goes well beyond the subject matter of "Working Girls," but it also follows directly from it, and from David's original encouragement and ideas.

I received substantial research assistance from Anne-Marie Jeannet, especially in the secondary analysis of some of the large data sets that make it possible for modern researchers to examine common trends across the world in a way that was impossible even twenty years ago. I also received research and bibliographic assistance from Saratha Rajeswaran, Scott Blevins, Harriet Paterson, Andrew Jenkins, Magdalen Meade and Sarah Battersby, and excellent transcriptions from Amanda Nicholas. Their assistance and competence are gratefully acknowledged. Russell Birkett provided some wonderful figures: any that are really imaginative and clear are almost certainly his. (The rest are my own.) John Gove contributed a brilliant title. Dr. Cath Mercer collaborated with me on the analysis and discussion of British women's sexual behavior, discussed in Chapter 8 and the Appendix, where a large number of analyses appear for the first time. I am enormously grateful for her interest in the project, for the high quality of her statistical work and comments, her willingness to scrutinize several drafts, and for spotting a number of errors of description and inference. Any remaining errors are entirely my fault and my responsibility.

The interviews used in the book were conducted at various times between May 2009 and June 2012. The women who agreed to be interviewed about their own lives and experiences were very generous with their time, and I am extremely grateful to them for their openness and frankness, for confirming some of my hunches and for making me think again about others. I have followed the common convention of using full names where people were willing to be quoted directly as themselves and a single name, normally a pseudonym, otherwise. In the latter cases I have also sometimes altered a non-significant fact or two in order to protect identities. I hope that Susan Chira, Sue Clarke, Alessandra Coppola, Lee Ann Daly, Deirdre Eng, Lawton Fitt, Vanessa Friedman, Karin Gilford, Merit Janow, Helen Joyce, Mary Myers Kauppila, Amanda Kramer, Caroline Marcus, Kathy Matsui, Lindsey McBrayne, Pat McGuire, Laura Mercadier, Kerry Miller, Jan Murray, Lynn Forester de Rothschild, Lauren States, Susan Stein, Liz Truss, Amy Wax and Governor Christine Todd Whitman, as well as my anonymous informants from Oxford University, the Asian University for Women, and from my home and my professional life, will find that the book resonates with their experiences and opinions.

Many academics and writers, some also named above, were generous with their time and in sharing findings, data, references and critiques. Peter Braude, Isobel Coleman, Lena Edlund, Kathleen McCarthy, Ashley Milne-Tyte, Theda Skocpol and Oriel Sullivan are quoted at some length. I drew directly on discussion and interviews with them, but also benefited greatly from the material and work in progress made available by Jonathan Gershuny (to whom special thanks for some of the data used in Figure 4.2) and Almudena Sevilla Sanz (Oxford University Centre for Time Use Research), Shireen Kanji (University of Basel) and Liam Wren-Lewis (Paris School of Economics). Many others helped in a variety of ways, including helping me to contact interviewees, finding archive material, suggesting sources, providing statistics and offering comments. With my apologies to anyone whom I have omitted inadvertently, I would like to thank and acknowledge the assistance of Gayatri Acharya, Pauline Adams, Isher Ahluwalia, Kemal Ahmed, Karen Arenson, Tony Atkinson, Marcia Bassett, Charles Beach, Jon Beveridge,

Acknowledgments

Jonathan Bloom, Raymond Butti Jr, Jane A. Callahan, Robin Carlaw, Lois M. Coleman, John Costin, Astrid Cravens, Padma Desai, Shirley Dex, Andrew Edgecliffe-Johnson, Leslie Fields, Anna Fifield, Chrystia Freeland, Paula Steisel Goldfarb, Elizabeth Goodyear-Grant, Heather Grizzle, Agnes Herzberg, Franklin Isacson, Saltanat Kidiralieva, Susan Lander, Richard Layard, Susan Lennon, Grace Martin, Scott Matthews, Sue Owen, Abby Peck, Anika Pratt, Adam Quinton, Dean Rogers, Holly Rogers, Mary Sansalone, Luca Solca, Lorett Treese, David Ward, Lindsay Whipp, Jocelyn K. Wilk, plus the Office of the University Registrar, Cornell University, and the anonymous admissions director of a top US law school.

I would also like to make special acknowledgment of both the encouragement and the substantive help I have received from my agent Zoë Pagnamenta, from Andrew Franklin, managing director of Profile Books, and Vanessa Mobley, my editor at Crown (Random House). Their responses, questions and criticisms have unquestionably made this a much better book, and, in Vanessa's case, stretched as far as providing me with a great interview about life as a New York City professional and parent. At Profile Books, I would like to thank, in particular, Penny Daniel, Rebecca Gray and my copy editor Lesley Levene, for calm efficiency, and also everyone who attended my seminar there and helped me to clarify my thinking.

Last, but very far from least, I would like to thank my husband and children, not just for forbearance but for ideas, argument and encouragement, and offer a special thank-you to my daughter Rachel, a classic product of this new female world I describe and also a superb critic of my chapter drafts.

INDEX

Index

Aubry, Martine, 99

Austen, Jane, ix, 206, 228, 258
  breaks off her engagement, ix, 151;
    differences between Austen's world
    and the modern one, ix–x, xiv;
    Emma, 151; *Pride and Prejudice,*
    x, 104

Australia
  childcare, 84, 300*n*63; higher
    education, 303*n*7; housework,
    300*n*63; median age for first
    marriage, 334*n*60

B

baboons, 213, 332*n*35

baby boomers (1940s and 1950s), 44, 64,
  165, 319*n*45, 320*n*56

babysitting, 46, 60, 255

Baden-Powell, Robert, 1st Baron, 145

Bali, Vinita, 113

Balkans: birth ratios, 233

Balls, Ed, 305*n*34, 341*n*53

Bandaranaike, Sirimavo, 307*n*22,
  337*n*16

Bandaranaike, Solomon, 337*n*16

Banerjee, Mamata, 117

Bangladesh: female prime ministers,
  117

banking crashes (2008), 195

Barclays, 191

Barnard College, New York, 44, 133,
  138, 287*n*3, 305*n*43, 312*n*12, 14

Bartz, Carol, 122

BBC, 146, 195

Beale, Dorothea, 135

beauty, 186–9, 196, 199, 327*n*28

"beauty bias," 187, 200

"beauty effect," 327*n*22

beauty industry, 200–1

Belkin, Lisa, 52

Belle de Jour, 183

Bennett, Arnold: *The Old Wives' Tale,*
  311*n*9

Bennetts, Leslie: *The Feminine
  Mistake,* 16

Bernhardt, Jeanne, 158

Bernhardt, Régine, 158

Bernhardt, Sarah, 157

Bettencourt, Liliane, 121

Bhutto, Benazir, 234, 307*n*22

Bhutto, Zulfikar Ali, 234

Big Brother (TV show), 154

Bigg-Wither, Harris, ix

"biological imperative," 220

Birth Cohort Study 1970 (BCS70), 33,
  283*n*27, 341*n*6

births out of wedlock, 27, 30, 209, 210,
  211–2, 215, 216, 217, 221, 223, 224,
  251, 316*n*2, 331*n*24, *n*25, 333*n*43

Blair, Tony, 329*n*9

Bloem, Iris, 262

"Blue Stockings," 127, 210

BNP Paribas, 192

Boleyn, Anne, 156

Bolick, Kate, 271*n*2

Bollywood film stars, 226

Booth, William, 140

Bossidy, John Collins, 336*n*77

"Boston Brahmins," 224, 237

Botín, Ana Patricia, 238

Boushey, Heather, 46, 52, 61

Bradley, Senator Bill, 118

Braude, Professor Peter, 41

breadwinner marriages, 13, 22

breast-augmentation surgery, 272*n*7

breastfeeding, 212, 214, 254, 332*n*31

Britain
  first industrial nation, 113; graduate
    parents of pre-school children,
    76; middle-class girls enter the
    professions, 129; "pupil teachers,"
    129; "rich list," 311*n*27, 306*n*8

Britannia Industries, 113

British Cohort Study 1970 (BCS70),
  283*n*27, 312*n*16

Brooks, David: *Bobos in Paradise,*
  208–9

Brown, Gordon, 329–30*n*9

Brown University, Rhode Island, 305*n*43

Brownmiller, Susan, 202

Index

Bryn Mawr College, Pennsylvania, 305*n*43

Buffett, Warren, 121

Bunny Girls, 158–9

Burdett-Coutts, Angela, 139

Burgess, Patricia, 303–4*n*14

Burggraf, Shirley, 38

Burmese independence movement, 234

Burnham, Andy, 305*n*34

Bush, George W., 118

C

Cambridge University, 159, 183, 304*n*26

    co-education comes piecemeal, 108; female undergraduate, 103, 104, 107, 306*n*44; and politics, 99

Cameron, David, 99, 329–30*n*9

Campbell, Mrs. Patrick, 168

Canada

    higher education, 303*n*7; volunteering, 136–7

capitalism, 236

Career Point, 106

caring professions, 9–10, 129, 274*n*26

Carroll, Cynthia, 110

Catholic Church, 135

Caucasus: birth ratios, 233

celibacy, 151

Center for the Study of Philanthropy, New York City, 144

Centre for Longitudinal Studies, 283*n*25

Chanel, 123, 204

charities, 128, 138–9, 193, 314*n*36

Charlottesville, Virginia, 244

Cheltenham Ladies' College, 135

Chen Lihua, 112

child mortality, 332*n*37

"child penalty," 288*n*17

child-bearing patterns, 24–42

    affected by money, 37–8, 39–40; birth out-of-wedlock, 27, 209, 210, 211–2, 215, 216–7, 221, 223–4, 251, 316*n*2, 331*n*24, *n*25, 333*n*43;

childbearing as an aspiration, xii, 29; cutting both ways, 31–3; fall in birth rates, 23, 24; larger families of less educated women, 24, 25; of new elite women, xi, 2–3, 23, 24–5; no delays and no regrets, 35–7; not often and early, but rarely and late, 33–4; parented by the state, 37–41; prime child-bearing age for graduate women, 34, 282*n*21; the retreat from child-bearing, 25–6; the road not taken, 30–1; roads taken and not taken, 26–30; too few, too late?, 41–2

childcare, 23, 57, 62, 71, 75, 254, 289*n*28

    "active," 83; and Australian men, 300*n*63; by professional graduate parents, 84–87; costs, 53, 59, 60, 61, 83, 241; "direct," 81; institutional, 61, 288*n*13; in London, 58; and non-standard work, 292*n*69; seen as women's role, 28; shared, 73, 213–4; subsidies, 18, 61, 279*n*63; time spent in, 84–5, 86, 119, 220, 244, 292*n*69, 300–1*n*63, 302*n*74

childlessness, ix

    in Asia, 27, 31; balance between men and women, 33; and divorce, 29; in elite men, 31, 33; graduate, xii, 26, 32, 33, 39, 40, 49, 210, 282*n*20, 284–5*n*39; in members of German Parliament, 32; and the Pill, 152; reasons for, 30–1; regret/lack of regret at, 30–1; stress-free, 152; of UK graduates, 27, 33, 281*n*6; of US graduates, 26–7, 32, 282*n*20, 283–4*n*32

children

    child fatalities, 83, 301*n*69; fatherless, 214; investment in high quality care, 86; as security for sickness and old age, 37, 38

Children's Garden, New York, 59

chimpanzees, 213–4, 332*n*35

Index

illegitimacy, 132, 152, 209, 214–15, 223, 332n33
Imperial War Museum, London, 98
in vitro fertilization (IVF), 41
India
 birth ratios, 233; female illiteracy, 111; growth rates and population, 306n1; second female prime minister, 117; servants in, 81; widows in, 114; women's role at top of job market, 114
Indian Institutes of Technology (IIT), 106
Indonesia, 114, 234
Industrial Revolution, 3, 108
industrialization, 128, 328n51
infant mortality, 214, 332n37
infanticide, 233, 333n42
inheritance, 121, 219
Institute for Industrial Therapy, 138
International Baccalaureate, 246
International Labour Organization (ILO), 7, 272n17
International Monetary Fund, 110, 204
International Wages for Housework Campaign, 294n3
Internet, 153, 175, 179
 dating, 226
investment banking, 22, 46, 49, 253
Iran, 95–6, 116
Iraq, 95
Islamic regimes, 95–6
Israel, 38, 207
Italy
 educational matching, 207; inequality in workload, 74, 242; Italian women's unpaid housework, 73–4
IUDs, 316–7n5
Ivy League colleges, 102–3, 107, 246, 252

J
James, Selma, 294n3
Janow, Merit, 79

Japan
 birth rate, 40, 62, 280n4, 316–7n5; and contraceptive pill, 316n4; equality in average total working hours, 74; female education, 62; fertility rates, 27, 63, 286n60; "floating world," 157; low marriage rates, 63, 336–6n74; median age for first marriage, 334–5n60; population levels, 280n4; very large companies in, 337n20; women in employment, 13, 62–3
Japanese Medical Association, 316n4
Jayalalithaa, J., 117
Jeannet, Anne-Marie, 278n50, 293n1, 313–4n34, 318n40, 322n75, 323n82
Jessel, Penelope, 314n37
Jewish Museum, London, 98
job pyramid, 7–9, 14, 16, 19, 32, 79, 99, 128, 153, 256
job satisfaction: low-paid workers in routine jobs, 19, 279n69
job-sharing, 50, 279–80n75
Joshi, Heather, 44, 46
Joyce, Helen, 217
J. P. Morgan, 123

K
Kagan, Elena, 99
Kapoor, Karisma, 226
Karabel, Jerome, 107
Katz, Lawrence, 32
Kauppila, Mary Myers, 237, 238
Kazakhstan, 240
kibbutz movement, 66, 253–4, 294n3
King's College London, 11, 41, 303n5
Kingsley, Charles, 94
Kinnock, Neil (now Lord), 87
Kipling, Rudyard: *Barrack-room Ballads,* xiv
Kogan, Stanley J., 208
Kohl, Helmut, 248

Index

religion, 129, 139
   religious attendance, 314*n*40
Rhode, Deborah, 187, 199–200, 202
Rich Man Poor Man (television series),
   181
Rinehart, Georgina, 121, 238
risk-aversion, 196, 238
Rogers, Mary, 230
Rose, Hilary, 31
Rosen, Ruth, 178, 179
Rosenfeld, Irene, 122, 310*n*45
Rous, Lydia, 135
Rowling, J. K., 121
Roxelana, 156
Royal, Ségolène, 99
Rumbelow, Helen, 18
Rwanda, 116
Ryan, Meg, 190

S

St. Hilda's College, Oxford, 135
Salvation Army, 140
Sanders, Teela, 179
Santander UK, 238
Sarkozy, Nicolas, 305*n*36
Saudi Arabia, 238
   emergence of top-class women's
      colleges, 116; women forbidden to
      drive, 111
Scandinavia
   cohesive, prosperous countries, 215;
      day care, 59; female employment
      statistics, 275–6*n*43; fertility, 40;
      high gender segregation levels in
      occupations, 7, 19–20, 293–4*n*2;
      high in "female legislators"
      rankings, 116; high level of female
      full-timers, 20; high out-of-
      wedlock births, 215; occupational
      recruitment, 7; and sexual equality,
      16–17, 107, 293–4*n*2
Schaeffler, George, 337*n*22
Schaeffler, Mariaq-Elisabeth, 337*n*22
Schaeffler engineering company,
   337*n*22

science: stereotypically male area, 20
Sebelius, Kathleen, 98
"second shift" argument, 70, 295*n*21
self-image, 325–6*n*8
self-made female fortunes, 121–2
servant classes, the return of the, 43–63,
   255
   different from us, 52–4; Eastern
      values?, 61–3; the end of history?,
      55–6; goodbye to the mommy
      track?, 43–7; heading out of the
      door, 47–51; holding the baby,
      56–60; "in service," 54–5; the
      opt-out that never happened, 52;
      tag-team parenting, 60–1
Seven Sisters colleges, 102, 133, 137
sex
   anal, 174, 324*n*98; casual dates,
      189; decline in high-risk practices,
      321*n*71; escorts, 327*n*26; female
      orgasm, 172–3; first sex, 160,
      318*n*39, 319*n*43, 45, 320*n*55;
      group, 173; heterosexual sex as
      a female monopoly, 155–6; legal
      age of consent, 160; long-term
      relationships, 189; one-night stands,
      323*n*87; oral, 173, 174, 324*n*98, 99;
      premarital, 152, 215; "risk-free,"
      152; the sex trade, 157–8; sexually
      active teenagers, 153; summers of
      love?, 161–4; underage, 160, 319*n*42
Sex and the City (TV program), 154,
   165, 168, 170, 226, 229
"sex deficit," 169, 171, 172
"sex-saturated" society, 166, 170
sexual attraction, 185, 186, 197
sexual revolution, 162, 170, 252
sexually transmitted diseases, 321*n*71
Shaw, George Bernard: *Pygmalion,* 68
Shih, Professor Victor, 240
Shinawatra, Thaksin, 234
Shinawatra, Yingluck, 234
short men, 199
Sidwell Friends School, Washington, DC,
   243

Index

signaling, 152, 189, 196, 197
  costly, 197, 204
Singapore
  fertility rate, 40; graduate
    childlessness, 40; high proportion of
    professionals in workforce, 286n60;
    single mothers, xiv, 37, 38, 209, 210,
    222, 223, 254–5, 292n73, 338n35
sisterhood, 3, 12, 64, 251, 252,
  328–9n55
"sisters under their skin," xiv, 16
Skocpol, Theda, 141, 145
  Diminished Democracy, 145
Slaughter, Anne-Marie, 48, 256
sleep, 80, 85, 299–300n58
Slovenia: educational matching, 207
Smith College, Massachusetts, 305–6n43
Social Attitudes survey, 290n58
"social desirability bias," 319–20n49
social housing, 37
social mobility, 340–1n52
social security, ix, 37
social work, 128
Somerville College, Oxford, xi, xii, 90,
  130
South Asia: female-male ratio for average
  length of education, 90, 302–3n3
South Korea, 40, 233, 234
Southeast Asia, 117
Southampton Industrial Therapy
  Association, 138
Soviet Union, disintegration of, 239
Spain: domestic workers, 291n67
spinsterhood, 5, 164–6, 171, 311n9
Spitzer, Eliot, 175
sports, 299n57
Sri Lanka: first female prime minister,
  117, 234
Standard and Poor's, 124
Stanford Law School, 208
Stanford University, California, 100, 108
state benefits, 47
States, Lauren, 58, 79
Stead, William T., 324n8
Stein, Susan, 59–60

Steinem, Gloria, 12
sterilization, 215
Stevenson, Betsey, 215
Stewart, Martha, 67
Strauss, Peter, 181
stress, 19, 21, 48, 57, 75, 76, 77, 152,
  168, 226, 246, 257, 297n37, 342n17
Suleiman the Magnificent, 156
Sullinger, Helen, 341n2
Sullivan, Oriel, 71, 73
Summer of Love, 162
Sunday Times Rich List, 121
surplus women, 15–16
Sussex University, 112
Suu Kyi, Aung San, 234
Sweden
  divorce rates, 335n68; domestic
    servants, 54, 290n51; extramarital
    birth rates, 221; family businesses,
    235; few marry young, 333n47;
    full-time workers, 18, 342n17;
    increase in marriage rate, 333n49;
    and marriage, 216; part-time work
    scarce, 19
Switzerland: votes for women, 116

T

tag-team parenting, 60–1, 255
Taher, Nahed, 113–4
Taiwan: birth rate, 40–1
Tajikistan, 240
tall men, 199
tall women, 328n45
tax credits, 38, 285n51
"Tea Party" movement, 316n63
teachers
  and home-teaching by affluent
    women, 128; loss of brightest female
    students, 312n17; mathematics
    and morality, 135–6; not being
    considered as a career currently,
    130, 134–5; Somerville alumnae
    records, 130; "Teach for America"
    and "Teach First," 313n19; teacher
    training in US, 91, 303n9, 311n2

ABOUT THE AUTHOR

ALISON WOLF CBE is the Sir Roy Griffiths Professor of Public Sector Management at King's College London, and director of its international center for university policy research. She writes widely for the broadsheet press, and is a presenter for *Analysis* on BBC Radio 4. She has worked as a policy analyst and academic in both the US and the UK, advised developed and developing country governments, and in 2011 completed a major review of vocational education ("The Wolf Review") for the British government.